Gandhi and the Contemporary World

Essays to mark the 125th Anniversary of His Birth

Edited by

Antony Copley and George Paxton

Indo-British Historical Society
21, Rajaram Metha Avenue,
Chennai - - 600 029,

Contents

Page No.

The Individual, Society and the State

Conflict Resolution

In Conclusion

To Two Committed Gandhians

Geoffrey Ostergaard

25 July 1926 – 22 March 1990

David Ennals

19 August 1922 – 17 June 1995

Edited by
ANTONY COPLEY
GEORGE PAXTON

Published by
Indo-British Historical Society,
21, Rajaram Mehta Avenue,
Chennai – 600 029 India.

ISBN 819 000 68 19

Designed and Printed at
Bhattarams Reprographics Private Limited
II/22, Dr. V.S.I. Estate,
Thiruvanmiyur, Chennai – 600 041.

Preface

Antony Copley

Editorial

The Directors of the Indo-British Historical Society had a wish to see how Gandhi's ideas still applied in the present. The Gandhi Foundation wanted to mark the 125th Anniversary of his birth. Hence this jointly sponsored collection of essays. Could we not, encouraged the Directors, seek the opinions of a younger generation? And if, as Editors, we have not disappointed them, we have also sought the views of those with a longer experience of the Gandhian movement. It was not for us to practice ageism. We are very much in debt to Gopal Gandhi, Director of the Nehru Centre, for his advice on whom to approach in India.

Ours is but one of several ways of marking the Anniversary, and I owe another debt to my attending a conference at Westminster College, Oxford, on Gandhi's Conception of a New Society, organised, with great panache, by Margaret Chatterjee.

Such is the extraordinary richness of Gandhi's ideas that they apply equally to societies at the outset of development as to those at or near its completion, or, as we now call it, at a stage of post-industrialisation. Gandhi himself speculated that his ideas might be taken up, or at least listened to more keenly, as much outside India as within. With very much the same vision as Alexander Herzen, his was a preemptive bid to spare developing societies that nightmare of industrial capitalism. And just as Herzen entertained both a minimalist and a maximalist programme, so Gandhi veered between endless pragmatic endeavours to ease the pain of the present and a readiness to turn revolutionary. And Gandhi's insights have also provided a bitter post-mortem on development. At either point, his vision of an alternative society carries conviction. But whereas it is nearly impossible to deflect impoverished societies from the pursuit of the capitalist pot of gold, those which have experienced the destructive consequences of this quest are more likely to be convinced of the perceptiveness of Gandhi's critique. Maybe it is not so paradoxical that Gandhi's ideas are taken as, or even more seriously in industrialised societies as in developing.

Humankind has just emerged from forty years in the moral maze of the Cold War. The West succumbed to the belief that by championing capitalism over communism it was sustained by some higher moral purpose. This was to take on quite frightening, even hysterical, proportions in Thatcherism and Reaganism in the 1980's when it scented victory. Today we live with the consequences of that materialism and consumerism. In the fall-out from the collapse of the communist experiment, it is a tragedy to discover that its populations have no other ambition than to share in this materialist culture. Can Third World countries, victims of the economic aggrandisement and power politics of the Cold War, be blamed if theirs is likewise a materialist ambition, to close the economic gap between North and South? Not that the concept 'Third World' has any longer the same validity. Countries of the Pacific rim are as advanced economically as anywhere. Yet some societies of the south have seemingly rejected this materialist culture, most strikingly so, Nyerere's Tanzania, but more disturbingly, those driven by a powerful reassertion of Islamic values. We live in a world of still chronic economic malaise and deep moral confusion. Can the legacy of Gandhi address this crisis of the late 20th Century?

Just as important as any economic solutions is whether Gandhism can equip us, psychologically and temperamentally, to meet this challenge. We are at risk from surrendering to a sense of powerlessness. Yet we are essentially problem solvers, and were we to abdicate, we would betray our humanity. In an essay which tells us where the Gandhian movement is at in India today, Thomas Weber, in an intriguing way, discusses the respective roles of optimism and pessimism. Gandhi saw himself as an inveterate optimist, though even he was to experience despair at the communal holocaust which accompanied partition. If, in Weber's view, there was a greater underlying optimism with the more idealist, other-wordly followers of Vinoba Bhave, even the more wordly, the more confrontational followers of J.P. Narayan did not despair, and this optimism is Gandhi's most dynamic legacy. Yet how can we acquire this sense of enpowerment?

One way in is to fashion a proper balance between the masculine and feminine in our make-up, between the animus and anima. Gandhi recognised the need for Indians, subject to the charge of effeminacy by the colonial state, to strengthen its masculine side, to recreate a Rajput or Kshatriya ethic of courage.[1] Gandhi always bridled at any accusation of weakness and rejected any account of *satyagraha* as mere passive resistance. Clearly he sought to do everything possible to strengthen the moral resolve of the Gandhians. Yet Ashis Nandy has perceptively queried whether we do not do an even greater harm to the psyche, both Indian and European, by this prioritizing of the masculine at the expense of the feminine.[2] And, of course, Gandhi's was a personality which strongly reflected the feminine. Were Gandhians to take Eysenck's famous personality test, almost certainly most would come out on the tender rather than the tough side. Gandhism is a movement which seeks to attune humankind to Nature rather than to seek its domination and exploitation. The spirit of Gandhism informs the whole contemporary ecological movement. Today we all claim to be Friends of the Earth. To be attuned to Nature, we have to be in touch with our feminine side. If, in so many ways, nationalist movements have emphasised the need for physical strength, Gandhi displaced this to the moral. He was himself a man of quite astonishing physical as well as moral courage. Of course this exploration of the male and female in the psyche would have a sexist character were it not to be recognised that here we have been looking at the issue largely through male eyes and a rather different emphasis would have to be made from a female perspective.

These essays range across those issues which most concern us today. There is the crisis of the environment, reflected in the ecological movement and the debate on development. There is a search for new values, both social and religious, one which takes us back to Gandhi's own dialogue with Ruskin, Tolstoy and Vivekananda and forward to today's debates on the nature of education and the need for religious pluralism. There is the perennial question on how the individual and the community relate to the state: here there are important articles on how Gandhi's vision of a decentralised political community can still work. Then there is the continuing and urgent matter of how to resolve conflict, both within our societies and between states. Can Gandhi's supreme emphasis on means provide an answer to such intractable conflicts as those of Kashmir and Northern Ireland? Can we rediscover our faith in the United Nations?

Ecology and Development

It is through the modern ecological movement that we stand up against the abuses of rampant capitalism and mindless development. Few phenomena have engendered so much anger, in both India and Britain. In India, for example, there is the sustained opposition to the Tehri dam and the whole Narmada scheme. In Britain there are now highly organised campaigns against those gratuitous infrastructure developments, such as those endless new road schemes which needlessly threaten the environment, and there is that extraordinary escalation of protest at cruelty to animals brought about by an inhumane market economics. We would be wrong, however, to see this as a highly coordinated movement, more a series of disparate, if connected, protests. Or will the Green parties yet convert these into a concerted political movement?

Of course there are difficulties in accurately presenting the needs of endangered communities. Within the *Chipko* movement, for example, where committed Gandhians have argued for an almost complete ban on the exploitation of forest resources, others, just as committed to their survival, such as Batt, see the need for some use by local hill people. Sunderlal Bahuguna, in his contribution, explains why he has gone for a complete ban. The women won him over, their seeing the forest as 'our mother's home, a place which a lady remembers when in trouble.' But such divergences always exist in any Gandhian campaign.[3]

Kamla Chowdry, in a wide-ranging piece, takes up the implications of Agenda 21 of the Earth Summit at Rio in 1991. Given the Malthusian nightmare of a choice between destruction and sustainable growth, we have to look for new paradigms for development. It is important to grasp that an awareness of ecological needs does not rule out all development. Any right thinking person looks for ways of alleviating poverty. New priorities will have to be set, to look at development in terms of individuals and communities, to let the poor define their own terms. If this requires a reduction of needs, they will be those of the rich, not those of the poor. New paradigms will require a 'a reassessment of the concept of progress.'

In a brilliant rereading of Gandhi's ashram life, Shahed Power illustrates how Gandhi sought a new relationship with nature, both through his vegetarianism and his concern for animals. This was never pharisaical. Even vegetarianism was a form of violence, and Gandhi insisted that the ashram had the right to protect itself from the nuisance of stray dogs, not to mention pilfering monkeys. He goes on to draw a comparison between the way of life in ashrams with those of simple, indigenous people.

With Professor Naidu's article we shift focus from issues ecological to developmental. Implicitly, this is a remarkable response to Barrington Moore's earlier highly acclaimed analysis of differing modes of development.[4] In Moore's account, a range of models are compared as possible paths for development, from those of democratic societies, to those of fascist and communist, with the Indian solution faulted for its lack of a tough state: in Naidu's, setting the Indian example to one side, all the other approaches are condemned, on the grounds that they have a built-in tendency to militarism and aggression. How, indeed, could India bring itself to follow models that lead to such rapine? India should, instead, adopt a Gandhian model. My worry here is that such advice may have come too late, as India has so clearly committed itself to a development process on other than Gandhian lines.

In another wide-ranging piece, L.C.Jain grapples with the character of Indian devlopment. There was an initial fatal divide between Gandhi and Nehru, with Gandhi's quest for a socialist society, Nehru's settling for a socialist state, putting his faith in the bureaucracy, and emphasising production over employment. He failed to attend to the needs of the villages by implementing effective land reforms. He did not grasp that real change could only come from below, if with the assistance of the state. Jain's bleak statistics on poverty and illiteracy might well induce despair. But he does not, so one way out lies in fashioning appropriate local level political institutions: 'a bucket without a bottom cannot hold water.' And if the State has marginalised Society, he can still point to 'many non-charismatic leaders who are continuing to translate Gandhian philosophy into action or organising social protest movements.'

Rex Ambler takes a wider look at how Gandhi responded to the concept of Modernity. In *Hind Swaraj* Gandhi's first and most sustained critique of 'modern' civilisation, not necessarily the same as 'western', his was a desperate plea that India should not embark on the destructive path of industrial capitalism. Ambler worries, however, that in his prioritizing the spirit over the body, Gandhi may not have set us too demanding an ideal and in failing to match this, we may be led into pessimism. Do we not need to be in closer touch with the needs of our bodies, the better to heal ourselves?

V.B.Eswaran explores a theme of Indian development as 'drang nach western', too technologically orientated. India fails to make proper use of her population. The centre, or the State, will never come to the correct decisions. Only at the local level, and through N.G.O.'s, Non-Governmental Organisations, will local needs be properly understood. No longer should the relationship between community and the State be one of supplicant but of client. He draws attention to the way new local level committees, the *gram sabhas*, reach even deeper into the community than *panchayats*, and may prove to be the makings of Gandhi's village republics.

It is very interesting to recognise how Schumacher lent a contemporary edge to Gandhi's ideas. In an essay jointly written with his brother, Mansur, first head of the Institute of Appropriate Technology, which Schumacher set up in India, Surur Hoda convincingly shows how economics based on 'goods' rather than on 'people' both leaves the mass of the population impoverished and destroys the environment. In Schumacher's analysis, a complex transport system for the distribution of goods merely demonstrated that goods were being produced in the wrong place. Together with J.P.Narayan, Schumacher updated Gandhi's vision of a decentralised village economy. It would provide both basic needs and full employment.

It is very much the contention of this collection of essays that Gandhi's vision can equally apply to the so-called developed world. In his piece, for example, Robert Hart, after describing a number of sarvodaya experiments in Maharashtra and Sri Lanka, links these to the programme of the Green Parties and goes on to to describe intriguing examples of how they might apply in Britain, with plans from the Scottish Green party for their application to the forest area of the Highlands, even schemes for bioregionalism in suburban Surrey.

Godric Bader beards Satan in his den. How can capitalism itself be modified along Gandhian lines? Of course Gandhi himself did not turn his back on Indian capitalists. They were far too remunerative as benefactors of his constructive programme. Through his concept of Trusteeship, he sought a corrective to the mere exploitation of capitalism and its pursuit of wealth. It was in the 17th Century, Bader suggests, that capitalism and morality parted company. J.P.Narayan took up the concept of Trusteeship. In 1965 he discussed the issue with U.K. industrialist, George Goyder. In 1973, he set up a Trusteeship Foundation in Bombay. A solution lay in bringing together capital, management and labour in cooperatives. Here was a middle way between market capitalism and state socialism. Though this was not recognised, here there were marked overtones of Louis Blanc's Nationalist Workshops of the 1840's, and not enough attention has been paid to the debt of Gandhi and the Gandhians to the 19th Century Utopian Socialists. Cooperatives could both be rural, though must be voluntarist, to avoid the pitfalls of the collectivist Chinese and Yugoslav models, and urban. Bader's own family firm, the Scott Bader Commowealth Ltd, set up in 1951, was run along these lines. But we have to accept the possibility that the concept of trusteeship was but a transitional one, but on the way to a more fully fledged socialist society.

Sarvodaya: Social and Religious Values

Gandhism is of a piece, and one can only artificially separate out his attitudes towards the environment and development from his social and religious values, those we subsume under the concept *sarvodaya.* Yet many who are otherwise sympathetic towards Gandhi here feel less at ease. Is it just that we are culture-bound? Is our more libertarian morality out of tune with his ascetic morality? Yet we remain acutely aware how little a materialist culture can answer our inner needs and that we neglect the religious impulse at our peril.

Tarlok Singh's essay admirably leads us into a discussion of these values. Complementary to the concept of *sarvodaya,* and, indeed, one which might have taken precedence, is that of *antyodaya.* This was in fact, Vinoba Bhave's invention, a rendering of Ruskin's *Unto the Last*–more literally, unto the least– a concept that profoundly influenced Gandhi, and one that prompts two chapter headings in this volume, *Gandhi and the last man, Gandhi and the last woman.* Tarlok Singh provides a very clear exposition of Gandhi's debt to Ruskin, not an easy writer to elucidate. The great Victorian moralist rejected the materialist, laissez-faire ideology of Victorian Britain in the name of a visionary, new, political economy, one shaped by 'social affection', and with a morally aware society, one in which all would share a sense of social obligation, though admittedly a nonegalitarian, hierarchical one. In a highly original contribution, Gerald Studdert-Kennedy explores the influence of Ruskin, though often Ruskin at one remove, on both the Christian Socialists and Gandhi himself. This created the possibility of some dialogue between Christian Imperialists and Gandhi, though also misunderstanding. Fulfilment-minded Christians–and this is a theological approach, a belief that the Christian message lay buried in other world religions–believed that the evolution of such a Ruskinian moral society lay within the developmental potentialities of other societies and cultures. Gandhi's friend, the missionary, Charles Andrews, was one. In Ruskin, Gandhi found the inspiration for one of his own key concepts, *varnashramadharma,* of an organically regulated society. A Ruskinian sense of duty became his *dharma,* Ruskin's social morality, his *sarvodaya.* It is Studdert-Kennedy's most paradoxical claim that Gandhi, whilst rejecting modernity, by pursuing this social vision, was to lead backward, rural, India into the modern age.

Christian Bartolf reminds us of Gandhi's debt to Tolstoy. In his *Letter to a Hindoo* December 1908, written in fact to a disciple of Vivekananda, Baba Premenanda Bharati, Tolstoy told Indians to free themselves from the pseudo-science of the Raj, its Social-Darwinism. A law of love should replace a law of force. They should create a new civilisation. Gandhi's correspondence with Tolstoy only commences 1st October, 1909. Tolstoy responded positively to Gandhi's condemnation of 'modern' civilisation and to his idea of soul-force. It was, in fact Gandhi's Jewish friend, Kallenbach, himself profoundly influenced by the *Letter to a Hindoo* and *The Kingdom of God* who sought the Russian writer's permission to name the ashram outside Johannesburg, Tolstoy Farm.

Although they neither met nor corresponded, B.R.Nanda speculates on Vivekananda's influence on Gandhi. Did he take over his role of revitalizing Hinduism? In all kinds of ways Gandhi was likewise to challenge the Sanataṇists, the orthodox Hindus. But did Gandhi share Vivekananda's belief that Indians should take on board some of the masculine dynamic of the West? Where they clearly differed lay in

Vivekananda's prioritizing a moral and spiritual revolution whereas Gandhi believed in the inseparability of religion and politics. Even so, Vivekananda's fierce pragmatism, his sense of outrage at the poverty of so many Indians, would have encouraged Gandhi in a this-wordly direction and hence towards politics.

If Gandhi's views on education were to be highly controversial, he had a very definite programme for spreading his ideas. Unfortunately, given his emphasis on both craft skills, interpreted as pro-caste, and his Hindu values, he managed to alienate both the low caste, especially the untouchable, and the Muslim. Another Gandhian, Rajagopalachari, when he attempted to introduce a Gandhian-style educational scheme during his second term as Chief Minister of Madras in 1954, was forced to resign. Julian Brotherton suggests, however, that Gandhi's educational ideas can travel and that we are today beginning to appreciate their virtue. In the class-room children are now encouraged to anticipate the adult world. The vocational skills which they learn, the technology, business studies, are all underpinned by a value system, *sarvodaya* no less, which encourages a 'true economics' and a sense of social justice. Admittedly, teachers have to be on their guard at too premature a symbiosis between the worlds of child and adult, of education and industry: theirs is 'the immensely demanding job of affirming the personal worth of all pupils.' No subject, Brotherton argues, is value free. Education has to have an environmentalist approach.

How would a Gandhian interpret Britain in the 1980's? The late Fred Blum, one of the inspirational figures in the early days of the Gandhi Foundation, especially of its Summer School, was clearly appalled by the obscenity of unemployment and the sickness of our dependence on nuclear weapons. How can a society with any concern for the truth rely on weapons of mass destruction? His was a passionate plea that people should never be used as a means to an end but always as an end in themselves, that work should once again become meaningful. We have to draw deep on the 'ground of our own being', to tap into a universal source of energy. Only this way can we draw on a Gandhian well-spring of non-violent resistance. Such an endeavour of raising Gandhian ideas to the level of consciousness is always in danger of slipping away from us.

One of the more controversial aspects of Gandhi's social and moral vision was on the role of women. Here he seems most culture-bound by his own society. There is, of course a huge gap between the real enslavement of women in traditional societies and those questionnings of patriarchy and sexism in a more emancipated West. It would be unreasonable to expect Gandhi to have anticipated, to have approved, many of the expectations of modern feminism. We have simply to live with the moral ambiguities of his ideal of *brahmacharya*. Clearly, those doubts about his male sexuality which led to a vow of abstinence are light years away from a western feminist concern with female sexuality and sexual libertarianism. Maybe all along, the 19th Century male-led reform movement in India for the emancipation of women was driven above all by a male quest for educated female companionship and insufficiently saw the struggle through the eyes of women. Ranjit Roy hints at this in his interesting exploration of Gandhi's attitudes towards women. And, he points out, Gandhi went beyond Bankim Chandra

Chatterjee and Vivekananda in linking womanliness with political emancipation. Gandhi sought to break down the barriers between the private and the public demesne and to encourage women to assume a greater responsibility in public life. But feminist doubts remain. Was his simply a way of tapping the power of women, their *shakti*, and did he really free himself from patriarchy? Roy believes he was wrong not to allow women to participate in the Salt March to Dandi. Would Gandhi approve that tendency in Indian feminism today to question the Hindu tradition of the Sita-style dutiful wife? If, as Roy claims, women were discouraged from politics and the professions after independence, it is a curious fact that after 1947 women could gain admission to the elite civil service, to the IAS. Some of the contributions to this volume show that the momentum for a larger involvement by women in modern political life, won through their being drawn into the civil disobedience movement, is still being sustained by Gandhians in their campaigns at village level.

In Norman Scotney's sensitive and exploratory essay on Gandhi's attitudes to inter-faith relationships, Gandhi emerges both inclusivist and pluralist. He spent part of his formative years in Christian England and Christian South Africa and one wonders if this did not lead him to pay too much attention to Christianity and not enough to Islam, where in India the real challenge lay. One has no doubt that in terms of the ideal, one should reach out for inter-faith transcendence in ways that modern theologians, such as John Hick, encourage. But to expect too great a degree of reciprocal concession, especially from overtly exclusivist faiths, may be over-ambitious, and one should possibly settle for no more than toleration, a live and let-live relationship at best. Did Gandhi get it right? He recommended loyalty to one's own religion in preference to any syncretism, and always opposed proselytism and any attempt to convert. Of course, with the rise of fundamentalism, few issues today have such a sense of harrowing urgency. Thomas Daffern, in his highly erudite piece, examines the way Gandhi's ideas have influenced Hindus and those of other faiths. One of the more worrying aspects of his research is the discovery that Muslims are the least susceptible to Gandhian values.

The Individual, Society and the State

Gandhi's attitude towards the centralised state is another controversial area. Could it be argued that the whole anti-statist character of the independence movement was its most dangerous legacy? There was Gunnar Myrdal's famous critique of India as a 'soft' state, one that warred against the needs of a developing economy. Gandhi looked at the State through the lens of colonialism. Had the Raj been less of a law and order state and more of a welfare state, maybe his response to the state would have been modified. But once he had associated the state with violence, his underlying anarchist quest for decentralisation proved irreversible. Here would be his basis for democracy. And as his oceanic vision led ever outwards to wider political associations, so it was not incompatible with Proudhonian models of a federal structure. But would it work?

In this volume we are encouraged once again to have faith in Gandhi's vision of *Panchayat Raj*, of a decentralised village democracy. In an invaluably clear account,

Sadiq Ali shows how recent legislation has put more flesh on this ideal, above all through the legislation of December 1992; these measures 'can go a long towards taking rural India towards the goal Gandhi had in mind.' His is an optimistic forecast. In an angry, though also optimistic piece, Bunker Roy reflects on his years of involvement with village India in Rajasthan. Maybe, he sadly observes, with the deaths of Vinoba Bhave and JP Narayan, the Gandhian movement is not what it used to be. How can we today fulfil Gandhi's demand of reaching out to help his putative 'last man', exploited, suppressed and never treated fairly or justly by the better-off in the village. Roy's is less a faith in *panchayat* institutions–indeed they often fail the villagers–more in the endless resourcefulness of the villagers themselves. They are often far more able to solve their own problems than those professional or 'educated' personnel sent to do the task. To be 'literate' in India is quite different from being 'educated'. Roy puts his faith, instead, in 'the barefoot mechanic.' Ways and means of finding solutions to village problems can always be found if the villagers are left to fend for themselves.

In a voice from the South, and the problem is of course pan-Indian, Lakshmi Krishnamurti also takes heart from recent legislative measures. The role of women, if by reservation, can be increased at the *panchayat* level. She provides telling examples of *sree shakti*, women power. Quite ordinary women are displaying initiative. This demonstrates the creative role of those new levels of local participation, the *gram sabhas*. The Satyamurthi Centre for Democratic Studies provides a training, especially for women, for those working at this level. In 1995 there are elections for these newly renovated *panchayat* institutions and here, she argues, will be a real test to see if local communities can rise above the divisive loyalties of caste, community and political party, a challenge, she suggests, as great as that of 1942 and JP's anti-Emergency movement.

'Can we, however, sustain a revisionist view of Gandhi's interpretation of the modern state? Is it correct to say that he saw the state as violence incorporated? Is it true that non-cooperation was driven by mere anarchism?

Anthony Parel presents a brave case for interpreting Gandhi's political outlook as 'inspired by a liberal view of the state, law and citizenship.' To what extent, indeed, did Gandhi part company from the Indian Liberals in the 1920's? Some Gandhians, such as Rajagopalachari, never really severed their links. But for those Gandhians who turned Responsivist in the 1920's and those who argued for office acceptance in the late 1930's, the prospect for strong parliamentary institutions in India would have been seriously weakened. So why should there not be a Gandhian liberalism? Is there in Gandhi's outlook, as Parel argues, a distinctive view of the individual and liberty, one which combines elements, with reference to Isaiah Berlin's famous essay, of both the negative and the positive concepts of liberty? At the least, this would be a rejoinder to Edward Shils' strange, but once influential idea that Indians experience a weak sense of the self. Was Gandhi's endeavour to transcend the sectional loyalties to caste and community in the name of individualism? Given his commitment to one man, one vote, in his show-down with Ambedkar, this may well have been the case. In Parel's persuasive analysis, Gandhi's belief in the possibility of an autonomous acceptance of *dharma*–a voluntary acceptance

acceptance of a communitarian ethic and hence a combination of positive and negative types of liberty–lifts the Gandhian concept of individualism over the merely self-seeking, egotistical, laissez-faire version. But where does this leave attitudes towards the State?

In Vasudha Dhagmar's lively piece, Indians are exhorted no longer to look on the state through the derogatory approach of the non-cooperation movement, but as a democratic state. Admittedly, she begins her article with a pretty bleak account of the break-down of the judicial system in Bihar and elsewhere: there are some truly shocking figures of those detained without trial. This cannot inspire confidence in the state. But a negative attitude towards the state gets one nowhere. There was the utter folly of murdering the young District Magistrate from Bihar, Krishnaiah. Even Gandhi had no wish to bring the law into contempt. How absurd, in Dhagmar's opinion, that when NGO's cooperate with the state, they are branded as collaborationist. Here is a significant attempt at a revisionism of Gandhi's political message.

Conflict Resolution

How viable is *satyagraha* today as a means of resolving conflict? Or has violence overtaken non-violence? Symptomatic of the latter is a readiness to see even in Gandhi a willingness on occasion to compromise with violence–how we interpret 1942 is here critical–and to speculate on the interconnectedness anyway of violence and non-violence in Indian culture.[5] Yet the old tried and tested means of struggle can still produce results. One outstanding example today is the Narmada Bashao Andolan (Save Narmada Movement), a nation-wide campaign against the huge irrigation schemes on the Narmada river. These, it is claimed, will canalise water from upstream to the drought zone of Kutch, Saurastra and North Gujarat. This is a protest against such white elephants of modern development and one in the name of an alternative approach to development, both decentralised, and one which looks to more environmentally friendly ways of water conservation. It also has profound cultural concerns. This is both an attempt to preserve the traditional culture of the forest people and to protect the ancient archaeological sites on this sacred river. It has not been without success. Already it has seen the withdrawal in 1993 of the World Bank from funding the linchpin of the scheme, the Sardar Sarvodar dam. Recently, the Government of Madya Pradesh is also beginning to rethink at least the height of the dam. This may add up to no more than a delaying action. But the struggle continues.[6]

In Sunderlal Bahuguna's personal narrative we hear the authentic voice of Gandhism in action. His has been a life-time of protest on behalf of Gandhian causes: his earlier campaign for prohibition, the *Chipko* movement, to protect the forest, latterly against the ecologically damaging scheme of the Tehri dam.

Is there a Gandhian solution for Northern Ireland? Did, indeed, Gandhi have an answer to Terrorism? Probably we still underestimate the appeal of Terrorism as a tactic during the freedom struggle and the degree to which Gandhi's *satyagraha* was its conscious rejoinder. Terrorism emerged as a tactic in 19th Century Russia and at the turn of the century in India and, common to both as an explanation, was a lack of democratic structures, an inability of the populists in Russia to make effective links with the peasantry and of the fledgling nationalist movement in India with the masses. In despair at expressing their beliefs, a minority element within these movements took to terrorism. In Russia there was a strongly pathological element to terrorism. In India it was a youth protest, often inept and immature. But, despite the more democratic structures brought about by Gandhi's leadership of Congress, it continued to exert an appeal. In Northern Ireland from the 1970's, terrorism threatened to become so engrained that it was tempting to give way to despair of any democratic alternative. One who did not do so was John Hume. 'From the beginning', he stated, 'I have argued that two mind-sets have to change if we are to solve the problem: Nationalists have to be persuaded that it's about people and not territory, and that people should be living not dying for Ireland; Unionists have to give up the view only their own exclusive possession of power can protect their interests.'[7] The only way out of the deadlock was to persuade terrorists that there was a viable democratic alternative. John Hume's conversations with Sinn Fein and the IRA were crucially instrumental in bringing about this change of mind.

In a penetrating piece, Peter Cadogan, the Gandhi Foundation's Coordinator for Northern Ireland Project, explores the frightening religious fundamentalism that lies behind the nationalism in Ireland. It was not always so, but he points to a tradition from Wolfe Tone, to Patrick Pearce, to Gerry Adams. It is an outlook that has warped both the Catholic Nationalists and the Protestant Unionists. Here lies the force behind the terrorism on both sides. But terrorism need not feature.

Interestingly, the IRA was disbanded in 1962 and it was only reincarnated as the Provos in 1969 following Protestant attacks, associated with the Unionist paramilitary organisation, the UVF, set up in 1966. This is a bleak environment. We are reminded of William Golding's parable, *The Lord of the Flies*, that thin veneer of civilisation. Beneath the fragile crust, a smouldering violence, Freud's dark vision of the unconscious. 'Today's fundamentalism', states Cadogan, 'is a greater killer than the Cold War ever was.' So what solution can there be, he asks, to a victory or death situation? As a good Gandhian, he has not given up hope. He believes that the solution has to lie in an agreement between the two communities in Northern Ireland. The answers lie in Belfast and Derry rather than in London, Dublin and Washington. He puts his faith in the very Gandhian Peace People, set up in 1976, and its three Nobel Peace prize winners, Ciaran McKeown, Mairead Corrigan (Maguire), and Betty Williams.

Does a Gandhian approach equally apply to the resolution of international conflict? Can it provide the basis for peace? According to Neville Maxwell, there was one extraordinary attempt at a Gandhian solution to a conflict, the way India defended its borders against the Chinese in 1962.[8] But India drew a non-Gandhian lesson from this crisis, the need to be far better prepared militarily. Possibly, from that point, one can date India's quest to become the superpower in the region. Ted Dunn has some very interesting proposals for peace in the region. An equivalent to the Council of Europe should be set up for South Asia. Rather than a market-led solution to its economic backwardness, there should be a Marshall Aid style programme for the region, with a readiness to accept inter-state cooperation the condition for entry. There should be a regional secretariat. A five to ten year programme of aid to village communities would follow, based on intermediate technology, forestation, and the provision of clean drinking water. The economy would be geared to self-sufficiency rather than export. Disarmament throughout the region would release the funds for development. The multi-nationals, claims Dunn, would welcome such a change, as it would be all the easier for them to market their goods. It is, of course, a utopian vision, and postulates an equilibrium between states all the harder to achieve now that India has achieved super-power status in the region.

Alison Williams, in a piece too long effectively to summarise here, invests an equal optimism in a vision of a world citizenship under the 'global governance' of the UN., a Gandhian global 'federation of villages' for the 21st Century. She recognises the need for fairly drastic reform of present-day UN institutions. It is underfunded. Its regular income is no more than that of a major US city. Its secretariat is no larger than that of Saatchi and Saatchi. How can the UN continue to take on major emergencies which occur every three weeks when anyone of them is beyond the capacity of any one member state? The composition of the Security Council has to be reformed. How can its institutions be so democratised that we become genuine citizens of the world rather than but represented as global inhabitants? She points to the work of CAMDUN, the Campaign for a more Democratic UN. Intriguingly, she sees cause for hope in current theories of chaos and complexity. Howard Horsburgh ruminates on these questions, exploring in a critical way different levels and methods of peace-keeping, from that of the diplomatic alliance, to a system of collective security, to an international peace-keeping force. His is a pragmatic approach. Often we have to settle for less. If capitalism be the world's choice, then we can but seek to mitigate its character, pointless to go on weeping in vain for socialism.

Conclusion

Gandhi was a this-wordly man, a practitioner of *karma yoga*. His was a never ceasing quest to solve problems in the here and now. This explains his emphasis on means over ends. There was, of course, a higher moral, indeed, metaphysical purpose. Such means are the way to self-realisation. Practical action took precedence over prayer (*bhakti*) or knowledge (*jnana*). Grappling with tangible difficulties lends an immediacy to the Gandhian imperative. It is this very insistence on the particular that almost converts Gandhi into a modern. Certainly, in every generation, he will never cease to be a contemporary. Should he be labelled a Utopian for endeavouring to spare India the travails of industrial capitalism, or, at the least, to mitigate its damage? But India has chosen a different path, and Gandhi in India has to a large degree been marginalised, or, even worse, pedestalized. This is not to ignore those brave and optimistic Gandhians in India who still seek to realize his ideals. Maybe his farsightedness will yet be grasped, for India is a long way into development, and it is in so-called developed countries that the perceptiveness of his anxieties have become all too painfully apparent. In the programmes of the Green movement, which could just as plausibly be called the Gandhian, his insights are very clearly spelt out. Did the world have to inflict on itself those very policies which Gandhi so passionately opposed to comprehend the full force of his vision? If anything, Gandhi is even more relevant to the contemporary world than to that of his own generation.

In conclusion, there are three articles: one by that most searching of contemporary critics and interpreters of Gandhi's thought, Bhikhu Parekh; one by *Mahendra Kumar*, Editor of *Gandhi Marg*, a wide-ranging piece, covering many issues raised in this volume, but an essay with grim conclusions; one by the present High Commissioner to the U.K., Dr Singhvi, a loyal supporter of the Gandhi Foundation, a lecture which opens up the relevance of Gandhi's ideas for the next century in ways which this volume as a whole has sought to do.

Notes & References

1. This is a theme the Rudolphs have explored. See L.I. and S.H.Rudolph Gandhi: *the Traditional Roots of Charisma* London and Chicago:1983.

2. Ashis Nandy *The Intimate Enemy: Loss and Recovery of Self under Colonialism* Delhi:1983.

3. I am very grateful to Antje Linkenbach for sending me her essay *Ecological Movements and the Critique of Development: Agents and Interpreters.* Thesis Eleven. Number 39, pp. 63-85.

4. Barrington Moore Jr *Social Origins of Dictatorship and Democracy: Lord and Peasant in the making of the modern world.* New York: 1966.

5. See Denis Vidal, Gilles Tarabout and Eric Mayer, *On the Concept of Violence and Non-Violence in Hinduism and Indian Society* South Asia Research Vol 14 No 2, Autumn pp. 196-213

6. I am very grateful to Alex Wilks, Editor of *The Ecologist*, for keeping me informed of this campaign.

7. *The Independent* 27 October 1993.

8. Neville Maxwell *India's China War* London: 1970.

George Paxton

The Gandhi Foundation

The wide appeal of Gandhi's personality and ideas as well as the historical connection between Britain and India would, one might think, have resulted in the formation shortly after Indian independence of a society to promote Gandhi's philosophy in Britain. And although from the Indian side, Radhakrishna, Secretary of the Gandhi Peace Foundation, and J.P. Narayan on several occasions urged such a step, it was not until the early 1980s that the catalyst appeared.

Richard Attenborough's film on Gandhi attracted enormous audiences around the world and some of the fascination of the real man was vividly conveyed by Ben Kingsley's sensitive portrayal. To meet the interest aroused by the film, biographies of Gandhi were brought back into print and his autobiography became readily available to the interested public. The time was obviously ripe for a Gandhi society and so Surur Hoda, an Indian working for the International Transport Worker's Federation and settled in Britain, made the vital contacts. One of the key figures was David Ennals, a former Cabinet Minister in a Labour Government, who had recently been given a life peerage. Another was a prominent member of the Society of Friends, Cecil Evans, Assistant General Secretary of Quaker Peace and Service. The Friends have a long-standing interest in Gandhi whose ideas and life are so compatible with the ideals they profess. These three then approached Richard Attenborough in the hope that he would agree to be the President of such a society, which he did.

Many other people thought likely to be sympathetic to this ver..ure were contacted and on 10th October 1983 the Gandhi Foundation was launched at a meeting attended by about 200 people in Friends House in London. In addition to Sir Richard Attenborough as President, the Rt. Hon. Lord Ennals became Chair, Surur Hoda the General Secretary, and Cecil Evans was called Adviser, later Vice-Chair of the Foundation. Eleven years later these four are still the office-bearers with the addition of Elizabeth Clarke in the vital role of Treasurer.

The aim of the Foundation was seen as essentially an educational one: to disseminate knowledge of Gandhi and his ideas and relate them to contemporary society. To promote these aims, within a couple of years there had evolved three annual events and a quarterly newsletter. On the anniversary of Gandhi's assassination, 30th January, there is held, normally in central London, a Multifaith Service bringing together people of different faiths such as Buddhist, Christian, Hindu, Jain, Jewish, Muslim, Sikh in remembrance of Gandhi and to share in words, music and dance something of their different traditions. In July there is held a Summer School in Oxfordshire where about forty people of all ages live together for a week, sharing the necessary tasks of cleaning, cooking and washing-up as well as attending daily workshops which take up different aspects of the theme chosen for that year. A variety of crafts are taught, and in general our lifestyles and attitudes are challenged. Many find this an enlightening experience and some return year after year. Some of the participants come from India and other countries. The third event of the year is a lecture which is usually held on Gandhi's birthday, 2nd October, but sometimes is different to suit the availability of the lecturer. Prominent Lecturers have included Professor Johan Galtung, the distinguished sociologist, Jonathan Porritt of Friends of the Earth, Ian Martin of Amnesty International, Professor Paul Blau of the Austrian Green movement, and the Dalai Lama who, not surprisingly, attracted an overflow audience. In 1989 instead of a lecture, a television Channel 4 panel discussion was broadcast, the majority of the participants being Gandhi Foundation members. This, of course, reached a vastly greater audience than the normal lecture.

All Friends of the Foundation receive a newsletter quarterly and this is the main means of communication with most subscribers. The first editor was Kathleen Jannaway who had been Secretary of the Vegan Society and then founder of the Movement for Compassionate Living. She was followed by Rosalind Schama for a short period, and then George Paxton who is the current editor of what is now called *The Gandhi Way*. A more recent service to the readers is the offer for sale of books imported from India and Gandhi's own writings have proved the most popular of those offered. A few pamphlets have been published by the Foundation: a bibliography of Gandhian titles and a lecture *The Relevance of Gandhi in the West*, both by Rex Ambler, and *Gandhi and Western Education Today* by Julian Brotherton. A video on cooperative games mainly for primary age children was made by Mildred Masheder.

Although most of the work of the Foundation is done by volunteers, there has usually been a part-time administrator located at Kingsley Hall in Bow in east London. Founded during the First World War by sisters Muriel and Doris Lester as a community centre, the present building became the base for Gandhi when he came to the Second Round Table Conference in 1931. Two small rooms used by Gandhi are the office of the Foundation today. The area in which Kingsley Hall is situated has been settled by immigrants from a variety of countries over a long period. Most recently large numbers of Bangladeshis have made their home here. Because it is an area of disadvantage and racial tension, at an early stage in the Foundation's life it was suggested that some sort of practical work ought to be done there. In spite of many meetings with local individuals and groups no on-going 'constructive work' has resulted yet. But at the time of writing, workshops on community peacebuilding are being held in Kingsley Hall organised by Tom Daffern.

Because of violent conflict within part of the UK itself, there has been for several years a Northern Ireland Project supervised by Peter Cadogan who has made an in-depth study of the problem and established many links with people in Northern Ireland and concerned people in other parts of Britain. As well as keeping Friends of the Foundation informed he has had many letters published in newspapers on both sides of the Irish Sea putting forward proposals towards a settlement of the conflict.

While the Gandhi Foundation remains a small organisation (around 500 Friends) it has carried out a substantial programme of education in its first decade of existence with prospects of further dissemination of knowledge of Gandhi and his philosophy in the second decade. Whether it has the resources in terms of personpower and finance to carry out community projects in particular areas remains to be seen.

Thomas Weber

Gandhism, Optimism and the Gandhians

Interestingly, when the current state of the Gandhian legacy is discussed, the examples tend not to come from India. And this appears to be not merely a cultural misappropriation - Indian Gandhians will often say to foreign inquirers that Gandhi has been forgotten in India, that he is being re-imported from the West. In these conversations names such as those of Attenborough and Schumacher loom large.[1] But there are still a great many dedicated Gandhians carrying on the work of the Mahatma in Bharat and in any discussion about the position of Gandhi today it would be instructive to examine their perspective.[2]

The Gandhians do not necessarily speak with one voice. The differences, over and above those of individual characteristics, often depend on the ideology of the individual, whether his or her world view has been coloured more by Vinoba Bhave or Jayaprakash Narayan, and whether they believe that the political situation in the country is deteriorating so rapidly that the "need of the hour" forces them to compromise on ideals (if not their fundamental principles) in the way that Gandhi often did.[3]

During the mid 1970s, as a result of the Bihar agitation and JP's campaign of Total Revolution which followed, the Gandhian movement split over fundamental philosophical issues. The two leaders of the Gandhian movement, JP and Vinoba, eventually came to differ in their interpretation of the use of *satyagraha*, in the methods to be employed to bring about societal change, the speed at which useful change was possible to achieve, the degree to which Gandhians should be involved in power politics, and the importance of spiritual versus humanist reasons for acting.

Until then the movement seemed united and appeared to be speaking with one voice.[4] JP's general deference to Vinoba's leadership finally ceased following JP's frustrating experience of grassroots work in 1970-1 in the villages of Musahari in Bihar. This had two marked consequences: first JP's realisation that the results of constructive peacebuilding work in the Vinoban tradition did not justify the effort.[5] This in turn led JP back to his pre-Gandhian roots in political activism. Secondly, his emergence from Vinoba's shadow into a position of rival leadership. This led to open differences and to JP taking active control of the movement.[6] The result was a split among the Gandhians that has still not quite healed. The lifting of measures aimed at suppressing the Gandhian movement during Mrs.Gandhi's "emergency" could have heralded a new high point for Gandhian influence in India, however the Janata debacle merely helped to marginalise an already weakened movement.

The Gandhians

Vinoba explained that with the progress of science and the creation of nuclear weapons humanity faced ultimate destruction. In order to neutralise this force of violence and to arouse the world's conscience Gandhi's nonviolence had to take on "more subtle and finer forms." *Satyagraha* could no longer afford to "create agitation or tension in the minds of the opponent," it had to avoid a "collision of minds and seek harmony in thought."[7] Until change was brought about through understanding and acceptance, rather than through imposition, "the seeds of violence, imperialism and world wars would not be rooted out."[8]

Satyagraha had to progress as the political situation progressed (from imperialist domination to "democracy" in India) and as science progressed. Consequently, Vinoba declared that Jesus' concept of "resist not evil" and Gandhi's "nonviolent resistance" were no longer adequate and what now had to take their place was "nonviolent assistance" in right thinking.[9] Without this all that could be achieved was legislative reform, and that could never lead to total revolution. Vinoba saw the use of political structures as a method of solving problems as doomed to failure: "When one problem appears to be nearing a solution, ten others crop up", and when a solution appears to have been achieved "soon it raises its head again."[10] In his analysis of the Bihar movement, Shah maintains that Vinoba had long been anxious to discover a new technique because of the traps of the false assumption that once an opposing leader is removed all will be well, and the "impassioned tensions" of political movements that distract people from their original objectives.[11] With *Bhoodan,* the land-gift movement, he had already provided the classical example.

The transformation to a *sarvodaya* social order was to be accomplished without directly challenging the legitimacy of the state, for, after all, in a democratic system, power had been entrusted to the state by the people. However, it could not be achieved through the ballot which Vinoba saw as either a farce that left real power in the hands of the few, or as a formula for disruption.[12] Vinoba's aim was to create conditions which would "do away with the need to use even the power of the State."[13] The achievement of this anarchist polity was to come about gradually – he was not anti-state; he, hoped to bypass the structures on which the state rested and thus allow it to wither away. Vinoba was fond of saying that politics disintegrates and spirituality unites.[14] He made it clear that for him there could be no outward revolution without a corresponding internal one, without a change in mental attitude: "All revolutions which take place, whether they are social or economic, have their roots in spiritual ideas. At first there is a change in spiritual values and later on social, political and economic values undergo change."[15]

Given his activist background, it is not surprising that at the time of this intellectual reassessment, JP's analysis of the political situation and his understanding of *satyagraha* would mature into something substantially different from Vinoba's, that unlike Vinoba he would embrace the position of Gandhi the politician over Gandhi the saint.

While still very much in the shadow of Vinoba, JP saw *bhoodan*, bringing about "changes of the heart", as the vehicle for the establishment of a *sarvodaya* social order. If this failed in the first instance, he looked to the experience of Gandhi to provide a path for further action. Subsequent steps were to include an attempt to educate the public to the evil that was being opposed, followed by the launching of movements to place moral pressure on the "wrong-doer" or "mistaken party" and finally by resorting to non-cooperation on the assumption that injustice was only possible with the cooperation of the wronged party.

In the diary that he wrote while in prison during Mrs.Gandhi's Emergency, JP noted that although Vinoba seemed to hold that "systematic change in the political order could be brought about without a struggle, even a peaceful struggle," after twenty years of effort nowhere had success been achieved.[16] He continued, pointing out that one of the reasons for this was a lack of *atmosphere* of struggle: "it seems to me that in such an atmosphere psychological forces are created that attract men and drive them to accept challenges and to change themselves and others." While conceding that during the *Bhoodan* movement through "Spiritual and moral appeals, the saintly influence of Vinobaji, did bring about some remarkable moral changes in some individuals," he concluded that these could "never become a social or psychological force"[17] that would be effective in securing a more just society. While Vinoba strove for perfect nonviolence, JP spoke of social change through a mass movement of peaceful people's power"[18].

JP's primary concern was the achievement of real democracy and a society devoid of inequalities where all lived in a state of freedom.[19] His concerns, like Vinoba's, were centred on the problems of the human condition – freedom of the human personality, of the mind and of the spirit – but his quest was a political, not a spiritual, one.[20] He was searching for the form of social organisation which would provide the masses with the maximum freedom, and the most appropriate way of bringing it about.

JP shared Vinoba's view of a village society and the way that it should be organised. In an open letter to his Praja Socialist comrades, when he finally announced his resignation from the Party in 1957, JP made the point that although he had withdrawn from politics, *sarvodaya* also had its politics - a politics of a different kind. Unlike the politics of party and power, *sarvodaya* politics rested on *lokniti* (politics of the people) as opposed to *rajniti* (politics of the state). He added that *sarvodaya* politics could have "no party and no concern with power." Its aim was to abolish all centres of power and to achieve a withering away of the state. As this "new politics grew" JP saw a corresponding diminution of the "old politics."[21]

In his analysis of the relationship of the Gandhian movement to politics at the 1961 All India Sarvodaya Conference, JP noted that, as Gandhians, they did not belong in political parties and should not "take part, directly or indirectly, in any political contest for position and power." He added, however, that this did not mean that they should be unconcerned with what happened in the political field with the working of democracy. He asked rhetorically whether, if democracy was in peril or if there was danger of political chaos or dictatorship, they should "sit back smugly and twiddle our thumbs on the ground that we have nothing to do with new politics?"[22]

JP was for a partyless democracy but he saw that there was no alternative to parties in the short term, not until a lengthy process of mass political education had managed to eradicate the distinctions of class and caste.[23] Rather than merely allowing the state to wither away he saw danger for the future if antidemocratic tendencies in power politics were not tackled. During the Bihar Movement he reiterated the partyless ideal while organising a party to oppose Mrs.Gandhi.[24] In his prison diary, in direct contrast to the position of Vinoba, JP wrote: "No one, at least no one who has no party affiliation and therefore no motivation to exploit every situation for partisan ends, and who is still anxious to start a peaceful revolutionary movement, i.e. a movement to bring about basic changes in society and in social attitudes, can ever, in the conditions of our country, avoid a confrontation with the kind of government we have."[25]

His rejection of Vinoba's "positive" *satyagraha* came from his realisation that it was inadequate to produce the psychological climate necessary to bring about the social revolution he desired. And to the charge that his change of direction was politicising the *sarvodaya* movement he answered that such politicisation "should give it immense strength and make it more relevant to contemporary society.[26]

Both Vinoba and JP knew that the nonviolent revolution they desired would only be achieved through the efforts of the people themselves. The differences centred around the means that would be employed by the people to bring this revolution about. Ostergaard makes the point that whereas Western anarchism is "immediatist", Indian anarchism is "gradualist" .[27] JP was more anarchistic in the Western sense, reverting to active struggle and "negative" *satyagraha*. Unlike Vinoba, he was also anti-state, pitting people's power *against* that of the state.[28] Vinoba, on the other hand, was a gradualist, far more concerned with the purity of the means than with any immediate ends that may be achieved. In this he was following the Gandhian dictum that the ends grew out of the means employed, and echoing Gandhi's statement that even if a Hitler's heart was not "melted" by the efforts of the pure *satyagrahi* it did not matter because intrinsic values were as important as any instrumental considerations.

The differing approaches of the two Gandhian leaders was dependent on their personal convictions, and perhaps even more on the differences in personality between

Vinoba and JP. Vinoba, stressing spiritual values, placed primary consideration on the conversion of the individual so that these individuals could bring about the hoped for changes in society. For him changes in the social structure would not come about without adequate moral development.[29] JP on the other hand, unsurprisingly given his lengthy association with Marxism, saw it as more practical and perhaps more logical that people would change once the environment had been changed.[30]

The perceived failure of Vinoba's approach to bringing about meaningful change led to the more confrontational position of JP. However, given the failure of tackling the government head-on as a way to usher in the nonviolent revolution (and in any case the lack of resources to do so), a further re-evaluation was to be expected. That efforts in India are again being concentrated on local peacebuilding as a way of bringing about change, which is a far longer-term project, seems to reflect a return to what may be termed Gandhian basics enabled by the stubborn optimism of the Gandhian fraternity. Perhaps this can be coupled with the simple fact that this approach embodies a more realistic interpretation of the current political circumstances prevailing in the country.

With the passing of the old guard of Gandhian politicians and the alienation of the weakened Gandhian movement from the central authorities, there is very little scope for the toleration of a highly organised group whose avowed aim is to make the state redundant – even if it were possible in some way to recreate the heyday of the Gandhian movement.

The Marginalisation of the Gandhian Movement

In his landmark work *Asian Drama*, published in 1968, Swedish economist Gunnar Myrdal provided an analysis of the social and economic factors affecting India's rate and level of development. There, Myrdal designated the country a "soft state", that is one where governmental decision making shies away from placing obligations on the populace, and if policies are framed in legislative terms at all, often they are not enforced.[31]

The Indian State bureaucracy did not have the ability to reach into every village. This, coupled with the Gandhian legacy, including that of resistance to governmental coercion and a philosophical commitment to the proposition "that democratic planning requires the people's participation and initiative.... in the course of creating the new institutions for self-government and cooperation,[32] ensured that *sarvodaya* workers would play a large part in the country's path to development. Myrdal believed that "rapid development will be exceedingly difficult to engender without an increase in social discipline in all strata and even in the villages."[33] And here he means state imposed discipline. In other words for effective "development" a "strong" or "hard" state was a necessity – the Gandhians, however, by very definition, were the champions of an even further "softening" of the state.

Much has happened since the words of Myrdal were written. During his inaugural presidential address at a 1972 Sarva Seva Sangh[34] conference, Siddharaj Dhadda stated that:

> The aim of the *Sarvodaya* movement is to make the people conscious about the reality of the present situation, to diminish their reliance on government, to help them organise their strength and take the management of their affairs in their own hands. We want the establishment of a real participatory democracy in the place of the present representative one. Representative democracy may have been good in the past when science and technology had not advanced to the extent as to enable the representatives to obtain a stranglehold on the lives of the people through state machinery. The exercise of the power of the Government in the old context was confined to performing its legitimate function of a peace-keeping and coordinating agency ... the people were masters of their own lives and destiny, without let or hindrance from outside forces. But the phenomenal advance of science has created a strange paradox. It has made possible and has actually led to an ever increasing concentration of power, political, economic, military, into the hands of an ever diminishing number of people – a smaller and smaller coterie.[35]

In short, India was rapidly losing its status as a "soft state".

With the passing of Nehru and the estrangement between the Gandhian movement and his daughter following JP's call for "Total Revolution", the *sarvodaya* establishment lost government support for, and was even actively obstructed in, carrying out its voluntary social work activities. As the nation increasingly took on the trappings of a "hard state", particularly under the regime of Rajiv Gandhi, the Gandhian movement (along with other voluntary agencies) was further pushed to the periphery in terms of the inputs it could provide to the shaping of social organisation and development.[36] This trend has been exacerbated by the ever declining appeal of Gandhian philosophy to the youth of the country with a rapidly swelling middle class desiring an increase in consumer goods, and the absence of a charismatic leader among Gandhians that could counter it.

Perhaps a strong Gandhian movement, as it worked in the 1960s and early 1970s, cannot be tolerated by a state where the political leadership no longer has a philosophical commitment to the values of the "Father of the Nation", where Gandhian ideas about societal organisation are often derided as being utopian and irrelevant as the country moves towards the Twenty-first Century, and where the organisation itself is the self-declared vanguard of a revolution aimed at a destruction of the Indian polity as it has evolved in the years since independence. Further, perhaps this type of organisation can only be tolerated where bureaucracy does not permeate all levels of society, where the state does not have the resources to provide its own rapid and adequate intervention in times of social turmoil. As states "harden", the operation of such groups becomes incompatible with a government that seeks to establish its position as legitimate and sole sovereign.[37]

In 1964, leading Gandhian Narayan Desai was already lamenting that the Sangh's peace brigade, the Shanti Sena, faced two problems that prevented it from being as "effective as it should be." He named them as a lack of means of quick communication and an extreme lack of finances.[38] The situation for the *sarvodaya* movement has deteriorated since. At a time when the ability of the state to move its own functionaries around the country has been aided by the increasing mobility of its armed forces, Gandhian institutions, ever further removed in history from Gandhi himself, are increasingly feeling the economic pinch. And, as the government moves inexorably into areas that were once the domain of Gandhian institutions, people are less willing to donate money to groups that are increasingly seen as costly and amateur parallel organisations.[39]

Erica Linton, an observer of the *sarvodaya* movement at the height of its power, made a telling point in this regard. Touring Gandhian pilgrimage sites in Pune with a non-Gandhian chauffeur, at the *samadhi* of the Mahatma's late secretary Mahadev Desai in the Agha Khan's palace, she turned to her escort and remarked: "'You know, I suppose, that Mahadev's son Narayan is the secretary of the *Shanti Sena*?' 'Oh, you mean the American Peace Corps', explained the driver. What a sorry state of affairs", she commented "when foreign volunteers make a greater impact on the community than their own young men."[40] It was this realisation that led to the setting up of a youth wing of the *Shanti Sena* following the Bihar famine of 1966-7. The attempts at Gandhian peace and constructive work, however, never reached the critical mass necessary to make the ignorance of Linton's driver anything other than the norm. And with the decline in, and marginalisation of the Gandhian movement in the years since, there is little evidence that there is any scope for optimism on the part of the Gandhian establishment that there will be any change in this situation in the foreseeable future.

Optimism

Dictionary definitions of optimism mention the inclination to take the most hopeful view of a given situation, the opinion that everything will turn out for the best, that good in the end will triumph over evil. This in turn implies that humans are basically good and therefore can control the evil in themselves and in society.

Gandhi often wrote of his optimism. He based his optimism on his belief in himself and on his personal expectations.[41] He placed himself among the "tribe of Columbus and Stevenson, who hoped against hope in the face of heaviest odds," noting that the "days of miracles are not gone."[42] And although he claimed to base his optimism "on solid facts,"[43] the more cynical observers of his life need only point to the mass killings in his homeland at the end of his long life of preaching the gospel of non-violence to claim that the optimism was misplaced. In the end Gandhi would perhaps have agreed with them, and given what has become of the India of his dreams,[44] perhaps pessimism is a more realistic attitude to hold.

The opening sentence of a recent book on pessimism informs us that "it is now difficult to be optimistic."[45] The book, *Pessimism*, was written just before the end of the

Cold War. It gives as the reasons for pessimism a declining faith in progress, the (now at least temporarily diminished) threat of nuclear war, and our destructive treatment of the environment with the resulting problems with feeding the hungry and generating safe energy. Since the heyday of the Gandhian movement, India has experienced increased communal violence, consumerism and centralising tendencies about which the heirs of the Mahatma have been able to do little.

Bailey, the author of *Pessimism*, sees new social movements, especially in the fields of ecology, peace and feminism as being the new sources of progressiveness. However, progressiveness and newness, or even popularity and persistence, are not measures of effectiveness. They do not of themselves demonstrate "success in shifting the old politics in a more benign direction." In his assessment of nuclear disarmament campaigns and "green" parties, he concludes that given the continuing arms race and exploitation of the environment, "there is little sign of encouraging success".[46] Bailey sees little possibility of success in situations where the movements cannot win in parliaments. And for social movements this is extremely unlikely – except in the case of the Gandhian movement, perhaps the archetypal social movement, which ushered in the Janata government in India. And that led to perhaps its last great failure.

Those descendants of the "irrepressible optimist" who threw their lot in with direct political action as the vehicle of change exhibit a noticeable level of pessimism. They saw a long-term view and strategy as inadequate in a rapidly deteriorating world – the "need of the hour" compelled immediate action.[47] However, this approach also meant short-term defeats. Without a charismatic leader they are unable to capture the imagination of the populace, their message is considered irrelevant in the light of a growing consumerist ethic, people's candidates fail in elections that are dominated by personalities rather than issues; and as the state takes on an increasing number of the functions that were previously the domain of the voluntary sector, and the Gandhians are categorised (or were during the Indira Gandhi government when they were still a force to be reckoned with) as a *de facto* opposition party, the *sarvodaya* movement has become increasingly marginalised. While they cling to their long-term vision the lack of direct short-term victories dampens their feeling of optimism.

The followers of Vinoba have a different history. To generalise, their optimism appears to be based on faith rather than experience and they tend to believe in the intrinsic good, regardless of the apparent instrumental applications, of their philosophy in action.

Conclusion

The walls of almost every Gandhian home or institution are adorned with pictures of Gandhi (who tried political and spiritual, long and short term approaches in his optimist's quest to bring about change), and the pictures of both JP and Vinoba (who, perhaps not unrealistically, tended to be polarised in their approaches). It is possible to see Vinoba's gradualist approach as being ultimately correct in a deep Gandhian sense– while still maintaining a desire for tangible results. The path of ignoring the government, of working outside its structures and letting it wither away ("worldly" success), can only be achieved if enough people follow it through, not merely the odd saint. The result-oriented confrontational approach has a far better chance of mobilising the masses and seems to have a better chance of at least limited success, and also a greater chance of ultimate failure. Its success cannot make government wither away or achieve the "other worldly" ideals inherent in "pure" *satyagraha*, it can only replace the political structure with a less oppressive one.

Confronting the power structure head-on, however, means that the government cannot ignore its antagonist and ensures that all the forces at its disposal will be directed at crushing any direct opposition. Some opted for the political approach of JP hoping that it could succeed, while maintaining the nagging feeling that in the long run it could not provide the ushering in of the Gandhian ideal. Since the failure of the Total Revolution the conundrum involved in the "this-worldly" versus the "other-worldly" manifestations of *satyagraha* is still being worked through.

Despite the objective reality of their present weakened position in Indian society, the Gandhians are nevertheless generally optimistic about the value of Gandhism as a force to be reckoned with, one which can bring about change for the good. And the most optimistic are the Vinoba supporters, who have not suffered the same tangible defeats as their colleagues who entered the political fray. They see that their message, if not necessarily their movement of old, is one for the ages. They realise that the process will be slow, that there will be setbacks, but are convinced that it will eventually win through, that with a continuation of grassroots work success is assured. By organic means, Gandhi's message will triumph. They firmly believe that all signs point to this outcome - the increasing number of social movements around the world now employing Gandhian methods and the approach of environmental collapse is forcing a re-evaluation of the hegemony of Western lifestyle and consumption patterns in a way that indicates a shift towards a Gandhian outlook. Although others may see them as anachronistic, and it is reasonable to be pessimistic about the future of the old Gandhians ever again being in the vanguard of a dynamic and influential social movement, they believe that the march of history is now coming the full circle and that they are merely ahead of the times. For life on the planet to continue a simple life is necessary, and in order to survive the rest of the world will catch up eventually. It is not a belief in the possibility of miracles, but one that says that humankind is wise enough not to destroy itself or its environment. This self-assured belief in being on the right path leaves no room for pessimism.

Notes & References

1. This traffic is not completely one way, West to East. There is at least one relatively well-known current example of Gandhism moving in the original direction: that of the Chipko movement. See T.Weber *Hugging the Trees: The Story of the Chipko Movement* (New Delhi: Penguin, 1989).

2. The generalised impressions that follow are based on interviews with leading Gandhians who were involved in the Gandhian movement at its peak in the 1960s and early 1970s, conducted between November 1988 and February 1989. The interviews form part of another, larger project: the chronicling of the history of the Shanti Sena. Without the assistance of the Gandhian old guard the following could not have been written – nevertheless responsibility for the conclusions drawn from what they said to me is entirely my own.

3. I have tried to explore some of the issues surrounding this question in the article "The Lesson from the Disciples: Is There a Contradiction in Gandhi's Philosophy of Action?" *Modern Asian Studies* vol.28, no. 1 (1994), pp. 195–214.

4. However, initial signs of differences between the two leading figures in the movement could be discerned as early as October 1962 when Chinese troops invaded territory claimed by India. See T.Weber, "Peacekeeping, the Shanti Sena and Divisions in the Gandhian Movement During the Border War with China" *South Asia*, vol. 1 3, no.2 (1990), pp.65-78.

5. See Narayan "Face to Face", in J.P.Narayan, *Towards Total Revolution*, vol. 1 1 (Bombay: Popular, 1978), p.246.

6. For a detailed description of the later history of the Gandhian movement see G.Ostergaard, *Nonviolent Revolution in India* (New Delhi: Gandhi Peace Foundation, 1985); R.Church, "Vinoba Bhave, Jayaprakash Narayan and Indian Democracy", *Gandhian Perspectives*, vol.1 1, no.2 (1980), pp.89-129; and T.Weber, *Unarmed Peacekeeping and Gandhi's Peace Army: The Shanti Sena* (New York: Syracuse University Press, forthcoming).

7. Quoted in V.Tandon (ed.) *Selections from Vinoba* (Varanasi: Sarva Seva Sangh, 1981), p.281.

8. *Harijan* 7 July 1951.

9. K.Shah, (ed.), *Vinoba on Gandhi* (Varanasi: Sarva Seva Sangh, 1985), p.52.

10. K.Shah *Vinoba: Life and Mission: An Introductory Study* (Varanasi: Sarva Seva Sangh, 1979), p-135.

11. Shah, p. 1 37.

12. V.Bhave, *Democratic* Values (Varanasi: Sarva Seva Sangh, 1962), p.67.

13. V.Bhave *Bhoodan Yagna* (Ahmedabad: Navajivan, 1957), p.87.

14. See Shah, p-135.

15. See Tandon (ed.), p.91.

16. J.P.Narayan, *Prison Diary* (Bombay: Popular, 1977), pp.21-22. At the time Nargolkar had summarised the position thus: "So far as Vinobaji's theory on non-violent revolution is concerned, it may be granted for the sake of argument, that it is impec-

cable. But in practice, it failed to deliver the goods in terms of revolutionary changes in the present social and economic structure ... the gramdan-gram-swarajya programme never rose to the pitch of a mass-movement. Later, it degenerated into a hopelessly local activity sustained with tremendous effort by a few dedicated workers, who were constantly goaded by Vinobaji. There was no enthusiastic participation by the people. There was no involvement of the people in gramdani villages in the difficult task of promoting Sarvodaya ideals in their individual and collective lives." V.Nargolkar, *JP's Crusade for Revolution* (New Delhi: Chand and Co., 1975), pp.86-87.

17. Narayan *Prison Diary* p.22. At times he was even more blunt when contrasting Vinoba's gentle/gentler approach with peaceful people's struggle for revolutionary changes by claiming that he could not "understand Vinobaji on this point", adding that Vinoba had not demonstrated in practice just how the desired progression could be made; see Narayan, *Towards Total Revolution*, vol.4, p. 1 87.

18. JP came to the conclusion that while Vinoba's aim was change through complete nonviolence "the observance of complete non-violence was not possible in a mass movement", consequently he declared his objective to be a little less ambitious: "social change through peaceful people's power." See "Why Total Revolution," in Narayan, *Towards Total Revolution* in, vol.4, pp.115-17 at p.115.

19. See "Reconstruction of the Indian Polity," in *Socialism, Sarvodaya and Democracy: Selected Works of Jayaprakash Narayan* ed. B.Prasad (Bombay: Asia, 1964), pp.192-239.

20. JP readily admitted that he had no knowledge of things spiritual in terms of religion or metaphysics. See Narayan, *Toward Total Revolution*, vol.1, pp.96-97. According to JP's friends and biographers, Allan and Wendy Scarfe, by the early 1960s Bhoodan was for JP primarily a way of alleviating the existing problems of landlessness in the quickest way possible rather than as a means of attempting to raise the moral tenor of society in a way that might, at some future time, help solve problems of landlessness and rural poverty. Interview with Allan and Wendy Scarfe on 20 November 1989, at Warrnambool, Victoria.

21. J.P.Narayan, *From Socialism to Sarvodaya* (Varanasi: Sarva Seva Sangh, 1958), p.48. JP did, however, admit that "though all my energies would be bent towards developing *lokniti*, I shall not shut my eyes to what happens in the sphere of *rajniti*." Narayan *From Socialism to Sarvodaya*, p.49.

22. See the published report of JP's "Presidential Address" at the Thirteenth All India Sarvodaya Sammelan (conference) at Sarvodayapuram, in Unguturu, Andhra Pradesh, 18-20 April 1961, p.21. For the argument that Gandhians should "consciously choose to participate in politics and take up positions of authority and power in State administration" in order to bring about a sarvodaya social order, see T.K.Oommen, "Rethinking Gandhian Approach," *Gandhi Marg* vol.1, no.7 (1979), pp.416-23.

23. See A. Bhattacharjea, *Jayaprakash Narayan: A Political Biography* (New Delhi: Vikas, 1975), p.120; and J.P.Narayan "The Revolt Against the System," in *Towards Total Revolution*, vol.4, pp. 121-32 at p. 122.

24. During a press club statement in October 1974 he admitted that this would not lead to a partyless democracy "but to a democracy which has parties. But these parties will be much better controlled by people themselves." *Sarvodaya* vol.24, no.5 (1974), pp.176-77. Elsewhere during this same period, JP noted that partyless democracy is "an ideal", "something for the future", that may come into existence "in the far distance" etc.; see Narayan, *Towards Total Revolution*, vol.4, pp.79-90.

25. Narayan *Prison Diary*, p.57.

26. J.P.Narayan, "The Path of Revolution," in *Towards Total Revolution* vol.4, pp.80-95 at p.94.

27. G.Ostergaard "Vinoba's 'Gradualist' Versus Western 'Immediatist' Anarchism" *Gandhi Marg* vol.5, nos.8&9 (1983), pp.509-530 at p.524.

28. Ostergaard, p.528.

29. See Vinoba's introduction to K.G.Mashruwala, *Gandhi and Marx* (Ahmedabad: Navajivan, 1951), p.12.

30. See Bhramanand, "Jayaprakash Narayan's Views on Peace: A Documentation Article," *Interdiscipline* vol.5, no.12 (1968), pp.78-96 at p.87; For a way this process of change may occur see T.Weber, "The Marchers Simply Walked Forward Until Struck Down: Nonviolent Suffering and Conversion" *Peace and Change* vol. 1 8, no.3 (1993), pp.267-289.

31. G.Myrdal *Asian Drama: An Inquiry into the Poverty of Nations* (Harmondsworth: Penguin, 1968), p.66.

32. Myrdal, p.891.

33. Myrdal, p.899.

34. Formed in 1949 as a confederation of constructive work organisations founded by Gandhi, in effect the governing council of the Gandhian movement.

35. Published report of the half yearly Sarva Seva Sangh conference at Ernakulam on 19 December 1972, p.7.

36. For an articulation of this complaint from the Gandhian point of view see M.Choudhuri *Threats to Liberty* Varanasi, Sarva Seva Sangh, 1983, pp.24.

37. Harris adds that because both sarvodaya and the government have the same clients (villagers), there is a real tussle over a conflict in values. The government has a vision of a high technology future for the country while the Gandhians oppose the technological revolution. The plans they have for rural development and their strong views about the operation of the industrial sector are incompatible. One is concerned

with "development", measured in terms of economic achievement, the other with a more spiritual concept of "uplift", the changing of the moral values of the people through work at the grassroots level. I.Harris "Sarvodaya in Crisis: The Gandhian Movement in India Today" *Asian Survey* vol.27, no.9 (1987), pp. 1036-52 at p. 1042.

38. N.Desai "While the Hearts were Scorched" in Sarva Seva Sangh *A Time to Speak (An Appeal for Rethinking our Communal Disturbances)*, a small pamphlet "Only for private circulation" (n.p.: Sarva Seva Sangh, 1964), pp.19-24 at p.24.

39. Interview with Sarva Seva Sangh secretary Chunibhai Vaidya on 30 November 1988, at the Sabarmati Ashram in Ahmedabad.

40. E.Linton *Fragments of a Vision: A Journey Through India's Gramdan Villages* (Varanasi: Sarva Seva Sangh, 1971), p.1 12.

41. See *Young India* 13 August 1925, CWMG XXVII:448-49.

42. *Harijan* 15 June 1940, CWMG LXXII:161.

43. *Young India* 23 October 1924, CWMG XXV:181.

44. See J.M.Brown *Gandhi: Prisoner of Hope* (New Haven and' London: Yale University Press, 1989), pp.389-391.

45. J.Bailey *Pessimism* (London: Routledge, 1988), p.l.

46. Bailey, p. 153.

47. Here the debate seems to mirror the one engaged in by Western alternative seekers between those who opt out of corporate society and its political processes to live a life of example, and those who see this approach as essentially escapist given that meaningful changes can only come about quickly enough in a rapidly deteriorating world through a direct involvement in the political arena.

Environment and Development

Kamla Chowdhry

Gandhi and Sustainable Development Earth Summit and Agenda 21

In the past twenty years considerable debate and discussion has taken place in various national and international forums about the environmental implications of industrialisation, economic growth, lifestyles and consumerism, waste, pollution, health, quality of life, etc. In June 1992, the United Nations Conference on Environment and Development (UNCED), popularly known as the Earth Summit took place in Rio. The Earth Summit marked the largest gathering of nations, to discuss the dangers to the future of our planet and life support systems, and to evolve policies and institutional mechanisms for sustainable environment and development. More than 170 leaders of countries participated in the Conference and committed their countries to environmentally sustainable development. The Rio Declaration stated "environmental protection shall constitute an integral part of the development process and cannot be considered apart from it."

Also emerging from the Rio Conference was Agenda 21, a master plan of action for moving towards sustainable development. The action plan includes sections on poverty, changing consumption patterns, international trade and cooperation, promoting sustainable agriculture, rural development, desertification and deforestation, protection of atmosphere, oceans and the mountains; toxic, hazardous, radioactive and solid wastes; women and development, indigenous people, the role of NGO's and multi-lateral agencies etc. etc. The Rio Conference also estimated that about $ 600 billion a year would be required for effective earth restoration and for its care and maintenance.

Two years after the Earth Summit and the plan of action as embodied in Agenda 21, the general feeling both in the developed and developing countries is that things are not moving towards the vision as articulated at the Earth Summit. In the earlier UN Conference in 1972, also nothing much happened. Dr Mustafa Tolba, in his State of the Environment Report, 1972-92 said that "time was running out", and that "none of the environmental problems identified by the Stockholm Conference twenty years ago have really been solved – and some of the key issues addressed in 1972 have gone from bad to worse". Crippling and degrading poverty and environmental degradation has spread in many parts of the world.

To many, Agenda 21 has grounds for hope, and to others, it is an empty symbolic gesture. Will Agenda 21 lead the earth's citizens to sustainable development and equitable sharing of the earth's resources? Or will the divide between the rich and the poor, the developed and developing countries increase? Underlying much of the thinking and recommendations of Agenda 21 is a wide-spread presumption that science and technology can overcome our environment and development problems, and allow us to continue expanding resource extraction and their use, producing products and indefinitely raising the material standards of living.

Throughout Agenda 21 there is little mention about the need for limits to growth. Milbrath, discussing the limits to growth concludes "the physical limits to growth in human uses of a finite planet indicate that we cannot sustain our present trajectory. In order to change our trajectory, it is imperative that we change our society. If we do not plan ahead and change thoughtfully nature will force change from us through pain and death."(1)

The hope of transforming society to a different form, one with a different vision and values is necessary if a sustainable and a more satisfying future is to be achieved. The world is at a cross-road, it can move towards sustainable development or its destruction. There are many difficult choices to be made if a transition to a sustainable world is to be made. Clear cut choices are often difficult and daunting. So much of the industrial culture of the developed nations – and now of developing nations as well – is built upon the premise of perpetual material growth that moving towards a different world seems difficult, almost inconceivable. And yet it has to be done if life on this earth has to be saved.

How do you move towards a sustainable world? Where do you find the necessary inspiration? Maurice Strong, the Secretary General of UNCED, in his opening statement at the earth Summit suggested: "The change in behaviour and direction called for here must be rooted in our deepest spiritual, moral and ethical values. We must reinstate in our lives the ethics of love and respect for the Earth which must be accompanied by a revitalisation of the values essential to all our principal religious and philosophical traditions. "

We turn to Mahatma Gandhi, a man not only of deep spiritual, moral and ethical values, but a man of action, who could transform the masses and could lead a non-violent revolution. Gandhi was deeply concerned about the poor of the world, about antyodhya, the poorest of the poor, about equity, about consumption patterns and life styles, and the nature of economic growth and industrialization as is Agenda 21. If the vision of the Earth Summit and a transition to a sustainable future is to be achieved, we have a great deal to learn from the Mahatma.

Present Picture

What is the present picture of economic growth, of development and environment, that Agenda 21 hopes to change into one of sustainable development. Sustainable development has been defined as "meeting the needs of the present generation without jeopardising the ability of future generations to meet their own needs." We look at the present world picture in terms of poverty and hunger, pollution, and the state of human development.

Poverty and Hunger

Out of a population of some 4 billion in 114 developing countries, more than 2.5 billion live in rural areas, and of these approximately 1 billion live below the poverty line – 633 million in Asia, 204 million in Africa, 27 million in Near East and North Africa and 76 million in Latin America and Caribbean.(2)

Although child mortality rates have improved in developing countries, mortality rates continue to be high – 200 per 1000 live births. Female mortality is particularly high. Some 180 million children, one in three, suffer from serious malnutrition. Nearly 3 million children die each year from immunizable diseases (United Nations Development Programme, 1990)

By the year 2000 world population would be more than 6 billion – it is now around 5 billion, and by the year 2020 it is estimated to be 8 billion. This increase in numbers will require food and agriculture production at least 100% higher than at present. With population growth pushing ahead of potential food production the future in terms of food security looks grim for developing countries. Food Agricultural Organization estimates that 64 developing countries out of 117, would be unable to feed their population adequately and that 38 of these developing countries would be able to support less than half their populations.

Lester Brown mentions that grain output per person has fallen 8% from the historical high reached in 1984 dropping roughly 1% per year. There are no new technologies in sight that can help farmers restore the 3% annual rate of growth in grain harvest that prevailed from 1950 to 1984. Starvation, violence, political unrest, are indicative accompaniments of the average grain availability predicted for the future.

The present average grain consumption per capita per year in India is 200 kgs, China 300, Italy 400, and USA 800 kgs, the bulk of it consumed indirectly through meat, cheese etc.

Drought in many developing countries but especially in Africa, devastated both land and people. The capacity of many national systems to deal with drought has diminished.

Increasingly, land is degraded from deforestation, overgrazing, overflowing, and erosion. Top soils, thinned by erosion and low in organic matter store little moisture to carry through a period of drought. As a result, the effects of drought are far more devastating today than they were a generation ago.

Northern Europe also suffered from drought in 1992. In their case shortfalls were easily off-set with imported grain – a step not likely to happen in many developing countries because of the debt burden.

Not only drought but increasing environmental degradation is also affecting agriculture productivity adversely. *The State of the World Report*, 1990, mentions that soil erosion has undermined the productivity of about one-third of the world's crop lands.

According to the international Soil Reference and Information Centre an area nearly Western Europe's size has lost most of its productivity from man's abuse. Another 2.25 billion acres, larger than Australia, has declined and needs restoration. Land degradation is proceeding so rapidly that few African countries can hope to achieve sustainable agriculture in the near future while serious food consequences could eventually be felt in Latin America and Asia, said Saouma, Director-General of FAO.

The International economic order is also so structured that it hinders the efforts of the poor countries to improve their economic lot. The South Commission report points out that the countries of the South are unfavourably placed in the world economic order and individually they are powerless to influence these processes and institutions – the South will need to organise itself for moving towards an economic order which promises greater equity and justice.

President Hurtado of Mexico voicing the concerns of Third World leaders struggling with their economies and international debt said: "The 1980's not only represent lost time in terms of growth but backward steps have unhappily been taken. The South has been virtually kept out of economic decisions that most concern it. Our raw materials are bought at prices less and less remunerative while products with higher value added find their access blocked by artificial obstacles with political overtones."

Global markets do not operate freely, the share of the least developed countries in the world trading system has been halved since 1960. The unequal opportunities cost the developing countries $ 500 billion a year – 10 times what they receive in foreign assistance.(18)

The rich and poor countries are a world apart.

The richest fifth have 84.7% of GNP, 84.2% of world trade, 85.5% of domestic savings, and 85.0% of domestic investment. The poorest fifth have 1.4% of GNP, 0.9% of world trade, 0.7% of domestic savings and 0.9% of domestic investment. And this difference is increasing. (UNDP)

The present world picture is that the poor countries are becoming poorer and the rich countries richer.

Pollution

Industry has coaxed many toxic substances from roçk and soil to use in manufacturing and has consequently released many toxic substances into the environment. For instance it has released 300 times the amount of lead, 20 times of cadmium, and 4 times as much arsenic into the atmosphere than is naturally present.(3)

According to OECD, Organisation for Economic Cooperation and Development, we have introduced 4 million chemicals in our environment, and 563,000 of these are in common use. We add possibly 1000-2000 new chemicals each year. Environmental health experts point out a clear link between certain industrial chemicals with cancer. Leukaemia has been linked to benzene, an ingredient in gasoline; and mesothelioma, a form of cancer, to asbestos exposure. Farmers in industrialised countries have increased risk of cancer due to the wide–spread use of pesticides, herbicides, fertilisers etc.

Frank Rauschel, Director of the National Cancer Institute warned "Given today's environment we are living with a time bomb that is going to explode in 20 to 30 years from now in the form of more persons being stricken with cancer."

A number of pollutants and toxicants endanger the nervous system. Solvents in many daily use products such as shoe polish, furniture polish, disinfectants etc. cause memory problems, dizziness, irritability and fatigue. Asthma has increased significantly because of air pollution.

Inspite of serious health hazards, the chemical industry advertises itself with "Better living, through Chemicals", and "without chemicals life itself, would be impossible".

Over a million people in urban areas are threatened with unacceptable levels of pollution and related health problems,

The EEC points out that in spite of all measures taken to control waste it is continuing to increase at a rate of 5% per annum. In one year the European community released into the environment 90 million tonnes of household refuse, 115 million tonnes of industrial waste, 950 million tonnes of agricultural waste, 200 million tonnes of sewage sludge and 150 million tonnes of waste from extractive industries.[3] Already waste disposal is a serious problem and if economic activity continues at the present rate, the Commission admits the quantities would be quadrupled by the end of the century!

An OECD report suggests that the OECD area is rapidly reaching the point where it must chose between industrial expansion and clean air.

Pollution trends are also changing climate patterns. Approximately 125 million tons of carbon dioxide, the prime ingredient of global warming, is thrown out by industrial pollution. Professor Flohn stated at the International Conference on Environmental Future, "that a global climatic catastrophe is unavoidable, if we continue to use energy at the current rate."[3]

Goldsmith suggests that it is not by making millions of deceptively precise measurements that we can understand how pollution is affecting our environment and lives. It is the effect of pollution on living systems, taken as a whole, that we must consider. Schubert agrees: "It is apparent that an overall approach is necessary if society is to control and minimise genetic and toxicological risks to the population. It is unproductive and self-defeating to repeatedly deal with an individual chemical on an emergency basis. Repetition of such piecemeal consideration eventually distracts the public and government from the general problem of how to deal with the myriad of chemicals to which the population is exposed."[3]

The developing nations, eager for economic growth, employment and meagre wages, are importing toxic industries and toxic waste in their countries. For instance, in Canada, when domestic sales of asbestos declined due to public health concerns, the industry, in collaboration with its government, promoted sales abroad. Ninety five per cent of the asbestos Canada produces is now exported, largely to the Third World countries. (3)

Pesticide producers pursue a similar policy of international expansion. The US General Accounting Office estimated that in 1989, 25 per cent of the pesticides exported were unregistered because of their harmful qualities. In Britain too John Madeley, in an article entitled *Britain and the Third World* writes: "Britain has continued to use the third World as a dumping ground for pesticides, which are either banned or severely restricted on health and environmental grounds in Britain and other countries. Banned pesticides often return on imported food, a phenomenon known as the circle of poison."

The dilemmas posed by the need for expanding trade and establishing safe havens for toxic industries are formidable and urgent. The urgency arises from the fact that environmental issues are becoming factors in regional and global trade negotiations.

The border region between USA and Mexico has been used as a haven for environmentally dangerous industries. In 1991, three-quarters of the companies in this region known as "maquiladoras" were found to have toxic discharges causing cancer, birth defects, brain damage, etc. The effluents were being emptied into open ditches running through settlements near the factories. A Mitsubishi Kasei Corporation subsidiary was forced to close down in Malaysia by a court order after years of protest by local residents for dumping radioactive thorium which led to high levels of leukaemia.

We live in a highly polluted and toxic world. The main solution of pollution problems seem to be to export it elsewhere. Goldsmith mentions that Britain prides itself on the fact that SO_2 levels have been falling, but this is only because high chimneys have been built which allow it to drift across the North Sea to Scandinavia where it is stunting the growth of crops and trees.[3]

In Gandhi's language there is violence in such development.

Human Development

With industrialisation and urbanisation individuals, families and communities have paid a heavy price. Institutional structures and values which kept the families and communities together have disintegrated leaving a host of human problems to be addressed.

Mahbub ul Haq, Chief Advisor at UNDP (UN Development Programme) has contributed significantly to the international development debate. He has emphasised the need to consider human development as an index of progress rather than GNP which was the standard measuring device used by economists and development agencies. Haq points out that human development is a process of enabling people to have wider choices, that income is one of those choices, but health, education, physical environment and freedom of action are also important. He designed a new development index called the Human Development Index (HDI) which combined life expectancy, adult literacy, and income in an innovative way to measure a country's progress. Hopefully HDI would shift the emphasis of planners from concerns of only economic growth to a broader spectrum of human concerns and choices.

The industrialised countries, in spite of great economic wealth and powers, have increasing social and human problems. The old family structure and social norms have broken down with no new cohesive and unifying force. There is evidence of high rate of drugs, HIV, cancer, divorce, suicide, accidents, rapes and assaults, etc.

Developing countries too in the process of industrialisation and economic growth are being afflicted by the same kind of problems – weakening of the social fabric, drugs, corruption, crime, terrorism etc. Many of these problems are no longer local or national, they have become international and global. The great Bombay explosion recently in which several hundred people died was an example of terrorism from across national boundaries; so was the explosion in the Trade Center, New York. As the UNDP Report 1994 mentions, "the battle of peace has to be fought on two fronts. The first is the security front from whose victory spells freedom from fear the second is the economic and social front where victory means 'freedom from want' ".

The social and economic problems in developing countries have a different "human face". There are starving and malnourished children, increased prostitution and HIV, lack of access to safe water sanitation, health, and education, homelessness, migration, slums, bonded labour, child labour etc.

There are, as the UNDP report points out, "the 'silent emergencies' of poverty -- water pollution, sanitation, health etc, and the loud emergencies of global warming, ozone depletion which usually dominate the headlines. Poverty as great an enemy of environment and peace as misspent affluence is."

One of the major problems in developing countries has been the top down bureaucratic structure of delivery services to the poor. The result has been that the poor have been bypassed inspite of major allocations. If participation is to become an important aspect of the human development process then new structures will be essential. In a recent workshop the participants agreed that the most readily identifiable reason for access difficulties centre in the bureaucracy. Case after case, country after country, cited the rebuffs and anxieties suffered by the poor at the hands of arrogant officials. The uneasy "supplicant" is curtly told to wait, often for hours, or to return again, pushed around, shouted at, and suffer other indignities. Corruption and harassment has increased. Gandhi understood that "the state represented a soulless machine which can never be weaned from violence to which it owes its existence".

It is important to move towards a strengthening of institutions of civil society. Many NGO's have shown that with greater participation costs have decreased, efficiencies increased and empowerment of people taken place.

There is much to be desired in the present social and human development picture in both developing and developed countries. The issue is no longer how much economic growth but what kind of growth, and what kind of price societies are willing to pay.

The need for a new paradigm

The UNDP Human Development Reports clearly point out that though economic growth is essential, it is not sufficient for human well-being. High growth rates do not automatically translate into higher levels of development. The Human Development Report 91 states "men, women and children must be the centre of attention with development woven around people, not people around development. Moreover, development must be participatory, and for this, people must have the opportunity to invest in the development of their capabilities – in their health education and training."

Further, the Human Development Report 1993 emphasises even more strongly for a shift in the development mode. It challenges traditional concepts of security and old models of development, as well as ideological debates on the role of the market and outmoded forms of international cooperation. It is clear, it says, "that the implications of placing people at the centre of political and economic change are critical, and require a new paradigm of development. The report calls for nothing less than a revolution in our thinking."

In 1971, the Club of Rome commissioned a study at MIT (The Massachusetts Institute of Technology) to examine the long term causes and consequences of growth in population, industrial capital, food production, resource consumption and pollution. A computer model called World 3 was created to simulate the various interacting factors. The results, which created a furore, were published in a book called *Limits to Growth*. Twenty years later the authors revisited World 3, updating the computer data and published their findings in *Beyond the Limits*. The main conclusions of the second study were essentially the same as the earlier one but the disquieting trends had strengthened further. The main conclusions as stated were :

1. Human use of many essential resources and generation of many kinds of pollutants have already surpassed rates that are physically sustainable. Without significant reductions in material and energy flows, there will be in the coming decades an uncontrolled decline in per capita food output, energy use, and industrial production.

2. This decline is not inevitable. To avoid it two changes are necessary. The first is a comprehensive revision of policies and practices that perpetuate growth

in material consumption and in population. The second is a rapid, drastic increase in the efficiency with which materials and energy are used.

3. A sustainable society is still technically and economically possible. It could be much more desirable than a society that tries to solve its problems by constant expansion. The transition to a sustainable society requires a careful balance between long-term and short-term goals and an emphasis on sufficiency, equity, and quality of life rather than on quantity of output. It requires more than productivity and more than technology; it also requires maturity, compassion, and wisdom.

The authors concluded: "we realised that in spite of the world's improved technologies, the greater awareness, the stronger environmental policies, many resource and pollution flows had grown beyond their sustainable limits. . . Like everyone else, we did not want to come to these conclusions. . . the present way of doing things is unsustainable. The future to be viable at all, must be one of drawing back, easing down, healing. Poverty cannot be ended by indefinite material growth; it will have to be addressed while the material human economy contracts."[4]

Goldsmith and several others identify industrialisation as the root cause of today's ecological and social problems. They point out that because of industrialisation and the way we use science and technology, we have persuaded ourselves that the "sky is the limit" in consumer goods and ingenious technologies, and that with further advances in science and appropriate technology, we could deal with social ills, unemployment, crime, disease, as well. Goldsmith, like many others working closely with people at grassroots, is asking for a fundamental reappraisal of conventional thinking. The social and ecological problems confronting us today, Goldsmith claims, cannot be solved with a little tinkering of the system. They are too deep rooted, having their roots in the very nature of industrialisation. Carrying his logic further Goldsmith sees the solution of the problem in de-industrialisation. It is difficult to move towards a sustainable society, he claims, "because we are unwilling to face the inevitable concomitant of trends we most highly prize – those we have been taught to identify with progress – the development of science and technology, industry and the global market. We would also have to face the still unacceptable conclusion that our problems can only be solved by reversing these developments i.e. by putting 'progress' into reverse – an enterprise that few would even be willing to contemplate, yet for which there is no alternative."[4]

Wolfgang Sachs too writing on the age of development says "the time is ripe to write its (development) obituary..... delusion and disappointment, failures and crimes have been the steady companions of development and they tell a common story: it did not work. If all countries 'successfully' followed the industrial example, five or six planets would be needed to serve as mines and waste dumps. It is thus obvious that the 'advanced' societies are no model; rather they are most likely to be seen in the end as an aberration in the course of history. The arrow of progress is broken and the future has lost its brightness; what it holds in store are more threats than promises. How can one believe in development if the sense of orientation has withered away?"[1] Wolfgang Sachs too wants a review of the existing development model and "to recognise that we all wear not merely tinted, but tainted glasses if one takes part in the prevailing development discourse".

Half a century ago when the alarm bell of environmental degradation and world poverty had not sounded as loud and clear as today, Gandhi, looking at the direction that development and progress were taking said: "I must not fear if the world is going in the wrong direction and like the proverbial moth burns itself eventually in the flame around which it dances more and more fiercely". "It is my bounded duty", he added, "to my last breath to try and protect India and through India the entire world from such a doom".

The movement of environment and sustainable development has a great deal to learn from Gandhi and his philosophy of *ahimsa,* non-violence, his concern for *antyodhya,* the poorest of the poor, and *satyagraha,* truth force, his methodology of struggle. Gandhi, in spite of his spirituality, was a man of action. We will now view sustainable development and the strategy of action for achieving social and political goals inherent in environmental concerns from Gandhi's perspective.

Gandhi and Sustainable Development

At the end of World War II President Truman said: "we must embark on a bold new program for making the benefits of our scientific advances and industrial progress available for the improvement and growth of underdeveloped areas. The old imperialism – exploitation for foreign profit – has no place in our plans. What we envisage is a program of development based on the concepts of democratic fair dealing".

And so development was born, based on the concept of fair dealing. Unfortunately, Truman's vision of exploitation – free development and fair dealing — was lost en route!

The concepts of development as they evolved and spread were based on a Western perception of reality, and led many developing countries to what Gandhi considered "a four-fold ruin:" social, economic, political and spiritual. The inter-relatedness of these provides the traditional and cultural modes of cooperation, of sharing and control over resources. With the four-fold ruin the very essence of communal life was eroded and with it went all restraint in the exploitation of people and resources.

Gandhi had asked: "why must India become industrial in the Western sense? The Western civilisation is urban. Small countries like England and Italy may afford to urbanise their systems. A big country like America, but with sparse population cannot do otherwise. But one would think that a big country with a teeming population, with an ancient rural tradition, which has hitherto answered its purposes, need not – must not – copy the Western model. What is good for one nation situated in one condition, is not necessarily good for another differently situated. One man's food is another man's poison."

Other world leaders too voiced their concern and the need of having development in terms of their objectives as expressed by their people. Thus, Julius Nyerere wanted development to be the political mobilisation of a people for attaining their own objectives, conscious as he was that it was madness to pursue the goals others had set. Other leaders had proposed "ethnodevelopment conscious of the need to look within and search for one's own culture instead of using borrowed and foreign ideas" Medha Patkar, Anisur Rahman, Orlando Fals Borda insist on participatory methods of development, conscious of the exclusion made of the poor, tribals and indigenous people in the name of development.

If concern for human development, participatory development, and sustainable development is to be relentlessly and vigorously pursued, it is likely that we will land ourselves at Gandhi's doorstep. Said Gandhi: "I am a searcher after truth....... the idea pursued must not be lowered because of our weakness or imperfections. I am painfully conscious of both of them. I must continue to bear testimony to Truth even if I am forsaken by all. Mine may be a voice in the wilderness but it will be heard when all other voices are silenced if it is the voice of truth."

We turn to the 'voice in the wilderness,' realising after 40 to 50 years of development experience, that perhaps it was the voice of truth.

Gandhi and Nehru

When Independence was around the corner Gandhi initiated a dialogue with Nehru about the future directions and development priorities for India. Wrote Gandhi to Nehru: "I want to write about the difference of outlook between us. I want our position vis a vis each other to be clearly understood by us....... I am now an old man. I have named you as my heir. I must, however, understand my heir and my heir should understand me. Then alone shall I be content." Gandhi felt that if the differences were fundamental then the public should be made aware of them, otherwise, he felt it would be detrimental to independent India.

The differences, as we shall see, were fundamental and these could not be resolved because Gandhi was assassinated on January 30, 1948, and Nehru had to undertake the burden of steering India without the tempering influence of Gandhi. Nehru was conscious of the tremendous influence Gandhi exercised on him inspite of his differences. "It was clear that this man of poor physique had something of steel in him, something rocklike which did not yield to physical powers, however great they might be. And in spite of his unimpressive features, his loin-cloth and bare body there was a royalty and kingliness in him which compelled a willing obeisance from others.... his voice clear and limpid would purr its way into the heart and evoke an emotional response. "Unfortunately, this clear and limpid voice could no longer purr its way in Nehru's heart and evoke an emotional response. India embarked on a development strategy very different from what Gandhi had hoped."

Nehru did try to clarify his position to Gandhi. "Regarding certain objectives like sufficiency of food, clothing, housing, education, etc. these should be the minimum requirements for the country and everyone........ It is with these objectives in view that we must find out how to attain them speedily." And, "speedily" to Nehru meant modernisation, industrialization, building of big dams, establishing institutional infrastructure for science and technology. In other words, catching up with the West for, according to Nehru, there was no way out of these but to have them.

Gandhi's priorities for development, were village development and village industries. Gandhi identified with the poor: "whatever cannot be shared with the masses is taboo to me..... My loin cloth is an organic evolution in my life. It comes naturally without effort, without premeditation....... service to the poor has been my heart's desire and it has always thrown me amongst the poor and enabled me to identify myself with them."

Development to Gandhi was abolition of poverty, misery and fear. "I shall work for an India in which the poorest shall feel that it is their country, in whose making they have an effective voice, an India in which there is no high class or low class of people, an India in which all communities will live in harmony. Women will enjoy the same rights as men. This is India of my dream."

Nehru, on the other hand, strongly believed that it was not possible for India to be really independent unless she is modern, scientific and technologically advanced. He believed in big industries, State owned. Nehru was reluctant to start the development process with villages and village-industries. Nehru wrote: "Is it not romantic.... to expect *khadi* and village industries to solve the long term problems of India's poverty? Is not Gandhi's emphasis on the spinning wheel overdone and foredoomed to failure in an industrialised world?," or, "A village normally speaking is backward intellectually and culturally, no progress can be made from a backward environment." Gandhi, on the other hand, thought of the Indian villager as the salt of the earth, the sheet anchor of democracy. In describing the Indian villager he said: "an age-old culture is hidden under an encrustment of crudeness. Behind the crude exterior you will find a deep reservoir of spirituality. You will not find such a thing in the West. Take away his chronic poverty and his illiteracy and you have the finest specimen of what a cultured cultivated free citizen should be." And then: "A semi-starved nation can have neither religion nor art nor organisation. Whatever can be useful to starving millions is beautiful to my mind. Let us give today first the vital things of life, and all the graces and ornaments of life will follow." The dispossessed millions haunted him. His great ambition was to "wipe every tear from every eye."

It was obvious there were deep intellectual and attitudinal differences between Gandhi's and Nehru's approach to development. Nehru said: "we cannot stop the river of change or cut ourselves adrift from it, and psychologically, we who have eaten the apple of Eden cannot forget the taste and go back to primitiveness."

Nehru's development ideas were derived from Fabian literature, Marxism, and other western liberal thinkers. "Inevitably we are led to the only possible solution – the establishment of a socialist order, first within national boundaries, and eventually in the world as a whole, with a controlled production and distribution of wealth for public good. How this is to be brought about is another matter."

Talking about Gandhi's emphasis on village industry, and especially the promotion of hand–spinning and hand-weaving (*khadi*), Nehru said: "(*Khadi*)....... is an intensification of individualism in production, and is thus a throw-back to the preindustrial age. As a solution of any vital present day problem it cannot be taken seriously and it produces a mentality which may become an obstacle to growth in the right direction." Nehru, however, agreed "there is tremendous unrecorded unemployment in India and even greater partial unemployment in rural areas. Economically *khadi* has been a help to these wholly and partially unemployed and because this improvement has come from their own efforts, it has raised their self respect and given them some feeling of confidence." Empowerment is what the modern development thinkers would call it.

Nehru readily agreed that the psychological benefits of *khadi* have been great. "It brought nearer each other the middle class intelligentsia and the peasants........ the adoption of the simple white *khadi* dress by the middle class resulted in simplicity, and a feeling of unity with the masses........... Even the poorest felt something of this dignity and self respect." *Khadi* was a great equalizer between rich and poor and became a symbol of equity to be pursued in India's development.

In spite of recognising the many advantages of *khadi* and other village industries at the stage and period of India's growth, Nehru firmly believed in changing over to a higher economy. "Only a radical change will do – an end to little holdings and introduction of organised collective farms and cooperative enterprises. The land will not and cannot absorb all our people – and others must turn to small scale industry but in the main to large scale socialised industries and social services."

Gandhi's approach to the future of India was based on his concern for the poor, in the 'here and now' situation of the rural poor – and not in some distant utopia. Writing in the *Harijan* Gandhi said: "Mechanisation is good when hands are too few for the work intended to be accomplished. It is an evil when there are more hands than required for the work as is the case in India......... the problem for us is not how to find leisure for the teaming millions inhabiting our villages. The problem is how to utilise their idle hours which are equal to the working days of six months in a year."

Economists argued against village industries and village development; they said that Gandhian economics would mean a return to primitiveness, a lowering of the standard of living. Not so, said Gandhi, "if by a high standard we mean that those who have not enough to eat should have plenty of fresh wholesome diet, those who are naked should have durable clothes, those who have no shelter should have cosy dwellings."

To Nehru and to the planners Gandhi's development ideas sounded primitive. Nehru expressed his frustration and said: "in spite of my close association with him for many years. I am not clear in my own mind about his objective. I doubt if he is clear himself. One step enough for me, he says, and he does not try to peep into the future or to have a clearly conceived end before him. Look after the means and the end will take care of itself he is never tired of repeating: or be good in your personal individual lives and all else will follow."

Gandhi was not swayed by the technological achievements of the West as Nehru seemed to be. Gandhi wanted India to follow its own path of development taking its realities, its own people and its own culture into account. In Gandhi's leadership of the masses, it was clear that there was a mutuality of the leader and the led in which the leader was guided by the reality of the led.

The reality of the Indian masses was their abject poverty, a sense of helplessness and fear – pervasive oppressive strangling fear; fear of police, the official, money lender, fear of unemployment and starvation. Gandhi's vision of development seemed to emerge from these millions. Speaking their language, voicing their concerns he drew attention to their appalling conditions. Nehru recognised the power of Gandhi and his hold over the masses, "Gandhi's words, his use of pious phrases, may sound platitudinous, but make no mistake there is power behind his words. Gandhi came to represent India to an amazing degree and to express the very spirit of the ancient and tortured land. To the millions he was India."

Independent India, under Nehru's leadership, chose a development strategy of big industries, big dams, big scientific institutions, state–controlled. The country made impressive progress in many directions. It established a strong and diversified industrial base, it established modern agriculture with assured irrigation through big dams, and increased food production and self–sufficiency in grain. In general, development planning followed a capital intensive strategy. Nehru's development changed the face of India but not in the way intended. The failures were in the neglect of issues relating to rural poverty, primary education and illiteracy, unemployment, increasing inequalities, and women's drudgery. The widening disparities in income and consumption have led to social and political unrest, wide-spread corruption and the decay of the social fabric.

After four decades of development experience, development agencies, like UNDP and other international agencies, are discarding many old concepts of development and moving towards a Gandhian focus on people as they are "here and now". Development strategies are UNDP writes "to be woven around people not people around development." Hear Gus Speth, the new UNDP chief: "all really basic and fundamental changes have been people-led, bottom-up movements". And: "Judging from past experience a durable solution to today's problems of poverty, unemployment, social disintegration and environmental deterioration cannot be achieved through just more of the development of the past kind. Development must have a new future – one based on a new understanding of real needs, in effect a new paradigm."

The importance of empowering individuals, groups and communities is now increasingly recognised. The political function of empowerment is the redistribution of power, to provide a voice to the voiceless. Gandhi, more than anyone else, empowered the millions, and through the process of sharing his lifestyle with the poor gave them an inner strength and courage to define development in their own terms.

Consumerism

Agenda 21 states that "...... the major cause of the continued deterioration of the global environment is the unsustainable pattern of consumption and production, particularly in the industrialised countries which is a matter of grave concern aggravating poverty and imbalances." And further notes that "developed countries should take the lead in achieving sustainable consumption."

In January '94 a Symposium on Sustainable Consumption was held in Norway where leading politicians, government representatives, scientists and environmentalists debated the issues relating to consumption and consumerism and considered what action should be taken. They discussed what can and should each sector of society do? What can and should governments do? And what can be achieved through international cooperation? They suggested more studies, and more detailed analysis for setting priorities for developing economic and administrative instruments; they advocated more education, training and public awareness; and pilot projects to demonstrate the effect of changed consumption patterns of production and environment, etc.[9]

Already there is considerable scientific data existing in the world to warn us of the dangers in further growth and consumption. According to Gro Harlem Bruntland, who chaired the World Commission of Environment and Development in 1972, private consumption of goods has been steadily increasing.

How to bring about the changes required for moving towards sustainable consumption patterns is an important aspect of the mandate of Agenda 21, and every environment conscious country is searching for its own solutions.

A recent study in the Netherlands identified the following four goals and changes required to attain a society based on sustainable consumption:[5]

- close process cycles: to ensure as far as possible complete reuse, recycle and repair.
- cut fossil fuel use by half.
- reduce transportation: provide goods and services as close as possible to consumers.
- improve quality of materials: use cradle-to-grave approach to get products which are more durable, repairable, and recyclable; avoid use of scarce or hazardous materials.

In order to cut the number of cars operating on roads, cycle courier services are becoming popular in Netherlands. Customers are getting used to the fact that a bike is being used. Also greater use of car rental services instead of owning a car. There are more than 80,000 Dutch people who work one or more days a week at home. In 1993 these ''teleworkers'' saved around 24 million car kilometers. Perhaps the most important development is the idea of ''eco teams''. These teams try to reduce their consumption level of raw materials and energy. They meet at regular intervals, encourage each other, (like alcoholics anonymous) compare results and plan future action. There are already 65 such ''eco teams'' in Netherlands alone, and in 12 other industrialised countries.[5]

The idea of self-discipline and of starting the change process with oneself is the Gandhian way. In the final analysis the solution lies not in more technological advances, but in the will to act in an environmentally sustainable and ethical way.

As Noel Brown of the UN Environment Program puts it: "It is no longer enough to lament over ecological vandalism characterised as global waste or the inequalities that currently exist in the exploitation and utilisation of natural resources by future generations or the denial to them of their natural patrimony. If the Rio consensus is to have any meaning it has to be morally grounded in the notion of human right and wrong in relation to the way the earth and its bounty are made to serve the interests of all. What is necessary now is a much clearer sense of the moral and ethical issues posed by Agenda 21."[6]

If the Rio consensus is to have any future then issues of human rights, equality, and access to natural resources must receive greater attention. These are moral and ethical issues. Consumerism and consideration of patterns of consumption and production in Agenda 21 takes us again to Gandhi's door.

Behind Gandhi's approach to consumerism was his concern for the poor and his praise for a simple way of life. Civilisation, he said, in the real sense of the term, consists not in the multiplication of wants but in the deliberate and voluntary reduction of wants. Further, Gandhi said "I hate privilege and monopoly. Whatever cannot be shared with the masses is taboo to me......" and "the golden rule is to resolutely refuse to have what the millions cannot. The first thing is to cultivate the mental attitude that will not have possessions or facilities denied to millions."

Gandhi believed in learning to put a curb on material wants. "The mind is a restless bird. The more it gets the more it wants and still remains unsatisfied. Our forefathers knew that if we set our hearts on such things we would become slaves and lose our moral fibre."

Agenda 21 hoped that the developed countries would take the lead in achieving sustainable consumption. Gandhi too hoped that "the rich should take the initiative in dispossession with a view to a universal diffusion of the spirit of contentment."

But he goes further and adds: "the incessant search for material comforts and their multiplication is such an evil, and I make bold to say that the Europeans themselves will have to remodel their outlook if they are not to perish under the weight of the comforts they are becoming slaves to."

There are other voices, from other parts of the world conveying the same radical message as Gandhi. Listen to André Gorz: "A richer life is not only comfortable with the production of fewer goods it demands it."

There are several movements emerging in Netherlands and other countries of simplifying life, of trying to curtail wants and other aspects of consumerism.

To Nehru Gandhi's utterances of sin and evil were full of paradoxes and confusion. Says Nehru: "the paradoxes and confusions in his utterances that trouble us are really due to entirely different premises from which he starts..... For him progress and civilization consist not in the multiplication of wants, of higher standards of living, but in the deliberate and voluntary restriction of wants which promotes real happiness and contentment and increases the capacity for service." Nehru adds: "I do not appreciate in the least the idealisation of the simple peasant life."

Gandhi understood, not only the deep poverty of India in the abstract but poverty in the real living sense. Gandhi also recognised their "deep reservoir of spirituality," under their chronic poverty and illiteracy. It is not surprising that Gandhi understood the masses and the masses felt understood by him. They could place their complete confidence in "this little man" who identified with their strengths and weaknesses.

Bergson, the philosopher, said: "we think with only a small part of our past but it is with our entire past including the original bent of our soul, that we desire, will and act". Gandhi's understanding of the masses was with his (and India's) entire past including the original bent of his soul!

Although Nehru was very close to Gandhi, he admits: "I have became a queer mixture of the East and the West, out of place everywhere, at home nowhere. Perhaps my thoughts and approach to life are more akin to what is called Western than Eastern, but India clings to me, as she does to all her children, in innumerable ways......... I cannot get rid of either that past inheritance or my recent acquisitions. They are both part of me and though they help me in both the East and West they also create a feeling of spiritual loneliness...... I am a stranger and alien in the West. I cannot be of it. But in my own country also, sometimes, I have an exile's feeling........... Sir Ramaswamy Iyer is absolutely right when he says that I do not represent mass feeling. I have no illusions on that point."

Although we all agree that the present consumption pattern and lifestyles especially as they operate in the developed countries, and in the more affluent parts of developing countries, need some kind of change as Agenda 21 has emphasised, the "soulforce" required for such change seems to be missing. More studies, more analysis, more computer models are not a sufficient recipe for change. We need a moral force.

We turn to Gandhi again to see how he applied moral force to change social and political realities. Einstein said of Gandhi : "in our age of moral decay he was the only statesman who represented that higher conception of human relations (and values) in the political sphere to which we must aspire with all our powers..... Generations to come will scarcely believe that such a one as this ever in flesh and blood walked upon this earth."

Satyagraha

Agenda 21 and its implementation would require many social and political changes. It is therefore worthwhile to look at Gandhian experience of achieving social and political changes through his *satyagraha* method.

The first time Gandhi used *satyagraha* was in South Africa to fight against an unjust law, a new registration measure introduced apparently with the object to humiliate and demoralise the Indians. It was in South Africa that he first used his weapon of *satyagraha,* and also realised the value and strength of women as *satyagrahis*. We shall, however, look more closely at the Salt *satyagraha* which Gandhi launched in 1930 for the repeal of salt taxes, though the primary and long term goal was of independence.

Gandhi called his method *satyagraha. Satyagraha* literally means holding on to truth. In his application of *satyagraha*, Gandhi explained, the pursuit of truth does not admit of violence being inflicted on one's opponent, and therefore also includes self-suffering. Essentially, *satyagraha* is a moral principle converted into a method to fight for social and political justice.

Gandhi knew his masses and knew what would appeal to them. "I claim to know my millions". He picked 'salt' as the symbol of oppression of the poor, a substance in which the poorest could participate in its liberation from the law. As Nehru recalls 'salt' suddenly became a mysterious word, a word of power. "We were bewildered and could not quite fit in a national struggle with common salt." But Gandhi's 'inner voice' was right, and as the struggle started it spread like a 'prairie fire'.

The first step in a civilised struggle is to inform the opponent about the steps you plan to take. he struggle is always open and transparent with no hidden agendas.

On March 2, 1930, Gandhi sent a long letter to the Viceroy, serving notice that civil disobedience would begin in nine days. The letter conveys Gandhi's style of confrontation and of dealing with a counter-player. He wrote: "And why do I regard the British rule as a curse? It has impoverished the dumb millions by a system of progressive exploitation and by a ruinous expensive military and civil administration which the country cannot afford. It has reduced us politically to serfdom....... The British system seems so designed as to crush the very life out of him. Even the salt he must use to live is taxed......."

"India must evolve force (non violent) enough to free herself from that embrace of death....... I know that in embarking on non-violence I shall be running what might be fairly termed as a mad risk but the victories of truth have never been won without risks often of the greatest character....."

Then he writes: "Take you own salary. It is over Rs 21000 per month besides many other indirect additions. You are getting over Rs 700 a day against India's average income of 'two annas' per day i.e. over 5000 times India's average income. The British Prime Minister is getting only 90 times Britain's average income......"

Gandhi himself led the band of *satyagrahis* carefully chosen. The 241 mile march to Dandi on the sea-shore started with 79 *satyagrahis*, but swelled as they went through villages into thousands. On reaching Dandi, after prayers, he symbolically broke the law on the beach. Thousands of villagers on the coast and in other places broke the salt law as well. Said Gandhi: "at present Indian self-respect is symbolised as it were, in a handful of salt in the *satyagrahi's* hand. Let the fist be broken, but let there be no surrender of salt. "

An American correspondent present during the salt *satyagraha* wrote: "In eighteen years of reporting in 22 countries I have never witnessed such harrowing scenes. Sometimes the scenes were so painful that I had to turn away momentarily. One surprising feature was the discipline of the volunteers. They were thoroughly imbued with Gandhi's non-violent creed."

The scope of civil disobedience spread like wild fire not only all over the country but to other things as well – forest laws, taxes, boycott of foreign cloth, banks, shipping, insurance, administration, education etc. Estimates of people in jail ran into hundreds of thousands.

Women from all walks of life joined the salt *satyagraha*. Women were especially encouraged because of their greater capacity for self-suffering. For women it was a way of declaring their independence, and in linking the buying and use of salt with the national struggle. Finally there were negotiations between Gandhi and Irwin on an equal basis; the salt laws were not repealed but sufficiently modified for the poor.

Gandhi had great skill in selecting something tangible, something symbolic, something that could be understood and appreciated by the common man and woman. The salt *satyagraha* tested the preparedness of the masses for a non-violent struggle, involving self-suffering for the longer term ordeal of fighting for independence – and yet the struggle against the salt tax was worthwhile in itself especially for the poor.

According to Louis Fischer, Gandhi achieved two things in 1930: "He made British people aware that they were cruelly subjugating India, and he gave Indians the confidence that they could by lifting their head and straightening their spines lift the yoke from their shoulders. After that, it was inevitable that Britain should some day refuse to rule India and that India should some day refuse to be ruled."

"The British beat the Indians with batons and rifle butts. The Indians neither cringed nor complained nor retreated. That made England powerless and India invincible." [7]

It is useful to distinguish between persuasion through reasoning and persuasion through *satyagraha*, non-violent coercion and self-suffering.

The Earth Summit and Agenda 21 depends largely on intellectual persuasion for achieving its objectives. To what extent intellectual persuasion will be effective in changing consumer behaviour, in reconciling to a new way of life, in industrialisation of a different sort, in changing relationships with Nature, and with the developing countries is highly questionable.

In everything that Gandhi did he introduced the spirit of religion into politics. Western observers often asked whether Gandhi was a saint or a politician. Gandhi explained: "I could not be leading a religious life unless I identified with the whole of mankind, and that I could not do so unless I took part in politics. The whole gamut of man's activities today constitutes an indivisible whole. You cannot divide social, economic, poverty and religious work in watertight compartments -- the spiritual law does not work in a field of its own but expresses itself through the ordinary activities of life".

Agenda 21 and its objective of achieving sustainable development, also requires social, economic and ethical choices, not in watertight compartments but as an indivisible whole. In Agenda 21 there is emphasis on the scientific and technical aspects, on social and economic aspects, but the ethical component is missing.

Einstein said of Gandhi: "He demonstrated that the allegiance of man can be won not merely by the cunning game of political fraud and trickery but through the living example of a morally exalted way of life..... It is my belief that the problem of bringing peace to the world on a supernational basis will be solved only by employing Gandhi's method on a large scale. "

We agree with Einstein that the problem of peace, as also of sustainable development and environmental concerns will only be solved by employing Gandhi's method on a large scale.

Gandhi and Implementation of Agenda 21

Amongst the major conclusions of the 178 nations attending the Earth Summit at Rio were that a change in the nature and practice of economic growth and development is urgently needed to deal with the ever widening scope of environmental degradation; that consumption patterns in rich countries must reduce, that poverty and population patterns must change if natural resources and world eco-systems are to survive, and that North-South relations need to be recast in the context of interdependence and mutual responsibilities.

Preliminary estimates for implementing Agenda 21 as indicated by UNCED to developing countries was $ 625 billion annually up to the year 2000. Development finance from external sources is $ 73 billion of which $ 57 billion is concessional official development assistance (1991 figures). Efforts at increased financial assistance has yielded negative results. Without taking anything else into account, the financial aspect alone seems to doom Agenda 21.

The international donor community is now calling or a departure from traditional notions of foreign aid in favour of new global partnership for transition to sustainable development! Partnerships only work on the basis of equity and mutuality, and even then there are many difficulties. Says India's Environment Minister, Kamal Nath: "for global sustainable development, a global partnership on the basis of equality, with equity as a prerequisite is imperative". Here again, it is difficult to see equity emerging as an international force for sustainable development. The countries of the South are unfavorably placed in the world economic order. The South Commission Report states: "The leading countries of the North use their power in pursuit of their own objectives. The fate of the South is increasingly dictated by the perception and policies of governments in the North and by the multilateral institutions which a few of these governments control. Domination has been reinforced where partnership for development was required."

As early as 1964, developing countries set up G 77 in order to achieve more equitable global economic structures and international relations. Its 30th Anniversary resolution admits that "today the picture looks less optimistic. Despite much bandying around the phrase there is no real Agenda for Development. Individual developing countries, even the most powerful and influential count for very little in the grossly uneven match with powerful nations of the North...... lopsided global power relations are unlikely to bring peace and prosperity to the bulk of the world's population." [8]

The relationship between international trade on an equitable basis and sustainable development is significant. The Third World countries inspite of their efforts are slipping backwards. Equity issues between the rich and poor countries are not likely to be solved by appeals of good will and long-term sustainability. The experience of G 77 amply proves this.

More science and more technology for dealing with problems of sustainable development are necessary, but are not a sufficient, condition. Sustainable development requires public awareness turned into political action; it requires igniting the moral and ethical values of a society.

Gandhi's great success in his various *satyagraha* movements was precisely in igniting the moral and ethical values of the Indian masses, values which are a part of the Indian heritage and Indian psyche Gandhi used the language of 'sin and salvation' and reintroduced values of austerity, service, non-violence etc. There is little doubt that his language and methods were peculiarly suited to Indian conditions and the Indian psyche, although it made Nehru and the intellectuals uncomfortable.

Nehru, however, recognised Gandhi's great insight and ability for mass action. "In his own peculiar way he had a knack of releasing powerful forces which spread out like ripples in the water's surface and affected millions....... he has changed the face of India."

It is this kind of releasing of powerful forces which Agenda 21 lacks and needs to learn. If the face of the Earth has to change, then there are lessons to be learnt from Gandhi.

We turn to Gandhi again to understand how moral issues of equity are to be fought and won. "Cowards", he said, "can never be moral, how can one seek truth without fearlessness?" And, one can add, how can we seek sustainability without fearlessness?

Where shall we start? With a new paradigm of development

Sustainable production and consumption will entail new development paths both for the industrialised and developing countries. The need for a new paradigm of development, a reassessment of the concept of progress, has been voiced strongly and widely.

Progress is not economic growth, is not higher efficiency, nor higher standards of living as measured by material goods. Catching up with the West and therefore the 'westernisation' of the world is also not progress or development.

The quest for a unified principle of development is perhaps contained in the Declaration of Cocoyoc (1974) emphasising that the purpose of development "should not be to develop things but to develop man...... Any process of growth that does not lead to the fulfillment of basic needs, or even worse, disrupts them is a traversity of the idea of development." The Declaration also emphasised the need for diversity and for pursuing many different roads to development. The Dag Hammarskjoeld Foundation also emphasises the need for an alternative development, another development, which is human centred development.

The UNDP Human Development Reports also widen the concept of development, moving from economic growth to human development. Gandhi's concept of progress and development also offers an alternative image of development.

If industrial civilisation and its values have polluted the environment and the earth that sustains us, we need to question the kind of industrialisation we want and reject. Gustano Estena, like Gandhi, calls for political action for a development that is relevant to the people, not borrowed development. "It is time to recover serenity. Crutches like those offered by science are not necessary when it is possible to walk with one's own dreams. Not the borrowed ones of development."[1]

We should start then with a new concept of development, a new paradigm of development, a people-led development, an alternative development, a development, which is "pro-poor, pro-nature and pro-women," not borrowed development.

Where shall we start? With a deep concern about consumerism and lifestyles.

At the core of the problem of global environmental degradation is the unsustainable pattern of consumption and production, especially in industrialised countries, aggravating the problem of poverty and imbalances. The solutions being considered in the developed countries are largely in terms of 'out there' - new and cleaner technologies with low environmental impact, green taxes, pricing policies, green labeling, and programs of public awareness, etc.

Gro Harlem Brundtland, in discussing Western levels of consumption, agrees that to sustain these levels for all, 7 billion people would need 10 worlds, not one to satisfy all our needs! And she admits that "as we strived in the World Commission on Environment and Development to agree on concepts that could gather global consensus, we realised it would be difficult to give support for global change if we had to conclude that countries and regions would have to sustain a significant decline in their standard of living." [9] Perhaps because of this fear the Commission concluded by saying "that the content of economic growth would have to change. Our economics would have to rely less on finite natural resources, and generate less waste." A very watered down statement from what reality demanded. One may ask here again, "how can we pursue sustainability without fearlessness?"

In the last 20 years, since the Report of the Commission on Environment and Development, *Our Common cause*, nothing much has happened. Consumption and consumer goods have increased, more waste has been generated and life-support systems have reached a critical point. As Mustafa Tolba mentioned in his review (1989-90), "none of the problems have been solved and some of the key issues have gone from bad to worse."

Elizabeth Dowdeswell, the new Executive Director of UNEP, agrees that "ultimately sustainable consumption is not a scientific or a technical question, and that it really is first and foremost a question of values." And, she points out, "that it is uncomfortable for many of us because that kind of self-examination and re-evaluation of lifestyles is not an easy thing for any of us to do." She continues: "I believe that what we are really talking about here, if we get past the definitional question is nothing less than a fundamental paradigm shift. How should we live? How much is enough? What way of life ought we to pursue? Those simple questions are often the most profound for they challenge the security of our accustomed norms." [9]

The 'simple questions' that Dowdeswell raises are also the questions that Gandhi raised but Gandhi's language makes Elizabeth Dowdeswell uncomfortable – as it did Nehru. Referring to Gandhi's statement that there is enough for everyone's needs but not for everyone's greed, she says: "that kind of a statement leads us to attempting to impose guilt and to lay blame and point fingers." Gandhi's language of "need and greed" upsets and confuses many people, especially people from a different culture. The interpretation of Gandhi's statements and the meaning we assign to them are bound by our own traditions, cultural imagery and terminology.

Perhaps the following statement which essentially means the same may cause less guilt to Dowdeswell. "Civilisation, in the real sense of the term consists not in the multiplicity of wants but in the deliberate and voluntary reduction of wants". Or "the mind is a restless bird, the more it gets, the more it wants and still remains unsatisfied." Or, is Thoreau's language more acceptable and free of guilt: "A man is rich in proportion to the number of things he can afford to let alone."

In spite of Dowdeswell's protest there are major conceptual similarities between Gandhi and Dowdeswell, although the language and imagery is different. Dowdeswell emphasises a fundamental paradigm shift; the unfolding of the potential of all people of the earth; the courage required to think and act differently; and the need for action. Gandhi too emphasises the unfolding of the poor villager's potential and of poor everywhere; the need for fearlessness for change; and moral action within a political framework.

I think Gandhi's answer to 'where shall we start?' is likely to be in a concern for the poorest of the poor; in moving towards a simpler lifestyle, a lifestyle which ultimately, can be shared with everyone; a fearlessness to fight for issues of sustainability.

Where shall we start? With oneself!

Gandhi practiced what he preached. If he was concerned about the "poorest of the poor" he adopted a lifestyle which reflected his constituency. "If I appear in my loin cloth it is because I come as the sole representative of those half–starved half–naked dumb millions" If Gandhi insisted on spinning it was to share the labour of the rural poor, especially of women. If the textile labour which went on strike under Gandhi's leadership complained of hunger and starvation, Gandhi himself went on a fast.

In his fight against untouchability also, Gandhi gave strong personal leadership. When Gandhi established his ashram in Ahmadabad, he invited a Harijan family to be a part of the ashram. The millowners of Ahmadabad who were willing to support Gandhi's ashram, said they would do so only if he would get rid of the Harijan family. Gandhi refused. The story goes that at a stage when there was no money left, an unknown young visitor came in a car and left a large bundle of notes with him for the ashram!

Further when Gandhi visited Delhi he often stayed in the sweepers colony, in the slums, where leaders, media persons, foreigners came to attend his prayer meetings and to visit with him.

Direct personal action was one of the keynotes of Gandhi's teachings. Help all you can on big things but do some little thing yourself. Sit down to eat with an untouchable, give up something, start work with the peasants, live in a village, learn to spin, plant a tree, etc.

Gandhi said: "I claim to be no more than an average man with less than average ability...... I have not the shadow of a doubt that any man or woman can achieve what I have if he or she can make the same effort and cultivate the same hope and faith..... I wear the same corruptible flesh that the weakest of my fellow beings wear and am, therefore as liable to err as any."

In the Salt March there were hundreds and thousands of people, ordinary people who were able to lay bare their 'corruptible flesh' to the batons and the kicks of the police. Where did this power for 'self-suffering' come from?

Gandhi said he learnt the power of passive resistance and self-suffering from his wife. But also from his ordeals in South Africa, where he learnt to reduce himself to zero. After that there was no fear, he said.

The liberation of women was set as a fundamental task for all Congressmen. Let the Congressmen begin with their own home, he said. "If they believed that freedom is the birth right of every nation and individual and if they are determined to achieve it, then they should first liberate their women from evil customs and conventions that restrict their all round healthy growth". And those who argued that the political struggle was much too important and should have priority over everything else, he countered, "to postpone social reform till after the attainment of *Swaraj* (Independence) is not to know the meaning of *Swaraj*".

Gandhi's insistence on doing spinning everyday himself and on everyone else taking to spinning, considered until then to be largely a woman's occupation, also helped to break oppressive stereotypes and weaning men away from images of so called 'manliness'.

Gandhi said that if women are to be free they had to be fearless – as he first learnt himself in South Africa. Gandhi helped women find a new dignity, a new self-confidence so that they themselves could fight against oppression – as he did.

To change the world we need to start with ourselves. We need an inner conversion, a coherence between the inner-self and the outer public self, between political action and ethical values. Gandhi said "My life is my message."

Can we do it?

Conclusion

If the face of the Earth has to change as is the mission of Agenda 21; if we need to know how to release powerful forces which Agenda 21 need to learn; if we wish to ignite the moral and ethical values of the people for sustainable development, then there are lessons to be learnt from the Mahatma, from his philosophy of *antoyodha*, truth and non-violence.

For Gandhi there was no difference between his personal and public life, no difference between his religion and politics; no divorce of the sacred from statecraft. His technique of *satyagraha*, incorporated religious, moral and ethical values. When someone asked Gandhi whether he was a saint or a politician he replied: "I am a politician trying my hardest to be a saint." His religion made him political and his politics were religious.[12]

The highest honour, Gandhi said, "that my friends can do me is to enforce in their own lives the program I stand for or to resist me to their utmost if they do not believe in it."

To follow Gandhi is difficult and yet millions have followed him in India, and his method of non-violence in other countries. He emphasised throughout his life that we must change ourselves before we can change others; that our real enemies are within, our greed and fears; that non-violence is a necessary weapon to change people, societies, and nations.

Toynbee, the historian, had said, "most civilisations died 200 years before they knew they died"! We hope the industrial civilisation is not in that process, and that we shall be able to move towards sustainable development, as envisaged at the Earth Summit and in Agenda 21 with some help from the Mahatma.

Notes and References

1. Wolfgang Sachs, (ed) *The Development Dictionary*, Zed Books Ltd., London, 1992.

2. Jazairy Idriss, *The State of World Rural Poverty* , FAO International Fund for Agricultural Development.

3. Goldsmith E and Hildyard N., *Green Britain or Industrial Wasteland*, Polity Press, 1986.

4. Meadows D TT and Meadows D L Randers Jorgan, *Beyond the Limits*, Chelsea Green Publishing Co: Post Mills, Vermont, USA, 1992 . Williams Maurice J and Petesch Patti L.

5. *Environmental News from the Netherlands* - A Quarterly Publication, 1994 No: 2.

6. Brown Noel J and Quiblier P (ed) *Ethics and Agenda*, United Nations Publications, New York, 1994.

7. Louis Fischer, *The Life of Mahatma Gandhi*, Macmillan Co., New York, 1966.

8. *South Letter*, Summer '94, The South Center, Geneva, '94.

9. *Symposium: Sustainable Consumption*, 19-20 January 1994, Oslo, Norway.

10. Nehru, Jawaharlal, *Mahatma Gandhi*, Asia Publishing House, 1965.

11. Nehru, Jawaharlal, *An Autobiography*, Jawaharlal Nehru Memorial Fund, 1980.

12. Nanda B R, *Mahatma Gandhi*, Oxford University Press, Delhi, 1989.

13. Ekins Paul, *A New World Order*, Routledge, London, 1992.

14. *Sustaining the Earth: Role of Multilateral Development Institutions*, Overseas Development Council, Washington D C 1993

15. During Alan, *How Much* is *Enough?*, W W Norton & Co, New York, 1992.

16. Chowdhry Kamla, *Population Growth, Food Security and Equity*. Symposium on Perspectives on India's Development, New Delhi, 1992.

17. Prabhu R K & Rao U R (ed). *The Mind of Mahatma Gandhi*, Navjivan Publishing House, Ahmadabad, 1945.

18. Human Development Report, UNDP, 1991, 1992, 1993, 1994.

Shahed Power

Gandhi, Nature and Indigenous People

Gandhi's life and work reveal that he felt a sense of affinity with nature. Throughout his adult years he sought a lifestyle that would meet one's needs and respect nonhuman creation. In this he came to see tribal or indigenous people as guides. There is a wealth of evidence from the first explorers and early settlers in North America describing how indigenous people had learnt to manipulate their environment so as to provide themselves with sustenance throughout the year. However, today that viable lifestyle itself has come under threat as indigenous people seek to survive within the dominant materialist society.

Early life

Given that the majority of rooms in the family home were small, low-roofed, airless and dark, it is not surprising that an energetic and mischievous child like Gandhi should spend much of his time out of doors, wandering in the streets of the old town or playing with other children on the beach. His sister Raliatbehn remembered him making friends with the animals that he met, even discovering the pleasure that dogs derive from being rubbed just behind their ears.[1]

The walled coastal town of Porbandar, Gandhi's birthplace, looks out over the Arabian Sea and has a rich maritime tradition. His early years in Porbandar, before the family moved in 1876/77 to Rajkot, in the hills to the north-west, gave Gandhi a knowledge of, and affection for, the sea that lasted the rest of his life. As he was to say, when writing about the extremely rough crossing to South Africa on the *S.S. Courland* in 1896: "I am a good sailor and do not get sea-sick."[2] He was at ease in and on the sea, and enjoyed swimming - something he continued well into his fifties.[3] At the age of 60, on the morning of April 6, 1930, before picking up the symbolic salt, Gandhi bathed in the sea at Dandi. But he also derived comfort and refreshment from the sight and sound of the sea. In 1924, released from prison after surgery, he went to convalescence at Juhu Beach, near Bombay. In a letter he made clear how important the sea was to him.

> In front of me lies the sea, murmuring gently. ... The sea has always been dear to me. This is the first time, however, that I have come to it seeking health. And, therefore, whether because of selfishness or for some other reason, it seems to have become dearer and I never tire of looking at it from the window.[4]

Juhu Beach became a favourite place of his for rest and recuperation, returning in December 1937 and for a month's convalescence in May 1944.[5]

As a child, gardening was Gandhi's chief delight and he became skillful at it. At Porbandar, by growing plants in flower pots, he created a garden on the terrace of the house. He had a kitchen garden in the courtyard of the house at Rajkot where he grew vegetables, fruit such as guavas, papayas and pomegranates, and flowers.[6]

Food and diet

Shy and gauche (he was only in his late' teens), Gandhi found it difficult to obtain vegetarian food on board ship on his first voyage to England in September 1888.7 Keeping to the strict vegetarian diet necessitated by the vow he had made before his mother was not easy in London either. He had to walk many miles before he discovered a vegetarian restaurant in St.Bride Street, next door to the offices of the London Vegetarian Society.[8] The discovery of this restaurant and of the English vegetarians he encountered marked a turning-point in his life. He was now a vegetarian by choice.

The membership of the Vegetarian Society of Manchester, founded in 1847, was dominated in its early years by the Bible Christian Church. The Bible Christians of Salford, heavily influenced by the writings of Emanuel Swedenborg (1688-1772), sought to quench humanity's "sinful, brutal nature" and "admit the full tide of Divine Influence". In this *contemporary* restoration of humanity the vegetarian diet was seen as a practical aid to independence, while the causes they espoused included civil, religious and commercial freedom. By the 1880s the influence of the Bible Christian Church had declined, as the bias in the membership shifted away from the northern industrial towns to London and vegetarianism became associated with clerical and retail workers. In 1888 the split away from Manchester came with the founding of the London Vegetarian Society.[9]

It is unfortunate that Gandhi was never to see his mother alive again. She could have shared with him her knowledge of what constitutes a balanced diet. Without her sensible restraint, Gandhi, once he had been persuaded by the reasoning behind any 'new' diet that attracted him, would often chop and change his eating habits with worrying suddenness and with deleterious effects on his health.[10]

Many of the works that he cited in the *Guide to London*[11], which he wrote on his return to India, were described in an 1852 review as exemplifying "physical Puritanism".[12] For example, Thomas Low Nichols's pamphlet *How to Live on Sixpence a-Day*, a bestseller in its day, extolled the frugal life.

> We have no right to eat more than is good for us .... while even one of our brethren has not enough to still the pangs of hunger .... Eat to live, and no longer live to eat.[13]

While these publications described the vegetarian diet as being practicable, economical, humane and aesthetic, many also made a link between stimulating food, such as meat and alcohol, and vice, and between simple living and sexual purity. Meat was injurious to both physical and moral health.[14]

It was while he was in England that Gandhi was introduced to the sacred texts of Hinduism, admittedly in translation, and in particular the *Bhagavad Gita*. For the rest of his life he would repeatedly turn to the *Gita* for both instruction and inspiration. In his own study of the Hindu sacred texts Gandhi did not feel himself bound by literal interpretations. The Bible Christians too had been sceptical of biblical literalism.[15] In South Africa, Gandhi was persuaded by the Jain poet, Raychandra Mehta, that the religious ideas he could accept were to be found within Hinduism.[16]

Food in India is not merely a substance vital to survival, it is "as much a subject for moral regulation and contemplation". 'Food in Hindu India stamps one's being and becoming'.[17] In Ancient India those upholding the ethics of non-violence *(ahimsa)* toward all beings were opposed to the priestly sacrificial cult. For Gandhi, an important contribution of Gautama Buddha to humanity was in the latter's compassion for all life.[18] *Ahimsa* and the perception of the sameness of life were connected with the ideas of *karma* and rebirth. *Karma* is the doctrine of causality while rebirth envisages the interchangeability of all life forms. Any act that is perpetrated against any other living being has ethical repercussions.[19]

Yet destruction of some life is inevitable since we depend on other living beings for our food.

> *Ahimsa* means not to hurt any living creature by thought, word or deed, even for the supposed benefit of that creature. To observe this principle fully is impossible for men, who kill a number of living beings large and small as they breathe or blink or till the land. We catch and hurt snakes or scorpions for fear of being bitten and leave them in some out-of-the-way place if we do not kill them. Hurting them in this way may be unavoidable, but is clearly *himsa* [violence]. ...When I eat cereals and vegetables in order to support life, that means violence done to vegetable life.[20]

> "Eating flesh and eating vegetables both involve violence but without the latter man can survive nowhere, while without the former he can ordinarily survive anywhere. If sensitivity to pain differs among creatures, the pain experienced by a cow in the throes of death cannot be experienced by plants. For all living beings, violence in some form is

unavoidable. The votary of non-violence will commit the minimum of violence.[21]

Since we cannot completely avoid violence, it is then important that we do not eat for pleasure but for survival, and imperative that we try to minimise the violence that we unavoidably inflict.[22]

The virtues on which all the other virtues depend are truth, *ahimsa* (nonviolence), and *brahmacharya (chastity)*. *Brahmacharya* is more than chastity for it seeks to bring the senses under our mastery, while *ahimsa* is not conventional pacifism. A *brahmachari* is one who practises self-restraint. The root verb *bhuj* can be translated as "experience", often refers to sexual enjoyment, and has strong connotations of "eating" or "consuming".[23] Gandhi eventually took the vow of *brahmacharya* in 1906.[24] *Ahimsa* involves love and compassion, and is not just a question of avoiding injuring others, but more positively, to stop harm being done to them and helping those who have been hurt.

Ashram life

The four ashram-type communities that Gandhi founded, two in South Africa (Phoenix Settlement and Tolstoy Farm) and two in India (Satyagraha Ashram, Sabarmati and Sevagram), provided a real-life context for the practice of *ahimsa,* for trying to fuse the eternal with the practical. In writing a history of the Sabarmati Ashram Gandhi admitted that the concept of an ashram was central to his life.[25] The community he envisaged would have an underlying spiritual basis, not something intellectually arrived at but involving "a heart-grasp".[26] These were communities where Gandhi and the other members could put to the test his ideas on community, right living with nonhuman creation, diet, health, faith, morality and service.

In 1913, in South Africa, Gandhi published a series of articles on health in its broadest sense,[27] revising them in India in 1942.[28] They summarise his ideas on a whole range of issues, such as diet, health, nature cure therapies and morality. A healthy state can only be attained and retained by obeying the laws of God. The human body is the universe in miniature, with the universe *within* reflecting that *without*. The Universe is seen as "the play" of the five gross elements: earth, water, *akash* [ether or space], light and air. Clean earth, pure water, open space, bright sunshine and fresh air are therefore essential for the preservation of the body.[29] Finally, the self-realisation of humanity is to be attained by the service of God through His creation.[30]

The first ashram was a farm near Phoenix Station, north of Durban, comprising a dilapidated cottage, an old orange grove, a few mango, guava and mulberry trees, and a stream running through the property. It was thickly overgrown with grass and inhabited by snakes.[31] Manual work, self- help and simple living were the guiding principles of the Phoenix experiment which began in 1904. Despite the infertility of the soil the settlement did eventually become self-sufficient in fruit and vegetables, while hedges were planted to protect the crops from roaming mules and donkeys.[32]

At the end of May 1910 a friend, Herman Kallenbach, a wealthy Johannesburg architect, bought another farm of about 1100 acres, named Tolstoy Farm, consisting of nearly a thousand orange, apricot and plum trees and a small house.[33] The entire acreage was to be cultivated jointly, to ensure more efficient production and build up team spirit. The soil here was fertile. Industry, economy and self-sufficiency were the watchwords of Tolstoy Farm. Oranges grown on the farm were made into marmalade, groundnuts into butter and even wheat for home-baked wholemeal bread. All rubbish was buried in trenches, all waste water was collected in buckets and used to water the trees, and all food refuse and excreta was covered in earth pits for later use as manure.[34]

As at Phoenix, there were a large number of snakes at Tolstoy Farm. Poisonous snakes at Phoenix had been killed when they got into the houses.[35] Gandhi put forward his own belief that it was a sin to kill snakes and won Kallenbach over. Kallenbach now set about collecting books so as to be able to identify the various species and make a rational assessment of the danger, since not all snakes are venomous. Snakes also perform a useful function in reducing the number of field crop pests like rats. Kallenbach even managed to tame a cobra, though Gandhi saw this as self-indulgence. Playing with the cobra when it was free, *that* would be to show real courage. But the cobra escaped. Another person would let young snakes play on his palm. As a result of these experiences, people on the Farm came to fear snakes much less.[36]

The founding in 1917 of the Satyagraha Ashram, on the bank of the Sabarmati River near the Sabarmati Central Jail, afforded the opportunity to formalise the nature of the community. Since *satyagraha* (literally, holding fast to truth) demanded long training and self-discipline, a code of rules and observances was necessary. Foremost among these was Truth which was more than just speaking the truth, but holding to it in the face of adversity. A central vow was that of non-thieving:

> I venture to suggest that it is the fundamental law of Nature, without exception, that Nature produces enough for our wants from day to day, and if only everybody took enough for himself and nothing more, there would be no pauperism in this world, there would be no man dying of starvation in this world. But so long as we have got this inequality, so long we are thieving.[37]

Gandhi once confided to Verrier Elwin that of all the ashram vows it was Control of the Palate *(aswada)* that he found most difficult, for he loved good food and sweetmeats.[38] He was continually seeking a cheap and nutritious diet, one the poor could afford, but also one that would be economical in terms of time. Cooking food involved considerable trouble and all needless processing was stained with violence. Uncooked food would save time and money as one needed to eat less dry food, while the vitamins would not be destroyed by cooking. However the various Raw Food experiments that he tried at different stages of his life all ended in failure.[39]

The Sabarmati Ashram grew its own vegetables and fruit, as well as grass for cattle. The absence of phosphates and small amount of potash in the Sabarmati soil made it suitable for fruit but inadequate for growing grain crops and cotton. Using the expertise of the American, Richard Gregg, Gandhi conducted experiments utilising human excreta and converting it to manure. Sanitation reform and the conversion of human excreta to manure were linked to the removal of untouchability.[40]

Ahmedabad in 1926 was afflicted with the problem of stray dogs, often mangy and some rabid. When consulted, Gandhi gave his opinion in favour of shooting the dogs. There were howls of protest.[41] He defended his opinion in print, asking whether it was better to have 5000 semi-starved dogs wandering about or 50 to be shot and the rest kept in a decent condition. "Merely taking life is not always *himsa."* The real solution to controlling the dog population was to learn "the art of keeping dogs", abetted by dog licences, collars and the killing of stray dogs "in the least painful manner".[42]

Monkeys were attacking the fruit trees and vegetables of the Ashram and were driven away by the use of "harmless arrows". Gandhi pointed out that, since it was one's duty to protect the fields on which many depended, the monkeys had to be deterred using the least violence, if possible, stopping short of killing. Stoning the monkeys was *himsa.* Petting and giving food to the monkeys was a mistaken humanitarian sentiment which would make us guilty of *himsa,* since we would have encouraged a pest of our neighbour's fields.[43]

A maimed calf in the dairy would not respond to treatment, just lying on her side in evident pain and unable to turn. Gandhi felt that "humanity demanded that the agony should be ended by ending life itself." His wife and a companion tried to nurse the calf and persuade her to eat, but without success. Accompanied by his family doctor, the dairyman and two others, Gandhi went to see the fatal injection administered. He gently held one of the calf's front legs as it died.[44]

A similar situation had arisen among the cats and dogs at Phoenix.

> A cat's skull became septic and white worms infested it. We applied many remedies, but to no effect. In a tone of despair and irritation, I was then asked what was to be done with the cat. We drowned it. ... [The] principal element that makes for non-violence is mercy, pity, compassion.[45]

The principle he had followed could also be applied to humans, where no aid could be given to a patient in agony and recovery was out of the question, and where the patient was lying unconscious.[46]

After the closure of Sabarmati in 1933, Gandhi eventually settled at Seagaon near Wardha in 1936, renaming it Sevagram 'Village of Service', and founding a centre for village development work there. With the ever present danger from snakes in the area, he wrote articles on snake poisoning, concerned that village workers should be well informed about snakes and what to do in the event of snakebite. He even started to build up a reference collection. Village workers were advised to wear shoes while walking in the dark and to carry a lantern, know how to identify the snakes, the nature of the poisons involved, the symptoms of poisoning and the necessary treatment.[47]

In attempting to coexist with the large number of snakes on the lands occupied by the four ashrams, Gandhi placed a high value on fearlessness *(abhaya)*.[48] As humans we are also responsible for other lives, either for the well-being of animals in our care (such as cows), or for the safety and survival of other humans (as in the case of the stray dogs) or protecting crops on which they depend (as in the case of the monkeys).

> [Once] a snake had crept into the Ashram cow-shed and coiled itself at such a place as made it impossible to bring it out alive. I would sleep at ease ... but others were worried. So Maganlal got it killed...[It] was my *dharma* [duty] to save the cows. However, let me say, that my nephew's killing the snake was as good or bad as my killing it.[49]

> All of us including myself are afraid of snakes ... We therefore as a rule catch them and put them out of harm's way. But if someone kills a snake out of fear, he is not taken to task....[In] my heart I do not harbour the necessary love, fearlessness and readiness to die of snake-bite .... It is possible that if I am attacked by a snake, I may neither resist nor kill it. But I am not willing to place anyone else's life in danger.[50]

Sevagram village had a population of 639, the majority of whom were harijans. Trying to improve the social and physical conditions in the village and the surrounding area was in the face of caste hostility and apathy. When ashram members tried to encourage local people to utilise the manure from earth latrines to improve crop productivity or to train people in the efficient skinning and complete utilisation of carcasses, as part of the cow protection programme, they were seen as failing to observe caste rules and were shunned.[51]

Composting and the compost pit had been an important feature of the Gandhian ashrams since Tolstoy Farm.[52] It utilised all the cow dung, human faeces and vegetable waste available in the villages for manure so as to increase the foodgrain yield. Fertilisers were expensive, destroyed the soil humus and caused erosion.[53]

Since the cow was for Gandhi a symbol for the entire nonhuman world, it was therefore a breach of cow protection to cause pain to the weakest, most insignificant creature on earth.[54] Cow protection meant the protection of everyone of God's creatures, and improving or repairing the roads would improve the lot of both villager *and* bullock.[55]

Since his South African days Gandhi did not believe that the way to protect the cow was through coercion or legislation, but by persuasion with respect for Muslim beliefs. He was aware of the cruelties practised on cows by Hindus: forcibly extracting the last drop of milk, starving, over-loading, over-working and goading their animals. Hindus needed to put their own house in order. Cow protection was a means of purifying Hinduism, while ghee manufacture, the economic use of hides and the other activities of cow protection such as cattle breeding to increase milk yields emphasised the economic rationale behind cow protection. Most of Gandhi's writings on cow protection date from the early 1920s and the mid-1940s, when Hindu-Muslim relations were going through critical phases.[56]

Seeing the effectiveness of both mass inoculation in tackling a cholera outbreak in the district and of skimmed milk and palm oil in treating keratomalacia among the village children caused Gandhi to revise some of his ideas.[57] He now admitted that, without a viable alternative, there should be some milk and milk products, such as curds, butter and *ghee*, in a vegetarian diet. But there were still drawbacks, both on moral and health grounds, to the consumption of milk and meat. If milk was to be taken, it should be skimmed milk.[58]

Learning from others

Gandhi was always open to the knowledge and experience of others. On a tour of the arid and treeless Cutch in late October 1925 Gandhi met Jaykrishna Indrajit, a forest officer, who was planting trees in Cutch.

> Digging of wells where water is scarce is a religion. ...It [Cutch] has a beautiful climate but some parts threaten to be a desolate waste unless there is proper rainfall in them. Rainfall can be almost regulated by deforestation or afforestation. Cutch needs conservation of every tree and every shrub. ...The conservation of forests, systematic plantation of trees, irrigation and many other things cannot be properly done without a common policy. ...In Cutch, Kathiawar, Rajputana, Sind and such other places a study of practical botany should be compulsory in all schools.[59]

During 1924 he had a series of long conversations with the singer Dilip Kumar Roy on the place of art and the ability of the poor to have easy access to it. Nature brought him wonder and awe, the presence of beauty, and the awareness of the touch of God. Spurred on to study the stars by D.B. Kalelkar, it became for him "one more method of seeing God."[60] He appreciated the beautiful in Nature – for example, Kanyakumari on the southern tip of India, the peak of Kanchengjunga through the clouds,[61] and the "glorious scenery" of Sinhgadh near Poona.[62] There can be "beauty in the speckless sky" and "beauty of colour in vegetables", for "what is useful can also be beautiful."[63]

> He [God] has granted us such climates and landscapes that we have natural scenes of entrancing beauty spread out before our eyes. The early morning sun of gold, moon-lit nights of silver, scintillating stars, superb sights on land and sea - these we all get to see in their original grandeur for nothing.[64]

Being greeted by flower petals strewn over him or garlands hung around his neck, Gandhi said: "How deeply it pains me that people should pluck masses of delicate blossom to fling in my face or hang round my neck! We should feel a more living bond between ourselves and the rest of animate creation." When someone brought him babul leaves to clean his carding bow at night, he said: "Look! all these leaves are folded up, asleep. Trees need sleep as we do. It's a wretched thing to tear leaves off a tree when it is resting.[65] All of creation has a claim on our consideration. We need to be able to distinguish between our 'basic' and 'peripheral' needs."[66]

In seeking a way of life that would satisfy one's need for sustenance yet not squander the earth's resources, Gandhi turned to indigenous people for instruction.

> You are fitted by nature to live on fruit and root and to eat in order to live, not to live in order to eat, and therefore best fitted to teach us that way of living.[67]

Indigenous knowledge

Seeing indigenous people as inheritors of ecological wisdom and living in balance with nature conceals the real processes of learning through trial, error and observation. Indigenous people are often also seen as having little or no impact on their environment. This is quite apart from the unfairness of looking to indigenous people to help solve our problems.

The first Europeans to settle in Island County, Washington Territory, on the west coast of America, in the late 1850s saw the region as a virgin wilderness. In fact, using fire and a simple technology, the Salish Indians had over many generations encouraged the growth of three dominant plants on the islands - bracken, camas, and nettles. These supplemented their regular diet of fish (particularly salmon) and small game, as well as creating favourable conditions for the great forests of Douglas fir.[68] Similarly, the open and parklike conditions encountered in southern New England were a result of American Indian management by fire. Fire could be used to drive game for hunting, to improve the quantity and nutritional quality of forage for herbivores as well as to clear fields for planting.[69]

Once American Indians had met the needs of their families for survival, with a small surplus for exchange, they would cease to hunt intensively, as traders often complained.[70] The arrival of European trade brought prestige goods and Old World disease epidemics, from which the Indians had been isolated, decimated social structures and broke the sanctions that had restricted individual accumulation.[71]

In 1807 Trout, an Ottawa visionary, conveyed a message from the Great Spirit to the Ottawa and Chippewa Indians.

"You complain that the animals of the Forest are few and scattered. How could it be otherwise? You destroy them yourselves for their skins only and leave their bodies to rot or give the best pieces to the Whites. I am displeased when I see this, and take them back to the Earth that they may not come to you again. You must kill no more animals than are necessary to feed and clothe you."[72]

For the present day Hopi, to farm as their ancestors did is to bring into being the fertility of the sacred as revealed in the formation of the world. Yet the Hopi do not always respect the earth as taught to do in the "long ago" by the god Maasaw. Severe overgrazing has resulted in wind and water erosion due to loss of ground cover. The dilemma is that they must earn enough money to keep their land and exist within the dominant society. They do realise that they are falling short. They are "trying to become Hopi." Hopi is an ideal to be striven for and periodically realised.[73]

The trouble is, as the elders of indigenous people realise, the old beliefs and traditions are intimately bound up with the old way of life. As indigenous people are stripped of their land so indigenous knowledge disappears. The forest from which they have derived their sustenance for generations, their way of agriculture and their religious ideas and culture are all bound up together.[74]

Conclusion

Indigenous people today are minorities within the world's nation-states, their cultures and ways of life under stress. Globally, the nations of the South too are under pressure, both economically and culturally, from the developed nations in the North where the scale of consumption is not commensurate with their population. For example, despite the fact that the United States has less than one third the population of India, its consumption of all sources of fossil energy is such that per capita emissions of carbon dioxide, a principal greenhouse gas, are 19 times those of India.[75]

Within the developed world a clear majority, having satisfied their basic survival and social needs, is now able to enjoy at least some material and non-material wants. But as expectations have risen in relation to actual improvements in material well-being, people have come to feel less affluent and less satisfied. The spread of affluence has come to be associated with growing divisions in society. Continuing rises in public spending have failed to prevent rising relative poverty and a growing crisis in many public services. Europe-wide, homelessness is on a rising trend and TB, a disease of poverty, has re-emerged in the USA and Europe. The USA has some of the highest child mortality rates in the developed world.[76]

As we have seen, Gandhi pointed out that in procuring food for our sustenance there will always be a certain amount of violence involved. Violence should then be kept to a minimum. Hence food should be to meet our need, not our greed. Also consuming much more than we need deprives someone else of what they need to survive and this Gandhi saw as theft. Gandhi repeatedly emphasized that to be concerned just with our own or our community's welfare is selfishness. One's own self-realization cannot be separated from the self-realization of those around us. If everyone cared for their neighbour, no-one who needed assistance,would be left unattended.[77]

Lowering relative, maybe absolute, living standards in the developed world is the only real alternative to continuing to create irreparable ecological damage or exacerbating the North-South divide.[78] Gandhi once defined real civilisation as that "in which the forces of nature are used with restraint."[79]

Notes & References

1. Pyarelal, 1965, pp.189,190-2,194; Devanesen, 1969, pp.12-13, 76.

2. Autobiography, Pt.III, chap. 1. Also the stormy 1931 voyage to England: Mirabehn, 1960, p.131.

3. Devanesen, 1969, p.170.

4. CWMG, Supplementary Volume 1, pp.266-7.

5. CWMG, Volume 77, pp.262n.,270,271,315; Mirabehn, 1960, p.258; see also Patel & Sykes, 1987, p.121.

6. Pyarelal, 1965, pp.195-7.

7. Autobiography, Pt.I, chap.13.

8. CWMG, Volume 1, pp.98-9; Hunt, 1978, pp.21,8 n.10,25.

9. Twigg, 1982, pp.66, 109, 112-118, 121-2; Lineham, 1982, pp.207-8, 216-7, 222.

10. For the many changes and experiments in Gandhi's diet, see Power, 1990, *passim.*

11. CWMG, Volume 1, pp.66-120.

12. Westminster Review, new series 1 (1852), pp.405-442.

13. Nichols, 1871, pp.43,46.

14. eg. Salt, 1886; Mayor, 1890. Also Just, 1988 - a South African discovery: Autobiography, PT.IV, chap.7.

15. Autobiography, Pt.I, chap.20. See especially Hay, 1989. Also Twigg, 1982, p.21; Lineham, 1982, p.214.

16. Autobiography, PT.II, chap.15; Hay, 1970, p.36.

17. Khare, 1992a, pp.16-17.

18. CWMG, Volume 35, p.246; Autobiography, PT.II, chap.22.

19. Jacobsen, 1994.

20. CWMG, Volume 50, p.205.

21. CWMG, Volume 35 [1927], p.380.

22. CWMG, Volume 30, p.537; also Volume 16, p.161. Cf.R.S.Khare, 1992b, pp.29-30.

23. see O'Flaherty, 1980, pp.31-2,18.

24. Autobiography, PT.III, chaps.7-8.

25. CWMG, Volume 50, p.188.

26. Autobiography, Pt.V, chap.9; CWMG, Volume 13, pp.225-26.

27. The articles are spread out in CWMG, Volumes 11 and 12.

28. CWMG, Volume 76, pp.411-12; Volume 77, pp.1-48.

29. CWMG, Volume 11, p.447.

30. see CWMG, Volume 50, p.80.

31. Autobiography, Pt.IV, chap.19; Pyarelal, 1986, p.436.

32. Thomson, 1993, pp.51-52,61-62,65-66.

33. CWMG, Volume 29, p.189.

34. Thomson, 1993, pp.71-72,75.

35. CWMG, Volume 29, pp.202-3; also Volume 12, pp.157-8; Pyarelal, 1986, p.441.

36. CWMG, Volume 29, pp.201-2.

37. CWMG, Volume 13, pp.225-35. See also Tagore, 'City and Village' in Tagore, 1961, pp.302-322 (see especially the passage about the earth having enough for our needs but not for our greed: p.314).

38. Elwin, 1964, p.53. See Autobiography, PT.III, chap.19 & chap.21; Pyarelal, 1980, pp.399-400.

39. For details see Power, 1990.

40. Thomson, 1993, pp.154-155.

41. Mirabehn, 1960, p.98.

42. CWMG, Volume 31, p.524; Volume 40, pp.229-30; Volume 90, p.150.

43. CWMG, Volume 37, pp.33,314-5; Volume 68, p.342. See also CWMG, Volume 50, pp.228-29; Volume 84, pp.62,392; and especially Volume 77, pp.207-8.

44. Mirabehn, 1960, pp.98-9; CWMG, Volume 37, pp.310-11,297-8; Volume 38, pp.139-40.

45. Diary, Volume 8, pp.282-4.

46. CWMG, Volume 37, pp.311,410.

47. CWMG, Volume 61, pp.338-9,471-72; Volume 62, pp'.50-1; also Volume 63, pp.254-55.

48. The importance of *fearlessness* is stressed in *Hind Swaraj* CWMG, Volume 10, p.53.

49. Diary, Volume 8, p.275.

50. CWMG, Volume 50, p.206. Once when a snake had crept onto his body he would not allow anyone to harm it: Diary, Volume 8, p.275; Kalelkar, 1950, pp.152-53.

51. Thomson, 1993, pp.186-87,207-8.

52. CWMG, Volume 29, p.192.

53. CWMG, Volume 90, pp.269-71,264,306,313,314; also Thomson, 1993, p.206.

54. CWMG, Volume 21, p.248; Volume 25, p.521.

55. CWMG, Volume 25, pp.518-21; Volume 33, p.76.

56. Juergensmeyer, 1985, p.12. Cf.McLane, 1977, pp.283,286,309. See e.g. CWMG,

Volume 10, pp.30-1,205;
Volume 20, pp.193-4,290,438;
Volume 21, pp.73-77;
Volume 24, pp.206,236,363;
Volume 25, pp.136-7,515-22;
Volume 26, pp.555-8;
Volume 75, pp.273-6;
Volume 87, pp.357-9;
Volume 89, pp.73-4.

57. Thomson, 1993, pp.206-208.

58. CWMG, Volume 77, pp.6-8.

59. CWMG, Volume 28, pp.457-9; see also Volume 88, p.425; Diary, Volume 6, pp.i9-20; Elmhirst, 1975, pp.42-50. Cf. his 1929 article on 'Tree Worship': CWMG, Volume 41, pp.292-3.

60. CWMG, Volume 49, pp.295-9,312-5; Volume 50, p.130.

61. CWMG, Volume 26, p.424; Diary, Volume 7, p.61. Autobiography, Pt.V, chaps.7-8.

62. Diary, Volume 2, p.140; CWMG, Volume 17, p.364.

63. CWMG, Volume 83, p.265.

64. Diary, Volume 4, p.286-7. See also CWMG, Volume 23, p.193; Volume 25, p.586; Volume 26, p.143; and Diary, Volume 8, pp.97,99,101.

65. Quoted in Patel & Sykes, 1987, pp.60-61.

66. VanDeVeer, 1979, see esp.pp.68-73.

67. Diary, Volume 9, pp.270,278; CWMG, Volume 33, p.162.

68. White, 1975.

69. Cronon, 1983, pp.49-50. For a discussion in a prehistoric context, see Mellars, 1976, and for a recent overview of contemporary indigenous agriculture, particularly shifting cultivation, see Brookfield & Padoch, 1994.

70. White, 1991, p.480.

71. Cronon, 1983, pp.98-99.

72. Cited in White, 1991, p.486.

73. Loftin, 1991, pp.9,110,117.

74. see Savyasaachi, 1993.

75. World Resources Institute, 1994, p.17. See also Power, 1992.

76. Lansley, 1994 [Report for the Henley Centre for Forecasting] pp.23,30.

77. CWMG, Volume 85, p.458; Volume 46, p.254; Volume 48, p.58; Volume 50, p.218; Gita III, 11-12.

78. Lansley, 1994, p.185.

79. [June 1918] Diary, Volume 1, p.145.

Bibliography

Autobiography: Gandhi, Mohandas K., 1982: *An Autobiography or The Story of My Experiments with Truth*, Penguin Books, Harmondsworth, Middlesex.

Brookfield, Harold & Padoch, Christine, 1994: Appreciating Agrodiversity: A Look at the Dynamism and Diversity of Indigenous Farming Practices', *Environment* 36 (5): 6-1 1 and 37-45.

Cronon, William, 1983: *Changes in the Land: Indians, Colonists, and the Ecology of New England.* Hill and Wang, New York.

CWMG: Gandhi, Mohandas K., 1958-1984: '*The Collected Works of Mahatma Gandhi*', Volumes 1 to 90 (Volume 1 in the 2nd edition of 1969 plus Supplementary Volume 1 of

CWMG: Gandhi, Mohandas K., 1958-1984: *The Collected Works of Mahatma Gandhi*, Volumes 1 to 90 (Volume 1 in the 2nd edition of 1969 plus Supplementary Volume 1 of 1989), The Publications Division of the Ministry of Information & Broadcasting, Government of India, New Delhi.

Devanesen, Chandran D.S., 1969: *Making of the Mahatma*, Orient Longmans, New Delhi.

Diary: Desai, Mahadev H., 1968-1974: *Day-to-Day with Gandhi: Secretary's Diary*, Volumes 1-9 [1917-19271, Sarva Seva Sangh Prakashan, Varanasi.

Elmhirst, Leonard K., 1975: *Poet and Plowman*. Visva-Bharati, Calcutta.

Elwin, Verrier, 1964: *Tribal World of Verrier Elwin: An Autobiography* Oxford University Press, London.

Gita: Zaehner, R.C. [Translator], 1966: *Bhagavad Gita*. In *Hindu Scriptures*. Dent (Everyman's Library), London, pp.247-325.

Hay, Stephen N., 1970: Jain Influences on Gandhi's Early Thought. In Sibnarayan Ray, Ed. *Gandhi, India and the World*. The Hawthorn Press, Melbourne, pp.29-38.

Hay, Stephen, 1989: The Making of a Late-Victorian Hindu: M.K.Gandhi in London 1888-1891, *Victorian Studies*, 30 (1): 75-98.

Hunt, James D., 1978: *Gandhi in London*, Promilla, New Delhi.

Jacobsen, Knut, 199-4: The Institutionalization of the Ethics of "Non-injury" toward All "Beings!' in Ancient *India, Environmental Ethics* 16 (3): 287-301.

Juergensmeyer, Mark, 1984/85: Gandhi & the Cow: The Ethics of Human/Animal Relationships, *Between the Species, 1:* 11-17.

Just, Adolf, 1988: *Return to Nature!*. [Translated by Benedict Lust.] Reprint of 1904 edition. Society of Metaphysicians, Hastings.

Kalelkar, Kaka, 1950: *Stray Glimpses of Bapu*, Navajivan Publishing, Ahmedabad.

Khare, R.S., 1992a: 'Introduction', in R.S.Khare (ed.), *The Eternal Food: Gastronomic Ideas and Experiences of Hindus and Buddhists*. State University of *New* York Press, Albany NY, pp.1-25.

Khare, R.S., 1992b: 'Food with Saints: An Aspect of Hindu Gastrosemantics, in R.S.Khare (ed.), *The Eternal Food: Gastronomic Ideas and Experiences of Hindus and Buddhists*. State University of New York Press, Albany NY, pp.27-52.

Lansley, Stewart, 1994: *After the Gold Rush: The Trouble with Affluence: 'Consumer Capitalism' and the Way Forward*. Century Business Books for the Henley Centre, London.

Lineham, Peter J., 1982: 'Restoring Man's Creative Power: The Theosophy of the Bible Christians of Salford', in W.J.Sheils (ed.), *The Church and Healing*, The Ecclesiastical History Society [Studies in Church History 191. Basil Blackwell, Oxford, pp.207-223.

Loftin, John D., 1991: *Religion and Hopi life in the Twentieth Century*. Indiana University Press, Bloomington

Mayor, John E.B., 1890: *Why am I a Vegetarian?*, (bilingual text: English & German), The Vegetarian Society, Manchester.

McLane, John R., 1977: *Indian Nationalism and the Early Congress*. Princeton University Press, Princeton NJ.

Mellars, Paul, 1976: Fire Ecology, Animal Populations and Man: a Study of some Ecological Relationships in Prehistory, *Proceedings of the Prehistoric Society* 42-, 15-45.

Mirabehn [Madeleine Slade], 1960: *Spirits Pilgrimage*, Orient Longmans, Calcutta.

Nichols, T.L., 1871: *How to Live on Sixpence a-Day*, Nichols, London.

O'Flaherty, Wendy Doniger, 1980: Karma and Rebirth in the Vedas and Puranas, in W.D. O'Flaherty (ed.), *Karma and Rebirth in Classical Indian Traditions*. University of California Press, Berkeley, pp.3-37.

Patel, Jehangir P. & Sykes, Marjorie, 1987: *Gandhi: His Gift of the Fight*. Friends Rural Centre, Rasulia.

Power, Shahed, 1990: *Gandhi and Deep Ecology. Experiencing the Nonhuman Environment*, Ph.D. thesis, University of Salford.

Power, Shahed, 1992: Development and the Cola Culture, *Gandhi Marg* **13** (4): 466-476.

Pyarelal, 1965: *Mahatma Gandhi: The Early Phase:* Volume I, Navajivan Publishing, Ahmedabad.

Pyarelal, 1980: *Mahatma Gandhi:* Volume II: *The Discovery of Satyagraha - On the Threshold'*, Sevak Prakashan, Bombay.

Pyarelal, with James D. Hunt (ed.), 1986: *Mahatma Gandhi: Volume Ill: The Birth of Satyagraba - From Petitioning to Passive Resistance*, Navajivan Publishing, Ahmedabad.

Salt, Henry S., 1886: *"A Plea for Vegetarianism, and other essays'*, The Vegetarian Society, Manchester.

Savyasaachi, Dr., 1993: An alternative system of knowledge: fields and forests in Abujhmarh, in T.Banuri & F.A.Marglin *(eds.), Who will Save the Forests? Knowledge, Power and Environmental Destruction'*, Zed Books, London, pp.53-79.

Tagore, Rabindranath, 1961: City and Village [19281. *In 'Towards Universal Man'*. Asia Publishing House, Bombay, pp.302-322.

Thomson, Mark, 1993: *Gandhi and His Ashrams.* Sangam Books, London.

Twigg, Julia M., 1982: *The Vegetarian Movement in England from 1847-1981: A Study of the Structure of its Ideology*, Ph.D. thesis, London School of Economics.

VanDeVeer, Donald, 1979: Interspecific Justice, *Inquiry*, 22:55-79.

White, Richard, 1975: Indian Land Use and Environmental Change: Island County, Washington - A Case Study, *Arizona and the West* **17** (Winter): 327-338.

White, Richard, 1991: *The middle ground: Indians, empires, and republics in the Great Lakes region, 1650-1815.* Cambridge University Press, Cambridge.

World Resources Institute, 1994: *World Resources 1994-95.* Oxford University Press, New York.

M.V. Naidu

Western Models of Development—their Relevance and Desirability for the Third World: The Gandhian Alternative

I. Definition of Development

The term 'development', has been traditionally defined as the attainment of unlimited economic affluence through unlimited industrialization, ad infinitum. This definition implies four elements-- materialism, industrialism, unlimitedness and timelessness. Materialism-industrialism has been presented as the panacea for all problems, from poverty to peace. The developed states of the West have constantly invited the Third World to build itself in the image of the West.[1] All the modern ideologies – capitalism, socialism, fascism and communism --- are completely committed to the goals of developmentalism through industrialism without limitations.[2]

The best typologies of Western development may be identified as the capitalist America, the imperialist Britain, the fascist Germany and the communist Soviet Union. In spite of their proclaimed divergencies and disputes, these four developmental models share certain common denominators that may be identified as the following:[3] (1) Colonialism / neocolonialism, domestic and external. (2) High science-technology. (3) mass economy based on mass production, mass distribution and mass consumption. (4) Media of mass communications. (5) Military industries and arms sales. (6) militarization and war. (7) Economic affluence (measured in such terms as incomes and consumption). (8) Chauvinistic nationalism. (9) The authoritarian 'Big State'. 10) A century of undisturbed industrial development.

II. Basic Elements of Development

The above elements may be elaborated as follows:

1. *Colonialism*: Industrialization needs--- (a) Raw materials in large quantity and variety; (b) Energy sources-- based on slaves, animals, wood, coal, oil, hydropower or uranium; (c) Labour power derived from slaves, peasants, workers and the unemployed; (d) Trade and markets, *i.e.*, free trade and captive markets with millions of consumers; (e) Free flow of capital and profits--*i.e.*, investment opportunities and immense and transferable profits.

   Countries or corporations undertaking industrialization without possessing the above ingredients will, therefore, have to develop, buy, exchange, or as is done most often-steal, rob or forcefully obtain the raw materials, workers, markets and profits. Colonialism is a system of unscrupulous exploitation of the economically and the militarily weak people by the strong, for the benefit of the strong. The victims of exploitation can be national minorities and regions, or foreign peoples and countries. The former may be called "domestic colonialism", the latter is foreign colonialism.

   Economic exploitation accompanied with military subjugation, political oppression and cultural dehumanization, constitutes imperialism.

2. *Science-Technology*: Closely integrated, science and technology inaugurated industrialization that has led to the modern production of consumer goods and military weapons. Improved machinery has led to massive industrialization.

   Energy production, machine-building, transportation, and communication were the basic products of science-technology that initiated and advanced the industrial age. Science-technology can be acquired through long-drawn national education and research, or through short-cuts, like purchase or industrial espionage.

3. *Mass Economy*: Mass economy, built upon mass production, mass distribution and mass consumption, requires the assembly line, mass transportation and mass communications.

   Monopolization, necessary for pooling raw materials, capital, technology and labour, gives rise to, among others, Big Business, Big Labour and Big Mass Media. Today's multi-national corporations wield powerful influence on national economies and governments.

4. *Media of Mass Communications*: Mass production necessitates mass consumption. Potential purchasers have to be informed on the availability of the goods, their quality and their prices. As the buyers reach level of satiety in consumption, they have to be induced and seduced into buying more things, "improved" things, and new things. Thus advertising and publicizing commercial products become crucial adjuncts to production. Hence the development of printing, telegraph, telephone, radio, film, television, computers and satellites.

5. ***Military Industries and Arms Sales***: From the beginning of industrialization, development has meant not only the production of consumer goods, but also of military weapons, because scientific or technological developments are always directed to armament making. Mass production of weapons necessitates mass distribution and mass consumption of weapons.

   At the initial stage of development weapons are marketed within the country of their origin. The citizens and the national governments are induced into buying more and improved weapons. Thus the more industrialized a nation becomes, the more militarized it becomes.

   To keep up the growth in domestic military industries, international sales of weapons become necessary. Today global sales of armaments average $70-80 billion *per annum*. Foreign arms sales, besides boosting national trade, also help in getting rid of surplus and obsolete weapons, in weapon experimentation in foreign countries, the development of military science-technology, winning and supporting military allies, or in punishing enemies or their friends. Military and non-military products are the "Siamese twins" of industrialization, sharing a single brain!

6. ***Militarization and War***: Militarization involves the acquisition and the expansion of troops, training of military personnel, conscription, bases, allies, military expenditures, and the like.

   Military industries enhance militarization. Besides, colonialism necessitates military power to suppress domestic opposition, the freedom struggles in the colonies, and the challenges of rival colonial powers. Wars and militarization reinforce each other. Both, in turn, strengthen "the industrial-military complex", a coalition of the militarists and the industrialists who are committed to militarization and military industries for power and profit. To this may be added the military scientists and the die-hard imperialists. The "industrial-militarist-scientific-colonialist complex" uses the mass media, the church and the school, to brain-wash the public on the need of militarization in the name of external threat, national power or prestige; weapons for individuals are legitimized on the pleas of crime prevention and self-protection, machoism and power.

   The industrial-military complex justifies the importance of militarism and war thus: Firstly, the risks of war are worth taking because the promises of economic affluence and political power are very worthy. Secondly, a defeat can always be averted by possessing a greater military strength than the enemy. Thirdly, wars are natural and necessary expressions of divine will, or national destiny, or dialectical determinism.

   Military defeats of an industrial state has often been used to inspire reindustrialization and remilitarization. Some believe that war is a boost to industrialization, because wartime industries develop innovative technologies, find substitutes or synthetic alternatives for raw materials, generate efficiency in resource utilization and produce economy of scale. This is like arguing that disease is good because it leads to the development of curative drugs. While Marxists believe that war is a boon to capitalists, Mao Tse Tung has argued that each war has helped an expansion of the communist system.[4]

In short, militarization and war are the inevitable and the necessary concomitants of massive industrialization in the modern state.

7. *Economic Affluence*: Industrialization has led to economic abundance, raising incomes and standards of living. Traditionally, industrial development is measured in terms of consumption of goods, like food, electricity or automobiles, while economic wealth is calculated in terms of gross national productivity, gross national income or individual earnings and expenditures.

   Material goods and monetary wealth constitute "the standards of living". This concept disregards psychological satisfaction, intellectual advancement, aesthetic fulfillment, and humanism that constitute, in Gandhian terms, "the standards of life."

8. *Chauvinistic Nationalism*: Massive industrialization cannot be initiated and advanced if the state is suffering from political instability and national disunity, caused by domestic conflicts, and foreign interventions or aggressions. Nationalism is the key to national unity and state power.

   By invoking and encouraging blind and emotional loyalty to tribalism, racism, religionism, or ethnicism, nationalism can be reduced to chauvinism. Chauvinism can be directed towards militarization and colonialization, as well as towards industrialization.

9. *The Authoritarian Big State*: The pre-industrial agrarian society is marked by three features: the individual enjoys maximum autonomy; the economic, political and military powers remain highly decentralized and non-governmental; and finally, the role of the government is minimal.

   The farmer in the non-industrialized agricultural economy is self-sufficient and self-reliant. Once agriculture becomes dependent upon industrial products, the farmer's autonomy and self reliance evaporate; he becomes dependent upon the resources, capital, skills, and the labour of thousands of people in hundreds of industries, in dozens of countries that are involved in the production and distribution of the industrial goods he uses.

   Every point of interdependency, in the complex chain of industrial economy, is a potential source of conflict and disruption. To avoid or eliminate such conflicts, the relationships have to be regulated through thousands of rules and laws. To enforce thousands of laws, there is a need for hundreds of bureaucrats, judges and policemen, and millions of tax dollars. All these activities mean increased governmentalization. Hence the rise of Big Government in the highly industrialized state.

Governmentalization increases with the rise of national and multinational monopolies, colonies, militarization and war. The growth of media monopolies, whether private or public, increases thought control and decreases citizens' freedoms. Colonialism embodies the extremes of governmentalization, centralization, militarization and thought-control.

The ultimate outcome of all the above factors is the rise of the Big State. The Big State is the authoritarian state; extreme authoritarianism is totalitarianism. Thus, the Big State is both the cause and the consequence of massive industrialization.

10. *A Century of Industrialization*: In the four Western models of development, the "initial" phase of industrialization was continuous, unlimited and more-or-less undisturbed over a period of a century. In other words, the early industrialization processes should not be shaken up by debilitating domestic wars, external aggression, or totalitarian global wars. Having had experienced industrial maturity, Britain, Germany and the USSR, were able to cope with post-war reconstruction. But the Cold War, through its intrusive nature and interventionist strategies, did prove damaging to the developmental plans of some countries. Even to reap the full benefits of colonialism, an imperial state needs a century of exploitation.

III. Relevance of Developmental Models to the Third World

From the points of view of reality and practicability, how relevant, transferable and replicable are the Western models of development for the Third World? To answer this question one must present a factual-empirical analysis of the basic features of developmentalism, especially during its "initial" phase, as represented in the case studies of Britain, the United States, Nazi Germany and the Soviet Union.

1. *Colonialism*: Britain's industrialization started with domestic colonialism over religious and ethnic minorities, and the poor. Still the small island could never have developed into a world power without imperialism. By 1914 Britain had captured 33.5 million square kilometres of territory and 384 million people;[5] it would declare proudly that the sun never sets over the British Empire. The Empire was the result of an unholy alliance of the "3Ms"–the Merchants, the Militarists and the Missionaries.

Suffering from limited resources and markets, Germany first acquired Schleswig-Holstein and Alsace-Lorraine in Europe. After in 1871, Germany resorted to building colonialism outside Europe. During 19th century, it acquired either political rights or economic interests in Africa, the Middle East, China and the Pacific. Population under German domain rose from 31.7 million in 1850, to 64.9 million in 1911.[6] After losing World War I, Germany lost some territories and all colonies. During the 1930s the Nazis openly demanded *lebensraum* i.e., lands for industrial development. When refused, Adolf Hitler launched World War II to build a world empire for the Third Reich.

The gruesome annals of genocide, enslavement, and violence in the Americas represent the phase of domestic colonialism that paved the way for American industrialization. The United States, starting with 13 ex-colonies, was eventually extended from coast to coast. Between 1895 and 1917, it had acquired 728,771 square kilometres of land with a population of 17.6 million.[7] Today, with the help of its world-wide neocolonialism, including Canada, Central and South America, the United States is able to acquire and use up 40% of world resources.

By 1914 the Tsarist empire had expanded to 17.4 million square miles and 33.2 million people. Under the Soviet Union, the Russians had, by 1924, domination over 90 million non-Russians outside Eastern Europe.[8] The Soviet domestic colonialism was built upon the massive slave camps, the liquidation of millions, enforced industrialization, and coercive thought-control. Eastern Europe provided neocolonies for Russian industrialization.

Between 1850s and 1910s, the colonies provided to the industries of the West huge quantities of raw materials. During this period the world's production of cotton went up by 127%, wheat by 67% and rubber by 44%, and so on. Similarly, production of coal went up by 1320%, copper by 1834%, gold by 1,218%, iron ore by 1,113%, and cast iron by 1,266%.[9] During the 19th and early 20th centuries all the colonial resources were either owned, or controlled and traded, by the Europeans. Any benefits that accrued to the peoples in the colonies were just minimal that *trickled down* as unstoppable *byproducts*.

In 1850 the world trade was $4 billion; in 1913 it jumped to $40.5 billion; more than 50% the trade was between the colonies and the metropolitan states.[10] By 1913 the British share of world exports of manufactures was 31%; of Germany, 28%; of the United States, 13%, and that of Russia, over 4%.[11] Between 1946 and 1956, the US companies in Latin America received $3.17 for every dollar they invested.[12]

During World War I, 1,800,000 soldiers and 400,000 labourers in India were recruited for the British armies overseas, while the British Viceroy of India "presented" to the British monarch a 'gift' of £100 million.[13]

Thus the colonies facilitated the *initial* stage of Western industrialization; today's neocolonies "sustain" that development. Since no Third World country can, at present, discover or conquer continents, or establish colonies, the colonial model of development is not at all relevant to the Third World.

2. *Science and Technology*: Britain, the United States, Nazi Germany and the Soviet Union were prepared to advance in industrialization, because they had attained high levels of literacy and education in science.

   One strong indicator of technological advancement in a country is the number of patents registered. Between 1760-1790, 976 patents for inventions were issued in Britain. The number grew to 21,910 during the years 1860-69. In the United States the patents rose from 473 in 1840 to 36,620 in 1907. Germany issued 8,784 patents in 1900; twelve years later, the figure rose to 13,080.[14]

   Science-technology brought about dramatic changes in transportation. By the year 1900 the railway mileage completed were as follows: Britain--19,000 miles (4% of the world total); Germany--32,000 miles (7%); Russia--28,000 miles (6%) and the United States--193,000 miles (42%).[15]

   Along with transportation came the revolution in mass communications. Science-technology produced such advances as paper-making, printing machine, radio, telephone, telegraph and television.

   Most of the Third World countries became independent with high rates of illiteracy (30 to 80%). This was a legacy of colonialism. To catch up with modern science-technology they need huge capital and a few generations of educated citizenry; or they have to become technological dependencies of the West and to pay the price of neocolonialism. Except countries like Brazil, China, Mexico and India, most of the Third World countries will not be able, in the near future, to produce science-technology that can be self-reliant, self-regenerating and self-directed.

3. *Monopolization for Mass Economy*: At the beginning of the 20th century in the United States, seven large industrial trust companies, headed by the giant corporations, such as the Standard Oil Company and the US Steel Corporation, had cornered, by 1908, most of industrial production, distribution and banking.[16] By 1900, the big monopolies in America were producing from 50% to 80% of the most important products, like food stuffs, chemicals, and iron and steel.[17] While the Eisenhower government, declared that "what is good for General Motors is good for America", other Americans had claimed that "what is good for General Motors is also good for the World."

   Between 1716-1793 the Bank of England had opened 400 provincial banks that helped the Industrial Revolution. In 1892 the National Trade Union Congress controlled 1.5 million workers. By 1911 a substantial part of the British economy (50-90%) had passed into the hands of monopolies like the Association of Portland Cement Manufacturers, the Cablemakers' Association, the Dyers' Association, the Salt Union and the Imperial Tobacco Company.[18]

During the same period, monopolization process started in Russia with the growth of corporations like Prodameta Company, the Krovlia, the Prodvagon, etc. Four oil companies, mutually interlocked, controlled almost the entire production of oil in Russia.[19]

In 1870 the German capital market was entirely in the hands of merchant bankers. In 1914 the four 'D Banks' – the Deutsche Bank, the Disconto-Gesellschaft, the Dresdner Bank and the Darmstadter Bank --- controlled 65% of the capital resources in all Germany. In 1904 the three major chemical industries – the Bayer, the Hoechst and the Ludwigshafen – fused into I.G. Farben.[20]

How many Third World countries have developed, or can develop, indigenous monopolies with huge accumulation of capital, technology, labour, and transportation and communication capabilities? Colonialism has left these countries with depleted capital, distorted trade and debilitating debts. Mass economy without monopolies is impossible.

4. *Media of Mass Communications*: The revolution in mass communication complemented and advanced industrialization, simply because goods produced had to be sold; advertising the products was necessary for selling. The first newspapers appeared in Germany in 1615, in England in 1622, in Russia in 1703 and in the US in 1704.[21] Books and newspapers inaugurated universal education.

Industrialization necessitated advertising and informing over long distances to unknown potential buyers, without the traditional messengers. Such advertising was facilitated by the inventions like telegraph and telephone, radio and television. During the 1970s the media available in the four developed countries under study were as follows:[22]

Country	Population (million)	Periodicals & Dailies	Telephones (million)	Radios (million)	TV (million)
Britain	54.0	10130	15	3.5	15.0
Germany	78.5	5500	13	25.0	20.5
USSR	242.0	8700	11	95.0	35.0
USA	206.5	2340	125	336.0	100.0

The developed world, holding 20% of the world population, has at its disposal about 60% of the world's newspapers, 65% of the world's radios and 65% of the books published in the world.[23]

During the 1980s the average annual investment in communications, as percentage of total GDP in the United States was 0.83%, in Germany, 0.82% and in Britain, 1.23%; while in India it was 0.17%, in Thailand, 0.30% and in the Venezuela, 0.51%.[24]

An interesting indicator on the close connection between mass production and mass consumption is the expenditure on advertisements. In 1971 the US, as a whole, spent $4 billion on radio and television advertisements.[25] Such spending presupposes the production and sales of goods worth many more billions. If mass media are necessary for industrialization, why cannot the Third World borrow or buy the media of communications from the developed countries? This is indeed being done now; unfortunately, this process has created numerous problems of inappropriate technologies, heavy costs of machine purchases and, most important of all, the issue of the media colonialism of the West on the values, ideologies, cultures, hopes, fears and frustrations of the peoples of the Third World.

In short, the Western models of mass media are irrelevant to the contemporary economic experiments of the Third World.

5. *Armament Industries*: Starting with rifles, revolvers, machine guns and new kinds of ammunition, the weapon industries in the West progressed, by 1914, to the making of cannons, the armour-plated battleships, submarines, tanks, hand and rifle grenades, bombing and fighter planes, and hundreds of varieties of poison gas.

Between 1855-1870 American Remington rifles and Colt revolvers were mass produced and sold all over the world.[26] During the 19th century the British companies, like Vickers, became suppliers to Europe, Latin America, Asia and the Middle East, for such weapons as the Dawson rifle, the Maxine machine gun, cannon, battleship, etc.[27] On the verge of the First World War, the Krupp Corporation manufactured 53,000 cannons; 26,000 were sold to Germany and the remaining 27,000 were sold to other 52 countries.[28] In spite of the restrictions of the Treaty of Versailles (1918), Hitler appropriated, in 1934, 800 million marks for German rearmament.[29] The Tsarist government invited many foreign arms producers to build military industries in the country, which the Soviet Union nationalized, attained military self-reliance, and then started selling weapons abroad.

For maintaining their domestic growth and profitability, the arms industries make patriotic appeals in the name of national security or national power. But when mass production of arms necessitates international sales, the arms industries propagate the economic benefits of foreign trade – employment, foreign earnings, disposal of obsolete and second-hand arms, financing of new inventions, opportunity of experimentation with new weapons and diplomatic leverage.

To the arms industries, war is profitable, as shown in the following figures on net profits:[30]

Arms Industries	Peace Years Average Profit (1911-1914)	War Years Average Profit (1914-1917)
Germany (in marks)	42,869,000	98,943,000
Austria-Hungary (in kronen)	11,425,000	36,176,000
France (in francs)	27,625,000	51,882,000
USA (in dollars)	164,076,000	475,406,000

The world exports in arms in 1921 were worth $43 million; in 1930 it was $55 million.[31]

Thus arms industry is an unavoidable concomitant of industrialization.

7. *Militarization and war*: As shown below, militarization increases as industrialization advances:[32]

Year	Increase in armed Personnel (1000)	Increase in military expenditures (millions)
USA		
1870-1914	47 to 164	$80 to $314
1921-1937	22 to 288	$748 to $992
BRITAIN		
1870-1914	345 to 582	$80 to $314
1921-1937	699 to 645	$1,144 to $1,263
GERMANY		
1870-1914	410 to 891	$80 to $314
1921-1937	115 to 766	$30 to $4000
RUSSIA		
1870-1914	716 to 1,352	$110 to $441
1921-1937	1,520 to 1,324	$402 to $5,026

Militarization inculcates militarism, the psychology of violence; militarism accentuates militarization.

The globalization of the arms industries and the militarization of the nation states, coupled with the colonialization and chauvinism, invariably leads to military conflicts. Between 1750-1945 Britain, Germany, Russia and the United

States were engaged in 54 inter-state conflicts: 44 wars in Europe, six in Asia, four in North America and one in Africa [the Spanish American war (1898) was fought in America and Asia]. Out of these 54 wars, Russia/Soviet Union was involved in 38, Britain in 28, Prussia/Germany in 17, and the US in 10.[33]

Between 1750-1945 the four states under study were involved in 36 colonial wars that were fought outside Europe--15 wars in Asia (including seven in India), ten in Africa, eight in the Western hemisphere, one in Ireland and two world wars.[34] The implications are--firstly, that the industrializing Western states went on a spree of conquering colonies and concessions to boost their industrial development, and thereby they dragged the non-Europeans into wars; and secondly, that many of the inter-imperial rivalries were fought out on the colonial soils.

The Third World countries, that are imitating the Western models of development, must realize that militarization and war are the natural outcome of industrialization.

8. *Economic Affluence*: The hopes, generated by the Western economists, that the Third World can catch up with Western affluence, were false. The economic gap between the rich and the poor nations is too big and too unbridgeable, as shown below in terms of trade, GNP and GDP.

Value of Exports (1965)[35]
(US dollars in millions)

Europe	$90,800	Africa	$ 9,000
USSR	$ 8,200	L.America	$12,700
N.America	$35,700	Asia (excluding communist states)	$26,700

In 1965, 154 states earned $49,000 million while four of the industrialized states earned $66,392 million through their exports.

Growth Rate of Real GNP[36]
(annual average)

	1913-38	1953-65
UK	1.1	3.1
W. Germany	1.6	6.2
Russia	2.8	6.1
USA	2.0	3.3

Gross National (1965)[37]
(dollars in millions)

Europe: GDP	$ 513,900	Africa : GDP	$51,100
per capita GDP	$ 1,600	per capita GDP	$ 170
N. America : GDP	$ 739,000	*L.America* : GDP	$216,900
per capita GDP	$ 3,450	per capita GDP	$ 510

In 1965, thirty of the developed countries had GDP worth $1,252,900 million, while 152 countries of the Third World together had $365,400 million: Not only was the GNP of the Third World very low, but its external debt also increased dramatically. While in 1975 the debt of the underdeveloped countries was $173 billions, the debt grew to $754 billion by 1985--*i.e.* within ten years the indebtedness increased by 336%.[38] In the year 1985 the number of the Third World citizens, living below the poverty line, was 30% of the world population.[39] In other words, while imitating the Western models of development, the Third World countries have incurred more debt and have failed in reducing their poverty. More fundamentally, should the Third World aim at the western "standard of living?"

8. ***Chauvinistic Ideologies***: The Western countries have had no hesitation in invoking chauvinism for mobilizing mass support for industrialization, colonialization and wars in the name of ethnicity, race, religion, country and empire.

"The White Man's Burden," became the racist rationalization for Western colonialism of 19th century. Karl Marx surmised that the Asian societies were "semi-civilized" simply because they did not satisfy his test of civilization-in-dustrialization![40] Franklin D. Roosevelt referred to Nazi Germany as the chal-lenge to "Western Civilization,"[41] as if Nazism and Fascism were not derivations of Western civilization. Regarding the Battle of Britain, Winston Churchill said: "on this battle depends the survival of Christian civilization."[42] Yet, he had no qualms of conscience in bombing millions of Christians in Europe and elsewhere, and in oppressing millions of nonwhite Christians in Asia and Africa. The American Senator, Albert Beveridge, mixing up race, religion and colonial exploitation, made a speech on 15 February 1889, in which he called the American Republic an answer "to the divine commands." Without any hesitation, Beveridge declared: "God has given us this Pacific empire for civilized administration." He proceeded to openly acknowledge the economic advantages of this 'empire'.[43] German leaders like Bismark and Kaiser Wilhelm II felt they were the favourites of God.[44] Even Hitler appealed to God in his speech to the Reichstag on 20 February 1938: "I now pray to God that He will bless in the years to come ..."[45] Hitler sought mass support, not only for anti-semitic racism, but also for German colonialism–*lebensraum*. While the Russian Tsars often used the Orthodox Church to manipulate the masses in the name of Christianity and Slav nationalism, to wage their imperial wars, the anti-religious communists preached Marxist ideology to mobilize the masses in the name of dialectical materialism and international proletarianism. In 1919, Lenin said: "History teaches that no oppressed class has ever come into power ... without passing through a period of dictatorship ... "[46] Advocating his theory of "permanent revolution" Leon Trotsky, in April 1919, referred to the growth of the proletarian revolution in Poland, Italy, Hungary and Bavaria.[47] Even though Marxism declares that patriotism is the opium administered to the masses by the ruling class, Joseph Stalin on 3 July 1941, talked of "The perfidious military attack on our fatherland..our patriotic war against German fascism.... "[48]

Racism, ethnicism and religionism, that helped Western industrialization and colonialization, are now tearing apart the new states of the Third World. How relevant are the 19th century chauvinistic ideologies of the West to the developmental aspirations of the Third World of the mid 20th century?

9. *The Authoritarian Big State*: Britain did not attain meaningful democratization until the middle of the 20th century. Until 1823 England maintained the death penalty for about one hundred trivial crimes; slavery was abolished in 1833; and only in 1829 were the Dissenters and the Roman Catholics allowed to hold public office.

In 1793, 162 feudal patrons controlled the majority of seats in the British House of Commons. The Reform Acts of 1832, 1867 and 1884 extended franchise to some extent. However, universal adult franchise for 21-year old men and women was not introduced until 1928, almost 150 years after the inauguration of the Industrial Revolution. Nevertheless, a woman could not become the prime minister until the 1970s. While Britain was being democratized during the 19th century, its non-white colonies were being denied similar reforms.

Germany had a long history of authoritarian regimes under kaisers. Chancellor Bismarck (1861-1888), acted as a dictator implementing the policy of 'the blood and iron'. Though post-war Weimar Republic introduced democratic reforms, within 14 years it was sabotaged by Adolf Hitler and the Nazi Party. Between 1933-39 Nazis swept away all traces of democracy and Nazi Germany became the first demonstration of how modern science, technology and industrialization can be combined to create a personality cult and totalitarianism.

Russian industrialization, that started in 1850s, was facilitated by the long-established autocratic traditions of Tsars. Most of them opposed reforms, parliamentary government, secular education and the free press. Usurping totalitarian powers, Stalin transformed the tsarist Russian Empire into the second most industrial, technological and militaristic power in the world, all within a span of fifty years. But, for this achievement, Stalin had to establish totalitarian dictatorship. This he only accomplished by liquidating thousands, by sending thousands to slave labour camps in Siberia, by generating fear and terror and by drawing the "iron curtain." The Soviet Union then gained control or concessions from Finland, the Baltic states, Bessarabia, Bukovina and from East European communist regimes; they all became appendages to the Soviet industrialization.

Would the new states of Asia and Africa want to replicate the violence and the totalitarianism of the Soviet system?

Though the founders of the United States raised slogans and wrote documents on human equality and civil liberties, they remained totally blind to the fate and the status of the white women, the black slaves and the aboriginal Indians.

Not until 1920 were the women given the right to vote. The aboriginal Indians, suffered mass killings, forceful evacuations and confinement in the reservations. Not until 1934 were the Indians even considered worthy of citizenship of the United States.

Worst was the situation of the black African slaves. In 1857 the US Supreme Court declared in the *Dred Scott* case that slaves were properties to be owned, sold or bought. Only after the Civil War were the black slaves emancipated in 1861. However, during the 1880s and 90s, the white Americans "lynched" about 100 blacks per year. Another 100 years had to lapse after the Civil War and slave emancipation, for the enactment of the Civil Rights Act of 1964 and the Voting Rights Act of 1965 that facilitated black voting.

Even today, minorities are not properly represented in the US Congress. The following data on the 1985 membership in the US Congress proves the point:[49]

	Population Ratio	Ratio in House	Ratio in the Senate
Women	51%	5%	2%
Blacks	12%	5%	0%
Hispanics	6%	2%	0%
Jews	4%	7%	8%
Millionaries	0.7%	16%	33%
Blue collar workers	30%	0%	0%

In the early stages of the American industrialization, the liberties enshrined in the Bill of Rights were often tampered with through laws like the Sedition Act of 1798, the Espionage Act of 1917, the Smith Act of 1940 and the anti-communist hysteria, known as McCarthyism.

American industrialization led to the rise of Big Government. In 1947-48 the Congress passed bills that constituted about 3,400 pages; during 1985-86, it approved bills that increased the pages to 8,000.[50] The federal employees in the year 1816 numbered 4,000; in 1980s their number rose to 3 million.[51] In 1984, the US federal government raised $800 billion in revenue, while it spent $1 trillion, or about $29,350 per minute.[52]

Is development through the authoritarian government, the ideal of the Third World that has emerged out of colonial authoritarianism?

10. ***A Century of Industrialization***: For two hundred years, between 1700 and 1900, the United States development remained undisturbed, excepting the period of the Civil War. Through its policy of isolationism (the Monroe doctrine), the US kept the European intrusions out of North America, while it extended its own neocolonialism over Latin America. Disregarding the Japanese bombing of the Pacific colony of Hawaii, North America was never attacked or aggressed upon by any foreign country during the last two hundred years.

Similar to the US, the industrialization of the United Kingdom remained undisturbed for almost 200 years. There were no political instabilities and civil wars in the British Isles, paralysing the socio-economic developments in the country. The creation of independent Ireland in the south, did not disrupt British industrialization. Even though Britain fought many a war during the 18th, 19th and the early 20th centuries, Britain was not directly attacked until Hitler bombed it during World War II.

While during the years 1830-1914 German industrialization remained undisturbed, the four years of World War I fought partly on German soil, greatly damaged German industries, armies, people, the territory and wealth. Under Hitler's dictatorship (1933-39), however, the reindustrialized and remilitarized Germany was ready to launch the Second World War. All this recovery was possible because of Germany's 100-year old scientific, technological and industrial legacies, that were interrupted and disrupted, but not erased or obliterated from the memory of the nation.

During half a century of industrial development in Russia, between 1860s and 1913, only two events generated destabilizing conflicts-- the Russo-Japanese War of 1904-1905 and the revolutionary movement of 1905-1906. Even though causing serious complications, these events did not stop Russia's industrial progress. The former event did, in fact, enhance industrialization. During the

Soviet era only two serious conflicts were threatening to Soviet industrial development: one, the civil war that threatened to split up the Russian empire; the other, the Nazi invasion of the Soviet Union in 1941. However, World War II not only gave a big boost to Soviet industrialization, but it also provided the Soviet Union a neocolonial empire in Eastern Europe. In short, Russian/Soviet industrialization took about 100 years to reach its maturity.

The mid-20th century world is a network of international interdependence and Cold War intrigues, in which neither isolationism is permissible nor escapism is possible. Even if the world were to allow the Third World an isolation of fifty years, are the peoples of the Third World willing to wait for fifty years on the promise that the Western style of industrialization will bring them Western standards of living? The poor of the world are hungry, unclothed and homeless now; they are unhappy and hopeless now! Losing patience, "The wretched of the earth" have already resorted to hatred, massacre coup d'etat, civil war and interstate war.

11. *The Total irrelevance of the Western Models*: The preceding survey of the basic features as the prerequisites of the developmental models of Britain, Germany, the United States and Russia/Soviet Union, provides the following conclusions.

First, the four developed countries under study were never victimized by foreign colonialism. In contrast, all the Third World countries are still suffering from the legacies of colonialism.

Second, the development in the four countries shows that, without mass education and highly developed science and technology, industrialization is impossible. The Third World is far from fulfilling this requirement; it cannot entirely depend upon imported education and foreign experts.

Third, as to the benefits of colonialism, the Third World countries are not going to discover and occupy new continents, to conquer old countries, to send millions of its poor citizens to settle in rich foreign lands, or to find captive markets.

Fourth, the industrial development of Britain, Germany, the USSR and the US has very much been tied up with their military industries, militarization and militarism. Most Third World countries have no arms industries. The import of military weapons is a big waste of the meagre resources of the poor countries. The supply of the Western weapons have exacerbated internal conflicts, and have dragged the Third World into staging "proxy wars" for the Western colonialists.

Fifth, can the Third World benefit by simply "borrowing" Western science and technology, instead of struggling to reinvent them? The current levels and typologies of Western machinery, weaponry, tools and techniques represent the 21st century. How can these products be applicable to the 18th and 19th century conditions of the Third World?

Sixth, the Western countries are now talking about "sustainable development." Whose development, one might ask? Of course, they are talking about the Western development. Should the poor countries submit themselves to be exploited to sustain the Western development?

Seventh, can foreign aid help the Third World development? Excepting fifteen to twenty percent, most of the foreign aid is pure business, not a free give away. The industrialized countries have the need to get rid of their surpluses in capital, agriculture, industries, weaponry, and the like. Over-production can affect prices, profits, wages and jobs. The profits from the sale of surpluses, the obsolete and the unhealthy goods, are used for further research. Foreign loans earn considerable interest, and foreign aid brings in political and diplomatic advantages to the giver over the receiver. Under "the tied loans," the recipient country is compelled to buy goods from the lender. Besides paying interest, the recipient has to make trade concessions, carry out political instructions or take diplomatic dictations. Thus, foreign aid is counter-productive to development.

Eighth, the formative phase of Western industrialization was facilitated by authoritarian regimes and limited democracy. The Third World peoples, however, have started with awareness and hope of the full democratic ideas of the mid-20th century. They have failed to realize, that in most cases, fullfledged democracy is antithetical to massive development. All highly industrialized states have authoritarian features.

In conclusion, all the four models of development are irrelevant to the plans, the realities and the hopes of the Third World; but, are they *desirable*?

IV. Gandhian Critique of Developmentalism [53]

The Western exponents and experts of industrialization have failed to point out the faults and failures of industrialization in the West during the last 200 years. None of the modern ideologies of capitalism, socialism, fascism and communism have questioned or rejected the fundamentals of industrialism.

Gandhism is the only ideology of the 20th century that has presented a serious critique of massive industrialization on Western patterns. According to Gandhian philosophy the Western models of development are not only irrelevant and inappropriate, but also undesirable and immoral.[54] The following pages contain an analysis and interpretation of Gandhism. They show that Gandhian philosophy is comprehensive, realistic and relevant.

According to Gandhism, industrial civilization is saturated with violence. Violence could be at the intellectual and psychological levels; it could be at the level of thought and feelings expressed in written or spoken language; it could be at the level of physical action that involves physical force; and violence could be structural when it is institutionalized as economic exploitation, political persecution and police coercion. Gandhism is opposed to all forms of violence.

To Gandhism nonviolence (*ahimsa*) is both the means and the end.[55] As an end, *ahimsa* becomes love, friendship and humanism, and as the means it implies empathy, sympathy, understanding, service and sacrifice.[56]

1. ***Gandhism on the Industrial-Military State***: Gandhian critique of militarism and war, is threefold: (a) Industrialism and militarism help and reinforce each other. Both feed on colonialism[57] and both are fed by science-technology and chauvinism. (b) Arms sales at home or abroad is an encouragement to violence. (c) Arms industries and arms race generate jingoistic chauvinism and wars.

   The following are the Gandhian alternatives to these undesirable consequences (a) Abandonment of the Siamese twins--militarism and industrialism. (b) Elimination of social injustice,[58] weapons and the worship of violence. Injustice can be fought through *satyagraha* that could consist of non-violent non cooperation or civil disobedience. (c) Instead of the weapons of war and destruction, Gandhism proposes the weapons of love (*prema*), service (*seva*) and sacrifice (*tyaga*). (d) The Gandhian alternative to offensive war is involvement in peaceful methods mediation, conciliation, arbitration and judicial settlement. The Gandhian alternative to defensive war is nonviolent defense (also called civilian defense).[59] Instead of armed force, Gandhism proposes peace brigade (*shanti sena*).[60]

   Gandhism on Economic Affluence: Gandhism points out two major negative consequences of massive industrialization: (a) Materialism has overwhelmed all aspects of life. The Gandhian antidote is spiritual, intellectual and moral development of the human beings. (b) Materialism enhances economic greed and selfishness of individuals and states.[61]

   The Gandhian alternative is the philosophy of *sarvodaya*, *i.e.*, sharing and caring among human beings.[62] For the implementation of this philosophy, Gandhism proposes the policies of equitable distribution of material wealth and the system of Trusteeship,[63] *i.e.*, the wealthy should consider their wealth as a trust for the benefit of the people and themselves as the trustees. The *Bhoodan* (land-gift) movement, that was launched by a Gandhian Vinoba Bhave, and that collected five million acres of land through appeal to conscience, was a demonstration of Gandhian theory of economic sharing.

3. *Gandhism on Mass Economy*: Gandhian critique of mass economy is based on three main issues:

   a. The domination of the machinery over the lives of the people, dictating workers' employment and wages, and citizens' needs and consumption.[64] The Gandhian alternative is the simplification and the scaling down of the mechanical devices. The *charkha* (the handmade and hand-driven wooden spinning wheel) can only produce a small-scale *Khadi* industry (the making of hand-woven cloth). *Khadi* economy is the antithesis of mass economy.

   b. Consumerism is the *sine qua non* of unlimited industrialization. The Gandhian alternative is "simple living and high thinking," *i.e.*, the fulfilment of the "basic necessities" and the avoidance of wastage and conspicuous consumption.

   c. Massive environmental damage has been caused by reckless industrialization. The Gandhian alternative is living in harmony with nature by eliminating industry and technology that are inimical to living things.

4. *Gandhism and Science-Technology*: Gandhian critique of the science-technology, that is aimed at mass industrialization, is based on three main arguments:

   a. Science is now dedicated to profits and dividends.[65] Science has not only become divorced from human needs, but it has become engaged in knowingly damaging human well-being, *e.g.*, adding poisonous chemicals to foods, and automating manufacturing so that workers could be fired.

   b. Science is also committed to power and prestige for countries. Today 'big' or 'super' powers are defined essentially in terms of their military power, their scientific-technological capabilities and industrial wealth. The Gandhian alternative is the subordination of science to ethical standards and human well-being.

   c. Enslaved to corporate gains and political and military power, science-technology has become dehumanized. The Gandhian alternative is its rehumanization--*i.e.*, science should not be employed to cause human exploitation, ill-health, or unhappiness; nor should science be employed for the destruction of animal life and nature, which constitute an integral part of human well-being.

5. *Gandhism on Colonialism*: Gandhism is totally opposed to any form of colonialism, at least for three reasons:

   a. Gandhism is opposed to any form of exploitation.[66] Colonialism is unscrupulous exploitation. Colonialism quickly leads to military conquest and occupation, to political persecution and domination, and to cultural subjugation and dehumanization. The Gandhian answer is decolonization--*i.e.*, the ending of slavery, serfdom, victimization and foreign domination.

b. Colonialism is always autocratic and repressive. The Gandhian alternative is freedom and democracy for the colonized people. Neocolonialism, that shapes economic dependency, military protectorate, foreign aid recipient, client state, communist satellite, Cold War ally, and the like, has since 1945, sponsored, aided and abetted, in the Third World, 149 proxy wars that have killed more than 23 million people, have turned 80 million into refugees and have cost the poor countries hundred of billions of dollars.[67]

c. The colonial power relies heavily and mostly on police, military, spies, jails, tortures and executions. Further, to expand its empire and to defeat the rival colonial powers, the imperial state resorts to police action, military intervention, aggression and war. Gandhism rejects violence and wars of all kinds. Gandhism proposes peaceful transformation through nonviolent freedom struggle[68] and nonviolent settlement of interstate conflicts.

6. ***Gandhism on Chauvinism***: The military-industrial-colonial state cannot be sustained and enlarged without the backing of the public that is willing to give blind, emotional and total loyalty to the nation. Such narrow-minded nationalism is chauvinism.[69] The Gandhian critique of chauvinism is threefold:

a. Chauvinism is built on the bases of ethnicism, racism or religionism.[70] Gandhism rejects all forms of bigotry, discrimination and narrow-mindedness. Gandhism advocates pursuit of truth (*satya*) that demands empathy and understanding and education in humanism. Gandhism proposes nonviolent struggle against narrow-mindedness.

b. Chauvinism exploits territorial, group, regional and imperial loyalty, to rationalize exploitative domination of other peoples and other lands. Militaristic chauvinism is jingoism. Rejecting chauvinism, Gandhism postulates universal well-being (*sarvodaya*)-*i.e.*, all peoples and nations equally deserve well-being, security, peace and happiness.

c. Chauvinistic ideologies rely upon propaganda and thought-control. Gandhism holds that public life should be devoid of lies, libel, slander and secrecy. The Gandhian alternative to thought-control is a free mind that is ever searching for truth (*satya*). Gandhism postulates pluralism in truth and non-conformism in the search for truth.

7. ***Gandhism on the Authoritarian Big State***: Massive industrialization causes and results in the Big State. The Big state implies--

a. Heavy governmentalization and centralization of the government. The Gandhian alternative is reduction in laws, bureaucracy and taxes, as well as the localization of government.[71]

b. Big Government is the response to the rise of monopolies of all kinds. Monopolization reduces individualism and freedoms. Hence the Gandhian antidote is demonopolization--*i.e.*, the decentralization of economic and political forces into small units: industries, businesses, unions, parties and constituencies. Demonopolization implies degrees of deindustrialization and degovernmentalization.

c. Big Government, according to the Gandhian critique, is invariably coercive. It relies heavily upon police and military powers and economic and social coercion.[72] The Gandhian alternative is a nonviolent government, under which the police assumes the role of the unarmed social workers and educators, while the military force becomes the nonviolent army of peacekeepers.

d. The Big State is an authoritarian/totalitarian state. The Gandhian answer is peaceful and democratic decentralization into economically self-reliant and politically self-governing village republics (*Panchayati Raj*).[73]

V. **Conclusion**

This article has dealt with four typologies of Western development--the capitalist model, the imperialist model, the fascist model and the communist model. After assessing the main features of Western developmentalism, the obvious conclusion is that the four Western models are not relevant and realistic to the contemporary scene in the Third World of the late 20th century.

Even if, for argument's sake, the Western models of development are relevant to today's Third World, are they desirable also? In other words, what have been the faults and the failures of Western development, and should the Third World repeat the follies of the West?

Excluding Gandhism, other modern ideologies have fully and unconditionally accepted all the fundamentals of massive industrialization, differing only on certain superficial and minor details. Only a handful of Western researchers have recently discovered the serious problems of environmental destruction, waste and depletion of earth's resources, the dehumanization of science, technology and industry, and the real danger of human annihilation at the hands of the nuclear technology and weaponry. They have realized the value of "peace dividends" at the close of the cold war, the power and practicability of nonviolence and that 'small is beautiful'. Some of these scholars have raised such issues as the "limits to growth," "appropriate technology", "common security," and "sustainable developments". Unfortunately all these ideas amount to tinkering with surface issues, because behind them all is the underlying faith in Western beliefs in industrialization, science–technology and materialistic interpretations of development. Sometimes it is argued that science-technology and industrialization are not destructive by themselves; they can be put to good use. It is like arguing that a sword by itself cannot kill, for only people kill people; however, the very purpose of the sword is killing; it cannot be used to till the soil. To till the soil, the sword must be "beaten into a ploughshare".

The developed world will not give up its wealth or power; the Third World, with two-thirds of the humanity, will never attain the Western levels of living standards. Nor will the West allow them to attain those standards. The Third World leaders must realize, sooner than later, that those who do not learn from history, are condemned to relive it.

Gandhism considers the Western models of development not only irrelevant, but also undesirable, for the Third World. Gandhian alternatives provide the most rational, realistic and practical answers to the crises of the Third World. Unfortunately the totally Westernized leaders of the Third World have been so brainwashed, that they are blindly, fanatically and thoughtlessly superimposing the Western models on their own countries, thereby causing tremendous failures and frustrations to their peoples. The frustrations of the Third World will surely visit the developed world; the fire-storm from the South could set fire to the North; the whole globe could go ablaze! The solution to this crisis lies in the Third World abandoning the Western concepts of development and discarding the Western models of industrialization. The Third World should re-define development in terms of "basic needs" and higher intellectual, cultural and moral standards of life, rather than the materialistic standards of living. The goal of basic needs can be pursued through small-scale and indigenized technology and industry, and through a self-reliant economy that does not depend upon foreign colonies or armament, and foreign trade or aid. Only a redesigned goal and a relevant pathway can correct and console the Third World; and only the contented Third World can save all other worlds!

Notes and References

1. Throughout this paper the term "West" means North America, Europe including Western and Eastern Europe, Soviet Union, Australia, New Zealand and South Africa.

2. See M.V. Naidu, Gandhian Perspectives on the modern Industrial State, *Peace Research*, vol.18, No.3 (September 1986), pp. 9-16, 70-74.

3. See M.V. Naidu, Gandhian Perspectives and Modern Ideologies on Industrialism, *Peace Research*, Vol. 19, No. 2 (May 1987), pp. 33-45.

4. See *Hung Chi* (Red Flag), a Chinese journal (30 March 1960). Cited by Ivo Duchachuk, *Nation and Men* (New York: Holt, Rhinehart and Windsor, 1971), p. 319.

5. Derived from N. Bukharin, *Imperialism and World Economy* (London: Merlin Press, 1972), p. 561.

6. Paul Hohenberg, *A Primer on the Economic History of Europe* (New York: Random House, 1968), p. 121. See also T.A. Neal, *Democracy and Responsibility: British History, 1880-1965* (Glasgow: MacMillan, 1969), p. 20.

7. Isaiah Bowman, *The New World* (New York: World Book Co., 1921), p. 561.

8. Brian Croziar, *Neocolonialism* (London: Bodley Head, 1964), p.89.

9. Bukharin, *op.cit.*, pp. 31-33.

10. John Strachey, *The End of Empire* (New York: Frederick Praeger, 1959), p. 177.

11. Adapted from A.K. Cairncross, *Factors in Economic Development* (London: 1962), p. 235.

12. Cheddi Jagan, *The Anatomy of Poverty in British Guyana* (Georgetown, Guyana: People's Progressive Party, 1964), p.50.

13. Ramesh Majumdar an H.S. Raichaudhury, *The Advanced History of India* (London: MacMillan, 1967).

14. Derived from Bukharin, *op.cit.*, p. 30.

15. *See Universal Directory of Railway officials and Railway Yearbook, 1961-62* (London, UK).

16. Derived from Bukharin, *op-cit.*, p. 43.

17. L. Goldstein, *Syndicates, Trusts and Modern Economic Policy* (Moscow, USSR: 1912), p. 51.

18. Herman Levy, *Monopoly and Competition* (London: 1911), pp. 226-267.

19. Goldstein, op.cit. See also L. Kafenhaus, *Syndicates in the Russian Iron Industry*- Both are cited in Bukharin, op.cit., p. 69.

20. Fritz Fischer, Economic Expansion and World Power, in Shepard B. Clough, Peter Gray, Charles K. Warner and John M. Camett, *The European Past* (New York: MacMillan Co., 1964), Vol.II., pp. 281-83.

21. John Bittner, *Mass Communications*: An Introduction (New Jersey: Prentice Hall, 1980), p. 21.

22. *Funk and Wagnalls New Encyclopedia* (New York: Funk and Wagnall, 1973) Vol. 11, pp. 165, 391, 394, 395; Vol. 23, pp. 437; Vol. 24, p. 81. Also see Charles R.Wright, *Mass Communication: A Sociological Perspective* (New York: Random House, 1975, p.48.

23. Sean MacBride et al., *Many Voices, One World* (London: UNESCO and Kogan Page, 1980), p. 125.

24. *Ibid.*, p. 131.

25. Charles R. Wright, *op.cit.*, p. 48.

26. Charles H. Fitch, Report on the Manufacture of Fire Arms and Ammunition, *Extra Census Bulletin*, (Washington, D.C.: Government of the USA, 1882).

27. See George Perri, *The War Traders* (London: National Peace Council, 1914).

28. H.C. Engelbert and F.C. Hanighan, *Merchants of Death*, (New York: Dodd Mead, 1934), p. 83.

29. *Living Age*, (October 1933), p. 126.

30. Derived from Moody's *Analysis of investments: Public Utilities & Industries 1912-1919*; cited in Engelbert and Hanighan, *op.cit.*, pp. 159, 179.

31. William Stone, International Traffic in Arms and Ammunition *Foreign Policy Report*, Vol No. 1 of 16 August 1933, p. 130

32. Derived from Quincy Wright, *A Study of War, 2nd ed.* (Chicago: University of Chicago Press, 1965), p. 671.

33. *Ibid.*, Tables 36-41.

34. *Ibid.*

35. *World Statistics in Brief*, (New York: United Nations, 1979), p. 224.

36. Derived from Angus Madison, *Economic Growth in Japan and the USSR* (New York: W.W. Norton, 1969), p. 36.

37. *World Statistics in Brief*, *op.cit.*, p. 158.

38. Ruth L. Sivard, *World Military and Social Expenditures 1986* (Washington, DC: World Priorities, 1986), P. 11.

39. Ruth L. Sivard, *World Military and Social expenditures 1993* (Washington, DC: World Priorities, 1993), p. 25.

40. Karl Marx, The British Rule in India, *New York Daily Tribune*, (25 June 1853).

41. Lewis Copeland and Lawrence Lamm, eds., *The World's Greatest Speeches* (New York: Dover Publication, 1958), pp. 522, 540.

42. *Ibid.*, p. 446.

43. *Ibid.*, p. 337.

44. *Ibid.*, p. 123.

45. *Ibid.*, p. 487.

46. *Ibid.*, p. 142.

47. *Ibid.*

48. *Ibid.*, pp. 494, 495, 498.

49. Susan Welch et el., *American Government* (St. Paul, MN., USA: West Publishing Co., 1986), pp. 249, 251.

50. *Ibid.*, p. 264.

51. *Ibid.*, p. 324.

52. *Ibid.*, p. 459.

53. The main sources of Gandhi's writings are the journals he edited—*Indian Opinion, Young India and Harijan*; other sources are his books--*Autobiography; Constructive Programme; Hind Swaraj; Speeches and Writings*, etc.

I am interpreting Gandhian opinions and writings for this assessment.

54. Gandhi named three ideologies--imperialism, communism and fascism, as threats to justice and peace. See Paul F. Power, *Gandhi on World Affairs* (London: George Allen and Unwin, 1961), p. 129.

55. *Young India* (17 July and 26 December 1924). Hereafter cited *Y.I.* Also see *Hind Swaraj* (Ahmedabad, India: Navajivan Press, 1908), Revised ed., 1951, p. 115. Hereafter cited *H.S.*

56. *Y.I.*, (31 December 1931).

57. Indian Opinion (24 September 1904). Hereafter cited I.P. Also see *H.S.*, pp. 24-27,31-34; *Y.I.* (5 November 1925).

58. Gandhism favours equitable distribution of wealth. Y.I. (17 March 1927); *Harijan*, (20 April 1940, 31 March 1946, 16 and 23 March 1947). Hereafter cited H.

59. *Y.I.*, (13 September 1928, 31 December 1931); *H.*, (15 February, 17 April and 24 May 1942).

60. *H.*, (26 March 1938, 21 July and 15 September 1940, 5 and 2 May 1946).

61. *H.S.*, Chapters VI and XIII.

62. *Y.I.*, (4 December 1924); 30 October 1925).

63. *H.*, (16 December 1939, 8 June and 25 August 1940, 16 and 23 February 1947, 25 October 1952).

64. *Y.I.*, (5 November 1925); *H.*, (30 November 1934, 29 August 1936).

65. *Y.I.*, (12 November 1931).

66. *Y.I.*, (October 1924, 12 November 1931); *H.S.*, pp. 24-27, 31-34.

67. Ruth Sivard, *World Military and Social Expenditures 1993,* (Washington, D.C.: *World Priorities, 1993*), p. 20.

68. *H.,* (17 February 1946).

69. *Y.I.,* (3 April 1924, 15 and 17 October 1925, 15 October 1931

70. Gandhi opposed racism. *Nonviolence in Peace and War* (Ahmedabad: Navajivan Press, 1948), Vol- II, P. 16. He was opposed to religious bigotry. *Y.I.,* (25 September 1924); *H.,* (13 July 1940, 1 and 9 August: 1942). He was against: theocracy and in favour of secularism. *H.,* (16 November 1947).

71. Gandhi advocated governmental decentralization. *H.,* (30 December 1939, 18 January 1942).

72. *Y.I.,* (November 1928); *H.,* (12 November 1938).

73. *H.,* (29 August 1936, 4 November 1939, 20 June and 28 August 1940, 26 July 1942, 28 July 1946).

L C Jain

Gandhi and Antyodaya : Society versus the State

We would explore here the relevance of Gandhi, if any, in the limited context of India's crucial and continuing problems and the paradigms attempted to solve them.

The Problems and Paradigms

During the freedom struggle, poverty and unemployment were listed as the foremost problems which were to be attacked wholesale after India attained her Independence in 1947. Gandhi underscored the critical importance of solving these problems:

> There may be work, there may be men to do the work and tools with which to do it, yet in my view a system that admits of poverty and unemployment is not fit to survive even for a day.[1]

Gandhi was of the firm belief that development effort must be addressed to the last person first – a belief that forms the basis of the concept of *Antyodaya* – or, unto the last.

He further held that two other conditions were essential to sustain a morally and materially sound attack on poverty, inequality and unemployment. First, austerity or consumption ethics: "He (who has made the ideal of equal distribution a part of his being) would reduce his wants to a minimum, bearing in mind the poverty of India". Second, a discerning and deliberate choice of technology – away from the imitative and addressed to India's own and unique problem: "If I could produce all my country's wants by means of 30,000 people instead of 30 million, I should not mind it, provided that the thirty million are not rendered idle and unemployed".[2]

Social ideas require appropriate institutions to translate them on the ground. This was Gandhi's forte. He proposed the institution of "village republics" in the political realm, and the pursuit of "village self-sufficiency" as the basis of economic development.

By the latter he meant that production and consumption should be as proximate as possible, and based as far as possible on the (proper) use of local resources[3]. To ensure that the goal of self-sufficiency at the village level was made an integral part of the planning process and the economic system, he repeatedly stressed that 'the first concern of every village will be to grow its own food crops and cloth".[4] Gandhi envisaged food-cloth led industrialisation and economic base.

The rest of the industrial apparatus was to be so designed as to reinforce such an economic base: "I do visualise electricity, shipbuilding, iron works, machine-making and the like existing side by side with village handicrafts. Hitherto industrialisation has been so planned as to destroy the village and the village crafts. In the state of the future, it will subserve the villagers and their crafts".[5]

Gandhi was killed within less than six months after Independence. The development scenario underwent a radical change. The "village republics" - the democratically elected decentralised bodies (*panchayats*, as popularly called) which were the very cornerstone of the Gandhian political, economic and social framework - were excluded altogether from the reorganised polity of the new Republic of India as enshrined in the Constitution adopted in 1950.

After Gandhi's death, the responsibility for giving shape and substance to political and economic edifice then rested principally with Nehru. However, Nehru was not in tune with Gandhi though he followed him through the thick and thin of the freedom struggle. Their contending views were[6]:

> **Gandhi:**
>
> Industrialisation on a mass scale will necessarily lead to passive or active exploitation of the villagers as the problems of competition and marketing come in. Therefore we have to concentrate on the village being self-contained, manufacturing mainly for use. The mere socialisation of industries would not alter this process in any way at all. Pandit Nehru wants industrialisation because he thinks that, if it is socialised, it would be free from the evils of capitalism. My own view is that evils are inherent in industrialism, and no amount of socialisation can eradicate them.
>
> **Nehru:**
>
> He (Gandhi) was a very difficult person to understand, sometimes his language was almost incomprehensible to an average modern. But we felt that we knew him well enough to realise he was a great and unique man and a glorious leader, and having put our faith in him we gave him an almost blank cheque, for the time being at least. Often we discussed his fads and peculiarities among ourselves and said half-humorously, that when *Swaraj* came these fads must not be encouraged.

Like Gandhi, Nehru had formulated his own approach to the solution of India's basic problems, far ahead of the dawn of Independence.

In his Presidential Address to the Indian National Congress (INC) at Lucknow in 1936 Nehru had articulated his own conviction.[7]

> I see no way of ending the poverty, unemployment, the degradation and subjection of our people except through socialism. That involves vast and revolutionary changes in our political and social structure, the ending of the vested interests in land and industry, as well as the feudal and autocratic Indian states system. That means the ending of private property, except in a restricted sense, and the replacement of the present profit system by a higher ideal of cooperative services. It means ultimately a change in our instincts, habits and desires. In short it means a new civilisation, radically different from the present capitalist order.

Nehru stood all out for industrial growth with prior emphasis being laid on heavy or capital-intensive industries. In his letter of October 9, 1945, to Gandhi he had gone on to say[8]:

> Then again we have to put down certain objectives like food, housing, education, sanitation, etc. which should be the minimum requirement for the country and for everyone. It is with these objectives in view that we must find out specifically how to attain them speedily. Again, it seems to me inevitable that modern means of transport as well as many other modern developments must have them. If that is so, inevitably a measure of heavy industry exists. How far (will that) fit in with a purely village society? Personally I hope that heavy or light industries should all be decentralised as far as possible and this is feasible now because of the development of electric power; if two types of economy exist in the country there should be either conflict between the two or one will overwhelm the other.

As Nehru became the steward of the Indian ship, it raised expectations among many, especially the socialists, that Nehru would move India on the socialist path as enunciated by him at Lucknow. But on becoming Prime Minister, Nehru opted for "mixed economy" (i.e., part socialism, part capitalism) and chose not the people-led village republics but bureaucracy as the principal instrument for delivering economic development and social justice. Also reversed was Gandhi's vision of food and cloth led industrialisation which was to subserve the villages. As India's first prime minister, Nehru contended that: the test of real strength is how much steel you produce, how much power you produce and use.[9]

This contention was given lasting expression in the model of development formulated by Professor P. C. Mahalanobis at Nehru's behest, its primary thrust being a concentration of resources in sectors such as steel, power and the like. Interestingly, this model was seen by its architects to be in perfect consonance with "the chief aim of planning in India is to solve the problem of unemployment as quickly as possible".[10] It is this very model that has shaped the basic character of development in India, over the large part since Independence.[11]

Jayaprakash Narayan (JP) – doyen of the Indian socialists – cautioned Nehru (December 1948) that his compromised strategy was misconceived and was bound to fail. "There is no doubt that you will hold fast to the faith that you are leading the country to socialism, but let me say without malice or rancour that in spite of your best intentions, the country is drifting in the opposite direction. You are trying to ride two horses, which may be possible in circuses but not in historical evolution. History can move only in one direction and not two at the same time. You want to go towards socialism, but you want the capitalists to help in that. You want to build socialism with the help of capitalism. You are bound to fail in that. If you want capitalism to play its role in industrialising the country, it will demand its price and if you pay the price, you will give the go-by to socialism. That is exactly what is happening today".[12]

Gandhi's associate, Vinoba Bhave, was invited by Nehru to meet the National Planning Commission and give his comments on the draft of the First Five Year Plan. "Nehru had never imagined that Vinoba would proceed to Delhi on foot to cover the long distance of over 1200 kms from his Ashram".

And, when he arrived, Vinoba did not mince words[13]:

> In the Constitution you have promised work and food to all citizens. But now you have totally forgotten this assurance. If you, on whose shoulders lies the responsibility of providing work to all, find it impossible to do so, you must resign.
>
> You ask village industries to support themselves. You first cut off my feet and want me to stand .... Village industries did not die themselves; they have deliberately been killed.
>
> Although both the Planning Commission and I are primarily concerned with the good of the Indian people, there is a difference in our basic approach. I am concerned mainly with two matters. First, we should stick to our pledge of stopping imports of foodgrains. The Commission visualises the continuance of imports for an indefinite period. I join issue on this point. We must fix a definite date for achieving self-sufficiency and abide by it. Otherwise, the will-power of the nation shall die. Secondly, an essential postulate of planning should be to provide work for all. The Planning Commission accepts this objective, but refuses to shoulder the responsibility of implementing it. If we do not accept this responsibility, our planning would not be national but only partial. If they agree to provide work for all, our villages will have to be made self-sufficient.

> Yours is a plan involving perpetual begging .... It cannot inspire anybody to produce more.

Nehru's response to Vinoba's criticism was equally severe albeit consistent with the views he held even during Gandhi's life time.

At the meeting of the National Development Council (NDC) in January 1956, Nehru said[14]:

> In the Standing Committee of NDC, greater stress was laid on the heavy machine-making industry being encouraged, as it was said to be the basis of industrial growth. If you do not do that, then naturally industrial growth is delayed. There is one approach which has sometimes been put forward that you should build up your consumer goods industries and gradually save money thereby, and build up something else, thereby getting some more employment. That, I believe, from the point of view of planning, is a discarded theory completely. Of course, it does some good here and there; I would not enter into the details but this approach is not a planned approach at all. If you want India to industrialise and to go ahead, as we must, as is essential, then you must industrialise and not potter about with old little factories producing hair and the like - it is totally immaterial what things are, whether they are small or big consumer articles. You must go to the root and base and build up the structure of industrial growth. Therefore, it is the heavy industries that count: nothing else counts, excepting as a balancing factor, which is, of course, important. We want planning for heavy machine-making industries and heavy industries, we want industries that will make heavy machines and we should set about them as rapidly as possible because it takes time.

At the meeting of the All-India Congress Committee, at Chandigarh on 28 September, 1959, he drove the nail, as it were, in the coffin of employment-centred Gandhian paradigm:

> The primary thing about an integrated plan was production and not employment. Employment was important, but it was utterly unimportant in the context of production. It followed production and not preceded production. And production would only go up by better techniques which meant modern methods.[15]

As for JP's criticism, Nehru was indeed unable to determine and regulate firmly the proportion of capitalism and socialism in his mixture (mixed economy). As a result, the concept of "mixed economy" degenerated into one of a "mixed-up economy". We had the worst of both. Remarkable progress was made with production – but employment did not follow production as Nehru expected – thus constraining demand for the rising production.

Further, while the ownership of farm land was tinkered with it was never taken to its conclusion. Ceilings were not enforced. Flagrant evasion was continuously overlooked. Tenancy security was pursued up to a point and then left mid-stream, making the situation worse for the erstwhile tenants. As a result, their relationship with the landowners deteriorated to the tenants' detriment. The helplessness of the tenants was compounded as even elementary education was not universalised which left millions drowned in the sea of ignorance and incapacitated from fighting their own battles for emancipation.

Thus, though Nehru presided over the Indian State continuously for seventeen long years, he could do little to alter the rural social landscape either in respect of education or land reforms. And, despite persistent failure in these crucial respects, he stuck to the bureaucracy to deliver socialism. Even the Congress Party was not mobilised as an instrument for advancing socialist goals – it was placed on duty only at election time to secure electoral victories once every five years. Thus there was scarcely any chance of the socialist pattern going much beyond the slogan stage. It was an unfertile journey for socialism.

The Indian National Congress made an attempt to rekindle socialism. At its session at Bhubaneshwar in December 1963, with Nehru present, it decided to amend its constitution to provide: The object of the Indian National Congress is the well-being and advancement of the people of India, by peaceful and constitutional means, of a socialist state based on parliamentary democracy, in which there is equality of opportunity and a political, economic and social rights, and which aims at world peace and fellowship [15]. In less than six months or before the ink was dry on this amendment to build a "socialist state" Nehru died in May 1964. Soon thereafter, the Indian National Congress itself was weakened by Nehru's successors who split the historic organisation into countless alphabets: Congress (J), Congress (R), Congress (O), Congress (S), Congress (I), etc.

Mark, the December 1963 resolution of the Indian National Congress was to build a socialist *state* – not a socialist *society*. This is the crux of the difference between Gandhi's position and that of Nehru. Gandhi believed in a society conducting itself on the egalitarian principles integral to socialism in its widest sense. Such a social order, Gandhi held, could be built essentially, if not only, by the people, the state assisting their endeavour if it could. JP explains Gandhi's position [16]:

> While the rest of the national leaders relied solely on the power of the State to accomplish their task of nation-building, Gandhiji was clear in his mind that the State could never be the sole instrument for creating the India of his dreams, or, for that matter, even the India of the dreams of the Indian National Congress of those days. To be sure, he did not underestimate the role of the State, nor was he disinterested in its proper and effective working. Indeed he was anxious to see that the State was in the best of hands available and that it followed the right policies,

programmes, and plans. Nevertheless, he saw clearly that even with the best of policies and the best of men in command, the State by itself could not deliver the goods.

Therefore, his plan was to create the power of the people alongside with the power of the State. Accordingly, he was preparing to go back to the people at the head of a large band of revolutionary workers, to serve the people, to educate and change them, to organise them and set them up on their feet, and to involve them directly in the process of social change and reconstruction. His means were going to be, as before, service through constructive work.

Impact on poverty, disparities, unemployment

For 44 out of 47 years of the career of free India, Congress has been the ruling party at the Centre with four Prime Ministers: Nehru, Indira, Rajiv, Rao. The impact its policies have made or not made, on poverty, unemployment and disparities is shown to all by independent scholars as well as official statistics and statements.

The July 1993, Report of the Expert Group[17] to estimate the proportion and number of poor, concluded that in 1987-88, the absolute number of poor persons was 313 million or 39.34 percent of the total population. Thus while the percentage of poor in the total population declined from 54.93 percent in 1973-74, including some of it due to definitional changes, the absolute number of poor remained more or less the same as 15 years earlier.

Observes the eminent economist, Dr. K.N.Raj, that though some progress has been made in India in reducing the scale of mass poverty in rural areas, particularly over the last two decades, it is evident that in most parts of the country the magnitude of poverty is still too large to be socially or politically acceptable. He adds[18]:

> Infant morality rate (i.e. the number of babies who die before they are one year old) – expressed in terms of 1,000 babies born during a year, which is the most sensitive index of levels of health – is still (in the early 1990s) as high as 124 in Orissa, 118 in Madhya Pradesh, 103 in Uttar Pradesh, and 88 in Rajasthan.
>
> They remain high in the 70-80 range even in Karnataka, Assam, Andhra Pradesh, Haryana, Gujarat, Bihar and West Bengal. These levels need to be compared with Kerala where it is now as low as 17. The higher levels of infant mortality rate reflect in most cases the failure to extend adequate health care facilities in rural areas. In Kerala, it is the State-wide extension of primary health centres in rural areas that explains its performance, and now the infant mortality rate there is comparable with that in developed Western countries.

All this he points out, has a bearing on the relentless demographic pressure India continues to face.

Rapid reduction in infant mortality rates to below, say, 30 or 40 per thousand births is the critical factor in, and in fact the clue to reduction in birth rates. For it is when most of the babies born are found to survive that ordinary people, particularly in rural areas, are convinced that two or three children will do to ensure that enough surviving children will be there to look after them when they themselves enter old age. In fact, it is this very factor that largely explains the very low rate of population growth already achieved in Kerala. Techniques of family planning may help them to prevent unwanted birth of children, but what is critical to their success is the emergence of strong motivation to keep low the number of children they wish to have. Where the objective conditions for such strong motivations exist, there is hardly any need for coercion or even moral pressure exerted through family planning campaigns. In fact, Kerala stands out as a State where such coercion and moral pressure have never been known and where therefore, reduction in the rate of growth of population has become a lasting achievement.

Over more than four decades from 1951 to 1993, the progress made in female literacy has not been impressive except in a few States like Kerala, Punjab and Haryana, despite the enormous amount of government funds that has been spent for these purposes in all parts of the country. 'Particularly striking are the differences between the few States mentioned above and the five States that have performed very poorly: Bihar, Madhya Pradesh, Rajasthan, Uttar Pradesh and Orissa. Thus, in respect of female literacy rates, while Kerala had a rate as high as 87 in 1991 rising from less than 39 in 1991, and Punjab a reasonably high rate of 64 by 1991 rising from 31 thirty years earlier, it was below 29 in Madhya Pradesh, 26 in Uttar Pradesh, 23 in Bihar and below 21 in Rajasthan even in 1991. The only feature one can observe in their favour is that the rate of female literacy was less than one in 1961 in all of them. So, if they continue expanding literacy at this rate, one may expected them to touch within thirty years the rate that has been achieved in Punjab in 1991 - even if not the very high rate of female literacy in Kerala.

Not only the adults, forty percent of rural Indian children fail to learn, read and write. One child out of two drops out after class four, not getting even the basic primary education. Nearly half of the drop-out rate occurs in class one and two. The drop-out rate is more more among girls, higher among rural girls and highest among tribal girls.[19] The reasons identified by a recent all-India study for high drop out rates are "poverty, helping parents in the household and fields, and unattractive school environment".[20]

The study by Dreze and Saran, which wore micro micro lenses and looked at just one village: Palam Pur in North India, found that "the government-funded village school is in the hands of a poorly motivated and effectively unaccountable teacher, and the quality of circumstances, many parents who would be glad, in principle, to send their children to school choose to make use of their labour services instead".[21] The community has no say in the management of the village school.

The only sphere in which significant progress has been made in rural development over the four decades from 1951 to 1993, argues K.N. Raj, has been in agriculture and related sectors like animal husbandry and forestry. In agriculture, growth in food grains output and the self-sufficiency in food grains gained thereby, have been among the major achievements of the country during this period. However, such rapid growth in food grains output has been evident mainly in a few States, mainly in the north-west of the country (covering Punjab, Haryana and some districts in Western Uttar Pradesh) in respect of wheat, and in some pockets in the South (as in the irrigated areas of Andhra Pradesh and Tamil Nadu in respect of rice).

This high growth is concentrated in 40 out of 440 districts. The gross regional disparities this skewed pattern of food production implies are obvious. There are studies which show that the access of the poorer sections to food is correlated to local availability which in turn is influenced by local production of foodgrains. Not far from Gandhi's proposition after all.

Growth of rural small-scale industries based on the increased purchasing power of the farming community has been even more limited- confined mainly to Punjab and Haryana. Rural development through expansion of commodity output has been there, essentially very patchy despite all the attention given to community projects, extension schemes, and village industries. "Indeed progress in India in this sphere appears very desultory", concludes Raj.

Another view of disparities is provided by the noted economist, Dr. C.T. Kurien. He concedes that the division of society into the many who are poor and the few who are affluent has been a very visible aspect of our country from time immemorial; it was so during the precolonial period, which accentuated the distinction. But he regrets that in spite of all the resolve and effort since Independence to remove social evils, mass poverty is still with us and the affluent few are becoming still more affluent[22]:

> Statistics relating to the distribution of income are less readily available than to the distribution of wealth, but according to a frequently referred private estimate, the bottom 40 percent of households in the country claim about 16.3 percent of the income while the top 5 percent claim 22.4 percent with the top one percent alone having 7.7 percent.
>
> The poverty line is the norm that is officially recognised in India for identifying poverty is what an Expert Committee set up by the Government of India in 1962 described as 'desirable minimum level of consumer expenditure'. The Committee arrived at a figure (average) of Rs.20 per head per month at 1960-61 prices as the cut-off line.

> The situation is actually far more distressing because the condition of large proportion of the people is much worse than the average would suggest. Judged against the standard of consumption expenditure of Rs.20 per month per capita, considered generally to be the bare minimum, it is obvious that half of the people live in *abject poverty*. (emphasis supplied).
>
> How abject it is can be seen from a recent study which recorded every day, for a period of six months, the consumption level and the living standard of those who were below the poverty line in one Indian state. Since rice is the staple diet in the state, the authors regarded variations in the consumption of rice as a better indicator of poverty than its average level. They found that for a third of the households surveyed the gap between the maximum and minimum per capital consumption of rice during the six month period was over 500 gms, compared with the overall average of 387 gms, showing that there must have been days when the consumption level must have been extremely low. The study found also that half the female adults did not have any vessels made of brass, steel or glass for cooking, serving or eating food. There is no reason to think that the findings of the study are exceptional. The fact is that the officially recognised poverty line is, indeed, a rock bottom level.
>
> Kurien concludes
>
> One way to ascertain who constitutes the affluent section is to seek what percentage of the households in the country accounts for the total household sector savings – which has been noted already, has been and continues to be the largest component of total savings of the economy. There are official estimates in this regard. But the findings of a national survey conducted in the mid-seventies by the National Council for Applied Economic Research, one of the leading private research organisations in the country, showed that out of the total savings of the household sector, the share of the bottom 70 percent was only over 6 percent, while that of the top 10 percent was about 68 percent and of the top 5 percent alone around 50 percent. On the basis what we have already designated as the 'top layer' of the Indian economy must be deemed to consist of about 10 percent of the households and thus, also of the total population. If the top 10 percent of households account for such a large share of the savings of the economy they should also be presumed to be the major beneficiaries of the economic growth of the past four decades or so.

So much for Gandhi's emphasis on unto the last.

Then there is the important question of impact of inflation on the purchasing power of different sections in society. Like growth, inflation also is not socially neutral, points out Kurien. "For instance, it is harmful to those with fixed incomes, because with increase in prices their purchasing power will go down; and is generally beneficial to those whose earnings (by way of profits, for instance) go up along with rise in prices. Wage earners, specially, tend to suffer on account of inflation because wage rates fixed in money terms tend to become sticky. Salary earners usually have some built-in mechanism to protect themselves against inflation such as dearness allowance and periodic revision of salary scales. The beneficiaries of inflation usually are business people, and traders. A creeping inflation of around 7 percent per year of the kind that we have been experiencing in recent years, would amount to a doubling of prices in a decade because of compound growth; and hence a rule of thumb is that all those whose money incomes do not double in a decade can be considered to be victims of inflation. On this reckoning, it is reasonable to conclude that post-Independence inflation, whether caused by structural factors or resulting from policy measures or a combination of both, must have adversely affected the poorer sections in the country and thus become a cause for continuing mass poverty".

In anguish S.Ramachandran notes : "the development process loses credibility in a situation where deprivation is growing."[23]

The overall employment pattern of the 1980s has been a matter of serious concern. In practically all major sectors of the economy the rate of growth of employment in the decade of particularly high growth (GDP rising to 5.3 percent over 3.5 percent in the previous two decades) has been lower than in the previous decade. The rate of growth of employment in the economy as a whole steadily declined from 2.82 percent in the 1972-73 to 1977-78 period to 2.22 percent in the 1977-78 to 1983 period and to 1.55 percent in the 1983 to 1987-88 period. Even in the agricultural sector which also witnessed significant increase in output, growth rate of employment declined from 2.32 percent in the first period to 1.20 percent in the second period and to a miserably low level of 0.65 percent in the third period. Only mining and construction showed higher growth rates in employment in the third period compared to the preceding two. The Seventh Plan document had estimated that the labour force would be increasing at an annual rate of 2.56 percent during 1985-90 and at 2.24 percent during 1990-2000. If the growth rate in employment during part of the Plan period was only around 1.55 percent as against the growth rate of labour force of 2.56 percent, there can be no doubt that the decade of high growth rate ended up with an unemployment (estimated 19 million person years) problem of very serious magnitude.[24]

Change of Stance

The powers that be may have failed to make an impact on poverty, but poverty particularly its persistence, has not failed to make some impact, albeit still limited, on the authorities; and forcing them to reconsider the past approach and strategies:

"Our experience of development planning has shown that developmental activities undertaken with people's active participation have a greater chance of success and can also be more cost-effective as compared to the development activities undertaken by the government where people become passive observers.... They are owned and managed by the users – stake holders, producers or beneficiaries themselves; are accountable to the community; have the capacity to become self-reliant over a period of time; have the capacity to diagnose the needs of the areas, interact with the governmental agencies in order to draw need-based local level plans and to implement those plans in close cooperation with the administration...." acknowledges the Planning Commission.[25]

The foremost task, the Plan says, is one of "strengthening of the *Panchayat Raj* institutions" to provide the requisite institutional underpinning for "reorientation and integration of all the village level programmes under the charge of the *panchayat raj* institutions".

It is a recognition that appropriate institutions are as much of a resource for economic development as policies and physical and financial resources. Hitherto, we have been having more of the latter, and little of the former. Consequently, vast sums poured on rural development, poverty alleviation, rural employment and minimum needs programmes have all failed, as seen, to produce commensurate results. A bucket without a bottom cannot hold water.

At long last, the authorities have awakened to this elementary fact of life. They have passed the 73rd Amendment to the Constitution to establish mandatorily a systematic network of *panchayat* institutions at micro-level, at each village and district, throughout the country – a necessary first step to ensure meaningful development as well as optimal use of available resources and to diversify and expand the resource base for development.

Besides, a totally new dimension is that one-third of the estimated three million elective seats in the *panchayats* are reserved for women and about one-tenth for disadvantaged sections (Scheduled Castes and Scheduled Tribes). The *panchayats* will thus acquire and act as an unprecedented social force vital for India's transformation towards greater equity.[26]

During the discussion of the 73rd Constitutional Amendment for *panchayats* in Parliament in 1992-93, the spokespersons of the ruling party and the opposition claimed that as the political power is being decentralised, the measure tantamounts to fulfilling Gandhi's dream.

Gandhi's dream was not a mere political personality for *panchayats* (or village republics). They were to be invested simultaneously with decentralised economic content: local production and consumption of food and cloth, in the minimum. Such local economic content was to foster social content through more assured food security, employment and income; and consequently little dependency and deprivation of the poor. Localisation of the economy to the extent feasible is an integral part of Gandhi's concept of *panchayats*.

True, *Panchayats*, even if not of the ilk Gandhi envisioned, are an important step forward for restraining unhealthy trends towards over-centralisation. They would help to improve the overall health of India's system of governance. But their effectiveness which is also dependent on 'localisation' of the economy is likely to be undermined by the simultaneous plunge India has taken for the 'globalisation' of its economy and its corollary of 'leave it all to the market' – to Indian and foreign investors; and the State going to the other extreme of near total withdrawal from one of controlling all investment decisions in the past four decades.

We may have a summary view of the globalisation–led reforms being pursued since 1991, vigorously[27]:

> The primary objective of economic reforms is to accelerate India's economic development. Rapid economic growth is considered necessary to deal with poverty by expanding productive employment and by providing resources for needed anti-poverty programmes in the interim.
>
> For rapid growth, efficient use of resources of the economy is essential and competition, both domestic and global, has proved to be the best means of ensuring efficiency. Trade liberalization, elimination of import licensing requirements, lowering of protective tariffs, reduction in the differential rates of tariff and devaluation can be expected to lead domestic industries to be appropriate to India's factor endowments and to be globally competitive. Deregulation has freed Indian industries to decide what to produce, how to produce, how much to produce and where to produce.
>
> To remain within the scope of this paper we would refrain from discussing the merits of this new paradigm except perhaps to point out that it can hardly qualify to be a new paradigm 'to deal with poverty' if, as in the past, the reliance is to remain on 'rapid economic growth'. How is that different from Nehru's – production, production and production paradigm – except the change in the actors i.e., the market replacing the state. It is the changes in the pattern of growth and its composition, that could make a difference to poverty – to the improved consumption of the poor and their participation in production and its rewards. Suffice to say here that, by definition, globalisation–led growth cannot be expected to pivot itself in the constituency of the poor; especially when top ten percent of India's 90 million offer an immediate and lucrative market.

A more serious implication of globalisation of the Indian economy would be to reduce, if not abort, the scope for "localisation" of the economy (that is, local production being proximate to local consumption needs, and local production drawing largely on local manpower and other resources) – which is the other side of the *panchayat* coin.

Gandhi - a little in, but essentially out

While the working experience of past 47 years has led India back to Gandhi's door – and his prescriptions seem considerably relevant to the objective situation and objectives of equitable and sustainable development, India is likely to be pulled away from Gandhi by the forces of globalisation.

It requires no microscope to see that Gandhi's prescription of proximate production and consumption through local decision-making is totally (if not, violently) at variance with the system of production and consumption determined at a global level with decision-making by remote control.

Globalisation may or may not leave Gandhi in the cold but that cannot be said with any certainty about the people of India and even their minimum expectations of liberation from poverty, unemployment and disparities in the foreseeable future.

To conclude, the equation between "State" and "Society" has undergone a sea change in the past four decades since Gandhi's death and India's Independence. The society has lost its primacy vis-a-vis the State. In the preindependence period the defiance of the imperial power generated extra energy and extra self-reliance in the body-politic of society. But in the post-independence period, this energy has sapped both absolutely and relatively. Moreover, in this period, the State has expanded beyond recognition, be it in respect of its authority, functions, financial and other resources or its administrative, police and armed might.

What has compounded the increasingly supplicatory role of society vis-a-vis the State, is the near total obsession of India's political parties with power politics and its centralisation. Political power is not being treated by them strictly as an instrument for promoting a new social order envisioned by the struggle for freedom. The political parties do have manifestos outlining their ideology and approach. But manifestos are a mere ritual. Few political parties have informed, awakened and committed membership. Fewer still observe democratic methods for the governance of their respective party, leaving a limited scope for openness, debate, discussion, self-criticism, which are an essential armoury for a force devoted to social change.

In the objective situation where the power of the State is rising and the self-assertion of society is diminishing, the scope for action by groups not seeking political power such as the Gandhians, is *prima facie* limited. But by the same virtue, their role has assumed greater social and strategic significance. There is a large and enlarging constituency of demand. However, the supply of political action (outside of power politics) by Gandhian and other socially aware groups, is still far too short of demand. A positive feature is that there are many non-charismatic leaders who are continuing to translate Gandhian philosophy into action or organising social protest movements. Of these, there are several specific examples, beyond the scope of this paper, which nevertheless show that the sustainability of political action outside political institutions improves when conducted in conjunction with constructive work.

The Emergency introduced in 1975 and its continuance for over one and a half years, revealed the serious failure of the Gandhian movement to build up adequate people's power as Gandhi had envisaged. 'Go to the root'.

There is still hope

The hope is that in the coming decade, the new emerging *panchayats* as an institution, and their new leadership of over three million may throw their weight towards a new 'structural adjustment' which allows for assimilation of political and economic interests of the masses of people on terms more equitable.

Notes and References

1. The Nehru-Gandhi Polarity and Economic Policy, Rajkrishna, Lecture delivered at the Nehru Memorial Museum and Library, November 15, 1977.

2. *Indian Socialism: Retrospect and Prospect*, VKRV Rao, 1982.

3. *Foundations of Gandhian Economics*, Amritanandan Das, Centre for the Study of Developing Societies, 1980.

4. *Gandhi's 'Hind Swaraj'- Its Appeal to Me*, T.S. Ananthu, Research Fellow, Gandhi Peace Foundation, 1982.

5. *Technology and Environment: Facts and Alternatives for India*, T.K. Oomen, Jawaharlal Nehru University, 1986.

6. *Nationalist Thought And The Colonial World - A Derivative Discourse*, Partha Chatterjee, United Nations University, 1986 (Second impression 1993).

7. India: Socialism Does Not Live there Anymore - Remembering Vaikuntbhai, a paper prepared in honour of V.L. Mehta, Chairman, Khadi & Village Industries Commission, L.C. Jain, October, 1991.

8. *Gandhi - His Life and Thought*, J.B. Kripalani, Publications Division, 1970.

9. The Nehru-Gandhi Polarity and Economic Policy, Rajkrishna, Lecture op cit.

10. *General Approach of the Second Plan Frame*, P.C. Mahalanobis, Planning Commission.

11. Poverty, Environment and Development - A View From Gandhi's Window, L.C. Jain, *Economic and Political Weekly*, February 13, 1988.

12. India: Socialism Does Not Live Here Anymore - Remembering Vaikuntbhai, op cit

13. *Vinoba: His Life And Work*, Shriman Narayan, Popular Prakasham, 1970.

14. *Economic Nightmare of India - Its Causes and Cure*, Charan Singh, 1981.

15. India: Socialism Does Not Live Here Anymore - Remembering Vaikunthbhai, op c.i.t

16. *Face to Face - Jayaprakash Narayan*, Navchetan Prakashan, 1970.

17. Report of the Expert Group on Estimation of Proportion and Number of Poor, Planning Commission, 1993.

18. Gandhi's Ideals and India's Progress in Rural Development. Dr. K.N. Raj, *Kurkshetra Annual Number*, October 1994.

19. Primary Education and Economic Development in China and India by Jean Dreze and Mrinalini Saran, *The Development Economics Research Programme*, London School of Economics, September 1993.

20. UNICEF, as reported in Delhi-edition of Times of India, November 18, 1993.

21. Primary Education and Economic Development in China and India by Jean Dreze and Mrinalini Saran, *The Development Economics Research Programme*, London School of Economics, September 1993.

22. *Poverty and Affluence*, C.T. Kurien, Madras Institute of Development Studies, 1992.

23. Poverty Line: The Line of Gross Unfairness, KS Ramachandran, *Financial Express*, December 3, 1994.

24. Trends in Employment, Planning Commission, 1990.

25. Eighth Five Year Plan, 1992-1997, Planning Commission.

26. The 73rd Constitutional Amendment, 1993.

27. Mid-Year Review of the Economy 1994-95, Kirit S. Parikh et al, Indira Gandhi Institute of Development Research, Reserve Bank of India, November 1994.

Rex Ambler

Gandhi against Modernity

Gandhi wrote only one book, strictly speaking: *Hind Swaraj*, or Indian Home Rule. He wanted to clarify what he meant by *swaraj*, a word that had come to mean a number of different things in the Indian political scene of that time (1909). Was it 'self-rule' in the sense that the Irish were then seeking it, a take-over of political power? Or was it something more profound and personal? Gandhi approached these questions by asking another, what was it that Indians specifically needed to be liberated from? He came to the conclusion that it was not British rule as such, but something deeper and more pervasive. It was modern civilization. This was a relatively new and somewhat shocking idea in an Indian context, and Gandhi clearly needed to justify it. But his justification of the claim was, if anything, more shocking than the claim itself. He argued that modern civilization, as presented in the west and more specifically in Britain, was an evil force that was entirely opposed to the true interests of human beings. 'The tendency of... the western civilization', for example, 'is to propagate immorality'[1]. The very things it boasts of, its medicine, its legal system, its parliamentary democracy, are in fact destructive and degrading:- far from establishing health and justice, they perpetuate immoral practice and deprive people of the self-knowledge and self-sufficiency to cope with the problems that face them. 'Hospitals are institutions for propagating sin'[2]; lawyers have 'enslaved India'[3]; 'That which you consider to be the Mother of Parliaments is like a sterile woman and a prostitute'[4]. And so with every practice and institution that can claim to be modern.

This wholescale condemnation dismayed many of his friends and admirers. His own political guru, Ghokale, according to Mahadev Desai, 'thought it so crude and hastily conceived that he prophesied that Gandhiji himself would destroy it after spending a year in India'[5]. But Gandhiji didn't. On the contrary, he publicly reaffirmed its ideas on many occasions afterwards, even as late as 1945, 36 years on, when he said, 'I withdraw nothing except one word of it, and that in deference to a lady friend' [6], the friend in question being Annie Besant.

What was going on? Why this vehement attack? And what exactly was he trying to say? Gandhi was not normally given to such vehement condemnation. He was usually balanced, judicious, ready to see the *good* in those things which he opposed. And in this particular case we may think he had particular reason to appreciate the civilization in which he himself had trained as a lawyer, learned to think through his philosophy (with the aid of such thinkers as Tolstoy, Ruskin and Thoreau) and discovered the power of organized campaigns for achieving justice (from such as Bradlaugh and Besant). Was he being entirely honest? Or had he taken on more than he could properly comprehend?

It could easily be argued that Gandhi had two lines of thought which are essentially quite different, and only tenuously related. There is the shrewd thinking of the lawyer and politician on the one hand, and the idealistic and faddish thinking of the religious seeker on the other. Both appear in *Hind Swaraj*, it could be said, which explains its muddle and extremism. He is shrewd about tactics and PR, but hopelessly idealistic and simplistic about history and civilization, where unfortunately he allows his religious and moral intensity to colour his judgments about the condition of the world.

But this won't do. It helps us to dispose of (what for us in the west may be) the difficult side of Gandhi, but it fails to come to terms with Gandhi's own account of his intention. It may be that the dualism of our own (modern western) thinking prevents us from seeing how politics and spirituality, analysis and morality can be woven into a whole.

Look at the context to start with. He was returning from London on a leisurely sea trip with two disappointments on his mind: the failure to win support from the British government for the Indian cause in South Africa, and the new threat of violence in the Indian Home Rule movement. He wrote a letter the following year (1910) to a Mr Wybergh of the Transvaal Legislative Assembly to explain why he had written the book in the way he had. 'The choice lay between allowing the readers of *Indian Opinion* (for whom it was originally intended), anxious though they were for guidance, to drift away in the matter of the insane violence that is now going on in India, or giving them, no matter how humble, a lead that they were asking for. The only way I saw of mitigating violence was the one sketched in the pamphlet'[7]. He knew that violence would not have achieved what these youthful anarchists had in mind and which Gandhi largely had in mind too[8]. The British were too powerful to be removed in this way, as Gandhi had been learning from his contacts in London with the Irish Home Rule movement. But how could Indians be persuaded to struggle without the violence that would surely let them down? And what precisely would they have to be struggling for? India was not South Africa with its very obvious injustice. It is evident that in setting himself to write such a book Gandhi had a difficult and sensitive task in hand.

Gandhi contrived his book as a dialogue between himself as 'editor' (of *Indian Opinion*) and the youthful but misguided revolutionary as 'reader', reflecting, he later claimed, the actual conversations he had in London that year.[9] He pointed out to his anarchist partner, among other things, the contradiction in using the weapons of the British to eject the British. Means and ends were not so easily separable. It was also naive to suppose that in getting rid of the British they would have got rid of the problems that had dogged them for 300 years. The oppression was not simply political: it was also, and more fundamentally, economic and ideological. If these youthful nationalists wanted to serve the true interests of India they should first identify her real enemy, which was not the British rule in India, but the civilization that the British had brought with them and had begun to impose on the nation. 'We saw in *Hind Swaraj*, he wrote some two months later in *Indian Opinion*,' that it is not so much from British rule that we have to save ourselves as from Western civilization'[10]. This might at first appear to to have increased what was already a near impossible task, but as Gandhi presented it the task was made easier. For Indians already had their own economic order, morality and culture – their own civilization in fact. So to oppose western civilization quite vigorously, as Gandhi did here, was, at the very least, tactically prudent.

It was also therapeutic, given the despondency and weakness of the Indian masses. This is evident from the continual emphasis in the book on the need for Indians to recover their moral strength and to find *Swaraj* for themselves. It is clarified by a letter he wrote to his friend and co-worker, Henry Polak, just before writing the book: 'If you agree with me, it will be your duty to tell the revolutionaries and everybody else that the freedom they want, or they think they want, is not to be obtained by killing people or doing violence, but by setting themselves right, and by becoming and remaining truly Indian. Then the British rulers will be servants and not masters. They will be trustees and not tyrants, and they will live in perfect peace with the whole of the inhabitants of India. The future, therefore, lies not with the British race, but with the Indians themselves, and if they have sufficient self-abnegation and abstemiousness, they can make themselves free this very moment'[11]. If we think of *Hind Swaraj* in these therapeutic terms, as helping Indians to 'set themselves right', we can see it as an psychological exercise in confidence building: it would be aimed, negatively, at liberating his fellow countrymen from paranoia (in relation to the British), a collective inferiority complex, and over-dependency; and it would be aimed, positively, at enhancing their self-confidence, maturity of outlook and freedom of thought and action. *Swaraj* could be defined precisely as personal freedom and maturity. 'We can see that if we become free, India is free. And in this thought you have a definition of *Swaraj*. It is *Swaraj* when we learn to rule ourselves. It is, therefore, in the palm of our hands'[12].

In that respect Gandhi's therapy is very close to Freud's, which was being developed at the same time. But Gandhi's depended on a polarisation of good and bad that would have given Freud some qualms. Indian civilization was not only better than the English, it was 'far superior to yours', he tells the English[13], it is 'unquestionably the best'[14], 'not to be beaten in the world'[15], and, indeed, 'has nothing to learn from anybody else'[16]. The polarization is sharpened in his preface to the English translation of 1910: 'The British government in India constitutes a struggle between the Modern Civilization, which is the Kingdom of Satan, and the Ancient Civilization, which is the Kingdom of God. The one is the God of War, the other is the God of Love'[17]. Is this delusion of grandeur, a compensation for a sense of powerlessness? Again, 'Control over the mind is alone necessary, and when that is attained, man is free like the king of the forest and his very glance withers the enemy'[18]. Freud has cited 'the withering glance' as an example of a self-deception designed to make up for feelings of weakness. But perhaps in the context of Gandhi's concern the compensation was part of the process of therapy that would end in a well-grounded self-confidence which was capable also of appreciating others. Gandhi gives a hint of this longer-term goal in his address to the English: 'Only on condition of our demands being fully satisfied may you remain in India; and if you remain under those conditions, we shall learn several things from you and you will learn many from us. So doing we shall benefit each other and the world'[19].

Polarization of good and bad also helped the actual struggle against the British, since it gave motivation to fight and at the same time gave some justification for the use of the very unorthodox weapons Gandhi had tried and tested in South Africa. Nonviolent resistance needed to be *seen* as worthy and powerful if it was to be effective in practice: it could not be a mere technique.

At this point the politics and the spirituality coincide exactly: the effectiveness of the *political* movement for Indian independence, relying on those resources that were peculiar to India and in which India had an advantage, depended precisely on *spiritual* values which enabled them to look beyond the politically expedient. For Gandhi himself, after all, *Swaraj* was always more than a political objective, though, as he admitted himself, he had little success in persuading others about this. He wrote of the book in 1921: 'I would warn the reader against thinking that I am today aiming at the *swaraj* described therein. I know that India is not ripe for it. It may seem an impertinence to say so. But such is my conviction. I am individually working for the self-rule pictured therein. But today my corporate activity is undoubtedly devoted to the attainment of parliamentary *Swaraj* in accordance with the wishes of the people of India'[20]. The commitment to both personal self-rule and political independence was not a conflict for Gandhi, however, since the two belonged together, and the one grew out of the other. Struggling for political freedom with nonviolent means would develop spiritual aspirations as well. His problem was only that India was not yet 'ripe'.

Part of the intention of *Hind Swaraj*, then, was to develop the *spiritual awareness* of his Indian readers so that they would not judge their situation in narrowly pragmatic or material terms. This in turn required a further criticism of the West since, on his understanding, it had rejected spiritual values in everything but matters of private life, Its tendency was all the other way, towards purely material welfare, and even then with the very crude notion that more material things meant greater human welfare. As he summarizes his view elsewhere, 'Western civilization is material, frankly material.

It assures progress by the progress of matter - railways, conquest of disease, conquest of the air. These are the triumphs of civilization according to Western measure. No one says, "Now the people are more truthful or more humble"'[21].

In addition to the politician, therapist and tactician in *Hind Swaraj* we also hear the prophet. He is outraged by what modernity has done to the world, in unemployment, tedium and war. It has a rhetoric of justice and equality, and some individuals who live up to these deals, but its basic dynamic ensures that these things cannot be achieved. On the contrary, its primary commitment to money through control of the market ('Money is their God'[22]) ensures that large numbers of people are kept in poverty. Its primary relation to India is also precisely that. The English 'hold whatever dominions they have for the sake of their commerce.... They wish to convert the whole w.orld into a vast market for their goods,'[23]. This perspective helps us to see more precisely what he understands by modern civilization. He is thinking of the way of life that came into being with capitalism and the industrial revolution. He is not thinking of the culture of the west in general, much of which of course he admired and even drew upon in the elaboration of his critique. It is modernity as such that worries him. And it worries him because of its devastating effect on human beings. This welcome refinement of the argument was made clearer in a speech of 1925: 'Do not for one moment consider that I condemn all that is Western. For the time being I am dealing with the predominant character of modern civilization, do not call it Western civilization, and the predominant character of modern civilization is the exploitation of the weaker races of the earth'[24]. He therefore wants to ask moral questions of it. 'Is the world any the better for those quick instruments of locomotion?', for example. 'How do these instruments advance man's spiritual progress? 'Do they not in the last resort hamper it? And is there any limit to man's ambition?... And what is all this worry and fateful hurry for? To what end?'[25]. It is therefore on moral criteria that he finally condemns it. 'The key to understanding *Hind Swaraj*', he wrote in the 1914 preface, 'lies in the idea that worldy pursuits should give way to ethical living'[26]. He demands that ethics be given the first consideration in public life, not the last. In this he followed some western critics, like Tolstoy, Ruskin and Emerson[27].

There was also an Indian ingredient to the critique: the idea that 'commitment to material progress was an intoxication, a *moha* (as in Arjuna's account of Krishna's state of mind in the Gita,[28]), or an illusion, *maya*. This in fact seems to provide the backbone to his reasoning. Note the crucial passage in the section on 'Civilization': 'Those who are intoxicated by modern civilization are not likely to write against it. Their care will be to find out facts and arguments in support of it, and this they do unconsciously, believing it to be true. A man, while he is dreaming, believes in his dream; he is undeceived only when he is awakened from his sleep'[29]. Perhaps some of the vehemence of Gandhi's language was intended to shake people out of a sleep, out of a state of intoxication. For only by seeing the truth, behind the glamorous llusion, would they be able to resist its hold on them. Gandhi wrote to Maganlal at about this time, 'Modern tyranny is a trap of temptation and therefore does greater mischief'[30].

Gandhi's talk, like that of a guru, was to help his disciples to wake up. When they did so they would naturally do the right thing.

Part of the (potential) subtlety of this analysis is that it saved Gandhi from writing off the English as morally despicable. His attitude is rather that of sadness and pity. 'They rather deserve our sympathy. They are a shrewd nation and I therefore believe that they will cast off the evil. They are enterprising and industrious, and their mode of thought is not inherently immoral. Neither are they bad at heart. I therefore respect them'[31]. The polarization is aimed at civilization, not people, which provides another important reason for not resorting to violence. It also provides the basis of Gandhi's boundless optimism, which can envisage not only the liberation of India from the illusions of this world, but also, through India, the liberation of the world!

However, it was not so important for Gandhi that this vision would ever be realized. It seemed to be enough that it was possible, for it then motivated the struggle to realize it and set the horizon for one's individual quest for liberation.

Even so, we might still wish to conclude, after considering this rationale of Gandhi, that he was caught in the trap of his own utopianism[32]. He can oppose modern civilization so totally only because he can seriously believe that its idealistic alternative is possible and feasible. But, it might be said, since the alternative is constructed on the basis of a purely spiritual understanding of the human and historical situation it cannot even begin to be feasible. (Gandhi's jibe about 'merely material' civilization might be redirected to him as 'merely spiritual'). Further, because he judged western civilization on the basis of its worst effects he was bound to judge it a total failure. In a revealing comment towards the end of *Hind Swaraj* he said: 'I cannot recall a single good point in connection with machinery' (p.96), not even the ship he was sailing on at the time, or the glasses he was wearing when he wrote those words. This is an example of the psychological polarization I spoke of earlier, which was as much a part of his personal mind-set as it was of the political and cultural struggle he led in India. In its original context of struggle, as I hope I have shown, it was justifiable and relevant [33]. Away from that context it is less secure: we need to introduce again categories of ambiguity and compromise which recognize that our ideals for society cannot be embodied in the world in a pure and unsullied form. But I am aware, in suggesting this, that I am reintroducing categories of analysis which are distinctly western, which admit of a tension, if not an opposition, between the worldly and the spiritual, the political and the personal. Our thinking in the west has undoubtedly been chastened by the modern experience of both astonishing success and appalling failure.

The question remains, however, whether the society Gandhi envisaged was, and is, ultimately possible, and whether modern society as he knew it was, and is, unsustainable. If the answer to both is affirmative, then it would make sense after all to oppose modern society in the name of something that can genuinely transcend it.

Notes and References

1. *Hind Swaraj* (hereafter *HS*), Navajivan Press, Ahmedabad, rev.ed. 1939, p. 63.

2. *HS*, p. 5 9.

3. *HS*, p. 5 4.

4. *HS*, P. 3 1.

5. Desai' s preface to *HS*, p. 14.

6. *HS*, p. 1 4.

7. Letter to Mr. Wybergh, May 10, 1910, in T*he Moral and Political Writings of Mahatma Gandhi*, (hereafter *Writings*) ed. Raghavan Iyer, The Clarendon Press, Oxford, 1986, vol I, pp.297f.

8. See the discussion of this background in Chandran Devanesan, *The Making of the Mahatma*, Orient Longmans, New Delhi, 1969, pp.364-376.

9. *HS*, p. 18.

10. *Writings*, I, p.333.

11. *Writings*, I, p.295.

12. *HS*, p. 6 5.

13. *HS*, p. 99.

14. *HS*, p. 64.

15. *HS*, p. 60.

16. *HS*, p. 61.

17. *Writings*, I, p. 272.

18. *HS*, p. 8 2.

19. *HE*, pp. 100f.

20. *Writings*, I, p.279.

21. In an interview for *The Friend*, 11 December 1931, reprinted in *Writings*, I, 328.

22. *HS*, p. 4 0.

23. *HS*, pp. 40f.

24. Speech to Meccano Club, Calcutta, 1925, in *Writings*, I, 345. On the later 'refinement' of his thinking on civilization see Madhuri Wadwa, *Gandhi between Tradition and Modernity*, Deep and Deep Publications, New Delhi, 1991, pp.65f, 89f.

25. An interview of 1926, in Writings, I, pp.281f.

26. Writings, I, p.277.

27. Cf. the 1910 preface in *Writings*, I, pp.271f.

28. I owe this insight to Bhikhu Parekh, *Gandhi's Political Philosophy*, Macmillan, London, 1989, pp.16f.

29. *HS*, p. 3 4.

30. A letter to Maganlal Gandhi, 2 April 1910, in Writings, T, P.3,17. Cf. the Calcutta speech referred to: 'The glamour of European civilization does not dazzle us. Scratch beneath the surface and you will find there very little to choose', *Writings*, I, p.345.

31. *HS*, p. 3 8.

32. Cf. Judith Brown, *Gandhi: Prisoner of Hope*, Yale UP, Newhaven and London, 1989.

33. Cf. Chandran Devanesan, *The Making of the Mahatma*, Orient Longmans, New Delhi, 1969, ch.6.

V B Eswaran

Gandhiji, Government and the Rural Poor

The political leadership in India, specially in the Congress party which was in the forefront of the struggle for Independence, and later has formed the Government at the national level almost continuously, has explicitly stood for economic growth with social justice. Measures to alleviate and eradicate poverty were therefore part of election manifestos and government policies. One makes a specific mention of this feature, because it is not always that countries which won their independence in the last few decades, with the bulk of the population living in the rural areas, set themselves this kind of broad goal, or put through measures such as land reforms which have been generally considered basic to helping the poor out of poverty.

Even after land reforms measures by which numbers of landless people in the villages were given some land, those without land are still a significant proportion of the communities in many States and regions. To their numbers one could add those with small or marginal landholdings which do not produce enough for the sustenance of their families for much of the year, with the result that they swell the ranks of the unemployed and underemployed in their villages for some months. In India an additional dimension of social justice was concerned with the caste divisions in the population. There are Scheduled Castes, meaning those notified in terms of a provision in the Constitution for the purpose. These were called *Harijans* by Mahatma Gandhi, treated as "untouchable" by the rest of the community. They live in all parts of the country. India also has Scheduled Tribes, communities who would be called 'indigenous peoples' in the current jargon of western development writers. These tribes have not really been part of the mainstream, and for about 20 years now, special development measures for their benefit have been devised and put into practice. Both the Scheduled Castes and the Scheduled Tribes have been exploited by other people -- the former by the so-called 'upper castes' in their villages, and the latter by the people who brought industry and business into their natural surroundings of forests which also happen to be rich in minerals and, of course, timber. It has been remarkable that the local tribal people have hardly been able to find space in the supervisory or managerial echelons in these industries.

The 1940's saw the preparation of a development plan for the country by the Congress party. The government of the day also drew up what were called in some provinces the Post-War Reconstruction schemes. When the Planning Commission was set up, after Independence, it was not writing on a clean slate. Specially it had the Gandhiji-inspired Congress Party's plan of 1946. The process of planning and designing its content were entrusted to very distinguished academic and administrative professionals. Prof. P C Mahalanobis, and Pitambar Pant were names to conjure with. Among the luminaries from the Administrative field may be mentioned V T Krishnamachari, C M Trivedi, and Tarlok Singh. However, the pre-Independence Gandhian element was largely lost in the "drang nach Western", as it were. The planners and Prime Minister Jawaharlal Nehru were keen that India should catch up with the West.

If one looks back into the first 28 years or so of planning, roughly till the crude oil price of 1973 hit India (and other oil importing countries), planning and the allocation of investment resources were directed mainly at building up economic infrastructure like electric power generation, and transport, and the capital goods and intermediate industries such as heavy machinery, steel, and the like, which were not labour-intensive. It became clear soon that where these industries were located they had also no particular impact on the surrounding communities by way of the new incomes and wealth percolating to the poor among them, other than wages for labour in mines or unskilled occupations. The more modern industries such as petrochemicals and fertilisers provided little scope for large numbers of employees, because of the very nature of the technology. Even in the agriculture sector, if one includes major irrigation reservoir projects with their canal systems in this sector, the tendency has been increasingly to mechanise construction activities where manual labour could do the job adequately - as was the case in the history of irrigation development in this country. In a discussion some years ago with a very senior engineer-manager concerned with the Narmada dam project in Gujarat, when I raised the question why even canals were to be dug by machines, the answer was that the job would be done much faster. Probably in a project financed by the World Bank, as the Narmada project was, the stipulations of the Bank governing the engagement of contractors on the basis of global bidding, as well as time-schedules laid down for the project, almost rule out manual labour. How is one to reconcile this result of the approach or policy of the department concerned with large irrigation works with that of other departments of the government engaged in planning and implementing schemes for providing work and purchasing power through the wages, also in the rural areas?

One could draw the inference that the academics and the administrators who were in key positions in the Planning Commission and the Departments concerned were not particularly knowledgeable as far as the conditions in the rural areas were concerned; where rural people had to be taken into account, more often than not they were numbers or statistics, more than *people*. On the other hand it was important to the planners and the departments of the Government that the country had to be 'modernised', meaning that industry had to be built up and an industrial revalution ushered in. This approach also led to somewhat grandiose planning. A 10 million ton annual target for steel production and consumption was mooted even in the 1960s. The result was investment resources being poured into such ventures, practically all in the public sector. The outputs were grossly delayed, because the project management was not the most efficient. Most of these undertakings also failed to make profits, and drained the exchequer of large amounts of the tax payers' money every year, for decades. The consequence, specially after the crude oil price increases of 1973, and later, upset seriously the availability of resources for the five-year plans, was that less and less investment went into the social services like health care, education, etc. Another kind of squeeze on the latter was a result of the higher expenditures in the defence budget from the sixties and seventies particularly.

Thus the mainstream of planning and government activity was concerned almost continually with the problems of 'modernisation' of the country and its economy, and this was in consonance with the mould of the first Prime Minister, Jawaharlal Nehru. One does not suggest that he was not concerned for the poor, but how much of his time and attention the ministers and departments concerned with rural questions could secure in practice is open to speculation. His successor, Lal Bahadur Shastri, was troubled by such questions, and the effectiveness of the administration in the field in dealing with them, but he was Prime Minister for too short a period to have much of an impact on the leviathan that the Government of India was well on its way to becoming. Indira Gandhi was a very shrewd politician, and from the late 1960s introduced a series of schemes for the poor, who were the largest vote banks in the countryside. The crash scheme for rural employment of about 25 years ago was a political move, rather than a design for poverty alleviation. She was the fount of a number of initiatives, incorporated into the '20 point programme' of the mid-seventies which has been continued. Her regime saw much land allotted to the landless, house sites were given to the needy, housing built for the Harijans, and so on.

These initiatives did activate most parts of the government machinery in the Central government and in the States, and get them to frame schemes and allocate resources for her programmes. This applied also to the Planning Commission, which in the early 1970s had refused to acknowledge or give any priority to the Maharashtra Employment Guarantee Scheme, even though the State Legislature had voted a taxation measure to meet part of the cost; or to the School Children's Nutrition Scheme of the Tamilnadu government. These schemes did not square with the Commission's economists' view of 'national priorities'! Both were for the poor, and the Maharashtra programme would have ameliorated the lot of the poor looking for work in the seasons when the dryland farming of the semi-arid areas needed no labour on the farms. Incidentally, similar programmes were started by the Central government some years later, with the same purpose!

Enough has been said to suggest that the Central government officialdom, and the Planning Commission pundits were quite far removed from the ground realities and circumstances of the rural areas and the poor who were not articulate or vocal. Curiously enough, politicians who were elected to Parliament, including those who became Ministers, seemed to be ineffective generally in voicing the legitimate needs of the poor in the decision-making forums such as the Cabinet. The Indian government system provides for drafting into the Central Ministries at senior levels, numbers of officials from the State administrations, so that their first hand knowledge and experience of the field would inform Central policy-making and decisions. Even this does not seem to happen. As an instance, the Deputy Commissioner (the head of the district administration) of a notoriously poor district in Eastern India told me in the late 1980's that Central Government schemes for the welfare of the poor were too detailed and inflexible, and, if modifications were needed to suit local conditions they needed to be approved of at the State Government level and often in the Central Government! Not all district officers would have taken the initiative, and the possible attendant risk of censure, to bend the prescriptions of the standard Central schemes, as she did.

If the measures of the 20-point programme were expected to be implemented with commitment, the official machinery fell short. Officials in the districts were required to report statistics of 'progress', that is the numbers achieved against targets given to them. It is well known that there was much fudging of such reports; a Secretary to the Government of India in a Department concerned with some of the 20 points told me that he had found this out when he went travelling to the field himself. I have also personally seen a district officer offering to sanction a gun licence to a villager provided he reported at the next 'family planning camp' where sterilization operations were scheduled.

Particularly for the *Harijans,* while legal protection and redress against 'untouchability' was provided by law, in real life the law could not help much. It has been the experience, on the other hand, that where *Harijans* earn significant incomes, their status in the community rose. For instance, one has seen *Harijans* who took works contracts in their villages and small towns, and earned sizeable incomes; they were more often referred to as Contractor so and so than as *Harijans*. They could more easily enter into social exchange and dealings with others in the community as they did with officialdom. The experience of NGOs whose credo is to work for *Harijans* and other 'dalits' (oppressed people) in many States also shows that their self-confidence can be built up by helping them to organise themselves. This spirit is strengthened and reinforced when they are also provided opportunities for earning money incomes, for instance, through schemes of the Government or programmes of NGOs. The passage of time, after the 1940s has also helped, for the younger generations of the 'upper castes', even in the villages, seem to have shed by degrees the old ways. Of course, the situation on the ground differs considerably from State to State. The answer for the *Harijan* problem, if one may call it that, is to be found in time and a steady widening of educational and economic opportunities for them.

Prime Minister Nehru was very keen on promoting modern science and technology, and saw to it that ample resource allocations here made to build institutions for research in agricultural as well as industrial fields. Indira Gandhi continued to provide her powerful patronage and support for these institutions and the scientists. One would therefore have thought that these institutions and the scientists would have studied and built up a comprehensive body of knowledge of how farmers in the countryside managed their land and water resources, the techniques they had inherited from the past and adapted to suit changing natural conditions, and their decision-making processes in agriculture, animal husbandry.etc; or of the traditional crafts and skills which used local raw materials and techniques, whether for the purpose of agricultural implements or textiles or baskets. But this has not been so. For the latter kind of knowledge, far more has been done by individuals and organisations than by the Government departments; for instance, perhaps Pupul Jayakar did more to bring the Madhubani painting to the rest of India and the world than anyone else, and incidentally put the women who had this art in the way of earning incomes from it. Currently there are voluntary organisations which are performing a similar service to rural folk who have the craft and the material to produce for the markets, in many parts of the country. Almost the same situation is to be found in the field of agricultural science, technology and research. More often than not the official Establishment in this area has proceeded on the basis that it was writing on a clean slate. The fact, on the other hand, is that over a hundred million farming families in the country have been practising crop and animal husbandry in innumerable local, situations with varying agro-climatic parameters and water regimes. These farmers, specially of the semi-arid and arid regions, have had relatively little research inputs, which would stabilise their economy to a point where they can cope better with rainfall variations than they can now. It is not that the research has not produced prescriptions. But these prescriptions tend to ignore ground truths, to be too generalised to fit localised resource conditions, and so on. Or, they are top-down prescriptions, say for treatment of a watershed of some thousands of hectares for the purpose of soil and moisture conservation, without consulting the couple of dozen resident rural communities and the many hundreds of farmers. Both fail to enthuse the people for whom they are intended, and no wonder.

Watershed treatment prescriptions are particularly relevant for the semi-arid and arid lands. For the irrigated lands, the research establishment produced the packages now referred to as the Green Revolution strategy. This called for high cost inputs by way of water, fertiliser, etc. But this strategy could benefit only about a hundred districts of the country out of 400 odd. Not only did the landowners in these districts benefit considerably by the new strategy; they also drew substantial subsidies from the exchequer by way of the pricing of the irrigation water, the fertilisers, and the electricity, as also the procurement prices offered for their produce by the official agencies. No such bonanzas came the way of the people in the semi-arid and arid areas where farming continued to be largely for subsistence, rainy season mono-crops were the rule, and for the rest of the year there was little or no work on the farms to keep the poor employed.

These sections of the people live chronically on the brink. A severe drought which results in large scale crop failures pushes them over into distress, dislocation of normal life, sickness, migration for wage earning, and so on. How little understood their condition is in distant Delhi, the centre of Government and planners and their like, may be illustrated by the following, extracted from the regular column of a well-known economic journalist in a national newspaper in March 1994:

> This does not imply that Government should forget about poverty altogether. First, as already noted, the State needs to be active in education, health, and infrastructure. Secondly, there is a problem of destitution – handicapped and aged people incapable of earning a living which cannot be tackled by growth. Third, and most important, sudden poverty and starvation can be caused by economic shocks like a drought.

That a drought is never 'sudden' or.that the poor who fall victim to it do so because they have been teetering on the brink, are facts of life; but not apparently known to many among those who call the shots in the Government circles or applaud them for 'structural adjustment' and 'industrial liberalisaiion policies'.

In sum, these poor, in the semi-arid and arid rural areas as well as in the high population-density regions with high proportions of landless labour, and marginal farmers, had really little by way of official programmes or measures of succour which would help them to achieve higher stable levels of living. The programmes of the last decade or more, such as the Jawahar Rozgar Yojana, did, and do provide employment and purchasing power for certain numbers and for limited periods in the year, but this is not quite the same.

The Government schemes tend, in practice, to be treated as independent in themselves, not connected with other schemes either in the course of implementation, or for the purpose of coordination between departments. For instance, when the Agriculture Ministry introduced, about four years ago, the National Watershed Development Programme in Rural Areas (NWDPRA), it did not consult the National Wastelands Development Board in another Ministry, though the character of the lands which were the concern of the two agencies was about the same. Again, the NWDPRA was to be implemented only in Blocks (a unit of development administration within a district) with at least 30 per cent of the area with 'semi-arid' rainfall conditions. The entire scheme was laid down in detail from Delhi, just months after the NWDB introduced its

Integrated Wastelands Development Programme under which local initiative for formulating projects was cardinal. Such instances can be multiplied, at the Central Government as well as the State levels. The outcome quite often is that these schemes produce less than the expected benefits or results. Less than a year ago, the Collector (administrative head) of a severely drought-prone district in South India told me that the NWDPRA in his district was a 'bloody mess'; and that from a Collector who had won the respect of voluntary agencies working in the district for his dynamism and commitment to his work.

Rather than explore the reasons for such a failure, it would serve our purpose better if we recognise that the Central Government is not the right level for making detailed programmes and implementation procedures for the poor and the disadvantaged. A realisation of this kind was perhaps one of the motive factors behind the number of voluntary agencies and non-government organisations (NGOs) which have come up in large numbers in most parts of the country. It is not a derogation of this view that there are a number of NGOs also which have been formed with an eye to drawing funds from Government sources -- since it became Government policy from the mid-eighties to finance NGOs for various development activities – and from the numerous foreign donor-agencies. Most of the serious NGOs working among the rural communities came to realise sooner or later the very strong linkages between people's livelihoods and their local natural resource endowment by way of the land, the water and the biomass, which provided their life-support. Specially the NGOs in the dry areas learnt this lesson very clearly in the successive years of drought in the mid-80s. Those NGOs which had sedulously helped the poor among the communities to build collective strength, but with not much stress on economic content by way of enhanced incomes or assets, found the edifice they had helped to erect collapsing under the impact of the drought-induced loss of economic staying power. These NGOs then reappraised their approach, and came to appreciate the central place of the health of the local land and water resources in sustaining the lives of the poor. For practical purposes this meant taking up projects for soil and water conservation through raising green cover on the land and other measures, depending on local contexts of land use, tradition etc. Where NGOs have been able to devise and put through such measures on the basis of watershed boundaries, and with the understanding and involvement of the local people, the effects have been remarkable by way of enhanced productivity of the lands.

NGOs generally have also been mindful of the equity aspect in such programmes, unlike the government schemes. The latter by and large have revolved around the technical do's and don'ts, without much attention to whether the benefits will flow to the rich or also to the poor, the women, the *harijans,* the landless and so on. Even where Government schemes incorporate equity prescriptions, they are usually conceived in the abstract, and not left to be decided at the level of the community. It is well known that a community's perception of equity vis-a-vis the poor could vary from year to year, because the problem of a poor family could vary from year to year; equity then is not theory but what practically would help the poor family. I have seen examples of such decisions or dispensations of equity in many parts of the country, from the Sunderbans to Rajasthan to Andhra Pradesh.

The case is clear now for the proposition that decisions and plans of work for the benefit of local communities and the poor and disadvantaged among them should be taken in those communities, with the helping hand of voluntary agencies which have taken root in those communities and have won their regard and trust. The Government departments would certainly need to play important roles, such as that of financing, arranging for external services and supplies if necessary, and providing technical advice. A difficult-transformation for them, and particularly for their officials who have always tended to treat the citizen and the community as supplicants and not clients. Things may not be as strikingly feudal as they were in the 1950s when I have seen village leadership in Bulandshahar district in Uttar Pradesh bend down and touch the feet of the Collector who looked not a bit discomfitted. But there are many parts of the country where the poor ask officialdom for charity, where officials still address villagers in the singular, corresponding to the French "tu". And, many of the citadels of agricultural research would not deign to treat with unpolished or illiterate farmers and herdsmen (though some do).

At the village level then should one look to the village *panchayat* (the elected local self-government body) for planning and implementing development programmes generally, and for the poor particularly? These *panchayats* have some features which should be noted as relevant in this context. In the first place they have jurisdiction over many communities or settlements, each with its own local natural resource (life-support) environment. Some *panchayats* are one-village bodies, but most are multi-village. This is a legacy of the law of the British days, such as the Bombay Village Panchayats Act of 1933, when these bodies were expected to look after street lighting, upkeep of the village streets and such other municipal chores. The present *panchayats*, in many States, as well as the new bodies which will be elected in accordance with the recent amendment to the Constitution, will have to do with all village affairs, including the management of the local natural resources. I would doubt very much whether the multi-village institution can do justice to its responsibility. Many in recent years, including myself, have been suggesting that the right body to deal with local matters of management of community resources and issues would be the *Gram Sabha*, that is the assembly of all families in the community or settlement; that the unit should be the settlement, and not the village which in terms of the law in India is one or more settlements within the boundaries of an area notified or recognised as a village in land revenue administration. It is the experience in the important field of forest management and protections, that, rather than elected *panchayat* bodies, the most effective have been village forest protection committees created by the village communities themselves. There are thousands of these now in some of the States, and discussions in the recent National Conservation Congress (New Delhi, November 1994) organised by the World

Wide Fund for Nature India, indicated that these informal creations of the community are more widespread and much larger in numbers than believed till now. Official policy has recognised these committees in recent years. I have myself seen some of those at work in West Bengal, and there has been considerable study and documentation of their composition and functioning in many States.

The cardinal feature, for my purpose, of these committees is that they are not elected an the one-man one-vote principle but they are nominated by the *Gram Sabha*, an all-community meeting. I believe that the conventional one-man one-vote desideratum of democracy is inappropriate for the village level body, whether it is the 'official' panchayat or a village forest committee, or the resource management society of the kind we have in many villages in the Siwaliks near Chandigarh, or Gram Vikas Mandals (village development councils) in many States in the country. These non-official bodies have been set up by the decision of the entire village community, usually in open meetings, with the help or at the suggestion of NGOs trusted by the community. The community itself usually does not hold with the one-man one-vote system for debating and deciding local questions of concern to the entire village or settlement. I once asked a very vocal and shrewd woman leader in one of the Siwalik settlements why they needed a natural resource management society for looking after the water in the pond and the trees and grasses in the catchment, when they had a *panchayat*. She replied, without a moment's hesitation, that the *panchayat* was for elections, but the whole community needed to participate in the resource-management. Clearly the present system of *panchayat* elections is seen to be divisive, and therefore not appropriate, where decisions have to be taken in the interest of the community as a whole. In a body elected in a divisive system, decisions are likely to be taken not necessarily on merits, in the interest of the whole community, but because the winning party and its votaries would like to decide in their own interest. There was an instance in the mid-eighties in one of the States, which was brought to my notice at that time, in which the Sarpanch (President) of a newly elected *panchayat* rescinded his predecessor's resolution making available part of the village land to the Government department for a fuel wood plantation. When this created a flutter in the Government department, the Sarpanch said that he had to get the earlier resolution cancelled as a demonstration of his victory, but he would arrange to pass another resolution to the same effect, now that honour was satisfied!

Gandhiji's village republics cannot obviously be found in the official *panchayat* system. But they do exist in the informal committees and such bodies which communities set up, when they are given the space to do so. The officialdom and the political executive, or parties, whether at the Central Government or at the State levels do not seem inclined to this point of view. A pity. These bodies have tremendous potential. They can see that local schools run well, and dispensaries; they can ensure transparency in the conduct of official business of all kinds, including public works, as a contrast to the present ways of the government departments and *panchayats* which do not like transparent functioning; they can see that the functions of the local body are carried out in a cost-effective manner, and are not loaded with the costs of inertia, inefficiencies and corruption as they often are now. Even now efficient and conscientious NGOs are able to execute large works at say two-thirds of the costs estimated by the government people, and of better quality, over large areas. I have seen these examples myself in more than one region in the country, e.g. Rajasthan, Andhra Pradesh, Gujarat.

Gandhiji saw that in order to secure the future of the country, its villages had to be helped to develop a degree of self-sufficiency and self-reliance. It now seems that there is this concern and thinking in the Government and outside it. There is also sufficient experience in the Government departments and with NGOs to point clearly to the efforts of the latter as more likely to succeed, and strengthen village communities. It has been a long circuitous route. It is clearly a start, economic liberalisation and the global economy notwithstanding; and a promise too, now that voluntary effort is pouring into this field, especially from committed local NGOS rooted in villages. It is good too that the governments at the Centre and in the States have recognised the value of these efforts, and are giving them room.

Surur Hoda

Schumacher on Gandhi

Gandhi's visions of *Gram Swaraj* ie self-sufficient but inter-linked village republics with decentralised small–scale economic structure and participatory democracy, left him immediately at odds with many in the Indian National Congress and outside who sought to develop India as a 'modern' industrial nation state. To Gandhi, political freedom was merely the first step towards attainment of real independence which entailed achieving social, moral and economic freedom for seven hundred thousand villages. 'If the villages perish India will perish' he had said. But the majority of academically trained, so called modern economists called his vision 'retrograde'. Some extremists even described it as 'reactionary' or 'counter-revolutionary' which aimed to put the clock back.

Many of those who admired his skill in leading the struggle for national liberation reluctantly tolerated his views as the price to pay for his political leadership. They were sold to the concept of large–scale urban industrialisation, mass production and economics of scale. They failed to understand Gandhi's economic insight and criticised him by saying 'Whatever Gandhi's merit as "Father of the Nation", he simply does not understand economics.'

Yet almost a quarter of a century after his assassination, Dr E F Schumacher, when delivering the Gandhi Memorial Lecture at the Gandhian Institute of Studies at Varanasi (India) in 1973, described Gandhi as the greatest 'People's Economist.' In his opening remarks, Schumacher told a story which went something like this. 'A famous German conductor was once asked who did he consider as the greatest of all composers. "Unquestionably Beethoven" was his answer. He was then asked "Would you not even consider Mozart?" He said "Forgive me." I thought you were referring to the others.'

Drawing a parallel Schumacher said the same initial question might be put to an economist as to who was the greatest. The reply might come 'Unquestionably Keynes.' 'Would you not even consider Gandhi?' 'Forgive me, I thought you were referring to the others.'

Schumacher indentified Gandhi as the people's economist whose economic thinking was compatible with spirituality as opposed to materialism. He said: 'Gandhi refused to treat economics as if people did not matter.' Gandhi had his finger on the pulse of the masses and therefore when someone put it to him that no religion was any good that did not make sense in terms of economics, Gandhi countered that no economics was any good that did not make sense in terms of morality and the poor masses. Schumacher therefore interpreted Gandhian economics as people's economics and explained the difference between economic reasoning based on 'people' as against 'goods', as was the case with materialistic economic thinking.

Schumacher explained that economic reasoning based on 'goods' would be solely concerned with increasing the supply of goods by means of advanced technology, scientific knowledge and modern equipment. Based on this line of thinking industries should be large scale, highly sophisticated, capital intensive and labour saving, even to the point of total automation. From the 'goods' point of view, human beings were not ideal agents of mass production because they tended to make mistakes, were unpunctual, argued back and joined trade unions. The ideal therefore was to eliminate the 'human factor'.

However, if the economic means of development was based on people, as with Gandhian thinking, one had to direct attention to people in need and start asking why are they poor; if it was because their productivity was zero, how then could this be raised.

With this line of reasoning eradication of worklessness was of paramount importance. The most disturbing aspect of most developing countries, Schumacher thought, was the fact that millions and millions of people were without work or at such a low level of productivity that it was negligible.

How could these people be helped to help themselves? It was in order to address this issue that Gandhi gave a call for 'production by the masses' instead of 'mass production.' While giving his prescription to the nation, he said that 'the salvation of India is impossible without the salvation of the villages and their poor inhabitants.'

The Gandhian Prescription

When asked how Gandhi, were he alive today, would view India's present situation after three decades of independence, Schumacher pointed out that the number of rich, even very rich, people in India had increased as had the number of desperately poor people. He added that the situation in India reflected the situation of the world as a whole and Gandhi would undoubtedly consider this a sign of grievous failure. The obvious question, Schumacher asked, was 'Why has it not been possible to help minions of unemployed and underemployed people to help themselves out of poverty?'

The answer, Schumacher added, was that an approach to economic problems which started from 'goods' and therefore aimed to eliminate the human factor from the productive process could not possibly lead to constructive job provision. Gandhi would not have found it difficult to understand this. Schumacher prophesied that if the next twenty-five years in India produced a continuation of the trends of development based on the Western model established since independence, the outlook for the mass of poor people was grim, even hopeless.

Referring to the Western world, Schumacher said that 'it is now widely accepted that there are limits to growth on the established pattern, so that, in all probability, the trends established over the last twenty-five years could not be continued even if everybody wished to do so. The requisite physical resources were simply not there, and living nature all around us, the Ecosystem, could not stand the strain. Gandhi had always known, and rich countries are now reluctantly beginning to realise, that their affluence was based on stripping the world. The USA with 5.6% of the world population was consuming up to 40% of the world's resources, most of them non-renewable. Such a life-style could not spread to the whole of mankind. In fact, the truth is now dawning that the world could not really afford the USA, let alone the USA plus Europe plus Japan plus other highly industrialised countries. Enough is now known about the basic facts of spaceship Earth to realise that its first class passengers were making demands which could not be sustained very much longer without destroying the spaceship.'

Schumacher summed up Gandhi's prescription for the salvation of India and indeed for the whole world as follows:-

1. Start all economic reasoning from the genuine needs of the people and help the poor to help themselves out of poverty.
2. Revitalise and foster not only agriculture as such but also all possible productive, non–agricultural activities in the rural areas such as cottage industries for potters, weavers, shoemakers, carpenters, blacksmiths etc.
3. Resist the further concentration of the growing population in large cities by reversing the trend of migration from rural to urban areas.
4. Develop systematic policies, based on the best available knowledge for the mobilisation of all productive resources, the greatest of which is the population itself.

Only by following the above mentioned prescription, Schumacher thought, would developing countries such as India hope to feed, clothe, house and provide the bare necessities of life for their teeming millions.

He then went on to identify the five main pillars of Gandhian economic thinking.

1. Non Violent
2. Simple
3. Small
4. Capital Saving
5. Rural-Based (Self Reliant and Employment-Orientated)

1. Non-Violent

Referring to the deep trouble in which the modern world found itself and the ecological crises facing it, Schumacher said that to most people this had come as a sudden shock. However, it would not have come as a surprise to Gandhi were he alive today. Gandhi perceived that the modern urban-based industrial civilisation was exploitative and violent. Gandhi did not employ nor did he require a computer to arrive at his conclusions. Common sense told him that Western style industrialisation was inherently violent and could never be implemented for the whole of mankind. 'It would strip the world like a locust' Gandhi had said and had warned that 'For India to change to industrialism is to court disaster.'

Gandhi abhorred the industrial civilisation because it was based on callous exploitation of non-renewable resources. It made bodily welfare the sole object of life, which reduced man to nothing but a clever animal. It was the tendency of Indian civilisation and Indian philosophy, however, to make man better than he was and Gandhi therefore wanted India to follow a different path of development. Today people particularly the young, in the rich as well as poor countries, are looking for just this: a different path of development, a different type of society, a different lifestyle.

Schumacher, describing 'Non-Violence' as a Gandhian term, widened its concept to include not merely the violence of man against man, but also the violence of man in his dealings with living nature around him and violence against the limited and finite resources of the Earth. Taking agricultural research as an example, Schumacher said that this was all based on violence – the use of insecticides, herbicides, fungicides, chemical fertilizers and the breeding of plants and animals which depended on the creation of highly abnormal living conditions. As a consequence modern agriculture had become a gigantic battle with nature instead of a careful, devoted striving to gear in with her unbelievably gentle and efficient methods. Organic agriculture based on the strict observance of biological laws, the proper recycling of organic materials, decentralising, diversification and good husbandry, was receiving virtually no support and attention. Yet there could be no disagreement that agricultural systems which depended completely and utterly on cheap availability of non-renewable materials such as oil had no long-term future. But a civilisation ruled almost exclusively by town dwellers was always in danger of forgetting this basic truth.

'As in agriculture, so in industry and in every other walk of life', Schumacher went on, 'we need to give our attention to the developing and perfection of non-violent methods to find answers to the threefold crises of the modem world – the crises of resource exhaustion, the ecological crises and the crises of man's alienation and disorientation. All this requires work ie Gandhian work with a spirit of truth and non-violence which inspired Gandhi.'

2. **Simple**

A simple lifestyle was Gandhi's hallmark. At his death his sole possessions were a pair of slippers, a watch, a pair of glasses and a few loin-cloths. He lived in poverty by choice most of his life in line with his motto 'Simple living and high thinking.' Quoting Gandhi's 'High thinking is inconsistent with complicated material life', Schumacher said that all real human needs were essentially simple, therefore only frivolities and extravagances like supersonic transport were inevitably complex. Complexity had to be seen not as a sign of progress but as a mark of failure. It entailed the need for extreme specialisation so that men became 'fragmentary', too specialised to be able to obtain wisdom. Schumacher maintained that the essence of the message of all the prophets and philosophers born in the East was a simple life-style.

In an attempt to emphasise this point Schumacher added that in the area of economics modern civilisation was moving at ever-increasing speed towards immense complexity and high capital intensity with the sole object of increasing gross national product, growth rate and per capital income. Referring to his experience in one of the Eastern countries in the early 1960's, he said:

> "This struck me very forcibly in Burma when I considered what my economist colleagues told me that the national income per head in Burma was £20 a year and I recalled wartime England, when a very effective official policy squeezed us down until the pips began to squeak and when the economists added it up, and the income per capital then calculated was £200. Now this is a comparison which ought to arrest our attention: with something in the order of £200 we could only just exist, and in other places of the world, with something called £20 they too can just exist. Are these genuine comparisons? They point not to differences in wealth but to differences in living patterns and life-styles. One pattern manifests and reflects itself in economists' calculations as £20 per annum per head and another at its minimum level, to basically the same job, ie just to carry the person through the year, manifests in the economists' book as £200 a head. If it were possible in the economy which has a pattern and is symbolised by the figure of 20 a head, to increase national income so that the 20 would become 30 or 40, while yet adhering to the same life-style, you would have transformed that country into the nearest thing to paradise on earth. But in doubling the national income

> and allowing the pattern to shift from your indigenous to an American one, which does not begin to function unless it is endowed with, in my symbolical statistics of £200, then the result would be simply disappointing although the economist will think that you have doubled the national income, but contrary to economists' estimation the country would rather slip into a slum economy than an economy of affluence, as the £40 a head income under altered conditions cannot even be enough to meet bare needs. Recognising that there are in fact two economics and two life-styles – and that is the trickiness of the problem we can recognise a twofold need, namely to make a success of the westernised sector and to make a success of the rest.

3. **Small**

Referring to his book *Small is Beautiful*, Schumacher said that when Gandhi said 'Not mass production but production by masses,' or when he talked about 'decentralised rural based self-reliant economy,' or when he demanded that 'production and consumption must be reunited,' he was talking the language of *Small is Beautiful*.

'Man is small and man is – or ought to be – beautiful and as such only the human scale economy of Gandhi's dream is appropriate', said Schumacher. The greater the size of the production unit, the greater the separation of production from consumption. Reuniting production and consumption units was only possible if production units were small. It would be easy to manage and adaptable to local conditions. One of the enormous advantages of small-scale production, reunited with small-scale consumption, was the minimisation of transport. Mass production entailed increased transport which added to the cost but never added anything to the real value of goods.

Modern economic thinking celebrated high speed and massive goods transport as wonderful achievements and included their costs in the gross national product as an indicator of economic progress. Post-modern thinking, according to Schumacher, would conceive the negative theory of transport, looking upon the need for goods transport primarily as an indicator of failure, proving that goods were being produced in the wrong places. This kind of thinking was already quite familiar to the factory planners and production agencies who strove for the minimisation of transport inside the factory and did not take pride in creating an elaborate infrastructure just for transporting goods from place to place.

The same thinking applied to society as a whole, which would never lose sight of the ideal, that things should be produced where they were needed. To use Gandhi's language: 'Production and consumption should become reunited,' or, to use another phrase of Gandhi's: 'Bring work to the people and not people to the work.'

Hence the need Schumacher emphasised for the development of small units, to fit into small scattered markets. 'Can we utilise science and technology to this end?' Schumacher asked. It was important to ask our scientists and technologists to use their knowledge and ingenuity not to make production units even bigger – seeking so called economics of scale – but to develop mini-plants so that people living in small communities in rural areas could again become productive, without being dependent on people already rich and powerful to provide 'job opportunities' for them. 'Economics of scale, which may well have been a nineteenth century truth, can be shown to be a twentieth century myth', said Schumacher.

4. **Capital Saving**

One of the pillars of Gandhian economic thinking was capital saving. Tragically, Schumacher pointed out, the world was moving at ever-increasing speed into large scale, immense complexity, high capital intensity, and elimination of the human factor: which was leading mankind into a crisis of survival. One of the reasons for Gandhi's opposition to capital intensive and complex machinery was the fact that it turned a large number of people into 'machine minders.' This did nothing to develop their personalities and merely robbed them of their creative power. Schumacher supporting Gandhi said that, in addition, highly capitalised modern, complex and gigantic technology had proved monstrously inefficient in solving the problems of the world. He added: 'If an ancestor of long ago visited us today, what would he be more astonished at? The skill of our dentists or the rotteness of our teeth? The speed of our transport or the length of time and the discomfort incurred in our travelling to and from work? The progress of our medicine or the overcrowding of our hospitals'! Our ability to land man on the Moon or our inability to find employment for people wanting work! The efficiency of our machines or the inefficiency of our system as a whole?'

Admiring Gandhi's sureness of touch, Schumacher said: 'Gandhi knew that a capital intensive economy could never solve India's unemployment problem, and went on to explain by giving an example. He said that in order to establish one work place it cost 100,000 Rupees and if you had 100 Crores (1 Crore = C Rs 10,000,000) you could establish only 10,000 work places. If one had to tackle an unemployment problem which ran into hundreds of millions, one could see the problem facing a poor country like India.'

Quoting another example, Schumacher said that he went to see a village potter, who was a marvellously skilled man but who had very primitive technical equipment worth Rs. 50. He then went to a city and met another potter minding a machine tool imported from Belgium, the price of which was in the region of Rs 500,000. Evidently the worker could never afford that kind of money to set himself up in business and as a consequence would be forced to go to a big city like Bombay, where there were already hundreds of thousands of unemployed people. It therefore followed that constructive job provision was only possible if one followed the Gandhian prescription, namely to design work to develop modes of production which fitted into the actually existing conditions in terms of capital availability relative to labour availability. In other words: systematic development of technologies cheap enough in terms of capital to give the chance of work to everybody.

5. Rural Based

As stated earlier, to Gandhi political independence was merely 'the first step' towards the attainment of real independence : ie social, moral and economic independence in terms of India's seven hundred thousand villages as distinct from its cities and towns. In a document which has become known as his 'Last Will and Testament' he provided a guideline to his followers to follow the *Sarvodaya* (Welfare of All) Movement for the uplifting of the villages. Quoting Gandhi 'You cannot build non--violence on a factory civilisation, the economy which I conceived eschews exploitation, because exploitation is the essence of violence. You have to be rural minded before you can be nonviolent......' Schumacher described him as a nonviolent social revolutionary.

Schumacher said: 'The grand objective of the *Sarvodaya* Movement as conceived by Gandhi and pursued by his followers was the total reconstruction of society. This meant that the village would become the basic unit of politics, economy and society. In such a unit agriculture would remain the basic industry but other small scale village industries using the most modern technology where it did not conflict with human needs would be developed. In short Gandhi's dream was to develop a decentralised economy in which each basic unit would be self-sufficient in meeting its main material needs – food, clothing and housing.'

Schumacher regretted that the Government of India in the post-independence period did not pay much heed to the Gandhian dream and sought to develop India as a modern, industrialised nation state. Though India was on the way to becoming the tenth largest industrial state, Schumacher thought it remained a predominantly rural based agricultural economy.

Despite the fact that almost 80% of the Indian people lived in the villages, no proper attention was given to improving the quality of life and creating employment opportunities in rural areas. As a result there was a large migration of people in search of employment from the rural areas to the cities where they only swelled the ranks of the slum dwellers. The only way to reverse this trend and save the villages of India from perishing was to create small village industries with the help of appropriate technology, thought Schumacher.

Big city-based industries and mass production methods destroyed the productive capacity of the rural inhabitants and robbed them of their means of livelihood. Citing an example of how villages had been deprived of their employment opportunity, Schumacher said: 'Once the paddy grown in the village was hand pounded in the village itself and consumed by the villagers, the surplus being sent to the nearest town or area where there was a shortage. Now all the paddy grown is taken by improved means of transport to the rice mills in a large city where it is pounded and sent back to the villages infected with all kinds of diseases. 'The village workers have lost their jobs and the net result remains the same, if not worse. What ought to have been done is to introduce improved paddy threshing equipment in the village itself.' 'Unless we put all the able-bodied young men and women to productive use in the villages it would not be possible to pull India out of the massive poverty in which it finds itself,' said Schumacher and quoted Gandhi as follows:

'If we tap all our resources, I am quite sure, we can again be rich, which we were I suppose at one time. We can repeat the phenomenon if we profitably occupy the idle hours of the millions.'

'To occupy the idle hours of the millions' was the most serious challenge facing a country like India, said Schumacher and added that no country could develop without letting the people work. The greatest deprivation that anyone could suffer was to have no chance of making a livelihood. He questioned the wisdom of maintaining an educational system with 50 million people in primary school, 15 million in secondary school and roughly 1/2 million in institutions of higher learning unless at the end of the pipeline there was something for them to do. One way to occupy the idle hours of the millions in the village of India was to embark upon self–help projects.

Giving an example of self–help, he said 'One of the greatest teachers of India, Lord Buddha, included in his teaching, the obligation of every good Buddhist to plant and see to the establishment of one tree every year for five years running. This in five years would give 2,000 million trees. The economic value of such an enterprise, intelligently conducted, would be greater than anything promised by five–year plans. It would produce foodstuffs, fibres, building materials, shade, water – in fact almost anything that is ready needed. And all this would have been done without a penny of foreign exchange and very little investment.'

According to Schumacher, Gandhi identified himself completely with the naked, hungry, starving millions of India and fought all his life to improve their lot. This is evident from the advice he gave to his followers which is know as 'Gandhi's Talisman.'

'Whenever you are in doubt, or when self becomes too much with you, apply the following test: recall the face of the poorest and the weakest person you may have seen, and ask yourself if the step you contemplate is going to be of any use to that person. Will that person gain anything by it? Will it restore that person's control over his or her own life and destiny? In other words, will it lead to *Swaraj* for the hungry and starving millions? Then you will find doubts and self melting away.'

This *talisman* is a challenge even today to all the decision makers of Gandhi's India.

Robert Hart

Gandhi and the Greens : Road to Survival

At this lost critical period in the history of the World humanity's only ultimate hope for survival lies in a worldwide movement for grassroots reconstruction on Gandhian lines.

Dr. Robert Muller, former Assistant Secretary-General of the United Nations and Chancellor Emeritus of the University for Peace in Costa Rica, wrote in 1993: "From all perspectives - scientific, political, social, economic and ideological - humanity finds itself in the kindergarten of an entirely new age: the global, interdependent, universal age, an incredibly promising age, a truly quantum jump, a cosmic event of the first importance that is perhaps unique in the universe .... Like it or not, this new age we are entering will be an age of communities and of co-operation."[1]

This vision accords with the great Constructive Programme that lay behind all Gandhi's activities. All the tribulations and suffering, which humanity is experiencing today, must be seen as the birth-throes of a new age of peace, justice, freedom and relative abundance, of which Gandhi had the audacity and incredible optimism to formulate a blueprint.

The keynote of Gandhi's system was *Sarvodaya,* a Sanskrit word meaning "welfare of all," which he coined after reading Ruskin's *Unto this Last*. It signified that the system was intended to fulfill the needs of every human being on a basis of complete equality, rather than the wealth and power of the few. While Gandhi's primary concern was with his own nations he made it quite clear that his system was also applicable to humanity as a whole.

The Constructive Programme sprang from the very core of Gandhi's philosophy of non-violence. Unlike other national liberators who used violent means to free their people from alien oppression, Gandhi saw independence, *Swaraj,* as an essentially positive concept. It involved the holistic development of the Indian nations with all its potentialities, talents and resources. A redeemed India, he believed, would bless the whole world, including the people of the oppressive power. In 1925 he wrote: "The constructive programme is the truthful and non-violent way of winning swaraj; it is designed to build up the nation from the very bottom."[2]

"Building from the bottom" meant forming small, democratic, exemplary groups of dedicated people as cells of a new body politic. Gandhi himself founded a number of such cells in the form of semi-monastic communities of a traditional Hindu type, or *ashrams*. The best known of these *ashrams* was that at Sevagram, where Gandhi habitually resided. It has been described as "a place of hope; a community where initiative and originality were fostered and where creative minds and hands were at work. In Sevagram men and women were not ashamed to speak of their ultimate goal as nothing less than 'the Kingdom of God within us and on earth.[3]'"

Gandhi occupied a small clay thatched hut, open to the weather, in the middle of a field. Among those who resided at Sevagram were an Indian princess, the daughter of a British admiral, the retired chief of one of the warlike tribes of the North-West Frontier, and a retired minister of state. All participated in the most menial tasks and all ate together, Gandhi himself preparing and serving the meals. Relations between men and women were completely natural but non-physical. When night came, all lay down to sleep where they wished, indoors or out-of-doors, some on a roof terrace in the middle of an orange-grove. Gandhi had a high regard for women, whom he regarded as "the better half of humanity."

The primary aim of all Gandhi's *ashrams* was to train social workers who would propagate his principles and practices in the surrounding villages and set as models of creative, non-violent living. Each trainee was required to take a number of vows: non-possession of material goods, apart from tools and other personal necessities; non-recognition of barriers between caste, class, race, colour or religion; simple living with abstention from all luxuries, and wearing only of *khadi*, handwoven cotton cloth. Training included periods of religious devotion and daily 33-minute sessions of silent, meditative spinning. The principal work comprised some form of manual Bread Labour, a concept which Gandhi derived from Tolstoy, who believed that it was the duty of each individual as far as possible, to provide his or her basic necessities by his or her own hands. Thus the individual would avoid being a burden on others, while acquiring concentration, precise thinking and strength of will by constructive work.

In the wider sphere of his all-embracing vision of the future of humanity, Gandhi envisaged the small, democratic, self-sustaining community as the basic unit of the new world order.

Gandhi's preferred model for such a unit was the traditional Indian village community, with its *panchayat*, an elected administrative body of five, which was responsible for all matters which concerned the village as a whole, such as irrigation and road building. The community was almost completely self-sufficient in basic necessities. In the early 19th century a British official, Sir Charles Metcalfe, reported: "The village communities are little republics having nearly everything they want within themselves and almost independent of foreign relations. They seem to last where nothing else lasts. The union of the village communities each one forming a separate little State in itself ... is in a high degree conducive to their happiness, and to the enjoyment of a great portion of freedom, and independence".[4]

This was the system which Gandhi wished to see revived. In contrast to the Marxist ideal of a "withering away of the State", Gandhi proposed a "Scattering of the State" that is, a decentralised distribution of State functions among India's 700,000 villages. Every village, he believed, should grow its own food and cotton for its own cloth, and contain a number of small workshops or factories, thus providing full, cooperative employment for all its inhabitants.

All goods which the village could not produce itself should be obtained, as far as possible from the immediate neighbourhood. This was in accord with Gandhi's doctrine of *swadeshi*. This concept, which has often been misunderstood and misinterpreted as implying a very unGandhian narrowness of outlook, simply means that a human being's first duty must be to her or his family or neighbours. This does not exclude the wider world. The individual or group can be seen as the mid-point of a series of concentric circles, indicating the biological entities – family, extended family, clan, tribe, nation and humanity as a whole – to which duties are owed. "Gandhi would patiently explain as he explained in one of his prefaces to his booklet, about the constructive programme that *swadeshi* seemed to him a necessary part of a truly universal outlook. There could be no genuine care for the welfare of humanity as a whole without a care for the well-being of one's own neighbours and neighbourhood".[5]

Gandhi called himself an Indian Nationalist but he was not a "racist". His patriotism was wholly constructive: a warm and unselfish love for the common people of India and an appreciation of the unique value of Indian tradition and culture to the whole world. His positive patriotism had no trace of negative feelings towards people of other races, even those who oppressed and exploited his own nation. In the last phase of his life, he strove with all his might to instil mutual tolerance and respect between Hindus and the people of the new state of Pakistan, even though, as a loyal citizen of India, he deeply deplored the dismemberment of his beloved homeland

Gandhi believed that every organic community, from the village to the nation, should strive to be self-sufficient in basic necessities, as competition for natural resources can lead to conflict and war. Self-sufficiency is an insurance against exploitation and victimisation by market forces. The individual, family or group can enjoy freedom for development, while avoiding being a parasitic drag on exporting countries, which, in many cases, sacrifice much of their best land in order to satisfy the needs of others, Also, exporters may be motivated by greed, as were the owners of Manchester cotton mills who tried to monopolise the Indian textile trade in the 19th and early 20th centuries. It was in answer to this threat of economic domination that Gandhi habitually carried a spinning–wheel and urged his followers to wear *khadi*.

The spinning-wheel, which was Gandhi's constant companion, symbolised not only self-sufficiency and Bread Labour but also his opposition to the big machines of industry which displace human labour and lead to the concentration of power and wealth in the hands of a few. He was not, however, opposed to small, labour-saving devices which could be assembled, worked and maintained by the average villager. It was in response to his pleas for the development of such machines that E. F. Schumacher established the Intermediate Technology Group in London. The spinning-wheel also stood for religious meditation, as Gandhi found its rhythmic movements were a stimulus to constructive thought.

Gandhi saw the self-sufficient community as the best matrix for the holistic development of human beings, allowing them to realise their full potentialities, physical, intellectual, emotional and spiritual. Unlike the fragmented conditions which are forced on those whose economic activities are divorced from their homes and social lives, the self-sufficient village allows its inhabitants to enjoy a wide variety of useful, constructive, co-operative activities which are beneficial to them all. They control almost every detail of their own lives, and thus practice a far truer and more basic form of democracy – comparable to that of the Greek *polis* – than that experienced by those who live under systems of "representative government." They are also able to enjoy diets consisting largely of fresh, home-grown food, with all its health-giving vitality unimpaired, rather than the stale denatured products of distant farms and factories.

An economy designed, on Gandhi's principle of *sarvodaya,* to satisfy the whole needs of whole human beings, must inevitably involve full employment for all. Workers are not restricted by the availability or non-availability of "cash," but are free to develop all sides of their natures in satisfying the multifarious needs of progressive human beings.

The creative, responsible life of a Gandhian-type community also provides a constructive answer to the problem of the "population explosion." Villagers do not feel obliged to have large families to support them in later life, as the community is a mutual-support system. Also, they do not wish to burden their friends and neighbours with excessive mouths which they may have difficulty in feeding.

In his vision of a new order for India and the world, Gandhi as far as possible ruled out compulsion or force in any form. In place of military or police forces he envisaged a *Shanti Sena*, a Peace Army, a body of highly trained and disciplined men and women, who would express the 'military virtues' of courage and devotion to duty (which Gandhi highly respected) in dealing with crime and disorder by non-violent means.

Gandhi's Constructive Programme was an expression of the precise and practical metaphysical system, derived from the Vedanta and the New Testament, which he called *Satyagraha,* Holding to the Truth. The Higher Truth, as he saw it, was God's design for a cosmic order dedicated to peace, justice, freedom and self-fulfilment for every living being, and God's main instrument for the working out of that Design was the Law of Love.

The basis of *satyagraha* was absolute and uncompromising monotheism, the undeviating conviction that, behind all the apparent conflicts of the material world, lies a single Supreme Power whose loving nature is expressed in the Cohesive Principle which maintains the form and unity of the galaxies, of the atom and of the living cell and which upholds the stability of organic communities, both in nature and among human beings. Wars and other conflicts arise because God allows a measure of freedom to His creation – freedom to deny himself and strive to wreck His designs in the interests of personal power, malice and greed. However, humanity must inevitably be forced sooner or later, by suffering, to realise that true happiness lies only in obedience to God's Law of Mutual Aid.

Two of Gandhi's living disciples who have done much to put the principles and forms of the Constructive Programme into practice are Murlidhar Devidas Amte of India and Ahangamage Tudor Ariyaratne of Sri Lanka. Both have great practical creative achievements to their credit, in the Gandhian tradition, which serve as living models for a New World Order.

The monumental legacy of Amte, his wife Sadhana and their family to the world is Anandwan, with its offshoots Ashokwan, Somnath and Hemalkasa, near Warora in Maharashtra, a great complex of farms, gardens, orchards, clinics, workshops, schools, and even a theatre, where those suffering from leprosy and other severely handicapped people, as well as aborigines, receive treatment and training in useful skills.

In the Anandwan complex, the total welfare of human beings, some of the most afflicted on earth, takes absolute precedence over every other consideration. If there is a "privileged class," it is that of people with the greatest need. No one is ever turned away; everyone is made to feel wanted and respected. This ethos gets to the root of the most painful symptom of leprosy, the greatest impediment to recovery: the sense of being unwanted and despised. Every patient is taught a useful skill. Following the recent earthquake in East-Central India, Dr. Vikas Amte, Murlidhar's eldest son, took a party of highly skilled building workers, all affected by leprosy to the devastated zone to erect specially designed earthquake-proof homes. In 1964 Anandwan patients constructed a university college for the neighbouring town, with provision for 1400 students.

All the Anandwan components are largely self-sufficient in necessities. Facilities include printing presses, a flour mill, a dairy, an agricultural seed farm, an engineering shop, a lamp factory, a tailoring shop, a cobbler's shop which specialises in footwear for patients with deformed feet and a carpenter's shop which makes all the beds and operating tables for the hospitals. Experiments are being made with Appropriate Technology devices and a forest garden is being established with 25,330 trees.

In 1993 Amte wrote: "At Anandwan we, outcasts living with outcasts, have built a world which embraces all who wish to join. A world where you do not stand alone, where you belong to others who belong to you. Where those rejected by an unconcerned and uncomprehending world realise their own worth with their own hands[6]."

Both Amte and his family see their great enterprise, inspired by compassion and geared to total human fulfilment rather than money and power, as a blueprint for a regenerated India, in line with Gandhi's Constructive Programme. Amte envisages an India in which "every area should be developed, using its own resources and in a manner relevant to its own conditions and problems. Clusters of villages with similar economies, similar resources and societies should be developed indigenously with one centre for every cluster. This centre should develop a stencil which everyone should copy."[7]

A similar comprehensive vision, with implications for the whole world, inspires the remarkable achievements of A. T. Ariyaratne, whose *Sarvodaya Shramadana* movement embraces 8,000 villages and six million people in Sri Lanka. By adopting the word *Sarvodaya* Ariyaratne declared his debt to Gandhi; *Shramadana* is a Singhalese word meaning "sharing of human energy."

The movement started in 1958 when Ariyaratne, then science master at a leading Colombo school, led a party of fellow-masters and pupils in the establishment of a work-camp to help the inhabitants of a deprived village. The group settled in the village for a while and helped its inhabitants to build a school, craft-centre and sanitary system, sink a number of wells, and improve their farming methods. This gesture of solidarity between the lowest and highest strata of Sri Lankan society, in which the intellectual has great prestige, led to the establishment of *Shramadana* camps in many parts of the island. Well balanced teams of experts and unskilled labourers work together to restore the villages' traditional self-sufficiency in basic necessities. These Ariyaratne identifies as freedom from poverty, clean and beautiful environment, an adequate supply of pure water, adequate shelter and clothing, a balanced diet, primary health care, basic energy and communication facilities, all-round education and opportunities for cultural and spiritual development.

Before the teams start work, "family gatherings" are held to allow all participants to get to know each other and to ascertain the villagers' most urgent needs. In an article in *Ceres*, the organ of the U.N. Food and Agricultural Organisation, Ariyaratne wrote: "Shramadana camps are the places where the young and old, the educated and illiterate, the privileged and the forgotten, all meet and serve one another as equals. The *shramadana* volunteers ... identify themselves with the traditional culture of the community and ... do not impose their will on the people ... The camp, with its songs and dances, work and study, truly becomes the ideal human family in microcosm, where self-fulfilment and joy of living become a reality...This type of experience, sometimes knee-deep in mud, brings about a new awareness."[8]

In a speech at the presentation to him of Japan's Niwano Peace Prize in 1992, Ariyaratne explained the worldwide significance of his efforts and aims. "The *Sarvodaya* objectives" he said, "is to create a society that is neither rich nor poor, where every individual, family and community is awakened to a more contented, peaceful and just life. These small units should be the fundamental human groups that should build a new, just and nonviolent world society. . . . The decisive factor in building such a society is the mutuality and the community that the people build to manage themselves, their resources and the environment. . . ."

"*Sarvodaya*. . . . has proved in practice that self-reliance, community participation and community self-development can be utilized to satisfy the most pressing needs of rural communities without destroying their spiritual, moral and cultural values. Sustainable development can become a reality only if we promote the development model, building from the bottom up. . . ."

"Now the time has come when science and technology on the one hand and spiritual wisdom an the other have to be synthesised on a global scale to build a nobler, more content, just and peaceful global community."[9]

The most effective system for achieving Gandhi's ideal of local sufficiency in basic necessities is the homegarden or forest garden, a very intensive form of multilayered cultivation in imitation of the natural forest which is found in many parts of the tropics. The Indian state in which there is the densest concentration of forest gardens is Kerala, which has had a succession of Gandhian-socialist governments since 1957, and in which there is a high degree of equitable land distribution. The Keralese forest garden is a very efficient and sustainable system of traditional agroforestry, characterised by a wide diversity of crops. This diversity is a deliberate strategy, designed to ensure continuity of supplies throughout the year as well as resistance to pests and diseases. Much of the state's industry is geared to the processing of forest garden crops, such as fruit, rubber, timber, herbs, nuts and vegetables.

With its systems of production for human need rather than profit, with its traditions of religious tolerance and social justice, high rate of literacy, quality of life and respect for women's rights, Kerala is widely regarded as a model worth studying by all who are striving for a people-centred world order on Gandhian lines.

In today's world generally Gandhi's truest political heirs are the Greens. Significantly the Green Parties of Eastern Europe are credited with being largely responsible for the great wave of non-violent People Power from 1989 onwards, which led to the overthrow of the Communist regimes and the end of the Cold War.

The Green Parties, with their intense concern for the infinitely serious environmental problems which threaten the very existence of all life, are the truest parties of survival.

The policy of the British Green Party, as stated in its European Election Manifesto, 1994 is firmly based on the Gandhian principle of *Sarvodaya*. "A Green economy promotes security and cooperation. We want economic policies based on production for human need, not on private profit, regardless of the exploitation of people and the environment."

In its constant emphasis on regional development combined with considerable degrees of self-sufficiency rather than centralised control and marketing the Green

Party also follows Gandhi's doctrine of *swadeshi.* The European Manifesto states: "Both in Europe and worldwide we need diverse, self-reliant local and regional economies which enable communities to meet most of their own needs locally. Strong local economies are less vulnerable than centralised ones to the fluctuations of global markets, and can guarantee basic economic security for all ..."

"Greens believe that the basis unit of democracy should be the region. Our objective is a European confederation of culturally diverse and economically self-reliant regions. Decision-making will be brought as close as possible to the people."

The last quotation shows that one of the Greens' reasons for supporting *swadeshi* is in line with Gandhi's assertion that higher degrees of democracy are possible where units are relatively small and decentralised. Another reason echoes Gandhi's opposition to big machines and over-elaborate technologies that pollute the environment. "Green policies encourage localised, rewarding production, making the best use of environmentally-friendly and socially-responsible technologies...

The Green Party is committed to using energy more efficiently, and to encouraging local production from renewable sources."

Another very important reason for promoting *swadeshi* – one that goes to the very root of human well-being – is its effect on nutrition. The European Manifesto says: "The excessive transporting and unnecessary processing of foods including irradiation, will be discouraged ... As far as possible, food needs should be met locally by fresh, organic food, and poorer areas must be helped to develop greater self-sufficiency in food rather than dependency on imports."

Greens are acutely aware of the threats to the environment posed by the internal combustion engine. This, too, leads to a *swadeshi* emphasis: "Our aim is to make transport greener and to reduce the total amount of transport required. This can be done by providing more of what people need closer to their homes."

The Scottish Green Party, in *A Rural Manifesto for the Highlands,* paints a detailed and extremely attractive picture of a redeemed forest economy to be developed for the sake of full employment and the whole interests of whole human beings – physical, intellectual, emotional and spiritual. Profoundly practical the principal aim of the "Greenprint" is stated to be to build up a sustainable land-use economy, with "local communities managing the total natural resource for their own benefit, providing... maximum potential for diversification." Intensively managed, the great new Highland Forest would yield up to its human population a great wealth and diversity of products as well as providing an incomparably more hospitable micro-climate and environment than presently afforded by the bleak and windswept moor. Its resources would include an enormous range of tree and shrub species, providing a correspondingly great range of food, fuels timber, industrial, craft and medicinal products. Agroforestry enterprises are envisaged: "a great deal of fruit growing would be integrated into the forest itself. In thinned forests fruit bushes would be the understorey and fruit trees interplanted amongst suitable wild trees. All would benefit naturally from the protection and fertilization of the forest trees."

A number of small industries and crafts could be established, it is suggested, to take advantage of the enormous stocks of timber that would become available. One can envisage sawmills surrounded by rings of satellite workshops, manufacturing tools, boats, furniture, paper, musical instruments and many other products. Energy could be provided by the abundant wind, water and biomass resources locally available. Summing up the programme, the writer affirms: "And so the forest economy could be created, transforming one of Europe's most severely ecologically and economically disadvantaged regions into one of great prosperity and beauty; one of lasting ecological and social stability."

A form of *swadeshi* which has caught the imagination of many environmentalists in the West in recent years is Bioregionalism. A bioregion may be defined as a natural area, integrated by land-form, climate or cultures which has traditionally constituted the main life-support system for a city, town or rural district. Examples include the watersheds of rivers and the 'green belts' round cities such as London. An interesting recent attempt to create a bioregional organisation in the Greater London area is Bioregional Surrey, which is largely the brainchild of a man of Indian origin, Pooran Desai.

The aim of the organisation is stated to be "to revive and create appropriately scaled industries founded on sustainable land-use." Within the broad guideline of "local production for local consumption," and making use of modern science and technology, 'it is a model of development that integrates conservation, heritage and community." The aim is the creation of sustainable livelihoods in the South-East of England and, by example, to lead the way into the next century.

"Bioregionalism," it is stated, "is about 'down-to-earth' solutions i.e. working from land-based industries upwards – fostering self-reliance and accountability."

Among the benefits of bioregional development are said to be:

- "rebuilding of community, regional character and sense of place, often involving the revival of traditional industries based on locally-produced materials";
- "low environmental impact including decrease in the need for transportation";
- "recycling of materials rather then their removal and export";
- "generation of a local and regional economy more self-reliant and inherently stable than the international financial systems."

Among specific projects already envisaged are one for the production of charcoal and one for the production of natural fibres.[10]

For a number of years, farsighted Greens have been talking of a Post-Industrial Society. Industry is causing so much harm to the environment and so much human misery that it must, in time, be superseded by systems kinder to nature and humankind. Blueprints for such systems and the life-technologies which they must involve exist in Gandhi's Constructive Programme and the writings of many members of the Green movement. At the same time, models, exemplary cells, of a New World Order are to be found in many areas, especially in tropical areas where traditional forms of Agroforestry are practiced. By a combination of traditional multiple cropping systems with new methods evolved by Western ingenuity, especially forms of Alternative and Wood Technology, all basic human needs could be met. Such systems would be indefinitely sustainable and would not pollute the environment. On the contrary, they would enhance the environment, counteract the Greenhouse Effect and feed the human soul by their beauty. If executed in accordance with Gandhian principles and lifestyles, they would make possible unprecedented levels of all-round human fulfilment, health and happiness.

Notes and References

1. *A Source Book for the Community of Religions*, Joel D. Beversluis, Project Editor (Council for a Parliament of the World's Religions, Chicago, 1993) P. IX.

2. *Gandhi: His Gift of the Fight*, Jehangir P. Patel and Marjorie Sykes (Friends Rural Centre, Rasulia, India, 1987) p. 31.

3. *Gandhi: His Gift of the Fight*, p. 136.

4. *Ecosociety: A Historical Study of Ecological Man* by Robert A. de J. Hart (Natraj, Dehra Dun, 1984) p. 68.

5. *Gandhi: His Gift of the Fight*, p. 39.

6. *Forest Gardening* by Robert A. de J. Hart (Green Books, Hartland, Devon 1991) p. 136.

7. *Ecosociety* p. 136.

8. *Ecosociety* p. 74.

9. *Program for the Ninth Presentation Ceremony of Niwano Peace Prize*, Tokyo 1992, pp. 29, 35, 51.

10. *Bioregional Surrey* March 1993, obtainable from Sutton Ecology Centre, Carshalton, Surrey SM5 3NX.

Godric Bader

Trusteeship : The Transforming Ethic

It is the purpose of this chapter to encourage those in industry and those who have responsibility for our world's assets of the value and vital significance of Gandhi's principles of trusteeship as the transforming ethic for the next century. It attempts to inform readers of the origins of the idea of Trusteeship, what has been achieved, and the ideals, ideas and aspirations for its future. The words 'man' and the generalised 'he' refer to 'mankind' and not to gender.

Gandhi 'sought first to change India and then through her the world so that humankind may attain a collective liberation from injustice, inequality, exploitation and war. He strove to dispel fear, cowardice, inertia and heartlessness so that people could be fit instruments for changing the world and worthy citizens of the new order' (M.M.C., *Sarvodaya,* Sept 1994 p 40)

One, and I would submit the leading, way Gandhi believed change should and would be brought about was through the development of his concept of Trusteeship. Change is too mild a word for the achievements of Gandhi. It would be better to describe them as transformations, as Gandhi brought change by transforming consciousness, changing mindsets and raising human awareness.

Trusteeship essentially means having faith and confidence in a process of taking responsibility for assets and social values, and administering their rightful and creative usage for the benefit of others, now, and in coming generations. This has roots both in East and West. Sushila Gidwani, writing about corporate management strategy in *Gandhi Marg* (Nov-Dec 1985 p 653), states that 'trusteeship [means] preservation of economic power for the benefit of the society as a whole'.

It is not widely appreciated that Gandhi's basic commitment to non-violence for which he is probably best known extended well beyond direct conflict resolution to the very root causes of violence inherent and endemic in our present economic, social and industrial systems. He explains this as *Ahimsa,* non-injury in thought, word and deed to all forms of life; non-violation of another person's essence, (but *not* passive resistance as often translated in the West) and *Satyagraha* – militant action with concern for the opponent; truth-force; life force. (Further reading 1 and 2). 'It consists not only in non-cooperation with the social evil, but also in preparing others for that non-cooperation, and, above all, in effecting a change in the hearts of individuals responsible for that evil (*Gandhi Marg*. vol 10 no 3 July 1966 p 200. Dayal Saran Verma). Bharatan Kumarappa, in his Editor's note at the beginning of Gandhi's *For Pacifists* (Bombay 1949) says: 'Gandhi goes much deeper [than just being non-violent in the sense of pacifism] and sees that war cannot be avoided so long as the seeds of it remain in man's breast and grow and develop in his social, political and economic life'.

The splitting away of economics from moral philosophy – around the 17th century – and the consequent study of economics quite separately from its original ethical grounding, eventually resulted in both capitalist and Marxist economists propounding the existence of immutable scientific economic laws and concepts. We all now live in collapsing ecological and socio-economic systems based on post-Industrial Revolution developments motivated solely by gain and power, so it is not surprising that such systems are unable to reflect or sustain man's true needs, purpose and identity. If man is to evolve he has an essential need to release the Divine spirit and purpose. Gandhi yearned to provide an environment in which this could be achieved. Influenced by his time and education in the U.K., he gradually developed his ideas on Trusteeship.

Undoubtedly the inspiration for this great concept was his unfailing guide, The *Gita*, and that inner spirituality that continually led him back to this source. "I understood the *Gita* teaching of non-possession to mean that those who desired salvation should act like the trustee who, though having control over great possessions, regards not an iota of them as his own...... Words like *aparigraha* (non-possession) and *somabhava* (equability)", he said "gripped me". (*Gandhi Marg*. vol 10 no 3 July 1966 p 199. Dayal Saran Verma). He had also undoubtedly been influenced by his study of British jurisprudence, and the Christian ethic of stewardship moved him strongly.

Gandhi's understanding of Trusteeship is clearly then a principle of economic conscience, a dynamic model of the concept of economic organisation and moral imperatives. Yet Gandhi was no economic determinist – indeed he was opposed to determinism of all kinds. His Trusteeship does not provide a prescription for giving the fullest release of human energy in the economic system, nor is it a concrete analysis, providing optimum economic and social organisation, as Marxism and systems of state control, or capitalism, claim to do. (Further reading 3)

"My theory of Trusteeship is no makeshift, certainly no camouflage. I am confident it will survive all other theories. It has the sanction of philosophy and religion behind it. No other theory is compatible with Truth and Non-violence". (Mahatma Gandhi, *To a Gandhian Capitalist* Letters between M.K.G and Jamnalal Bajaj, p 10).

I see Trusteeship through Gandhi's eyes, as having the greatest ultimate strength and power because, through its basic spiritual truth, it is able to regenerate such moral and political energy that it will eventually overtake capitalism, socialism, and even the more recent developments, "socially responsible capitalism" and "democratic socialism" (both of which are now adopting elements of Trusteeship).

J.D. Sethi wrote in *The Awakening*, the monthly journal of Lok Sevak Sangh, (*Vol 1 No 2 Nov 1978*). "Of all Gandhiji's ideas and concepts, Trusteeship was the most original, as it was also the most tentative since he did not have time to experiment with it on a scale that would match the grandeur of the concept. He did not have time enough to define it precisely, not to speak of spelling out its full implications in concrete terms. Nevertheless he was laying firmly the principle for achieving something very big, a comprehensive system which would eliminate capitalism and bureaucratic statism.

Trusteeship rejects both the capitalist and communist systems as practised today, along with their respective ideologies. It claims to be a system, with its own ideology, different from that of capitalism and communism and is definitely based on participatory democracy. Trusteeship is a fraternal partnership between all factors of production who aim at achieving larger social benefit rather than work for a narrow economic objective such as profit."

Influence of Gandhian Values in Practice

One of the more significant attempts to promote Trusteeship was the launching of the Trusteeship Foundation in Bombay in early 1973. This was due to the inspiration of 'J.P.'. Jayaprakash Narayan was a very influential, revered figure throughout India. Originally a Marxist, he was convinced by Gandhi to support his views, for which he was jailed again by the British, before working in Congress with Nehru, but declined to be considered for President, and was "detained" by Indira Gandhi. The principal objective of the Trusteeship Foundation was, and is, to propagate the concept and ideal of Trusteeship as advocated by Gandhi. Eminent economists, industrialists, Trades Union leaders, social workers, and professionals have been associated with the work of this Foundation. The goals of the Foundation are:-

a) The ultimate aim is to introduce into our public life, and especially in the field of business and industry, the Gandhian concepts of self-discipline and non-exploitation and to propagate the idea that an enterprise be run with the consensus and participation of all the partners, such as Capital, Management and Labour. It is the Foundation's endeavour to bring the local community and the consumers into the process.

b) In view of the national need to increase production and productivity, to ensure millions of our countrymen freedom from want and the right to work, the Foundation aims at making every section of our society aware of its social responsibilities and to look at and solve our problems with the help of Gandhiji's insights.

c) To achieve the above aims, the Foundation will try to promote a continuous study of the concept by professionals, academicians, intellectuals, journalists and students of affairs.

The 'Specific Plan of Action' was:-

a) To set up Study Groups of economists, professionals and others to help promote conceptual clarity;

b) To help the Government and Legislators to draft, frame and promote an enabling legislation on trusteeship, so that those who wish to implement it in their units may be encouraged to do so;

c) To help evaluation by social scientists, social workers and professionals, of those units who wish to submit themselves to a social audit;

d) To help the existing or new units to implement the concept by working out different patterns and models and helping them through consultancy and training of personnel.

e) To educate public opinion through National Conferences, seminars, public meetings, discussions on T.V., radio and in the newspapers;

f) To bring together representatives of Capital, Management, Labour and Consumer at discussion meetings, study camps to consider the concept and work out the details with a view to help implementation in phases.

g) To publish newsletters, books, pamphlets etc. for dissemination of knowledge and information on the subject and world trends;

h) Lastly, to help industrial houses and units to express their social obligations and prepare project reports through rural area development projects, and to promote the necessary study and research.

Gandhi is quoted in one of the Trusteeship Foundation publications *Humanised Society through Trusteeship* (1973) as saying that everything belonged to God and was from God – therefore it was for His people as a whole and not for a particular individual. When an individual had more than his proportionate portion he became a Trustee of that portion for God's people.

J.P. had earlier concerned himself with the very practical Gandhian principles in industry by inviting George Goyder, a leading U.K. industrialist and author of *The Future of Private Enterprise* and *The Responsible Company* (the first of several books), to India in 1965 for a Conference opened by the then Prime Minister, Mr Shastri. J.P., in his key introductory speech responding to the P.M., said that Gandhi had hoped his 'theory and practice of Trusteeship might be a gift that India could make to the world'. The proceedings of the conference were recorded and published in book form in 1966 by Manaktalas of Bombay under the title *The Social Responsibilities of Business*. The book contains a photo-print of the hand-written amendments of Gandhi to a document enunciating the Fundamental Principles regarding Trusteeship, alongside those of Professor Dantwala (author of *Gandhism Reconsidered*). Reading them now one can understand how attempting to formulate the practical application of the principles was enormously difficult at that time.

Following Independence the forces of the old mind-sets relegated and scorned the principles of Trusteeship and Gandhi's hopes of decentralisation and building up village life, and were finally lost through Nehru's adoption of Western industrial practices.

Gandhi knew his ideas would be scorned after his death, but predicted that they would be relevant again in 30 or so years. Nehru found them practically and politically impossible to follow. (Further reading 4)

The Trusteeship Foundation of Bombay organised an International Conference in 1979 which resulted in the development of a small number of industrial companies who endeavour to live out Trusteeship. (see *Business India* Nov 5-18 1984, Special Report 2, p.96).

1985 saw a special issue of the magazine *Gandhi Marg* totally devoted to Trusteeship, reporting a three day seminar held at the Gandhi Peace Foundation from 29th November to 1st December. I will quote much of the introduction as it is not easy to find a copy. Commenting on India's mixed economy model of that time it says :-

"The Seminar examined at great length the philosophical, ideological and theoretical aspects of Trusteeship as propounded by Gandhi and his colleagues and comrades..... [it] threw up a lot of questions and doubts about the practicability of the idea of Trusteeship. ...it was not left to others to answer the questions [but the questioners] tried to answer them ... without losing faith in the idea itself. This is characteristically a Gandhian way of analysing problems.... The argument is that mixed economy [modern capitalist corporate structures and communist state-bureaucratic socialism] without any normative moral objectives attached to it can become a dangerous and corrupt pragmatism. The normative principles could only be those which are derived from Trusteeship. Even the third prevailing system or principle, i.e. of cooperatives, which both systems tried to absorb in their respective models, was weakened in its force and thrust.

There has been no pure economic model of management and ownership. Each model has its own mixture. Each had its own dominant paradigms..... On the other hand, a deliberately designed mixed economic model has been found to be the most difficult to handle because the mixture could not formulate clear cut alternative paradigms.

Nevertheless.....the idea of cooperatives comes nearest to Trusteeship and .... can be made a starting point of a great thrust towards a new economic system.....the cooperative principle should be applied wherever it is feasible to do so as a substitute for market capitalism or state socialism.

The main issues of crises of the prevailing modern systems are unemployment, concentration of economic power, alienation, exploitation and militarisation. Gandhi claimed Trusteeship was an answer to these problems......Both the capitalist and the communist nations are examples of heavy concentration of economic power by which a small minority exploits a vast majority.....Trusteeship can....break up the .....concentration of economic power.... Those who participate in production without any sense of greed for wealth or income are unlikely to suffer from alienation.

The basic philosophy of Trusteeship is that it does not have to await a situation when a full-scale model will or can be imposed. The overall Gandhian approach is that whatever is good does not have to wait. One step at a time is good enough. If taken by a large number of people it can have great impact......somebody has to [start. It can be] an individual.....a home, a school, a farm, an ashram, etc.....strengthening [and democratising] cooperatives, [*and new industrial*] *management techniques and reforms. Those who believe in Trusteeship have a responsibility to identify the reforms which may ultimately help the transformation of the existing system towards a new one*''. (My italics).

These last two sentences are particularly interesting as the World Business Academy, (and the Social Venture Network) has realised the importance of the ability of today's industry to transform existing systems. The World Business Academy is a predominantly American concern which works at a deep, fundamental level to encourage the apparent paradigm shift from the socio-economic system which takes no account of the people trapped within it, to a caring, viable, economic, value-driven global society, while its offshoot, The Social Venture Network, works at a more immediate level to achieve the same ambitions, aided by the academic work of the Society for Business Responsibility into the promotion of business ethics. The influence of Gandhi's Trusteeship is not obvious, until you come to look at the principles which inspired the W.B.A.: ''the modern world undergoing a period of fundamental transformation, the extent and meaning of which we who are living through it are only beginning to grasp.......the role of business in that transformation is absolutely crucial'' (Willis Harman *Why is there a World Business Academy?*). The W.B.A. outlines some of the modern tendencies, the concept of work as life enhancing, not a market commodity, with businesses dedicated less to financial goals than to fulfilling work, smaller and more informal, alternative economics and emphasis on cooperative global developments, recognition of the disbenefits of vicious competition, and the support of values and incentives which foster ecological care and consideration.

Sethi continued on what is becoming another concern of companies in the current decade, that of social accountability. The R.S.A. have formulated a Network to enquire into ''Tomorrow's Company''. One of the Work Groups focus on ''Ownership and Governance'' issues has endeavoured to clarify their views on the company and the 'stakeholder' issue. Michael Nisbet's draft of their thinking states: ''A company, in the sense of a business, has several characteristics. It is a private enterprise for profit, and it is a community of people with a purpose, and it is an institution in society. It earns its revenue from customers who can (usually) choose to take their custom elsewhere. It seeks to add more value to the resources it buys than the cost incurs of adding such value – when it doesn't it is a drain on society. In the face of such competition (i.e. alternatives) through time, the company is like a living system, striving to survive and justify the use of resources. It undertakes its activities in the context of society. Its collective behaviours flow from the actions and mindsets of its owners, its managers and employees, and the members of that society...."

...'stakeholders' are those with direct or contractual connections with the Company - owners, customers, employees (and suppliers and lenders). Relationship with the community and the environment are best reflected in the 'corporate citizenship' approach, whereby the actions of the company are like those of a responsible and active citizen, but no more than an active citizen".

Whilst clearly such a statement is typically cautious and still a far cry from a Trusteeship conception, it is now admitting a Company is not an activity totally in its own right. Other Work Groups in the R.S.A.'s Network are looking at the Company as a "Living System", "Employees as People", "Ethics", "Measures of Success", and examining the social auditing, that companies such as Traidcraft U.K., B.S.O.-Origin-Holland, Sparekassen Nordjylland Sbn Bank of Denmark (Ethical Accounting Statements 1993), and others are now pursuing. Even conventional company auditing (supported by E.C. directives) is now requiring certain social reporting criteria, such as the extent of workforce participation.

The *Gandhi Marg* "Introduction" is noteworthy for recording Trusteeship as requiring such practices. He wrote: "Along with this widening participation, another reform needed is the social accountability of the enterprises. For this, maximum horizontal autonomy will have to be provided to the enterprise. The business community has resisted outside inspection but it can no longer escape the challenge of finding a way for establishing and accepting their responsibility to the society as consumers. Otherwise the society can take them over through the state or some other coercive mechanism. Some kind of social auditing is necessary. This will require a large number of honest, dedicated and competent technical people. This too is not an easy exercise, but, once begun, it can generate its own momentum, given the purpose. It is dangerous to believe that there are not enough honest men in society."

Society is unlikely now to "take them over but there are increasingly coercive legal requirements and regulators" to curb exploitative practices. "Are there enough honest men?", Sethi asks, and this is now a leading question (highlighted by the Cadbury Report, a study undertaken by Sir Adrian Cadbury to bring ethics into plc's and the city,) which points up the absolutely crucial and fundamental necessity of Basic Education, a pre-requisite of Trusteeship, the keystone of Gandhi's building. Sethi continues: "Workers' education through their own organisations lies at the root of..... reforms. Workers have to be educated not only about others but about themselves and their trades union. Without proper education..... their participation in management and ownership can become a source of corruption and greed [and they] can be easily manipulated. Trades union leaders who have developed vested interests in the existing system .... are bound to resist reforms. That is no reason for postponing the training..... Reforms will ultimately come only through the growing consciousness of the workers. If the so-called proletarian consciousness has not developed anywhere according to the Marxian model, it is because the proletariat has not been educated about their responsibility as a class to society and the need to resist vested interests within their own ranks and leaders."

Summing up this need for in-depth, if not "soul force" education of those with responsibilities over the workforce and the Trades Union, Sethi states: "the producers and those who analyse the economic situation, i.e. the economists and those who make policies [directors, managers, pension fund managers, investment/shareholder groups, etc.] and bureaucrats, all have to listen to the voice of their conscience before their self-interest. That is why it was said that Trusteeship has to be a *Satyagraha* or a movement towards invoking conscience of those who are involved in the system."

To complete the quotations from Sethi's introduction, the penultimate paragraph contained a reference to the land problems. "The participants in the Seminar said that they were not clear how Trusteeship could be applied in rural societies. Gandhi had made it absolutely clear that Trusteeship was a principle of universal application. The commune system in China was in a sense an example of Trusteeship. However, because it worked within a dictatorial political system and lacked the voluntary component, it lost its political force as it became an instrument in the hands of the leaders who held the political monopoly and power. [The same thing happened in Yugoslavia.] (Further reading 5) The principle of cooperative farming as against collective or individual farming is .... nearest to Trusteeship. Another important principle of Trusteeship is to organise and make the rural society responsible for health, education, and sanitation for which no-one seems responsible today. All these experiments can be started at any place and at any time."

The work in particular of the Intermediate Technology Development Group and the Plunkett Foundation (an agricultural co-operative movement started by Horace Plunkett over 70 years ago) has taken this direction, with a more holistic concern for the land.

The foundation of the Scott Bader Commonwealth Ltd was the direct result of the restructuring of an industrial manufacturing company towards the realisation of Trusteeship principles, founded in 1951 by Ernest Bader and his family. Professor Fred Blum, who studied S.B.C.W. for a number of years in the 60s, and wrote the first book on the company (*Work and the Community, The S.B.C.W and the Quest for a New Social Order*), says: "Whoever will make a real breakthrough by using modern technology within an organisation which will foster man's development and make work part of a meaningful life will have found the key to the new order..... The S.B.C.W must be seen in this perspective." (*Humanised Society through Trusteeship, Trusteeship Foundation publication, 1973*)

Ernest Bader was a Swiss emigre who preferred the freedom and wider horizons in England in 1912, and after marrying Dora Scott in 1915 founded Scott Bader Co Ltd in London in 1920 to import Swiss celluloid, later expanding into synthetic resins. Ernest Bader had become a Quaker and, as a contribution to making a less violent world, stimulated by the influence of Gandhian non-violence, he and his family gifted the company into a Trusteeship in 1951, forming a cooperative common-ownership company. Two previous attempts to develop a value-driven company had failed, but due principally to the influence of George Goyder OBE and the writings of Wilfred Wellock, restructuring took place and trusteeship for the previously privately owned company developed.

To illustrate the inspiration of Quaker concern the minute of Social Witness in 1944 is exemplary:

'Deep in each human soul lies the seed of the eternal divine life. Its flowering to the glory of God is the aim and purpose of man's being.... To all men [the resources of the world] are given, to all men in common ownership they belong, and although these resources may be administered by particular individuals, groups or nations, any system which limits their availability for all men and women, regardless of colour and creed, is hindering Christian fellowship and the divine order.... No man is a 'hand' to be kept in or thrown out of the economic life of the community as suits the needs of any system. The community is a system wherein each man and woman should find a place of significant service and creative living. All are members, all share in the duty and should enjoy the right of helping to determine its policies, whether political or economic, industrial or social. For its foundations rest on a democracy based on the brotherhood of man and drawing its reality from the Fatherhood of God.'

In 1965 the S.B.C.W. had the singular pleasure and recognition to be visited by J.P. who had been following the developments at Scott Bader with interest. I had the privilege, through friends in the Trusteeship Foundation, of meeting J.P. again, when he was under house arrest by Indira Gandhi in Bombay in 1977.

It is interesting to read Wilfred Wellock's booklet *Gandhi as a Social Revolutionary* (1950). Essentially it is the report of a conference in India in 1949, which should have involved Gandhi, but was postponed following his assassination. Some of the thinking and wording appears in the preamble to the S.B.C.W. constitution: "We must ask ourselves to what extent violence resides in the demands we make upon the earth's resources by reason of our self-indulgent existence, and what is to be our own personal contribution to the realisation of peace". (Further reading 6)

Writers in *Gandhi Marg* (Nov-Dec 1986), notably Kahil Gilbran and Shan Turnbull, see the Mondragon Co-operatives in Spain also practising Trusteeship principles. Hopefully more Trusteed Companies will develop as, in our current predatory industrial society, these courageous attempts to challenge present practice are under intense pressure to conform with conventional industry and need the encouragement of new Trusteeships. (Further reading 7)

Gandhi was aware of this risk and for this reason considered what he called Basic Education to be a fundamental building block. Wellock (*Gandhi as a Social Revolutionary,* p 21) describes it as follows: "Basic Education is a way of life, a method of learning and living, of learning through living, an art which ought to begin on the day of birth – even before – and continue until death."

Mondragon has been helped by its early schooling through the founder Father Arizmendi, who started a training college. S.B.C.W. has not yet achieved a learning centre, but has made many attempts at raising the awareness of its members to their responsibilities and Commonwealth purposes. Learning organisations are now the vogue, an attempt by 'leading edge' companies to deal with the highly turbulent pressures in commercial life, although not yet developing Trusteeship principles, but becoming aware of their wider 'stakeholder' responsibilities.

The Future

What are the prospects of seeing the World's resources held in common for the peoples of our planet?

We are finding ourselves now in the closing decades of the 20th century in great need of remotivation by ethical principle. Trusteeship provides just such an ethic, and it is vitally necessary that those who are aware of Gandhi's principle strive to pursue his unfinished task. *Sarvodaya* (September 1994), (quoted above) mentions a Save Freedom Movement dedicated to the purpose of continuing Gandhi's transforming work as the best way to celebrate Gandhi's 125th anniversary. Unhappily 'M.M.C.' considers the national committee constituted by the Indian Government to celebrate this occasion to be, in its manner, purpose and constitution, "nothing but an affront to the memory of Gandhiji."

Apart from India, where there are many stalwart workers, consciences are being stirred across the world. Ethics are being taught in business schools. Market economics, currency speculation, soil vitality, air pollution, the destruction of historic social cultures and marginalisation of human relationships are all under intense discussion in the media and elsewhere. The continuing violence to the human condition and its environment is being challenged, but often the answer is to apply further violence as a restraint.

Possibly even more insidious, as Gandhi would have seen it, is the violence which results from the pressure for more intensive growth via capitalism and the many forms of privatisation. The real fact of economic life is that the world's resources, (notably fossil fuels, minerals, and the land, dependent on sun, rain and wind), are the seed-corn of the future, which must be husbanded, recycled, and replaced, as one conserves capital, not expended as income. This world-wide headlong rush for economic gain by many business men still blinded to these facts is sadly also being pursued in India, and the likelihood of change, sufficient to introduce Trusteeship, now looks increasingly distant. The forces of multi-national businesses are rapacious in forest destruction, decimation of fish stocks, and the earth's raw material resources in India as much as elsewhere on the planet. Nonetheless, if human life is to continue and become sustainable, the irreversible violation and degradation of our water, soil, flora and fauna has to stop, and the adoption of the Trusteeship principle on a local basis has to be urgently inaugurated on a global scale. Every country is now involved. I believe that Trusteeship is the only way that is able to provide a viable way out of these impasses for either the developed or developing countries on any kind of sustainable basis. Quakers, who had strong links with Gandhi, made a statement recently in Canada containing these words: "To base an economic system on self-interest is fundamentally contrary to the teachings of all the great spiritual leaders of the world." (*Marilyn Manser, CFSC, 1993*).

It is now abundantly demonstrated that neither the capitalist nor the state socialist economies can create viable conditions for the people of the world, nor have they been able to help developing countries to determine their own destinies. Clearly both systems are still a far cry from giving material expression to the paramount need of the working out of the Divine Spirit in man. Currently it is seen that capitalism is on top in creating worldly goods and services, but only by undermining future resources, creating increasing pollution, widening the gap between rich and poor and unhealthily concentrating the wealth and power in fewer hands. The statement "living off the future inheritance of our children" sums it up. Endeavours through 'regulatory' forces, or wider shareholding in ever larger corporations, are largely ineffective. In many quarters a strong, morally driven, legal system is requested, but is sadly lacking in formulation. Until the moral motivation becomes one of holding man-made assets and world resources 'in trust', exploitations of man by man and of planet earth generation by generation will continue. Trusteeship can provide a way to avoid not just violence between humans but also between humans and their environment, and has to be the ethic for the next century.

Developments in Antarctica have had such a concept vaguely behind them. There has also been talk for a number of years that the U.N. should take responsibility for the incredible mineral wealth in the seabeds of the oceans. (See Brian Parkyn's letter to *The Independent* 09/11/94). Malta promoted the U.N. conference on the law of the sea, and the proposal that space, atmosphere and the sea bed should be seen as the common heritage of man.

J.P. wrote in *Humanized Society through Trusteeship* (p 28): "Wherefrom will come the motivation to work for a Trusteeship economy, and how can that motivation become a social force so as to be able to transform society?"

He went on to say "[in] the drive towards a Trustee economy, the pioneering and pathfinding efforts should come from idealist outsiders - intellectuals and persons with social concerns - whose passion in life is to bring about a more sensible, ethical and satisfying economic order than both private enterprise (of the 19th and 20th century) and state enterprise (communist or democratic socialist)" He cites Lenin pointing out that "the working class left to itself could not have gone beyond trade unionism. It was the intervention of the outsiders that lifted up a mere struggle for better wages and conditions of work to a theory and practice of social revolution of international scale. The outsider (Marx, Engels, Lenin, and the others) was not driven into it by any class or economic or power motivation; but by emotional identification and intellectual conviction". This is, as I see it, the main purpose of writing in celebration of Gandhi's 125th anniversary, as if we are to believe in his purposes then we too are required to act.

J.P. used similar words, as his chapter ended with the following: "Whether this hope can be realised, no one can tell. . . . . All that can be said is that there is reason behind the new forms of economic enterprise . . . . [and] shared interest between the community and . . . . enterprise. . . A combination of these ingredients should prove to be a fairly powerful social force."

This was written in the early 1970s. Environmental awareness, and phrases such as 'Space-Ship Earth', the work of the Baha'i, (stating 'The earth is but one country and mankind its citizens') and the World Citizens' Movement are all moving in the right direction; there seems to be no one focus on progressing Trusteeship, even of the world's major resources. Yet the idea shines through in, for instance, the work of the Club of Rome, and the world conference in Rio. Space exploration has given us visual images of "one world' and the work of Dr Karl Robert Hendrik has highlighted how all our planetary life depends on the sun and the green cells. Awareness is growing in schools where Agenda 21 and its follow-up involves the development of global thinking in young school children, almost the kind of Basic Education Gandhi had in mind.

Robert Muller, former Assistant Secretary General at the U.N. and now Chancellor of the new University for Peace in Costa Rica, has written a book entitled *The Birth of a Global Civilization*. He describes a "World core curriculum", convinced by his U.N. experience of the crucially urgent need to establish a universal educational curriculum designed to "help the birth of a peaceful, happy and fulfilled human civilisation". The curriculum is centred on the belief that "some cosmic force, or law, or God, or Creator in the Universe has put on the human species certain objectives, functions, expectations and destinations". Clearly here are deep echoes of Basic Education which had at its core the purpose of raising a motivating awareness of spiritual forces within each individual. It is heartening to note that this curriculum has been adopted in places as disparate as Texas, Mexico and Russia.

We do not yet know what combination of social forces brought down the Berlin Wall, and de-legitimised communist structures in Eastern Block countries. Maybe similar forces will de-legitimise the "unacceptable faces" of capitalism and exploitation. I would like to believe forces developing Trusteeship principle will be paramount in transforming our industrial society in the next century.

Bibliography

The Awakening, the monthly journal of Lok Sevak Sangh, (Vol 1 no 2 Nov 1978)

Professor Fred Blum. *Work and the Community, The S.B.C.W and the Quest for a New Social Order* Routledge Kegan Paul. 1970.

Business India Nov 5-18 1984, Special Report 2, p 96

Mahatma Gandhi, *To a Gandhian Capitalist,* Letters between M.K.G and Jamnalal Bajaj, p 10.

Gandhi Marg, vol 10 no 3 July 1966 p 199-200. Dayal Saran Verma

Wills Harman *Why is there a World Business Academy?*

Humanised Society through Trusteeship, *Trusteeship Foundation publication 1973.*

London Yearly Meeting of the Religious Society of Friends, 1944.

Marilyn Manser, Statement at the Canadian Friends Service Council, 1993 "M.M.C". *Sarvodaya* - Sept 1994 p 40.

W. Wellock. *Gandhi as a Social Revolutionary,* p 21.

Further reading 1. *Gandhi's Truth,* E. Erikson, p 410-415

Further reading 2. *Gandhi as a political strategist* G. Sharp, chapters 2 + 4

Further Reading 3. Second and Third Cantor Lectures *Tomorrow's capitalism in a Japanese perspective,* Dr Kiichi Mochizuki, *R.S.A. Journal* October 1994 p 378 and New game, new rules, new strategies, Professor Lester Thurow, *R.S.A. Journal* November 1994 p 50.

Further reading 4. *From Gandhi to Guevara* C.R. Hensman, Hazel Watson & Viney, 1969.

Further reading 5. *Industrial Partnership: Utopia or Necessity?* Professor Branko Horvat. Scott Bader Commonwealth Lecture 1986.

Further reading 4. London Yearly Meeting: Social testimony 1944.

Further readings 6. *The practice and experience of the Mondragon Basque Co-operatives* Josu Irigoien.

Scott Bader Commonwealth Lecture 1984.

The Trusteed Corporation Carl Rieser, The Servant Leadership Library.

Stewardship Peter Block, The servant Leadership Library. Indianapolis.

Democracy Accountability and Participation in Industry, Brian Parkyn, MCB General Publications Ltd, Bradford. 1979.

Equality through Trusteeship Valdilal Mehta, McGraw Hill 1977.

Sarvodaya: Social and Religious Values

Tarlok Singh

Sarvodaya and Antyodaya in Gandhian Thought and Practice

Mahatma Gandhi lived a life of intense activity, continuous exposition of thought, and zealous experimentation to give practical shape to ideas which could help lift the mass of the people in the villages. His life was as restless as it was purposeful and, following his day to day work through the pages of the multi-volume biography begun by Pyarelal and now being carried to completion by his sister Sushila Nayar, one observes with amazement how Gandhi filled each day of his life with ceaseless endeavour and deep meaning. The ninety odd volumes of his Collected Works contain but few complete pieces of composition from his pen, for in the main they were a record and a by-product of the work in which he was engaged, whether in the struggle for political freedom or in constructive activity or by way of letters and interviews and writing for *Young India* and later the *Harijan,* or speeches in his evening prayer meetings. His systematic writings are easily counted: *Hindi swaraj* or *Indian Home Rule,* the *Autobiography,* the paraphrase of John Ruskin's *Unto This Last,* interpretation of the Gita, and the pamphlet on *Constructive Work: Its meaning and place.* Each of these was an expression of his inner faith and conviction. Each was an exercise in synthesis, a summing up in its own context of his life and experience and view of the future.

The idea of *Sarvodaya* or Welfare of all, came to the surface from Gandhi's reading of Ruskin's *Unto This Last,* which his friend and comrade, Henry Polak, gave to him to read on a long train journey, As he has said in his Autobiography, the book kept him awake through the night as he found his own deepest convictions reflected in it. Later, he paraphrased it and translated the book into Gujarati, giving it the title *Sarvodaya.* Compained with the original, the paraphrase is more or less faithful. He went beyond the paraphrase to sum up its teachings, as they struck him, in the form of three propositions.

1. That the good of the individual is contained in the good of all.
2. That a lawyer's work has the same value as the barber's in as much as all have the same right of earning their livelihood from their work.

3. That a life of labour i.e. the life of the tiller of the soil and the handicraftsman is the life worth living.

Gandhi observes in his autobiography:

> The first of these I know. The second I had dimly realized. The third had never occurred to me. *Unto This Last* made it as clear as daylight for me that the second and the third were contained in the first. I arose with the dawn, ready to reduce these principles to practice!

Ruskin's main attack was on the ideas and assumptions underlying the prevailing political economy of the time. This had some influence on Gandhi's own thinking, but he passed by much of Ruskin's critique. The concept of Bread Labour, which he later advocated, specially through the spinning wheel, was sparked by his reading of Ruskin. The first of the lessons he drew from Ruskin was already part of his being, since the idea was long ago expressed in the Gita and the Upanishads and indeed in the scriptures of most ancient faiths. Vinoba explained that the idea of *Sarvodaya* as preached by the Gita is to merge oneself in the good of all. Vinoba cited Tulsidas as saying that 'generally, people desire their personal good. A few desire the good of their own people, but only the servants of God desire the good of everyone.' What was new was the name Gandhi gave to the idea, calling it *Sarvodaya,* meaning welfare of all. Gandhi went beyond this. In due course *Sarvodaya* merged into Gandhi's rendering of Truth and Non-violence and the practical expressions he gave to it, within the limits of what was possible at the time, in various forms of constructive activity.

In later years, the expression *Sarvodaya* did not figure much in Gandhi's writings, and most of Gandhi's repeated emphasis was on Truth, Non-Violence and Trusteeship, into which the idea of *Sarvodaya* had come to be transmuted and absorbed or on various forms of constructive work or on *Satyagraha* and non-violent passive resistance as part of the struggle for freedom.

Dr. Rajendra Prasad's interpretation was that in Gandhi's thinking Non-violence merged into Truth and Truth stood out as 'the one great fundamental to which he held fast'. He suggested that Gandhi applied this principle to practical problems as they arose and various items in the constructive programme as conceived by Gandhi were but steps in the direction of and leading to the great summit which had to be reached by individuals and society at large. This wider meaning does not emerge from what Gandhi himself wrote about the constructive programme, but may well have reflected the perception of so distinguished a follower of Gandhi as Dr. Rajendra Prasad and others among Gandhi's immediate disciples. In the main Gandhi's followers wrote about *Sarvodaya* after his death, not so much while he was himself doing most of the expounding.

More than a year after Gandhi's death, leading constructive workers, including Vinoba, Mashruwala, Kaka Kalelkar and others met at Sevagram and agreed to form themselves into *Sarvodaya Samaj,* a kind of Brotherhood but essentially a loose organisation.

Their aim was 'to strive towards a society based on Truth and Non-violence in which there will be no distinction of class or creed, no opportunity for exploitation and full scope in the development of both individuals and groups'. The programme was largely based on Gandhi's brochure, *Constructive Work: Its Meaning and Place,* which he had first published in 1941 and revised in 1944. However, each worker of the Sarva Seva Sangh continued to pursue whatever tasks he was engaged in and not much was heard of the *Sarvodaya* Samaj as an umbrella organisation in later years. It was during this period that Vinoba spoke on several occasions on *Sarvodaya,* Mashruwala wrote about Gandhi and Marx, and Dr.Rajendra Prasad, then President of the Constituent Assembly, spoke at some length on *Sarvodaya* and Gandhi's thought. Jayaprakash Narayan's conversion to *Sarvodaya* came some years later, under the influence of Vinoba's dynamic search for forms of non-violent revolutionary social action called for by conditions in the villages. However, after a period, he parted from Vinoba and came to be immersed in mass action to cleanse public life and to work for a partyless democracy at the grassroots. He called it *Total Revolution.* The most original commentaries on *Sarvodaya* thought came from Vinoba, who gave to it over a decade or more a new social content in the form of *Bhoodan* and *Gramdan* movements. He also carried forward Gandhi's thinking through works such as *Swaraj Sastra, Democratic Values, The Third power; Thoughts on Education, and Women's Power.* These were in addition to his reflections at the moral and religious plane such as *Talks on the Gita, The Steadfast Wisdom* and short syntheses and interpretations of the texts and teachings of Islam, Christianity and other faiths. Acharya Kriplani also wrote on Gandhi's thought, but mainly in its bearing on politics and the freedom movement. Thus, in the interpretation of *Sarvodaya* as a social concept, we need to turn mainly to Gandhi and Vinoba, Gandhi's practical applications of *Sarvodaya* have a unique interest, considering the limitations under which he had to work. Vinoba's efforts through *Bhoodan* and *Gramdan* were ambitious and far-reaching in conception, while the practical results achieved were relatively small. The idea of *Gramdan,* suitably adapted to the present-day needs of a changing rural society and rural economy, has potential significance for the future. Several principles underlying *Sarvodaya* as philosophy and as practical action still need to be and can be assimilated into the broader strategies of national developments planning and economic and social change. However, *Sarvodaya* ideals as Gandhi conceived and formulated them could well remain largely as beacons or points of reference for the future.

II

To return to the concept of *Sarvodaya,* as welfare of all, it is interesting to recall that the expression *Antyodaya,* meaning 'Welfare of the Least' - an almost literal translation of Ruskin's 'unto this least' was first used by Vinoba. As he put it in 1949,

> The proper rendering of 'Unto This Last' would be *Antyodaya* (uplift of the last) rather than *Sarvodaya.* Of course the last man's uplift is included in the uplift of all, but in emphasising the last, the object is that work should begin from that end. I agree that the *bhangi* (sweeper) should be

> our first concern. But the word *Sarvodaya* should stand; for it is not that all others have been uplifted and only the *bhangi* remains. In this unfortunate world of ours, we are all fallen and everyone needs to rise. The rich are fallen long since, and the poor have not risen at all. The result is that, both need to be uplifted. In one of his hymns Tulsidas says, "Lord, Thou alone knowst the right method of Grace. Thou takest away the smallness of the small and the greatness of the great."

From this explanation, Vinoba went on to stress, following Gandhi's own thought, the importance of non-possession and the need to remove 'possessiveness' in the same way as scavenging, and physical labour. 'Every one', Vinoba observed, 'must take part in physical labour and put a limit to his possession.'

We may now turn to Gandhi's view of *Sarvodaya* and its expansion or transformation to some far-reaching concepts of moral and social philosophy, it would seem that these transitions arose primarily from Gandhi's own integral world view. As a social concept, *Sarvodaya* could have held its own ground and served as a guiding principle for the organisation of society, going beyond the idea of welfare state as it has evolved and is evolving in the West under the conditions of democracy, Gandhi carried the thought further when he argued that only a non-violent society could secure the welfare of all. In 1940 Jayaprakash Narayan, then leading Congress Socialists within the Indian National Congress, drew up a draft Resolution for the Congress Session at Ramgarh. On technical grounds the Congress Working Committee did not agree to its circulation but, at Jayaprakash Narayan's request, Gandhi agreed to publish it and to comment on it in the *Harijan*. Gandhi's own observations, reproduced as an Appendix in Jayaprakash Narayan's volume *Towards Struggle – Selected Manifestoes, Speeches & Writings* (Yusuf Maherally, ed. Padma Publications, Bombay, 1946), are revealing:

> I have claimed that I was a socialist long before those I know in India had avowed their creed. But my socialism was natural to me and not adopted from any books, It came out of my unshakable belief in non-violence. No man could be actively non-violent and not rise against social injustice, no matter where it occurred.....
>
> 'I have always held that social justice, even unto the least and the lowliest, is impossible of attainment by force. I have further believed that it is possible by proper training of the lowliest by non-violent means to secure redress of the wrongs suffered by them. That means non-violent non-cooperation. At times non-cooperation becomes as much a duty as cooperation. No one is bound to cooperate in one's own undoing or slavery......
>
> It therefore gladdens me to find Shri Jaya Prakash accepting as I read his draft, non-violence for the purpose of establishing the order envisaged by him. I am quite sure that non-violent non-cooperation can secure

what violence never can, and this by ultimate conversion of the wrong-doers. We in India have never given non-violence the trial it has deserved, The marvel is that we have attained so much even with our mixed non-violence.....

Shri Jaya Prakash's propositions about land may appear frightful. In reality they are not. No man should have more land than he needs for dignified sustenance. Who can dispute the fact that the grinding poverty of the masses is due to their having no land that they can call their own?....

But it must be realised that the reform cannot be rushed. If it is to be brought about by non-violent means, it can only be done by education both of the haves and have-nots. The former should be assured that there never will be force used against them. The have-nots must be educated to know that no one can really compel them to do anything against their will, and that they can secure their freedom by learning the art of non-violence, i.e., self-suffering. If the end in view is to be achieved, the education I have adumbrated has to be commenced now. An atmosphere of mutual respect and trust has to be established as the preliminary step. There can then be no violent conflict between the classes and the masses.

In the passage quoted above, *Sarvodaya* as a strategy for social change and reconstruction of society is linked with non-violence. After the warnings by Milovan Djilas in *The New Class: An Analysis of the Communist System* (Praeger, New York, 1961) and by Theodore H.Von Laue in *Why Lenin? Why Stalin? A Reappraisal of the Russian Revolution, 1900-1930* (Lippincott, New York,1964), the documented excesses of the Cultural Revolution in China, and the breakdown of the economic, social and political system of USSRs and the Communist States of all countries in Eastern Europe who can say that Gandhi's reading of the dynamics of revolution brought about by violence was wrong?

In comparing the doctrines of Marx and Gandhi, Mashruwala raised the issue of class war and its place in the reconstruction of society and the economy. Gandhi held that in India a class war is not only not inevitable but is avoidable if we have understood the message of non-violence. Gandhi did not love Zamindari or capitalists or even the Princes, but he did not look upon them as enemies and gave them the benefit of being basically patriots and well-wishers of their people who would not fail to respond sooner or later if approached with understanding. He turned the searchlight inwards and asked, how much has each of us done to identify ourselves with the masses. 'Let us who live in glass houses', he said, 'not throw stones' To what extent do you share the life of the masses? I confess that with me, it is still an aspiration. we ourselves have not completely shed the habits of living that we say the capitalists are notorious for?'

Asked if class war could be avoided, Gandhi argued back:

> It can, most decidedly, if only the people will follow the non-violent method. By the non-violent method we seek not to destroy the capitalist, we seek to destroy capitalism. We invite the capitalist to regard himself as a trustee for those on whom he depends for the making, the retention and the increase of his capital. Nor need the worker wait for his conversion. If capital is power, so is work. Either power can be used destructively or creatively. Either is dependent on the other. Immediately the worker realizes his strength, he is in a position to become a co-sharer with the capitalist instead of remaining his slave. If he aims at becoming the sole owner, he will most likely be killing the hen that lays golden eggs. Inequalities in intelligence and even opportunity will last till the end of time. A man living on the banks of a river has any day more opportunity of growing crops than one living in an arid desert, but if inequalities stare us in the face the essential equality too is not to be missed. Every man has an equal right to the necessaries of life even as birds and beasts have. And since every right carries with it a corresponding duty and the corresponding remedy for resisting an attack upon it, it is merely a matter of finding out the corresponding duties and remedies to vindicate the elementary equality. The corresponding duty is to labour with my limbs and the corresponding remedy is to non-cooperate with him who deprives me of the fruit of my labour. And if I would recognize the fundamental equality, as I must, of the capitalist and the labourer, I must not aim at his destruction. I must strive for his conversion. My non-cooperation with him will open his eyes to the wrong he may be doing. Nor need I be afraid of someone else taking my place when I have non-cooperated. For I expect to influence my co-workers so as not to help the wrong-doing of the employer. This kind of education of the mass of workers is no doubt a slow process, but as it is also the surest, it is necessarily the quickest. It can be easily demonstrated that destruction of the capitalist must mean destruction in the end of the worker; and as no human being is so bad as to be beyond redemption, no human being is so perfect as to warrant his destroying him whom he wrongly considers to be wholly evil.

In the passage cited above, we can see the transition from Welfare of All, to Equality and, as means, to Trusteeship and the sanction provided by organised non-violent non-cooperation with what may be conceived as wrong and those responsible for the wrong. Even in categories familiar to social science, we have here an interrelated and powerful set of ideas serving as the instruments of far-reaching social engineering. In Gandhi's time India was yet struggling with all the limitations within which he worked, yet his confidence in his system of revolutionary social change was complete and unshakeable.

Did Gandhi put excessive faith in the idea of Trusteeship?. Perhaps that was so. Gandhi was leading India through a great transition when all the available forces in favour of freedom had to be held together. At some point, in a democracy, pressures for change in relationships of income, wealth, property, status, class and caste must take the form of legislation binding on all. Therefore, Gandhi's trusteeship could be viewed as a transition rather than as a final stage in the evolution of society. The makers of India's Constitution, above all Jawaharlal Nehru, provided for the concepts of social change in a free, democratic India in the Directive Principles and Fundamental Rights. With the concern for right means to all right ends which he shared with Gandhi, Nehru had faith enough in the people and in the processes and pressures of democracy to insist that the goals would be reached even if they took a little longer than one wished. The goals themselves were unmistakable even though there might be tortuous turns and temporary reverses on the way, As Nehru put it in 1952 when India's economy was barely emerging from the travails of the Second World War and the tragedy of Partition:

> Our economy and social structure have outlived their day and it has become a matter of urgent necessity for us to refashion them so that they may promote the happiness of all our people in things material and spiritual. We have to aim deliberately at a society which is not dominated by the urge for private profit and by individual greed and in which there is fair distribution of political and economic power. We must aim at a classless society, based on cooperative effort, with opportunities for all.

The word *Sarvodaya,* as Vinoba said in 1948 soon after Gandhi's death, expresses a lofty and all-embracing sentiment. Therefore, he wanted Gandhi's day of martyrdom the 30th January, to be celebrated each year as Sarvodaya Day. As he put it,

> We do not want the rise of the few, not even of the many, or for that matter of the greatest number. We are not satisfied with the greatest good of the greatest number. We can be satisfied only with the good of one and all, of the high and the low, of the strong and the weak, the intelligent as well as the dull, only then will we be satisfied.

As a man of God, it was natural for Gandhi to write and speak continuously about God and Truth as the ultimate source. The objectives he sought gained strength from his profound thinking but could, equally, be considered and pursued in terms which were wholly moral and secular.

This brings us to the place of *Antyodaya,* or welfare of the least, in Gandhi's thought. The expression, as stated earlier, was Vinoba's. The practical content of *Antyodaya,* as expressed in the Constructive Programme, was Gandhi's own and was drawn from his deep understanding of the village and the villager, of the needs and potentials of women and of workers, of the common man everywhere. Through all his travels from the day he returned from South Africa, he was constantly observing, listening, arguing, reflecting, and devising practical ways of lessening pain and poverty and arousing a greater sense of confidence and self-reliance within each individual, each group and each community, in village and town alike. He knew the limitations of time and circumstance, and took note of them in devising his specific programmes of action. The Constructive Programme was largely Gandhi's own creation. It was implemented and carried forward through a galaxy of outstanding associates, dedicated men and women whom he had inspired, who spent their lives in the service of the masses as he bad wished them to. It was in essence the programme of *Antyodaya*. Through it, those specially were to be served and raised whom society had placed at its lowest rungs or left weak and deprived.

Except for the passages on Communal Unity, Economic Equality, National Languages and Students which deal with critical conditions for nation-building, all the items of activity are addressed to sections of society which need to be strengthened in a variety of ways or to means by which rural communities can prepare themselves to move forward as a whole. There is now an enormous body of literature on all the activities comprised in Gandhi's Constructive Programme. Many new programmes and activities have been introduced since Independence. Much legislation has been enacted. Vast administrative organisations have come into existence. Democracy is being carried to the grassroots and everywhere there is a common commitment to empower the people. Much still remains to be done. Therefore, the underlying spirit rather than the content of various items of activity as proposed by Gandhi through years of practical experimentation has to be infused into programmes and organisations which have taken shape over the past decades. In response to unresolved problems and new challenges, changes are constantly taking place. Therefore, in each period, the content of what constitutes *Antyodaya* and the practical shape that can be given to it will go on evolving, sometimes by design, sometimes under compulsion, but always under stress of challenge, from within and without.

The impact of the ideas of *Sarvodaya* and *Antyodaya* is not limited to India. The *Sarvodaya* movement in Sri Lanka is primarily concerned with village reconstruction and harnessing of the energies of the people. Spread now through 6000 villages and more, it stands for 'awakening' and traces its roots to values imbibed from Buddhism. While *Sarvodaya* and *Antyodaya* in India, with the strength and weakness that go with these concepts as applied in real life, influence action and thought elsewhere, in turn they continually absorb lessons from other lands, notably from countries with similar conditions and aspirations. Neither concept is to be viewed as static. Each will go on absorbing new insights and new possibilities. The legacy left behind by Gandhi through *Sarvodaya* and *Antyodaya* will go on unfolding itself in a hundred ways which cannot yet be foreseen. The message of welfare of all, of welfare of the least, and living in harmony with nature and environment which Gandhi urged and practised is profound in its simplicity and universal in its application. It holds the key to India's future.

Gerald Studdert-Kennedy

Gandhi, Ruskin and the Christian Imperialists

> '... The strange, enigmatic figure of Mr Gandhi put himself at the head of the *Satyagraha* (soul-force) movement of protest, which the left wing adopted as their own...'[1]

The registration in some such terms of a sense of baffled uncertainty in relation to Gandhi is a cliché in commentaries published for the relatively small 'India Public' in Great Britain between the wars, as it is in the correspondence of British politicians concerned with the nationalist movement. Of course there were impatient, simplifying voices from the imperialist right wing. Thus, Sir Harcourt Butler of the ICS, speaking on the BBC in 1931:

> ... Autocracy and revolution are in the blood of the East. What has happened to representative government in Egypt, Persia, Turkey, China? What is Mr Gandhi's attitude today? Autocracy prevails ... [2]

From the opposite flank came persistent clarifications from the small coterie of British Gandhians. Thus, H.S.L. Polak to the same patient BBC audience:

> The Indian masses see in Mahatma Gandhi, now an elderly man weakened and emaciated by prayer, fasting and heavy labours, as they see in no other leader in his generation, their saviour from oppression and poverty, the spokesman of their unformed thoughts and unuttered hopes, their guide to freedom ...[3]

Nevertheless, both the political 'right' and the more liberal 'left' also acknowledged a residual ambiguity, the former in regular references to Gandhi's oriental inscrutability and cunning, the latter most often in uneasiness over his 'non-violence' and his apparently unstable drifting from 'social reform' to 'political' intervention. Whilst for the broad middle ground that backed the White Paper proposals in the 1930s, the ambiguity was pervasive: Gandhi was at different moments both 'saint' and 'fox', national leader and subverter of the historical achievements of the Empire.

As we are now bound to acknowledge, it would be quite unreasonable to expect anything else. A substantial and continuing development in the historiography of the nationalist movement has demonstrated that in India itself Gandhi meant very different things to different people and different groups, that specific situations, confrontations and failures imposed shifts and expediencies and reversals on him, and that his syncretic and pragmatic intellectual approach both generated and tolerated serious contradictions and inconsistencies.[4] This volume is itself only the latest acknowledgment of the recurrent rediscovery, reinterpretation and critique, in a changing world, of a Gandhian discourse which had served initially to provide the political idiom that assimilated the rural masses into a nationalist movement. For a great many people it had seemed to promise much more, before being abandoned by the consolidating state nationalism identified with Nehru.[5]

This particular essay is reflexive and backward-looking in the first instance, since it is less concerned with Gandhi than with 'Gandhi', less with the historical figure and his substantive complexity than with an alien, imperial discourse within which an ambiguous idea of him took shape, and therefore with the prior assumptions, beliefs and expectations which the British brought to bear on the Raj and the prospects for an Indian nation, and specifically on Gandhi as a nationalist leader.

To a very great extent these perspectives have long since evaporated, and survive now in a merely archival kind of existence. The Empire no longer exists. Nationalism for the British today, both at home and abroad, is disturbing and threatening, even intermittently encouraging perhaps, in quite different ways. However, it is still worth considering what functions the defunct imperial discourse, with its confusions and contradictions, may have served. The phenomenally complex process to which we currently attach the label of 'nationalism' emerges out of that past and out of confused and heterogeneous perceptions and misperceptions, in themselves both imperial and nationalist, of other people's 'nationalisms'.

Partha Chatterjee has well emphasised the fluid and open-ended, but nevertheless dependent nature of the evolution of Indian nationalism in the colonial period. He has stressed the function of Gandhian discourse in facilitating the transition of a rural colonial society into the state nationalism and the attempted 'scientific' construction of a modern society in the Nehru period. The crucial mobilisation of the peasantry behind the nationalist movement was achieved, he has argued, through Gandhi's *Ramarajya*, which provided a moral conception that articulated demands in the peasant-communal consciousness for political justice. Gandhi thus created a moral community at the grass roots which made national political development possible. At the same time

> the working out of the politics of non-violence also made it abundantly clear that the object of the political mobilisation of the peasantry was not at all what Gandhi claimed on its behalf, "to train the masses in self-consciousness and attainment of power".[6]

On the contrary, the national organisation of a dominant class, itself fostered by the imperial order, consolidated itself within the institutional structures of the new state, whilst no all-India organisation of *kisans* and labour was allowed to emerge, and there was therefore no basis for a politically effective challenge to the existing structure of society. The peasantry in the pre-Independence decades became a component of the emerging modern nation, but on terms dictated by others.

In the course of developing this argument, though for good reason, Chatterjee 'held constant' the complicating ingredient of the imperial discourse itself, as a given, against which Non-Cooperation, Civil Disobedience and Congress Raj pitted themselves. But the imperial vision was not so simple, and the complex and shifting nature of the imperial discourse is clearly relevant to an argument such as Chatterjee's. The ambivalences of 'Gandhi', as a figure taking shape within it, – conjured up for the disparate components of the British public by an intrigued western press and its photojournalism, and by the contradictory assertions of public figures – needs to be identified along with the substantive ambiguities of Gandhi himself in our consideration of the historical process to which he made his extraordinary contribution. They are part of the network of mutual perceptions, misapprehensions and judgments that described the imperial relationship, and they affected the behaviour of both parties to it.

The readings or misreadings, furthermore, of Gandhi and the nationalist movement contained in the imperial discourse were not of transitory significance. The threads connecting nationalist politics then and now will not be pursued here, but it is, for instance, from as full an understanding as possible of the imperial relationship that we should approach the profoundly un-Gandhian implications of the contemporary situation addressed by Chatterjee in a more recent analysis. Here he considers the implications of the prospective insertion, by a movement of the political right, of an exclusivist 'Hindu' national culture into the controlling structures of an interventionist, modernising Indian state.[7] The assertions of this contemporary 'Hindu nationalism' indirectly but undoubtedly owe a great deal to much earlier imperial assumptions about Hinduism and its 'reform' (and of course about both Christianity and Islam,) and their bearing on nationhood and nationalism in the subcontinent.

Hindu revivalism has a long history in the imperial period, as a sectarian and proto-nationalist ideology, which rejected secular, western and 'liberal' values imposed on the colonial situation. Its legacy was an important component of the context in which, and on which Gandhi had to work as a popular leader. Today however, the more sophisticated contemporary forms of 'Hindu nationalism' that have evolved from such earlier developments represent a challenging accommodation to the 'modernity' rejected by Gandhi and, in different ways, by other influential figures in the past. This challenging accommodation takes the form of an appropriation and redefinition of the concept of secularity. Secularism was of course a shibboleth of the Nehruvian era which would, so it was assumed, in due course dissolve any residual threat of political conflict based on religious exclusivism. But Secularism is now, paradoxically, being used to justify the homogenisation of a national culture in terms that are exclusively Hindu and therefore implicitly threatening to non-Hindu communities in India. In its current form, however, it is very explicitly located within a discourse of modernisation driven by market opportunities. The compulsions of this modernity are a legacy from an imperial past, and so is this movement's recycled rhetoric of Nationalism, including its appeal to an exclusive, national religious culture.[8]

II

It is well known that Gandhi acknowledged a particular kindred spirit in the John Ruskin of *Unto This Last* (1862), a copy of which was given him by Polak, and which he adapted into Gujarati as *Sarvodaya* (1908). It is not clear what else of Ruskin's he ever read,[9] but Ruskin is a particularly appropriate point of entry to a consideration of the British response to Gandhi himself. Sales of *Unto This Last* were nearing a hundred and six thousand copies in the year following *Sarvodaya's* appearance. Ruskin founded no school, but with Carlyle and Morris, made a powerful contribution to the critical strand in Victorian sensibility which was, in Collini's summary, 'uneasy with modernity, suspicious of the reductive tendencies of science, hostile to the soulless reasonings of political economy'.[10]

However, as Bernard Shaw cheerfully informed a distinguished audience assembled by the Ruskin Centenary Council in 1921, those Ruskin appealed to, 'the educated, cultivated and discontented' took from him considerably less than he offered. They found him difficult.

> But what really puzzled his readers -- and incidentally saved his life, because he certainly would have been hanged if they had grasped what he was driving at, and believed that he believed it--- was that he was incredible. . . .
>
> They could not bring themselves to believe that he meant what he was saying, and indeed shouting.[11]

Shaw explains why:

> They were educated at our public schools and universities; they moved in a society that fitted in with those public schools and universities. . . Ruskin's political message to the cultured society of his day, the class to which he himself belonged, began and ended with this simple judgment: "You are a parcel of thieves".

Saturated in class complacencies, this was a message they spontaneously diluted.

The sprightly Shavian exaggerations sugar a serious point. Shaw is accurate about Ruskin's readership. He liked to address the thoughtful 'working man' but most of his readers came from the middle class, from which of course was recruited what I refer to here as the India Public, a constituency based in the social networks of the Raj connecting ICS, Military, Education and Church (both the missions and the expatriate's Indian Ecclesiastical Establishment). Ruskin was absorbed, but in a selective reading, into a middle class public moralism, as was Gandhi in the Indian context. He made this easier, as Gandhi for the more well-to-do Indians did not, by never himself 'living in a garret' , a failure he ruefully acknowledged, and by the very qualified radicalism of his political ideas, which were less subversive of 'modernity' than Shaw suggests, and certainly far less radical than Gandhi's.

So, if it can be shown that Ruskin was selectively appropriated by Gandhi himself, he was also selectively read, though with a significantly different focus, by many of his own more thoughtful countrymen. One can go further than that, because Ruskin and Gandhi, or rather 'Ruskin' and 'Gandhi' unquestionably converged for specific sectors of the India Public. If Ruskin was tutor to a British middle class social moralism, he served also as a model to which the exotic orientalism of an ascetic nationalist leader in dhoti and sandals could be approximately assimilated; and insofar as that took place, 'Ruskin' obscured the reality of Gandhi as a politician.

As a source of social wisdom in the context of this public philosophy, 'Ruskin' was by no means alone. But one can emphasise the point that his was a voice in the discourse of imperialism that was particularly important in conditioning British perceptions of Gandhi, who was seen as his disciple in a more thoroughgoing sense than was in fact the case, an embodied repudiation of the *soi-disant* science of political economy[12] against which Ruskin fulminated. An imperfect image of Ruskin as prophet came to be superimposed on a yet more shadowy image of Gandhi himself.

Though he led no effective movement, the discourse to which Ruskin was assimilated by his British readers rested on an institutional base that survived well into this century, in the face of the much advertised Victorian 'loss of faith' and the subsequent cataclysmic impact of the Great War, namely the Church of England itself and the so-called Free Churches of nonconformist 'dissent', particularly the Methodists. Certainly these institutions were in long-term decline, but among Shaw's cultivated and educated, the discontented or guilty among them particularly, they continued to provide familiar and well-established bearings for many.

In the brutal summary necessary here, the important point to make about organised religion in England in Gandhi's life-time is the accelerated attenuation of what might be described as fundamentalism in terms of Christian doctrine and belief. What came to be established in its place was a broadly interdenominational 'social christianity', which interpreted Christ's injunction to look after one's neighbour less in terms of individual charities than in terms of collective obligations. These were to be recognised, for instance, in legislation affecting employment, education, health and general social needs. Indeed, a factor facilitating his readers' domestication of Ruskin's 'incredible' message was the conviction that his core point – that the political economy should be based on the 'social affections' rather than on competition – was steadily being attended to as liberal social legislation was put into place.

The broad label of 'christian socialism' covers a number of diminutive radical fractions, but a much larger general tendency which was socially conservative. This turned in mid-century to clerics such as F.D. Maurice, from a Unitarian background, and social thinkers such as Ruskin particularly. In 1889 a successor, Bishop Brooke Foss Westcott of Durham, emerged as founder of the Christian Social Union (CSU). (One of his devoted sons was for many years the Metropolitan or Primate of India, as Bishop of Calcutta, and a severe, though personally friendly, sparring partner of Gandhi's in the 1930s.) The CSU was 'a large and respectable body of academic churchmen who sought to replace what they supposed *laissez-faire* economic practice to be with 'brotherhood'. It is hard to quarrel with Edward Norman's argument that if their conception of 'brotherhood' was nebulous, their grasp of economic theory was weak, whilst their assumption that the one contradicted the other was not thought through.[13] They were, however, earnest, vocal and socially and politically active. They eagerly picked up Ruskin's argument that apparent conflicts of interest need never be antagonistic, if the spirit in which they are confronted celebrates the quality of life of a community instead of the pursuit, and institutionalisation, of competitive advantage. This orientation amplified, and, so to speak, sanctified, the claims of 'cooperation' against those of class war as the moral basis for political activity. It served to divert arguments about the structure of economic exploitation onto a consideration of the *affective* quality of relations between types and conditions of men and women.

There was little uniformity, and precious little 'socialism' in the usual sense in this public moralism. Maurice, for instance, managed to combine favouring *laissez-faire* as a trading principle with denigration of selfish competition, and he even believed that a pure national identity was established through war. Organised liberal Christianity, in any event, came to be dominated by a number of powerful and stable assumptions, articulated most authoritatively by figures such as Maurice, Ruskin and Westcott. Later, particularly in the decade immediately after the First War, these assumptions were energetically mobilised to blunt the edge of industrial conflicts that seriously threatened political stability in the United Kingdom.[14] At the same time these same assumptions had a significant bearing on perceptions of the threat to imperial order from the Indian nationalist movement.[15] The same educated public that looked uneasily at British society looked beyond it, to see Britain's global and historical responsibilities as an extension of the one set of universal, 'religious' obligations.

The evolution of mainstream liberal Christian discourse towards an increasingly nondoctrinal and interdenominational 'social christianity' needs to be understood in relation to three fundamental categories. These are, firstly, an idea of History; secondly, an idea of a natural, organic social structure; and thirdly, the idea of a Nation.

Ruskinism and liberal Christian teaching, and their popularisations, were preoccupied with all three.

The liberal India Public tended to exaggerate the congruence between its own sense of these categories and the content of the Gandhian message to India and the Empire. A congruence can certainly be identified in relation to the second, the model for a natural and organic social structure. The India Public was comfortably located in a stable society, organised round well-recognised and apparently accepted hierarchies of class. Its European enemies preached material equality and class revolution, as Gandhi certainly did not. Gandhi was at his most Ruskinian here. His substitution for the existing caste system of a purified functional hierarchy of the four *varnas* virtually transcribes key passages from *Unto This Last*.

The liberal India Public was seriously adrift, however, over the congruence it tended to assume between its own and Gandhian assumptions about the nature of History. Its concept of a Nation, the third of the fundamental categories required here, was a logical product of the first two. That is to say, a Nation was taken to emerge as an organic fact out of a purposeful and organic historical process. Conventional ideas about evolution here blended very comfortably with the whiggish providentialism that saw History as a process that liberated a larger purpose interior to itself, though not in a deterministic way, since the process could be obstructed by unenlightened human agency and social malformation.

It is difficult in this connection to exaggerate the hegemonic status of the idea of European History as a purposive, evolutionary and progressive process. There were multiple formulations of it. One version, which enjoyed wide popular appeal and the authority of Maurice, of the respectable 'christian socialist' tradition and of the English Hegelians (also, it is worth remembering, of the great liberal leader William Gladstone), was explicitly Providential in a Christian sense: History was the instrument of God's purpose, and indications of the divine will could be read out of contemporary tendencies by the perceptive and informed. Political Science, supposedly established as a positive science by Sir John Seeley, author of *The Expansion of England* (1883), promised to become the discipline of the perceptive and informed in this sense.[18] This conviction was central to the activities of important imperialist politicians with a close interest in India.[17] As for Ruskin, Chatterjee points out that he too was

> a historicist, influenced in important ways by German idealism and particularly by Hegel. Despite the contradictoriness which he shared with all the other critics of industrial civilization in Victorian Britain, Ruskin was, in the fundamental elements of his thought, a 'modernist'. Collingwood points out, for instance, that 'he cared intensely for science and progress, for political reform, for the advancement of knowledge and for new movements in art and letters. . . .'
>
> (But) all of these concerns were quite far removed from Gandhi's theoretical world.[18]

So Ruskin's moralism was read by the British middle class in the context of an historiography which celebrated successes and potentialities in industrial society which Gandhi actually repudiated.

In this perspective, Gandhi's contingent, non-historicist and 'experimental' understanding of politics was simply baffling. So it could not be acknowledged as a coherent alternative perspective. Instead, when it was impossible to ignore its manifestations, it was explained away, most often either in essentialist terms, as an 'oriental' inability to sense the fundamental reality of inherently purposeful change, by definition taking place in a linear rather than some kind of cyclical historical process, or it was explained as the product of local and contingent political pressures. The attribution of wayward activities on Gandhi's part to an inherent potential for irrational action of course relieved one of the obligation to explore them more fully.

Whig historicism, whether it was Christian and providentialist or secular and evolutionary, identified the Nation as the encapsulating organism, the articulated commonalty of natural groups and communities, occupations and professions, towards which forces within the historical process unevenly but purposefully move. The issue of the actual emergence or otherwise, through this evolutionary process, of any specific mature nationality could be reduced in principle to an empirical question. A claim could be assessed against familiar, European criteria of cultural, linguistic and political integration. Allowing for areas of overlap, the specific organic characteristics constituting the British, or the French, or the German or, more problematically, the Italian nations were taken to be a matter of general knowledge in Europe, where they had been fully analysed by many thoughtful observers, among whom Seeley seems to have been particularly important to the more liberal India Public. The question of the existence, or otherwise, in India of nationality so conceived was central to the series of twentieth century debates relating to constitutional reform.

Right wing leaders and activists in the British political arena pointed to the communal divide in India, to linguistic and cultural diversity and the structure of caste domination as conclusive evidence that its claim to authentic nationality was bogus. C.F.Andrews and the Quaker Gandhians, on the other hand, argued that we risked failing to catch the moment of historical ripeness, with consequences no less damaging to the moral cement of British society than to India herself. As the brisk voice of responsible imperialism, Samuel Hoare as Secretary of State presented the 1933 White Paper as a well timed and daring act of faith in the collective judgment of a conscientious and perceptive imperial and national leadership. Its supporters argued that the hour had come for India's next graduation towards nationhood. The devout High Anglican Lord Irwin, for instance, was in no doubt that there was an ultimate and transcending imperative calling for constitutional concession. It is highly significant that the India Bill was presented in the House of Lords, at length and with formidable assurance, by the Archbishop of Canterbury, Cosmo Gordon Lang, Lord Irwin's close friend, and the most active member of the Joint Select Committee on the White Paper.

But for all three positions, left, right and the broad official centre, the rigidity, social fragmentation and political exploitation associated with caste generated serious anxieties. It was on this crux that the visions of Ruskin and of Gandhi seemed most obviously to converge, because the idea of a natural and organic social structure provided the operational link between, on the one hand, the obscure impulsions of the evolving historical process and, on the other, its evident, though doubtless intermediate goal, the organic Nation.

Ruskin's contribution to an understanding of the nature of the social structure, was to derive a normatively rich ideal type from his most basic insight. This had a powerful appeal, because it provided a realistic and pragmatic rejoinder to the intolerable judgement identified by Shaw as the core of Ruskin's political thought, the unbelievable message for his well-meaning readers that 'you are a parcel of thieves'. Ruskin's non-material perception of social value, and of social order itself, moralised, and indeed spiritualised the pragmatically functional structure of his vision of the political economy:

> THERE IS NO WEALTH BUT LIFE. Life, including all its powers of love of joy and of admiration. That country is the richest which nourishes the greatest number of noble and happy human beings; that man is richest who, having perfected the functions of his own life to the utmost, has also the widest helpful influence, both personal, and by means of his possessions, over the lives of others.
>
> A strange political economy; the only one, nevertheless, that ever was or can be: all political economy founded on self-interest being but the fulfillment of that which once brought schism into the Policy of angels, and ruin into the Economy of Heaven.[19]

Ruskin is specific in the light of this resonant premise about the *functions*, and therefore the obligations of professional groups, for instance where he retrieves the function of the merchant or manufacturer from the nullity of the political economy of self-interest.

> . . . . the merchant's function (or manufacturer's. . .) is to provide for the nation. It is no more his function to get profit for himself out of that provision than it is a clergyman's function to get his stipend.[20]

This is a doctrine with an obvious appeal to an established and conscientious professional class, particularly taken in conjunction with another, which also seemed in a particular sense self-evident to Gandhi:

> . . . if there be any one point insisted on throughout my works more frequently than another, that one point is the impossibility of Equality.[21]

The relevance of this perspective to a nondoctrinal social christianity is obvious. Salvation through Christ had ceased effectively to be an unpredictable reward in a life after death. It had become a process to be rationally and collectively pursued in this world. Its eventual achievement depended on a functional division of labour, an ideal of social service which was shared by all, but interpreted by each in terms of his or her contribution to the life of society as a whole. It depended, too, on the essential structures of morally and practically competent leadership. Behind the mature nation lies an ultimate, transcendent validation. Functional integration is itself an index of national maturity and evidence of that validation. To be sure, leaders and led will drift away from the integrative moral cement of national functional integrity: human selfishness and frailty are the root premiss of an orthodox theology. But if we all at least recognise the moral imperative of *service* in the place and function allotted to us, we can be secure that the social collectivity itself is authentically informed by the transcendent purpose that drives historical change,and is actively engaged in the process of redemption most completely proclaimed by Christ.

III

India, needless to say, was not Christian, and neither was Gandhi. This fact was heavily underlined by the die-hard opponents of constitutional reform, and it would be quite wrong to suppose that on their part this was a cynical or merely conventional genuflection to the imperial state religion and 'the Tory party at prayer'.[22] They pointed to the ultimate incompatibility of Hinduism and Islam, and to the inability of either religion to provide the moral basis for an authentic national community. They mocked a caste structure in a condition of ingrown and disfunctional paralysis.

But the liberal mainstream and Gandhian 'left' could draw on more flexible theological resources. An important aspect of the development of a social christianity, as a religious faith concerned with a struggle, simultaneously moral and material, for the good life in this world, was a much increased sensitivity to the achievements of other religions. C.F.Andrews was only one among a number of articulate missionary theological thinkers to interpret Christ in terms of a 'fulfilment' of religious insights which had also been arrived at independently of Christian revelation. So Ruskin's religious vision of a functional community need not be seen as a possibility exclusively for a nation as mature as his own. The transcendent reality was universal and immanent in many forms. It could find expression in a transformation and realisation of very different possibilities, specifically, for instance, in those drawn out of Jain and Hindu traditions by the Mahatma.

This doctrinal reconsideration, of course, made it very much easier to contemplate a gradual withdrawal of imperial control prior to the establishment of a confident Christianity in India. The ultimate establishment of Christianity was a goal which had been widely considered by the British as a prerequisite for authentic national integration of the subcontinent. In the light of this 'fulfilment theology', an Indian nationalist leadership, though indifferent to the doctrinal content of Christian belief, could be seen in its performance of desirable social functions, underwritten by a Christian imperial order, as an effective expression of authentic nationhood.

It is unlikely that many in the India Public were aware of Gandhi's transposition, into the classic idealisation of the non-conflictual, non-competitive *varnas*, of Ruskin's vision of a rightly integrated hierarchy of social functions. The correspondence between Ruskin's conception of duty and Gandhi's of *dharma*, however, is remarkably close. Gandhi redefined the four traditional occupational categories of the *varnas* so radically, Parekh has pointed out, that his 'well rounded or fully moral man engaged in all four activities ... served his fellow-men, fought against untruth and injustice, earned his living and engaged in manual labour'[23]. This redefinition brings him even closer to Ruskin. But the technical distinctions between *varna* and *jati* would not have been general knowledge in the India Public. In the literature produced for the India Public caste receives a rather general treatment, on the one hand stressing the extravagant multiplicity of its divisions, and on the other its rather straightforward and generally, but not entirely, negative implications for the possibility of organic social evolution.

However, everyone knew that Gandhi was against the corrupt involution of contemporary caste, and sought to raise and give self-respect to the underdog and untouchable by valorising their practical service to the community. Everyone knew also of Gandhi's ashrams, the New Testament readings, the commitment to non-violence and, more uneasily, of the Christlike rigour of his personal asceticisms and his routine indifference to poverty – the cause of some solemn self-criticism on the part of British clergymen but understandably little imitation. There was general awareness of his early loyalty to the British Empire and the durability of his good-will towards Britain. He was almost too good to be true.

But not quite. That is to say that the British saw in him what they had learned to see. What they saw was national movement of social reform behind a remarkable leader, with a humbling commitment to a Ruskinian vision in exceedingly adverse circumstances. Gandhi rejected the soulless values of political economy, but he also rejected the competitive selfishness inherent in a confrontational class politics. In these respects his vision seemed both admirable and reassuring to the imperial middle class, as did the inherently apolitical functionalism of Ruskin's ideal social order. But doubts about the Mahatma surfaced very fast when Government encountered his moments of 'political' obduracy, the fast that looked like blackmail, the refusal to concede where reason appeared to cry out for concession. These had to be explained away in terms of pressure from 'extremists' and more generally in terms of his fatal, 'oriental' lack of historical realism, his romantic retreat from the conditions of political order, production and commerce, that constitute History's legacy to the age.

But History, one could assume, would take care of that. The prophet exists to remind us of values we are inclined to forget, of the direction in which we should face. The Mahatma lived out an uncompromising dramatisation of those values. In India one could see that his particular task was to bring an amorphous and traditional rural mass into the modern nation. That was something he could sense was required of him by a transcendant purpose. He was no doubt only able to do so by repudiating in his own life the 'modernity' to which in reality 'history' inescapably committed them. This reality his successors and most of his political allies had been willing to learn from their colonial mentors. He was unable to do so, but his religious insight into an underlying and organic social transformation had made possible the orderly transition of a vast society into the larger community of modern nations.

Notes and References

1. L.F. Rushbrook Williams, The Indian National Congress in its various phases, Ch III in Sir John Cumming, *Political-India, 1832-1932: a Cooperative Survey of a Century*, Oxford University Press, 1932, p. 60.

2. Sir Harcourt Butler, Achievements of the British Raj, *The Listener*, April 29, 1931, p. 717.

3. H.S.L. Polak, What Gandhi Stands For, *The Listener*, June 10, 1931, p. 977.

4. It seems invidious to select references, but pioneering studies include Judith Brown's *Gandhi's Rise to Power: Indian Politics, 1915-1222*, Cambridge University Press, 1972, and *Gandhi and Civil Disobedience: The Mahatma in Indian Politics, 1928-1934*, Cambridge University Press, 1977. Also the studies collected in R. Kumar, *Essays on Gandhian Polities: the Rowlatt Satyagraha of 1919*, Oxford University Press, 1971. For a critical exposition of the complexities, and inadequacies, of Gandhi's political discourse, see Bhikhu Parekh, *Colonialism, Tradition and Reform: an analysis of Gandhi's Political discourse*, Sage, 1989.

5. Partha Chatterjee, *Nationalist Thought and the Colonial World: a derivative discourse*, Zed Books, 1986.

6. *Ibid*, p 124.

7. P. Chatterjee, Secularism and Toleration, *Economic and Political Weekly*, July 9, 1994, pp. 1768-1777.

8. Chaturvedi Badrinath has shown, in a series originally published in the *Times of India*, how the Hindu nationalism elaborated by M.S.Golwalkar reproduced almost in parodic form the European common places about nationalism from the imperial period, in terms of an exclusive identification of Indian Nation with Hindu culture. *Dharma, India and the World Order*, Edinburgh, 1993, pp 280 ff.

9. Elizabeth T. McLaughlin, *Ruskin and Gandhi*, Lewisburg, 1974, p. 23.

10. Stefan Collini, *Public Moralists: political thought and intellectual life in Britain, 1850-1930*, Oxford University Press, 1991, p 185.

11. Bernard Shaw, *Ruskin's Politics*, Oxford University Press, 1921.

12. *Unto This Last*, London, 1862, Section 1.

13. E.R.Norman, *Church and Society in England, 1770-1970*, Oxford University Press, 1976, pp. 175 ff.

14. Gerald Studdert-Kennedy, *Dog-Collar Democracy: the Industrial Christian Fellowship, 1919-1929,* Macmillan, 1982, and a condensed account in '"Woodbine Willie": Religion and Politics after the Great War', *History Today,* December 1986. Maurice's grandson, a distinguished retired soldier, represents the sustained transmission of this perspective, and its decline. Like his father, also a distinguished soldier, he became Principal of his grandfather's Working Men's College in London, was a devout admirer of Ruskin, a leading figure in the ICF, prominent among the more naive 'Appeasers' of Hitler, - and father of Joan Robinson who, as a Marxist economist, represented the second theoretical antithesis to Ruskin's (or of course Gandhi's) political economy.

15. Gerald Studdert-Kennedy, *British Christians, Indian Nationalists and the Raj,* Oxford University Press, 1991, and a condensed account in 'Gandhi and the Christian Imperialists', *History Today,* October 1990.

16. The secret of Seeley's success was not in his ideas about political science, but in his fluent articulation of standard assumptions. e.g. 'It might appear that in this (Mahratta) confederacy there lay the nucleus of an Indian nationality, that Brahmanism was now about to do for the Hindus what has been done for so many races by their religion. But nothing of the kind happened ... There is then no Indian nationality, though there are some germs out of which we can conceive an Indian nationality developing itself'. *Expansion of England,* Lecture IV, 'How we Govern India'.

17. Studdert-Kennedy, *British Christians, op cit,* Ch 2, and 'Political Science and Political Theology: Lionel Curtis, Federalism and India', *Journal of Imperial and Commonwealth History,* May 1996.

18. Chatterjee, Nationalist Thought, *op. cit,* p.99. For R.G. Collingwood see his *Ruskin's Philosophy,* 1922, also (Chichester, Sussex) 1971.

19. *Unto this Last, op cit,* Section 77.

20. *Ibid,* Section 21.

21. *Ibid,* Section 54.

22. Gerald Studdert-Kennedy, The Christian Imperialism of the Die-hard Defenders of the Raj, *Journal of Imperial and Commonwealth History,* October 1990.

23. Parekh, *op cit,* p.229.

Christian Bartolf

Tolstoy and Gandhi

Undoubtedly the dialogue between Gandhi and Tolstoy was not only a correspondence of letters but also a correspondence of minds. Gandhi's reading of Tolstoy's writings can be dated back to the year 1894. Significantly the young lawyer first read Tolstoy's *The Kingdom of God is Within You* after humiliating experiences of racial discrimination in South Africa. Thus Gandhi was not attracted by Tolstoy the famous novelist, but by the Tolstoy who expounded the doctrine of Non-resistance in his three essays of confessions *My Confession, My Religion, The Kingdom of God is within You or Christianity Not as a Mystic religion but as a New Theory of Life*. Tolstoy had found a way out of his mid-life crisis through a new understanding of the Christian Gospel. Assisted by a Rabbi, Tolstoy had found a clue to a new understanding of the Gospel and of his life in a radical interpretation of Matthew's verse (5;38,39): "You heard that it was said: an eye for an eye, a tooth for a tooth. But I tell you not to resist the evil person." This Non-resistance however, according to Tolstoy, does not mean the victory of evil accepted with fatalism, but on the contrary, its destruction by the refusal to cooperate with injustice. According to the doctrine of Non-resistance it is necessary to struggle using just means against injustice in all social, political and economic fields of human life.

Gandhi did not however initiate the correspondence with Tolstoy until some years later. But as early as 1901 Tolstoy responded to the request of the Indian journalist, A. Ramaseshan, to take a stand and find encouraging words against the British colonial power.

In his letter responding to Ramaseshan, Tolstoy recommended refusal of military service and service within the colonial administration – resistance not as an armed uprising in the form of revolutionary struggle – but by "non-doing", "non-participation" in the political administration. Tolstoy combined his statement with a vehement rejection of the unjust caste system in India which he considered to cause disharmony between the ethnic groups and oppression of one group by another.

In 1903 in correspondence with the Muslim Mufti Muhammed Sadiq who wanted to confront Christian missionaries with Muslim missionaries in India, Tolstoy clearly stated that he disapproved of the activities of Muslim priests in India, because they might also contribute to communal disharmony.

In 1905 the famous Indian philosopher and pupil of Vivekananda, Baba Premananda Bharati (Surendranath Mukherji), sent a pamphlet from his exile in the USA to Tolstoy warning against the "White Danger" (adapted from the hypothetical "Yellow Danger" of Chinese and Japanese supposedly threatening European civilisation) as a reaction to the Russian-Japanese War. Tolstoy was not only concerned about the corrupting influence of the British rule in India, but also about the passionate tone of the letter addressed to him. Bharati sent, along with a second letter of 7 January 1907, his book *Shri Krishna - the Lord of Love.* Tolstoy was so fascinated by Krishna's philosophy of benevolence and love that he introduced each of his chapters of his *Letter to a Hindoo* (which he wrote in 1909) with a quotation from the Krishna book. Gandhi asked for permission to reprint Tolstoy's *Letter to a Hindoo* in his weekly *Indian Opinion.* That is why this *Letter to a Hindoo* will be quoted without denying that Tolstoy considered the miraculous legends, the cosmological myths and historical legends about the origin of the world to be fanciful. Bharati always published Tolstoy's letters of response in his magazine *The Light of India* so that another Indian contemporary, the journalist and sociologist Taraknath Das, took note of this correspondence and sent a letter to Tolstoy.

Letter to a Hindu

On 22 May 1908 the Bengali journalist, Taraknath Das, sent two issues of his magazine *Free Hindustan* to Tolstoy from his Canadian exile together with a letter in which the social revolutionary from Vancouver conveyed something of the Indian situation to Tolstoy. Taraknath Das pointed out that during the years 1891 to 1900, 19 million Indians had starved to death, whereas in the wars from 1792 to 1900 only 5 million people had died:

"You hate war, but hunger in India is more terrible than any war. It occurs in India, not due to shortage of food, but because of the plundering of the people and by the ravaging of the country by the British Government. Is it not a shame that millions of people in India are hungry, while the English traders export from India thousands of tons of rice and other foodstuffs ?"[1]

In the name of the millions of Indians starving to death, Taraknath Das asked Tolstoy for support. Tolstoy started writing his letter of reply to Taraknath Das on 7 June 1908; but it took half a year, 29 versions and 413 manuscript pages, which are kept in one of Moscow's museums on Tolstoy, before Tolstoy had composed his *Letter to a Hindoo* in December 1908 after having informed himself in more detail about the social, economic and political situation in India. Only the additional letter of an Indian teacher (G.D.Kumar) dated 21 August 1908, and further information which Tolstoy asked Taraknath Das for, enabled Tolstoy to write his statement.

Tolstoy started his article by expressing his deep concern about the misery of the oppressed Indians:-

The reason for the astonishing fact that a majority of working people submit to a handful of idlers who control their labour and their very lives is always and everywhere the same – whether the oppressors and the oppressed are of one race or whether, as in India and elsewhere, the oppressors are of a different nation.

This phenomenon seems particularly strange in India, for there more than two hundred million people, highly gifted both physically and mentally, find themselves in the power of a small group of people quite alien to them in thought, and immeasurably inferior to them in religious morality.[2]

Tolstoy saw the reason for this unnatural and inconceivable phenomenon in the fact that the enslaved do not look for an indigenous means of liberation from the intolerable oppression but rather assimilate "the anti-religious and deeply immoral social disorder in which the English and other pseudo-Christian peoples live". Science as a substitute religion was as much castigated by Tolstoy as the obedience to authorities like Tzars, Sultans, Rajas, Shahs and other heads of state who claim privileges for themselves.

Among the pseudo-legitimations of the ruling class Tolstoy first discovered the scientific justification for using violence as a 'law of history' in Darwin's theory of the survival of the fittest transferred from the world of animals to the social sphere (Social Darwinism):

The only difference in this justification by pseudo-science consists in the fact that, to the question why such and such people and not others have the right to decide against whom violence may and must be used, pseudo-science now gives a different reply to that given by religion – which declared that the right to decide was valid because it was pronounced by persons possessed of divine power. 'Science' says that these decisions represent the will of the people, which under a constitutional form of government is supposed to find expression in all the decisions and actions of those who are at the helm at the moment.[3]

This scientific superstition criticised by Tolstoy would however conquer even Japan and India and would make the oppressed commit the same mistakes as their oppressors so that Tolstoy doubts the truth of *Free Hindustan's* thesis: "Resistance against aggression is not only justified but demanded: Renunciation of resistance harms altruism as much as egotism". And Tolstoy replies to Taraknath Das:

You say that the English have enslaved your people and hold them in subjection because the latter have not resisted resolutely enough and have not met force by force.

But the case is just the opposite. If the English have enslaved the people of India it is just because the latter recognised, and still recognise, force as the fundamental principle of the social order. (....)

A commercial company enslaved a nation comprising two hundred millions. Tell this to a man free from superstition and he will fail to grasp what these words mean. What does it mean that thirty thousand men, not athletes but rather weak and ordinary people, have subdued two hundred million vigorous, clever, capable and freedom-loving people? Do not the figures make it clear that it is not the English who have enslaved the Indians, but the Indians who have enslaved themselves?[4]

Tolstoy finishes his *Letter to a Hindu* on 14 December 1908 with a comprehensive criticism of civilisation:-

What are wanted for the Indian as for the Englishman, the Frenchman, the German, and the Russian, are not Constitutions and Revolutions, nor all sorts of Conferences and Congresses, nor the many ingenious devices for submarine navigation, and aerial navigation, nor powerful explosives, nor all sorts of conveniences to add to the enjoyment of the rich, ruling classes; nor new schools and universities with innumerable faculties of science, nor an augmentation of papers and books, nor gramophones and cinematographs, nor those childish and for the most part corrupt stupidities termed art – but one thing only is needful: the knowledge of the simple and clear truth which finds place in every soul that is not stupefied by religious and scientific superstitions – the truth that for our life one law is valid – the law of love, which brings the highest happiness to every individual as well as to all mankind. Free your minds from those overgrown, mountainous imbecilities which hinder your recognition, and at once the truth will emerge from amid the pseudo-religious nonsense that has been smothering it: the indubitable, eternal truth in man, which is one and the same in all great religions of the world. It will in due time emerge and make its way to general recognition, and the nonsense that has obscured it will disappear of itself, and with it will go the evil from which humanity now suffers.[5]

Gandhi in South Africa

When Gandhi took up his correspondence with Tolstoy from London, he had gathered experience as a lawyer and political advocate of the Indian minority in South Africa for more than 15 years. With his wife Kasturba he had four children (Harilal, Manilal, Ramdas, Devadas) before he decided in 1906 to live his marriage in celibacy. Gandhi became a *brahmachari,* a seeker for truth in renunciation, through his experiences in a stretcher-bearer corps. He no longer dressed as an English gentleman but began to appreciate his Indian origin. From an assimilation always compromised by racist oppression he proceeded to the laborious work for the emancipation of ostracised Indian indentured labourers. His path and that of numerous seekers for truth, *satyagraha,* led to prison because they deliberately broke humiliating and unjust laws. In January 1908 Gandhi was in a Johannesburg prison for 20 days because he disobeyed an order to leave the Transvaal. An agreement with General Smuts did result in a preliminary release from prison at the end of January 1908; Gandhi however took up the campaign of civil disobedience again when General Smuts broke his promise. In October 1908

Gandhi was in Volksrust and Pretoria prison for about two months, in prison clothes, together with black jail inmates and ordinary criminals.

Satyagraha campaigns in South Africa started in 1906 in Johannesburg. An amendment bill to the so-called Asiatic laws was drafted to curtail the rights of Asiatic settlers. About 3,000 delegates of Indian settlers then held a meeting in Johannesburg and pledged "with God as witness" to resist the bill by non-violent means in the event of it being passed. 200 *satyagrahi* were sentenced to various prison terms because of their non-violent resistance. The *satyagrahi* expected mass arrests, fines and prison sentences. The Transvaal Indian struggle for emancipation led by Gandhi was the starting point for the first letter to Tolstoy.

In addition, Gandhi had edited the weekly magazine of the Indian minority in South Africa, *Indian Opinion*, during his farm experiment, Phoenix Settlement near Durban, an ashram where Gandhi practised his own life reforms with *satyagrahi* families. Gandhi was strongly influenced by John Ruskin's ideas whose plea for manual labour, handicrafts and agriculture as 'good labour' had impressed him. Similar ideas by the Russian peasant writers Bondarew and Sjutajew were borrowed by Tolstoy who propagated them as "bread labour" in his pamphlets. Gandhi was attracted by Tolstoy's The *Kingdom of God*:

Tolstoy's *The Kingdom of God is Within You* overwhelmed me. It left an abiding impression on me. Before the independent thinking, profound morality, and the truthfulness of this book, all the books given me . . . seemed to pale into insignificance[6].

In addition he read Tolstoy's writings on social ethics, *What is Art?, The Slavery of Our Time, The First Step, What Shall be Done? and the Letter to a Hindoo.*

Tolstoy and Gandhi

While in London for negotiations about the withdrawal of the so-called Black Act, Gandhi sent a letter to Tolstoy on 1 October 1909 giving an account of the situation of the Indian minority in Transvaal. He told of racial discrimination against 13,000 Indians and how half of them withdrew from the Transvaal so as not to bow to the unjust law, with 2,500 *satyagrahi* going to prison, some more than five times. The prison sentences were from four days to six months, in most cases with hard labour. The sentences also meant financial ruin for many of the prisoners. The delegation from the South African Indians hoped to publicise these facts in Britain.

Gandhi asked Tolstoy for permission to publish a translation of his *Letter to a Hindoo* with a certain modification, namely deleting a passage in which Tolstoy refuted the belief in reincarnation and transmigration, because millions of Indians and Chinese set great store by this religious conviction. This concept of rebirth was taught and affirmed not by scientific proof but by experience, and would thus explain some mysteries of life. To many a *satyagrahi* who was detained in the Transvaal prisons this belief had been a comfort. Gandhi did not want to persuade Tolstoy of the validity of this belief, but only asked for permission to remove the passage. In addition, Gandhi asked Tolstoy the title of the book from which he quoted Krishna.

On 7 October 1909, Tolstoy responded to Gandhi from Yasnaya Polyana:

May God help all our dear brothers and co-workers in the Transvaal. This fight between gentleness and brutality between humility and love on one side, and conceit and violence on the other, makes itself ever more strongly felt here to us also – especially in the sharp conflicts between religious obligations and the laws of the State – expressed by the conscientious objection to render military service. Such objections are taking place very frequently.[7]

Tolstoy gave Gandhi permission to publish his letter, even with changes, but pointed out that the immortality of the soul and the belief in divine truth and love would be more deeply rooted within a universal religion than the belief in rebirth. In addition, religious enterprises should be free from financial matters. That is why Tolstoy did not want to accept a fee for the publication of his letter.

On 10 November 1909, Gandhi thanked Tolstoy in another letter from London in which he added Joseph Doke's biography of Gandhi and stressed the importance of the Transvaal struggle in which half of the activists had to endure much suffering and hardship because of their principles. In this letter Gandhi pointed out that one of his sons had been arrested for the fourth time and had been sentenced to six months forced labour. In another letter of 4 April 1910, Gandhi reminded Tolstoy of a reply and also sent him his dialogue *Hind Swaraj or Indian Home Rule,* his radical criticism of modern civilisation.

Hind Swaraj

In the seventeenth chapter of *Hind Swaraj* which Tolstoy appreciated most and which Gandhi translated from Gujarati into English in 1909, Gandhi, in his dialogue, stresses the superiority of "soul force" over "brute force". In his plea for the power of truth and love, Gandhi criticises history as record of an unbroken chain of wars; historical description was nothing other than a report of the interruption of the natural path, the interruption of the power of soul force. In this chapter Gandhi elaborates the method to secure innate rights by voluntary suffering, as an alternative to armed resistance. He describes the calculated breach of law as "soul force", eg the prison term which the *satyagrahi* endures as "self-sacrifice". Instead of sacrificing other people, self-sacrifice was superior to any other sacrifice. Even if the issue proves to be unjust and a mistake, no one else has to suffer irreparable damage by this way of solving a conflict. Conscience does not allow submission to unjust laws.

Gandhi stresses the principle of 'home rule' or 'self-rule' in opposition to tyranny. Gandhi criticises the principle of decisions of majorities against minorities, because the majority might be "a gang of thieves" and the minority "a pious man". Gandhi also asks: who has got courage? The violator or the person who refuses to bow to violence? Equanimity and control over passions decide. The nonviolent resistance of a truth seeker was "a sword to all sides" which calls forth far-reaching results without blood shedding. The search for the truth of a situation leads on to a continuous quest for truth. Truthful people do not follow unjust laws eg peasants ignore unjust political restrictions and abandon them by non-cooperation. Special physical exercise for such a kind of resistance was not necessary, but weakening of the physical condition by a luxurious life style and child-marriage was unreasonable. Such "soul-force" was for the sick and frail as well as for the healthy. Complete liberation from sexual passions, voluntary poverty and cultivating fearlessness are preconditions for *satyagraha*. A celibate life, even in marriage, prevents men and women from being weak and cowardly. No financial ambitions but indifference to money shall be combined with the search for truth. One should be free of concern about relatives. A fearless person does not need a sword:

> A man with a stick suddenly came face to face with a lion and instinctively raised his weapon in self-defence. The man saw that he had only prated about fearlessness when there was none in him. That moment he dropped the stick and found himself free from all fear. [8]

Meanwhile Gandhi had published Tolstoy's *Letter to a Hindoo* in which he calls himself a modest and humble follower of Tolstoy. Following the comprehensive information Gandhi had sent Tolstoy, the latter replied from Yasnaya Polyana on 8 May 1910 that the biography of Gandhi had fascinated him and had given him the opportunity to know Gandhi better. On 23 April 1910, according to the diary of of Tolstoy's doctor, Dushan P. Makovitzki, Tolstoy had said that *Hind Swaraj* had been of exceptional interest to him, being a thorough condemnation of modern European civilisation from a religious Hindu. In a letter, 22 April 1910, to his secretary Vladimir G. Chertkov, Tolstoy said that Gandhi was very close to him. Tolstoy wrote to Gandhi, 25 April 1910, concerning *Hind Swaraj* that "the question you are dealing with in this book – passive resistance –. . . is a matter of utmost importance not only for Indians but for the whole of mankind". Gandhi replaced the term "passive resistance" with *satyagraha* about this time.

Tolstoy Farm

Meanwhile the nonviolent resistance of the Transvaal Indians escalated. Hundreds of Indian families who did not want to bow to the colonial administration were ruined and deprived of their property. Gandhi, together with his German-Jewish friend and architect Hermann Kallenbach, had acquired a piece of land near Johannesburg for cultivation. Kallenbach had bought the land, a settlement with agriculture, fruit trees and gardens, for the Indian refugees. Kallenbach had been impressed by Tolstoy's

Confession which concerned Tolstoy's mid-life crisis and spoke to his own situation. Kallenbach asked Tolstoy for permission to name the settlement after him since he hoped to develop a community life according to Tolstoy's ideals. In a letter of 15 August 1910, Gandhi also asked Tolstoy the same and expressed his deep friendship with Kallenbach. Through the name Tolstoy Farm, Gandhi gave Tolstoy the opportunity to participate in the campaign of noncooperation and nonviolent resistance of the Transvaal Indians.

Tolstoy's Legacy

In a letter sent by Kotschety on Tolstoy's behalf and dated 7 September 1910 (the letter was received by Gandhi after Tolstoy's death) Tolstoy revealed his thoughts arising from his reading of Gandhi's letters and reports:

> The more I live – and specially now that I am approaching death, the more I feel inclined to express to others the feelings which so strongly move my being, and which according to my opinion, are of great importance. That is, what one calls non-resistance, is in reality nothing else but the discipline of love undeformed by false interpretation. Love is the aspiration for communion and solidarity with other souls, and that aspiration always liberates the source of noble activities. That love is the supreme and unique law of human life, which everyone feels in the depth of one's soul. We find it manifested most clearly in the soul of the infants. Man feels it so long as he is not blinded by the false doctrines of the world.[9]

In his last letter Tolstoy gives the example of conscientious objection to military service and points to the 'manifest outrageous contradiction' between Christian teaching and political logic by ending his letter as follows:

> That contradiction is felt by all the governments, by your British Government as well as by our Russian Government; and therefore, by the spirit of conservatism natural to these governments, the opposition is persecuted, as we find in Russia as well as in the articles of your journal, more than any other anti-governmental activity. The governments know from which direction comes the principal danger and try to defend themselves with a great zeal in that trial not merely to preserve their interests but actually to fight for their very existence. With my perfect esteem, Leo Tolstoy.[10]

Notes and References

1. Letter from Taraknath Das to Leo Tolstoy (22/5/08). Quoted from Alexander Shifman: Tolstoy and India, New Delhi 1978. p.71.

2. Leo Tolstoy: *Letter to a Hindoo* (1908). Documented by Kalidas Nag: Tolstoy and Gandhi, Patna 1950, p.82.

3. Leo Tolstoy: *Letter to a Hindoo* (1908). Documented by Kalidas Nag, p. 90.

4. Leo Tolstoy: *Letter to a Hindoo* (1908). Documented by Kalidas Nag, p. 92f.

5. Leo Tolstoy: *Letter to a Hindoo* (1908). Documented by Kalidas Nag, p. 98.

6. M.K.Gandhi: *An Autobiography* or The Story of My Experiments with Truth, Ch. 15.

7. Letter from Leo Tolstoy to M.K.Gandhi (7/10/09). Documented by Kalidas Nag, p. 63.

8. M.K.Gandhi: *Hind Swaraj* (1908). Ch. 17.

9. Letter from Leo Tolstoy to M.K.Gandhi (7/9/10). Documented by Kalidas Nag, p. 71.

10. Letter from Leo Tolstoy to M.K.Gandhi (7/9/10). Documented by Kalidas Nag, p. 75.

B.R. Nanda

Gandhi and Vivekananda

For nearly a hundred years Vivekananda has occupied a unique position in the history of India as the prophet of a resurgent Hinduism. He had shot into fame with his address at the Chicago Parliament of Religions in September 1893. His exposition of classical Hinduism thrilled his countrymen, as it satisfied a deep and long-felt psychological need of the Hindu intelligentsia. Throughout the nineteenth century Hinduism had been on the defensive, believing itself to be beleaguered by erosion from within and assaults from without. The problem, as the founders of a new religious society, the 'Tatbabodhini Sabha' had posed as far back as 1839, was: 'How to propagate an ancient, dignified and intellectual form of Hinduism... to put a ban to the spread of atheism and Christianity.' Experienced British observers openly said that English education, railways and modern communications would undermine Hinduism. A senior British civilian, Sir Alfred Lyall, predicted in 1872 that 'the old gods of Hinduism will die in these elements of intellectual light and die as a net full of fish, lifted up out of water.' The Hindu response to this challenge was two-fold: efforts at internal reform and a reassertion of religious identity. In the mid-1890s there were signs of a religious revival. 'A dozen years ago,' the *Amrit Bazar Patrika* wrote on 4 October 1895, 'when educated men sat together they talked of politics; now, generally speaking, they talk of religion.'

It was against this background that we should appraise the role of Vivekananda. He sought to purify and revitalize Hinduism so as to fit it for the twentieth century. As his ardent disciple, Sister Nivedita, said, he was the first to formulate the basic character of Hinduism as a system of thought and way of life in the modern age. He expounded the Vedanta of the Upanishads not as a life-negating and other-worldly philosophy, but as 'a universal and practical creed which was to be carried into everyday life, city life, the country life and home life of every nation.' His Vedanta was based on eternal principles and did not depend on any particular book; it embraced all the scriptures of the world; going beyond toleration and brotherhood, it recognised 'God in every soul and God immanent in nature.' He looked forward to a universal religion which would be 'infinite like the God it would preach and whose sun would shine upon the followers of Krishna and of Christ, on saints and sinners alike, which would not be Brahmanic, Buddhist, Christian or Mohammedan, but the sum-total of all these and still have infinite place for development.' There would be no conversions and upon the banner of every religion would be inscribed; 'Help and not Fight', 'Assimilation, not destruction' and 'Harmony and Peace and not Dissension.'

To the Hindus, Vivekananda presented Vedanta as an instrument of a spiritual and moral revolution in which reason was to be an active agent of change. He felt India had a strong rationalist tradition, but over the centuries rationalism had been pushed to the background. He ridiculed the mumbo jumbo of ritual and superstition in which an ignorant and selfish priestly class had entangled the Hindu masses. 'Think of the last six hundred or seven hundred years of degradation' he said, 'when grown-up men have been discussing for years whether they should drink a glass of water with the right hand or the left, gargle five or six times ... Our religion is in the kitchen. Our God is in the cooking pot.' He blamed the priests for 'doling out ditch water, overlooking the eternal fount of amrit (nectar) that lies behind us.' He denounced the degeneration of the caste system and the curse of untouchability. What sense did it make, he asked in preaching *Advaitism*, after reducing *bhangis* and *pariahs* to their degraded condition? He condemned child marriages and called the opponents of the Age of Consent Bill 'religious hypocrites, as if religion consists in making a girl mother at the age of twelve or thirteen.'

Vivekananda had the courage to clash head-on with Hindu orthodoxy. Once, while he was explaining at a meeting in Madras the nuances of Vedanta, somebody from the audience interjected: Why if this was so, it had never before been mentioned by any of the old masters. 'Because', Vivekananda shot back, 'I was born for this and it was left for me to do so.' When the code of Manu was invoked, Vivekananda declared that all social rules which stood in the way of unfolding freedom must be destroyed. He wanted to raise the status of women in Indian society; the level of a civilization, he said, was judged by the way it treated its women: 'With 500 motivated men it will take me 50 years to transform India, with 50 motivated women it may take me only a year.' He considered 'the great national sin' was the neglect of the masses. Priestly power and foreign conquest had trodden down the poor of India for centuries. No amount of politics would be of any avail, until the masses were 'well-educated, well-fed and well-cared for. If we want to regenerate India, we must work for them ... I do not believe in a God who cannot give us bread here, giving eternal bliss in heaven.'

As for relations between adherents of differents religions, Vivekananda was not for *tolerance*, but for *acceptance* of other forms of worship. 'If you are born a Christian', he said, 'be a good Christian. If you are born a Hindu, be a good Hindu. If you are born a Muslim be a good Muslim.' Mankind had to realise, he said that 'religions are but the varied expressions of *The Religion* which is *Oneness*, so that each may choose the path that suits him best'. Vivekananda especially commended the spirit of equality in Islam, and in a letter dated 10 June 1898 to a Muslim correspondent, even envisaged 'a junction of the two great systems, Hinduism and Islam, into a Vedantic brain and an Islamic body.'

Vivekananda's pleas for religious harmony did not mean that he agreed with or commended everything that had been said or done in India or elsewhere in the name of any religion, whether Hinduism, Buddhism, Islam or Christianity. As we have already seen, he did not spare his own co-religionists. He had a knack of applying a sort of shock-therapy to jolt the orthodox, the complacent, the arrogant, and the bigoted out of their grooves. Some of his critics in the Parliament of Religions had argued that since the Hindus had never been conquerors of other lands, and were also poor, he had no business to preach his religion in western countries. Vivekananda told them that he admired the life and teachings of Jesus Christ, but wondered whether they understood the religion they professed. 'All this prosperity,' he said, 'all this from Christ! Those who call upon Christ care for nothing but to a mass riches!. Christ would not find a stone on which to lay his head among you. . . .'

Vivekananda pooh-poohed the idea that the adoption of western ideas, western language, western food and western manners would make Indians as strong and powerful as the western nations. 'Does the ass in lion's skin' he asked, 'become a lion?' At the same time he rebuked those of his co-religionists who advocated a revival or restoration of India's past. What he wanted was 'the strength of old India finding new applications and undreamt of expression in the new age.' He longed to see Hinduism imbibe something of 'the masculine vigour and dynamism' which had so much fascinated him in the European nations.

II

Gandhi was the most charismatic Indian leader of the twentieth century as Vivekananda was of the nineteenth. They were contemporaries though they never met, nor had any interaction while they lived. Their public life started about the same time. Gandhi's South African odyssey began in 1893, the year of Vivekananda's triumph at the Chicago Parliament of Religions. The two men vastly differed in their family background and educational and social milieu in which they grew up. Vivekananda was a religious leader, the proclaimed heir of the great saint of Bengal, Sri Ramakrishna; Gandhi plunged into the political arena at the age of twenty-four and for the next fifty years led struggles against racialism and imperialism. Vivekananda was only six years older than Gandhi, but died young in 1902 at the age of 39.

Despite these obvious differences it is possible to detect remarkable similarities between their thought-patterns and teachings, so much so that it seems as if it was Gandhi's historic role to carry forward the work for reform and revitalization of Hinduism, which Vivekananda left unfinished.

Unlike Vivekananda, Gandhi's life was not suddenly transformed by contact with a great saint. His religious quest really began soon after his arrival in South Africa when some missionaries tried to convert him to Christianity. He had a sceptical streak in him and decided to study not only Christianity, but other religions, including the religion of his birth. A decisive influence on him during this formative period was that of

Rajchandra, a young jeweller, poet and savant of Bombay, who was (in Gandhi's words) one of the 'three moderns' who had influenced him most, the others being Tolstoy and Ruskin. Rajchandra gave a sense of direction to Gandhi's religious quest; he stressed the importance of accord between belief and action; it was the way a man lived, not the recital of a verse or the form of prayer which made him a good Hindu, a good Muslim or a good Christian. Himself a Jain, Rajchandra restored Gandhi's faith in Hinduism.

The book which became Gandhi's strongest bond with Hinduism was the *Bhagavad Gita*. Two words in the *Gita* opened to him limitless vistas. *Aparigraha* (non-possession) implied that he had to jettison the material goods which cramped the spirit; *Sambhava* (equability) required that he must remain unruffled by pain and pleasure, victory or defeat, and work without hope of success or fear of failure. After pondering day after day on the *Gita*, he came to believe that what could not be followed in day-to-day life could not be called religion. Meditation and worship 'were not exclusive things to be kept like jewellery in a strong box'; they had to be seen in every act of the religious aspirant.

Gandhi's religious quest triggered off his metamorphosis from an upper-middle class barrister into Churchill's 'half-naked faqir', a *sanyasin*, all but in name. Religion transformed Gandhi, but he also transformed religion.

Like Vivekananda, Gandhi threw down a gauntlet to Hindu orthodoxy, and questioned the validity of some centuries-old dogmas and practices. He condemned animal sacrifices, child marriages, the dowry system and the greed of the priests and dirt around the temples. His severest strictures were reserved for the aberrations of the caste system and its monstrous progeny, untouchability. When an eminent Hindu Mahasabha leader, Dr. Moonje, cited verses to prove that untouchability was part of Hinduism, Gandhi told him: 'I do not accept everything written in Sanskrit as gospel truth. No book,' he said, 'could be limited to a single interpretation, irrespective of time and place, and every formula of every religion must be subject to "the acid test of reason".' He reinterpreted both in theory and practice several Hindu concepts to suit the changing times. For example, fasting was not merely a necessary ritual for the pious; it could be used a tool of social action. An ashram was not merely a place for prayer and meditation, but for training workers for service of the country.

Gandhi worked ceaselessly for the breaking of barriers between various castes, communities and religions and even nations. Like Vivekananda, he called for a new deal for women, and for the 'naked hungry mass' in the villages. It is curious that the word *daridranarayan*, which Gandhi often used, was coined by Vivekananda; it was not meant to idealize poverty, but to bring out both the cruel predicament and essential nobility of the poor of India. Like Vivekananda, Gandhi also attempted to shift Hinduism from its predominantly individualistic and other-worldly moorings. 'The way to find God,' he said, 'is to see him in his creation and be with it.'

Vivekananda had taken his lessons in religious tolerance from his master, Sri Ramakrishna. Gandhi delved into the scriptures of major religions and discovered an underlying unity in their teachings. 'God's grace and revelation,' he said, 'is not the monopoly of any race or nation; they descend equally upon all who wait upon God.' No religion was absolutely perfect; but every religion was to be judged not by its worst specimens, but by the best it produced. 'If you read the Koran,' Gandhi wrote, 'you must read with the eye of the Muslim; if you read the Bible, you must read with the eye of the Christian; if you read the Gita, you must read it with the eye of the Hindu. What is the use of scanning details and then holding up a religion to ridicule?'

For Gandhi communal harmony was not an academic issue; it was vital for success of his struggle against the imperial power which claimed that it was the discord between the religious communities which barred India's progress towards self-government.

Like Vivekananda, Gandhi, while deriving sustenance from the unsullied fount of ancient Indian spirituality, responded to western influences with judicious discrimination, accepting what was life-giving and rejecting what was deleterious.

In one important respect, Gandhi differed with Vivekananda, and it was fortunate that he did so. Vivekananda had rejected politics. 'The Greeks had sought political liberty,' he had noted in one of his lecture notes, 'the Hindus had sought spiritual liberty.' Vivekananda called for a spiritual and moral revolution to precede a political revolution. He neither used the word nationality, nor proclaimed an era of nation-making. 'Man-making', he said, was his task.

Gandhi's political mission and religious quest began simultaneously when he was in his twenties, his religious convictions gave him the strength and the stamina for a half-century of a crowded political career. He was accused of introducing religion into politics, but it was not the organized religion of dogmas, rituals, superstition and bigotry. In the very passage where he said that politics could not be separated from religion, he had made it clear that religion in this context was synonymous with ethics: 'Here religion does not mean sectarianism. It means belief in the ordered moral government of the universe. This religion transcends Hinduism, Islam and Christianity.'

In a recent book, *Creating Minds*, Howard Gardner, has profiled seven geniuses of the modern era - Einstein, Freud, Gandhi, T.S. Eliot, Stravinsky, Martha Graham and Picasso who, among other things, not merely solved existing problems but identified new ones. Looking back from the vantage point of the 1990s, it seems remarkable that, in the first decade of this century, Gandhi should have launched his crusades against racialism, colonialism, runaway industrialism, religious fundamentalism and violence. A good deal of Gandhi's agenda is likely to spill into the next century.

Julian Brotherton

Gandhi's Educational Message for us Today

In general, the Western World follows India in rejecting Gandhi as a social reformer. We regard his view of society as utopian, or at least romantic and against "progress". His work for education, although he called it his best gift to India, is quite unknown in the West, not even receiving a mention in otherwise outstanding biographies.

Why is this? A bigger mistake could hardly be conceived. The essence of Gandhi's educational thought is of crucial relevance to us in the West at this time of need, and possibly of even more importance for India. At least, here in Britain, more and more people's eyes are being opened to this fact, as we watch our schools becoming forcing-houses for consumption of "subject-matter", while education is treated as a package to be delivered to the consumer.

But if Gandhi was speaking for the Indian villagers of half a century ago, how can his words also be so modern? He was not even an educationalist! It is true that, on the face of it, much of his advice might seem culture-bound and only of remote, historical curiosity. But this is what is so exciting about Gandhi: we have to look a little more closely at his words. What he was asking from teachers, in conditions unrecognisably different from ours today in the West, contains an essential core which is entirely free from any culture or period of history and which comes purely from his understanding of human nature. We can hardly claim to have transcended this since his time!

It becomes crystal clear how relevant it is for us after a little "unpacking" and reformulating for our times, so as to apply it to the exigencies of the educational scene today. In what follows I shall attempt to explore how this might be done.

There are two interlinked themes in his recommendations – first, his insistence that school should not be separated from "real-life" and second, that a teacher's central purpose should be "the education of the heart": personal and moral development. He saw this as part of growing closer to God, our spiritual path.

In the village India of the time, ''real-life'', of course, was manual labour and such life-skills as carpentry or leather-work.. If a child could become expert in contributing through "crafts" to his community in a direct and visible way, at the same time as pursuing his academic learning through his work, an integration of personal and intellectual growth would result. We are, of course, very far from linking these two aspects of education today. The child's self-esteem and sense of joy in giving genuine service (for which he would be expertly trained) would be a firm psychological basis for moral responsibility as well as the best framework for academic progress.

Gandhi realised that meaningful practical work could generate wide-ranging intellectual possibilities. Mathematics, geography and so forth would emerge, with careful planning, from the experience of manual work (which ''sharpens the mind''). Thus properly chosen practical work, for Gandhi, embodied a potential for academic, psychological, emotional and spiritual development. Gandhi deplored the demoralising experience which school children have of being mere passive consumers, parasites on the adult world, the artificial separation of child and grown-up. At this point, the practising teacher of today might well sigh and read no more! Especially if he knows the parallel story of Dewey's work in America, around the same period, for similar (but not identical) objectives; in spite of Dewey's eloquence and professionalism, and his principle, like Gandhi's, that preparation for life cannot be separated from life itself, he was not publicly accepted in the end. Like Gandhi, he was accused of diluting standards of academic achievement. In the modern world there was no time to connect school with ''real-life''!

The difference between Dewey and Gandhi lay in Gandhi's more profound vision of human potential. His ideal was not simply the "all-round person" with open mind and curiosity about life, but a deeply compassionate individual with real longing to serve humanity and commitment to non-violence. How realistic at the present time is Gandhi's determination to find this point of interaction with 'serious adult work"? As work becomes more specialised and complex, further and further removed from anything in which a child could participate, it is not automatically evident how the world of school and the world outside could meet, in any real collaborative sense.

But already it is happening, and far more than it was a few years ago. Even the youngest children are often involved in assessing and planning improvements to their environment and the workings of school life. Recently, in Britain, all age groups have begun to study technology in their curriculum. This may involve advice and cooperation with experts outside. For pupils over 14, there are the National Vocational Qualifications, as well as Business Education. This is (for better or worse) very close indeed to ''real life'', but what would Gandhi have had to say about it? Can it be seen as an example of ''learning through crafts''? As a matter of fact when questioned about older children and city schools, Gandhi explicitly advocated such studies, under his concepts of ''crafts''. He often spoke of industrial training and commercial skills for school pupils. So, it seems, he was actually recommending, fifty years ago, what we are encouraging now.

Gandhi was under no illusions about the aims of industry, or about the philistine and materialistic tendencies of young people, alongside their innate idealism. Quite commonly now on the ordinary curriculum we have children studying stocks and shares, advertising, marketing and "profit-sales maximisation". In other words, children are actually studying how to make money and compete with their rivals.

What Gandhi was recommending then, (and, by extension, what he would be telling us now), evidently runs a big risk of promoting the very reverse of his objectives– a culture of commercialism.

But Gandhi knew this. Unfortunately, teachers of these subjects are most unlikely to have read his own stern warnings. If education is to have a vocational foundation, he insists, it must be based on "true economics". This means on social justice and equal good for all. "If economics enables the strong to exploit the weak, it spells death". Education "should not result in material power, but spiritual force". What he wrote in the 1930's is today of much more urgent significance, not less.

The modern form of "Craft Education", which has been suggested runs a much greater risk than the "crafts" of Gandhi's India. It is the risk of turning children into crude utilitarians and opportunists, or at best providing nothing more than a work-force for the economy.

Presented from another perspective, with a quite different set of principles, the very same experiences could provide children with highly effective exercises in consciousness-raising, about service to others and the importance of individuals. Gandhi himself pointed to urban industry as having this potential.

In spite of being fully aware of the dangers of "materialistic" industrial activity, Gandhi actually chose this field to teach moral and personal development as well as academic work. It is a kind of paradox which well illustrates his extraordinary originality.

The most successful and radical initiatives at the present time for bringing children and the adult workplace together are in New York (the City as School scheme). School-age pupils are based in businesses or industries, newspaper offices, hospitals and so forth, but at the same time they receive general academic teaching. There is, of course, no guarantee that this symbiosis of education and industry will result in anything more than speeding up the "rat-race". The potential for much more than that is formidable and exciting.

Gandhi perhaps wisely, left everything to the individual teacher, who might attempt to practise his vision "as far as possible". If one cannot succeed, another will perhaps carry it further, he remarked. He trusted teachers to discover what is practicable for them. A Book of Rules or Handbook would have been abhorrent to him. Education cannot be dispensed on prescription. It is not a commodity.

This may be true, but it is necessary to consider how the various elements of a modern curriculum can be given at least some Gandhian tone or flavour, under the limitations of our present-day school conditions and pressures. In every subject or field of study, even in those which are necessarily classroom-based, there is an ethical dimension. There are social and moral aspects to it. Take mathematics as an example, an area which appears quite value-free. But behind the figures, underneath the bank-rates, mortgages, tax-rates, discounts, profits and book-keeping are human decisions. Money was, after all, invented by us and every movement of it brings some benefit or damage to us or to others. How can a teacher discuss this? Covetousness, generosity and fairness are an inseparable part of this subject. Values are inescapable, even in mathematics. The slightest move in this direction and we enter discussion of *sarvodaya*, justice, freedom, equality. Knowledge on its own, as young people know better than we do if anything, can never mean much. If this is the case with mathematics, how much more so, perhaps, with the sciences and the humanities.

An obvious example of how we can edge towards a less violent society, as many schools are already trying to do, is by, bringing out the values of an environmental approach, sustainability, the oneness of creation, and our very real responsibilities to other life-forms sharing the planet. The received view of Nature as little more than a "resource" can only be transcended by inspiring children with a real love of place and of creatures; to stir and awaken the heart first. Such 'romanticism' may be distrusted by educational purists as indicating bias, but the plain fact is that exploitation will continue unless resisted with deep commitment.

We follow Gandhi only in so far as we can persuade or win over opponents, instead of becoming polarised against them. This involves the kind of work done in Peace Education, which covers conflict situations and mediation work within school itself, using well-tried techniques. Peace education, like environmental studies in schools, has been worked out now for many years and a large variety of teaching material has been evolved. Gandhi would have approved, but we are only at the edge of what he envisaged in education unless we include some practical involvement in the local community. We may or may not be able to integrate classwork with genuine service outside. The structure of adult work and society now makes anything further than intermittent and partial integration very difficult.

Closely related to this approach is the area known as "multicultural" work, which is also highly developed and researched now. Knowledge of different customs or life-styles of particular communities is an essential precondition for equality in the Gandhian sense, but "uplift for all" does not necessarily result from it. A feeling for our common humanity is much more than knowledge. Well-meaning attempts to glamorise "ethnicity" can exclude, rather than include people. Teachers have an immensely demanding job of affirming the personal worth of all pupils. Some interesting techniques are being tried now for reducing bullying and for structuring a more democratic involvement of pupils in schools.

All these initiatives, broadly speaking, do contribute to an updated form of Gandhi's "Constructive Programme", for the Western world. The spirit of *Ahimsa*, Gandhi's indefinable "extra", cannot be formulated or packaged, even though there are practical manuals on how to employ it as "a weapon of matchless potency". Gandhi called it "an attribute of the brave . . . . it doesn't come within the reach of the coward" (*Harijan*, 1938). He saw the development of it as the ultimate, if perhaps unreachable, goal of education.

Experience of the creative arts would seem to be closely supportive of Gandhian objective, although indirectly. The arts develop pupils' emotional and intuitive range of understanding, a necessary precondition for "the education of the heart" – in other words, for the caring personality.

Literature widens our perception of relationships and motivation. The arts may not lead directly to any conviction that virtue is beautiful or desirable, but if such conviction is to appear, art education will enrich it.

The arts are also recognised as involving faculties very similar to religious awareness, as if there was a kind of experiential continuum between them.

Not only this, but it is now argued that the most important capacities required today for entering the world of industry are adaptability, imagination and creative thinking. Such qualities are valued more by industrialists than technical knowledge in the school-leaver. This can be imparted later while at work.

Clearly, for all these reasons, the arts should play a large part in any school aspiring to some Gandhian ideals. The curious fact is that Gandhi seems to have rather underestimated the arts in education. He describes art as too far from "reality", or "a poor copy of nature". His extra-acute perception of Goodness and Truth perhaps overshadowed Beauty (and its effects).

Very few people would now disagree with Gandhi that the essential facts about world religions should be taught to children. But the implications of his philosophy and of his prayerful life indicate much more than this. We fail, surely, unless children can feel a true reverence for the thoughts and practices of (say) Judaism or Islam?

Gandhi used prayers and devotional songs from various faiths. But, as with so much in teaching, the teacher's attitude is the key. Vinoba Bhave writes (in *Thoughts on Education*), "My only plan for religious teaching is to choose good men/women as teachers". Gandhi saw religion, or coming closer to God, as practised through human interaction. The ideal teacher resembles the *karma Yogi*, who does not work for personal reward (even though he may receive it!). If we feel discouraged by this lofty ideal, we have to remind ourselves of Gandhi's thoroughly pragmatic nature too, and the fact that he knew his own inadequacies.

Since Gandhi's time, many types of 'self-development courses' have been devised to build awareness, self-esteem and inter-personal skills, both for children and for adults. Teachers can benefit from these before embarking on the road into the rather crude and discouraging atmosphere of many schools today.

We may only catch a glimpse of the personal qualities of Gandhi's picture of the community, the teacher and the child, but this does not mean we make no progress. Many schools do understand that personal growth and its "deep syllabus" are functions of the school as community. It is hard to prescribe in detail. As Vinoba said about Gandhian education: 'If they turn it into a system, they will kill it'.

Gandhi's advice about education is universal. It is as fresh as ever. Translated in terms of our present situation, it is the purest form of realism we have to work with.

Bibliography

Bhave, Vinoba: *Thoughts on Education* (Sarva Seva Sangh Prakashan, Varanasi, India)

Biswas, A. & Aggarwal, J. (1968). *Seven Indian Educationists*. New Delhi.

Brotherton, J. (1993) *Gandhi and Western Education Today* (The Gandhi Foundation).

Cenkner, W. (1976). *The Hindu Personality in Education*. Delhi.

Educational Reconstruction. (All India Educ. Conference, 1973).

Gandhi, D.N. & Sharma, R. (1965). *Educational Theories*. Agra.

Gandhi, M.K. (1951). *Towards New Education*. Navajivan.

Gandhi, M.K. (1951). *Basic Education*. Navajivan.

Gandhi M.K. *True Education* (Navajivan).

Patel, M. (1953). *The Educational Philosophy of Mahatma Gandhi*. Navajivan.

Ramanathan, G. (1962). *Education from Dewey to Gandhi*. London.

Rawat, P.L. (1965). *History of Indian Education*. Agra.

Ways and *Means*: *An Approach to Problem Solving*. The Book Centre, Friends' House, Euston Rd., London NW1 2BJ.

Wilson, J. (1990). *A New Introduction to Moral Education*. Cassell.

Fred Blum

Does Gandhi's philosophy of Non-violent resistance have any place in 1980's Britain?

The philosophy of non-violent resistance is an aspect of the more comprehensive philosophy of non-violence which is best expressed in the world *Satyagraha* which means "the power of truth" or "truth force". Gandhi himself used this word to express what was for him the essence of non-violence. We must, therefore, begin with the question asked by Pilate: "What is truth?"

I

The truth which Gandhi had in mind was not simply the absence of untruth, of a life. Nor was it simply the factual truth about a phenomenon which could be readily comprehended by our five senses and be expressed in a logical scientific way (though it was certainly not in any conflict with such truthfulness). Gandhi's understanding included this kind of truth but went much deeper and comprehended a space-time dimension other than that of the clock and measuring rod. The truth of non-violence was for Gandhi the truth of a universal reality, a truth which transcends the peculiarities and boundaries of a particular culture or national heritage. It is the true way of life, the true way of relating to other persons and to the human community of which we are part. Indeed, it includes our true relationships to nature, to our environment and ultimately to the universe in which and of which we are an infinitesimally small speck. Ultimately such truth is expressed in love.

To be true to ourselves in the *Satyagraha* sense of truth – as well as the Biblical sense of the Truth – means to be free to live our lives according to our deepest insights into the kind of people we essentially are. It means to be free to act accordingly, free to relate to others in terms of the best in us, and thus truly to love, free to partake in building a human community which gives to every human being the opportunity to develop his or her creative potentialities and to give one's fruit for "the good of all."

Truth thus understood is something intimately personal. Only I and those who truly love me and hence truly know me - and God - know this uniquely personal truth. Yet at the same time this truth is universal in a twofold sense: all human beings share the characteristics, tendencies or energies which in each of us take a unique expression. The building stones from which we are made are, so to speak, universal, though each building has a unique form and a unique expression. These buildings, furthermore, are built on a ground which is universal in the sense that it is the same, no matter what the differences in the patterns of culture may be and no matter what period of history we are concerned with. The "ground of our being" is timeless and universal, that is eternal. The forces or energies which are alive in the depth of our souls follow a lawfulness of their own, different from the laws which a given culture or a nation state may legislate at a certain period of history. In this sense there is a transpersonal truth, expressing the lawfulness of a deeper reality of life – a reality which transcends the logic of death by opening the gates to resurrection – to eternal life.

Non-violence as Gandhi understood it – *Satyagraha* – expressed this twofold quality of truth in the communal political life of India. It was the instrument that enabled an unarmed country, subjected to British rule for centuries, to resist non-violently and thus to bring about national independence. It is again important to emphasise that though independence was of decisive importance in the non-violent struggle for Indian freedom, it was in no way an exclusive objective for Gandhi. It was part of a struggle which was concerned with a total transformation of the Indian way of life - of politics, of society, indeed of all relationships whether personal, intrapersonal, interpersonal or concerned with work or nature.

II

An understanding of this "totality" of transformation is essential for an appreciation of the relevance of non-violence in Britain today. The very essence of non-violence is expressed in the unity of Gandhi's world view. He rejected the Niebuhrian dichotomy between "Moral Man and Immoral Society" by proclaiming the inseparable unity of our personal ethical values and of our public ethical standards. To resist non-violently meant to act with ethical responsibility in politics. It meant to accept the same ultimate values for our public life as citizens as we do for our private lives in our personal and familial relationships.

This fundamental unity and oneness of ethics is most powerfully expressed in the Sermon on the Mount. Gandhi knew the New Testament well and though he never became a Christian he always acknowledged his love of the Gospel. This love was most concretely expressed in his insistence on the harmony of means and ends if we are to live and act in truth. Non-violent resistance is an expression of this unity which implies that we take suffering upon ourselves rather than inflict it upon others.

Like everything in life which touches an ultimate truth, the acceptance of suffering as an aspect of non-violent resistance brings up to the resort's edge which separates good and evil, truth and falsehood. The taking-upon-ourselves of suffering, to be true, must be the flower of strength rather than of weakness (which in its extreme form may become masochism). The kind of strength which is a prerequisite for a true voluntary acceptance of suffering must be rooted in a living relationship to a deeper universal reality of life. We may or may not call this reality God but its hallmark is its ability to provide nourishment and sustenance from the universal "ground of our being" and thus to reach a level of consciousness which is most beautifully expressed in St. Francis' saying: "It is in giving that we receive, it is in pardoning that we are pardoned, it is in dying that we are born to eternal life."

For these words to have flesh and blood rather than being pious pronouncements we must have reached a stage in the development of consciousness which enables us to move from the realm of the opposites (most drastically expressed in "an eye for an eye, a tooth for a tooth") into the realm of the paradox (where we will find our true self by losing our little self). Non-violent resistance implies a movement towards such a mode of consciousness. It implies an ability to transcend the psychological mechanisms which determine much of our ordinary daily life and to be nourished by the energy of a universal source which enables us realistically to become agents of transformation of "what is" into "what is meant to be" - if the true essence of nonviolent resistance is to be realised.

To sum up: unity of our ethical standards, unity rooted in a living relatedness to the universal energies alive in all human beings, a striving for the highest and deepest we are meant to be, these are the foundations of non-violent resistance. The latter presupposes a development of consciousness which makes truth a force animating our whole life rather than a philosophical idea or a theological postulate. Being centred in our true selves as individual people and relating in terms of our true self to others as well as the human community and organised society is the core of non-violent resistance as Gandhi understood it.

III

Non-violent resistance thus understood has a twofold place in 1980's Britain. First, it provides a way of transformation which unites us rather than deepening existing cleavages and conflicts. Secondly, implicit in non-violence and the way of transformation is the goal of a social order which can resolve some of the most urgent problems of our time. In order to clarify these statements we must first say something about Britain in the 1980's. What are our most pressing problems? Where are the greatest dangers we must be aware of?

The 80's are a watershed in British history.

We witness the end of this final phase of an era which has freed the productive resources of humankind and proven the possibility of creating wealth unheard of in human history. Indeed we have been so successful in creating wealth that we have reduced the need for "labour" to such an extent as to be confronted with an unemployment problem which cannot be resolved within the present organisation of the economy. We have, furthermore, been so much concerned with wealth and material standards of living as to give only secondary importance to the impact of work which is organised on the basis of technical efficiency rather than human productivity. Hence new ways have to be found to create meaningful work opportunities if major social unrest and chronic illness of the body politic is to be avoided.

This diagnosis of Britain in the 1980's is not contradicted by the policies of the present government. Regardless of our party-political position, we are witnessing a phenomenon of historical significance. As the age of the classical free market mechanism reflecting the divine harmony of the universe is coming to an end, we are attempting to re-live once more its essence. This is an aspect of a period of transition to a new era which we are called upon to bring into being.

The basic choices which we are facing are: an attempt to cling to outmoded forms, reacting against the old forms, or creatively transforming the old forms while preserving the true values which they represent.

The desire to cling to outmoded forms is always a temptation when the way to new forms is difficult or obscure. The temptation simply to react against the old and to "do" the opposite is equally strong for those who despair of any solution within the existing framework of society. Yet neither is adequate to meet the real challenge of our time: to preserve those values of personal freedom rooted in truth as understood by Gandhi – and the Gospel, values which are the essence of a truly democratic society, at the same time finding new ways of living them and hence new forms of organizing society.

No society can endure for long periods of time the kind of meaninglessness of work and leisure combined with the unemployment prevalent today which is but a symptom of a seriously – and chronically – ill social body. New ways and forms are imperative. The only real issue is: do we create these new forms while preserving the universally true values which we have embodied in our personal, social and political lives, or are we to violate these values either by attempting to preserve old forms which have lost their power to give life to these values or by trying to overcome our present difficulties by a kind of reaction which is unable to differentiate between what is good and what is bad in what we have inherited.

IV

Nonviolent resistance, understood in the Gandhian sense as an expression of a philosophy of non-violent transformation, has a decisive place in resolving these problems because it shows both a way and a goal. The latter is, so to speak, implicit in the former just as when

Jesus spoke about the Way, the Truth and Life, the end or purpose was implicit in the direction which the choice of a Way implies. To resist non-violently is never primarily opposition to something. It is always subsidiary to a struggle for the realisation of a vision of a true human order.

To be truly human, a social order must reflect a universal truth. Gandhi was undoubtedly one of the few statesmen of our time who was universal in the sense of penetrating to a depth of understanding which transcends the cultural and historically unique aspects of a particular religious or national heritage. The vision which animated his struggle for truth and the light which guided him in finding his way was universal. The central tenet of non-violent resistance – the unit of life as expressed in the interrelationship of means and ends – is a universal truth which transcends the manifold time – and culture – bound ways of justifying actions which are recognized as evil in themselves. The recognition of this interdependency unifies the different realms of life by applying what we may call religious values to daily political life. This one-ness means at the same time a penetration to the ground of life – to that depth which we all share by virtue of being truly human.

In the Western world the striving for a universal truth which is also timeless found its classical expression in the natural law tradition of the Church. An important tenet of this tradition is that human beings must always be ends in relation to each other and never become means for the purposes of other people. This universal proposition implies a recognition of the interdependence of means and ends, of the way and the goal. It is indeed a universal guide for the development of a true human order - an order which enables everyone to develop his or her true God-given potentialities and thus to contribute to the human community.

To take non-violent resistance seriously means to take seriously the universal laws which guide our personal and social development. I want to illustrate what this means for overcoming the ills of our society as embodied in larger-scale chronic unemployment which I already mentioned and the threat of nuclear weapons.

In a society which recognizes the interdependence of means and ends and which does not prostitute human beings to be means for the purposes of other people, unemployment as we know it would be an impossibility. One of the fundamental principles following from the universal natural law tradition of the Churches as well as from the Truth of Satyagraha is that as long as there are human beings willing to work who have unsatisfied need, and as long as there are instruments to work with, "unemployment" is due to ills of the body politic expressed in shortcomings in the organisation of society rather than being an incurable phenomenon. As soon as we recognize this, the way is open for building a healthy society without unemployment.

Equally far-reaching is the recognition of the interdependence of means and ends with regard to atomic weapons. If Truth is the central value guiding our life, instruments of mass destruction cannot possibly lead to any good purpose. 'Deterrence' is indeed a phenomenon of illness–an attempt to gain security by having a button in my house which enables me to detonate a bomb destroying my neighbours house, knowing that my neighbour has the same possibility as regards my own house and will indeed be bound to use it as soon as I push my button. Such is indeed the security "modern men" derive from their arsenal of atomic weapons.

To resist non-violently such key phenomena of ill health and destruction – be they the destruction of human values implicit in unemployment as well as meaningless work or the outright mass destruction of life – means first of all to change ourselves, to become rooted in a universal reality and truth which in its ultimate expression is love. This implies a profound transformation of consciousness. We must begin by taking "the burden of change" upon ourselves. Only then can we approach "the other" by showing a way which is not directed against her and him as persons or groups. Ultimately this way frees her and him too though it often involves the abandonment of false privileges and more deeply of false crutches hitherto necessary to maintain personal integrity. This is the essence of non-violent resistance as an aspect of a non-violent transformation which transcends the destructive conflicts and tensions of the 80's and opens the way for building together a truly human order.

Gandhi has penetrated to a depth of understanding which the essential truth of West and East and thus opens the way for building a truly planetary human consciousness.

Ranjit Kumar Roy

Gandhi on Women: Their Role in the World of Politics

The question of women's status was considered as one of the indices for the measurement of modernisation and traditionalism in India by both Indian and British reformers and politicians in the late 19th and early 20th centuries. In the early 19th century, a woman's place in the society invariably meant her place in the household under the rule of the elders, her in-laws or her husband. Devoid of any opportunity of education or vocation and deprived of economic and political rights the Indian woman remained virtually caged in the 'andarmahal' (inner chambers) and her fate was determined by the male members of the family. While there was a modicum of freedom in the lowest rung of the society, the lot of the middle and upper class women was hardly enviable. This however, was not because the lower rungs of Indian society 'were more liberal or permissive' but because dire financial stress forced a peasant woman to participate in the process of production or to perform odd jobs as substitutes for their husbands. On the other hand, the hiatus between the rights and opportunities of a male and a female in the upper classes was vast. Men and women virtually belonged to two groups – the ruler and the ruled.[1] What worsened matters was that most women were reconciled to this lot, accepting it as the 'will of providence'.

Even if some silent resentment arose in their hearts, Indian women, steeped in tradition and bound by orthodox rules of social life, could not muster enough courage to give expression to it. With the advent of Western education and the impact it had on society, the position of women started undergoing subtle changes. The banning of *Sati* and the Widow Remarriage Act were important milestones in the process of change. The impact of reform movements (such as the *Brahmo* movement) on women in particular was considerable. It brought about an awareness of the various social limitations which impeded the progress of the country. The national movement provided the women of India a unique opportunity to break free from social conservatism. The *Swadeshi* era roused positive hopes. However, as the raising of women's political consciousness was the result and not the aim of the movement, it was neglected once it had served its immediate purpose.[2] In their arduous task of surmounting numerous obstacles the women of India were helped by Gandhi. He realised their problems, recognised them as 'repositories of moral strength and stamina' that could constitute an important ingredient in his conquest by non-violence, and drew them into the main focus of public activity. Gandhi's aim was wider than just gaining freedom for the country. He wanted to effect a complete restructuring of society in which women, and other depressed classes, would be given due recognition. He also knew that unless Indian women were drawn out of their homes now they would never be able to shake off role shackles of socio-religious orthodoxy which had bound them for centuries. Indeed, it was with Gandhi's arrival that the process of emancipation of Indian women truly began. For the women of India, on the other hand, political participation contributed considerably towards their overcoming of social inhibitions.[3]

Gandhi's concern for the women's cause is testified to by women on whom the impact of his words and deeds was considerable. There are some who on looking back see nothing but the 'Gandhi magic' as the single important factor which drew them out of the inner confines of the household. Some others, however, consider him to be one among several factors which changed their lives. Women belonging to the first category go so far as to credit Gandhi with successfully effecting a 'gender revolution' by placing women side by side with men. Kamaladevi Chattopadhyay wrote that 'never perhaps since Buddha preached his message has any single individual swayed and transformed the destinies of millions as did Gandhi'.[4] Rajkumari Amritkaur believed that of all the factors that contributed to the awakening in India, the most potent had been the field of non-violent action which Gandhiji offered to women in his battle for India's political freedom. It brought them out in their hundreds from sheltered homes to stand the furnace of a 'fury trial' without flinching. They came through the test well and proved to the hilt that woman was capable of leadership and just as well able as man to resist the evil of aggression. Their participation on equal terms with men in the freedom struggle gave women a definite place so far as salvation of India was concerned.[5] These women believe that, had it not been for Gandhi's 'wide vision and practical sense', women in India would have had to plod the slow way to emancipation. Since Gandhi valued women and regarded them as genuine colleagues and comrades their response to him was spontaneous. Indeed, when the Mahatma planned a non-violent movement for the country's freedom, these women took it as an open invitation for them to join the movement – not only because the technique suited them eminently but more because they considered it their moral duty to assist the Mahatma. While some women claim to have had rudimentary knowledge of nationalist activities[6] others attach more importance to the general political climate of the age which acted on them as a great stimulant.[7] What they all admit is that though the climate had been created, what was required was a major thrust and this force was provided by Gandhi.

Gandhi first realised the power of women in South Africa. Kasturba and other women of the Tolstoy and Phoenix farms joined the men in a *Satyagraha* to protest against the Immigration Regulation Bill and the Three Pound tax.[8] The immediate effect of women going to jails, undergoing hard labour and bearing untold miseries, was the miners' strike. Gandhi realised that the success of this *Satyagraha* had been due to the new moral force that women's entry brought into the movement. Indeed, the presence of women had generated public support and mobilised the 'apathetic and the marginally interested' to join the movement. Gandhi was quick to understand that women could become 'the leader in the *Satyagraha* which does not require the learning that books give but does require the stout heart that comes from suffering and faith'.[9]

On coming to India, Gandhi tried to forge a link between the Indian National Congress and women. He appealed to the Congressmen to make women's liberation their fundamental task and, in trying to end the social injustices from which they suffered, they should begin with their homes. If freedom was the birthright of every nation and individual and if the Congress was determined to achieve it, then it should first liberate their women from the evil customs and conventions that restrict their all-round healthy growth.[10]

It is necessary here to trace the origins and circumstances in which Gandhi's views on women took shape. A L. Basham says that this can be traced to the influence of Western feminism on him.[11] In 1898, Gandhi first described women as 'helpmates' and the vow of *Brahmacharya* which he took in 1906, may be regarded as a further step in his endeavour to understand and respect all women, including his wife. Another event which profoundly impressed Gandhi was the Suffragette struggle of British women. He was so moved by the dauntless spirit of these women in courageously braving the insults of the streets and police brutality, that he wrote an article in *Indian Opinion* highly commending their role.

At home, Gandhi was greatly influenced by his mother, Putlibai. Her austere personality, boundless love and iron will, left a permanent impression on his mind. Her qualities of head and heart proved an undying source of inspiration for Gandhi, whose life was to be one long struggle for self-mastery, and whose battles were to be waged and won in the hearts of men. The image of woman he imbibed from Putlibai was that of love and sacrifice and this explains the attitude of respect and the understanding of women's problems that he exhibited later in life. Putlibai's maternal love he imbibed and as age advanced, 'it flowed out in ever increasing measure, bursting the bonds of family and community until it embraced the whole of humanity.' He owed to his mother not only a passion for nursing but also an impetus for his technique of appealing to the heart through self-suffering[12], a technique which Indian woman have practised since time immemorial. Years later, Gandhi admitted the influence of his mother on his mind and work. While in Yeravada jail Gandhi told his secretary-companion Mahadev Desai: 'If you notice any purity in me, I have inherited it from my mother and not from my father'.[13]

Gandhi's marriage with Kasturba brought to him experiences which counted much in the shaping of his ideas and in the creation of a new method of action – non-violent passive resistance through *Satyagraha* or truth force. Gandhi is said to have admitted to John S. Hoyland that he learnt the lesson of non-violence from Kasturba when he tried to bend her to his will. 'Her determined submission to my will on the one hand and her quiet submission to the suffering my stupidity involved on the other, ultimately made me ashamed of myself and cured me of my stupidity in thinking that I was born to rule over her; and in the end she became my teacher in non-violence.'[14]

In formulating the concept of non-violence Gandhi seems to have been greatly inspired by the image of Mirabai. Time and again he cited Mirabai as a symbol of passive resistance who had the courage to break out of the traditional familial role, be undaunted by persecution, and remain steadfast in the pursuit of her goal. Gandhi hailed her determination to continue on her chosen path in defiance of all norms of social behaviour. In a letter to Esther Falring in 1917, Gandhi wrote: 'For me truth and love are interchangeable terms. . . . . What one has to do is to live a life of love in the midst of the hate we see everywhere. . . . . A great queen named Mirabai lived two or three hundred years ago. She forsook her husband and everything and lived a life of absolute love. Her husband at last became her devotee. We often sing in the Ashram some fine hymns composed by her.'[15]

In his first speech on the women of India to the members of the *Bhagini Samaj* (1918) (literally, Sisters Society) Gandhi asked them to build up leaders who could work for the uplift of women and give them their due. These leaders were to inculcate the qualities of purity, firmness and self-control and awaken in women a sense of their essential equality with men, their right to freedom and liberty and their right to a supreme place in their own sphere of activity.[16] Being equal, however, did not imply that women had necessarily to prove their strength in performing the same tasks as men. Rather, Gandhi felt that 'men and women should generally follow different vocations suitable to their different physical and emotional temperaments.'[17]

To Gandhi, woman is the companion of man, gifted with equal mental qualities. She has the right to participate in very minute details of man's activities and has an equal right of freedom and liberty with him.[18] But the truth is that man has dominated woman from ages past and so woman has developed an inferiority complex. She has come to believe in the truth of man's self-interested teaching that she is inferior to him.[19] Travelling all over India, Gandhi came to realise that the existing agitation for the regeneration of women was confined to an infinitesimal section of the people. In order to be meaningful, this question had to be considered in relation to men. Since legislation in India was the handiwork of men in which man has not always been fair, Gandhi suggested that efforts should be made to awaken in as many women as possible a proper sense of their present condition and inspire a self-confidence in her so that she could initiate her own regeneration.[20] The remedy to women's problems, Gandhi believed, 'is more in her own hands than man's. Women must cease to consider herself the object of man's lust or his play thing. She must refuse to adorn herself for men, including her husband if she is to be an equal partner with men.[21]

Gandhi believed that by taking part in the nationalist struggle, women of India could break out of their long imposed seclusion. His non-violent agitation was particularly suited for women for it required not physical strength but moral courage and spiritual determination. According to him, a woman is more fitted than man to make explorations and take bolder action in *ahimsa.* 'For the courage of self-sacrifice, woman is any day superior to man as I believe man is to woman for the courage of the brute'.[22] To Gandhi, non-violent agitation was a great equaliser, for women could play the same part in it as men. Moreover, as non-violent war called for.extreme self-suffering, none but women could live up to the task. The three essential qualities required.of a *Satyagrahi,* namely, capacity for love, non-violence and self sacrifice Gandhi found the women to embody. Quite naturally, women came to occupy an important space in his scheme of non-violent agitation.

During the non-cooperation movement, Gandhi consciously tried to involve women so as to link their struggle for social emancipation with the larger movement for national independence. At this time, Gandhi's emphasis was not so much on women's role outside home. He attached more importance to their constructive contribution from home. The programme centering around boycott of foreign goods, spinning and wearing of *Khadi,* was taken up so that women could participate from within the household. His programme for women, in fact, complemented the humdrum of household chores and gave them a mission within their prosaic existence. In his appeal to the women of India Gandhi pointed out that the use of *Khadi* was not only necessary for the success of the *Swadeshi* programme but was imperative for the economic regeneration of the country --- for the middle class, it should supplement the income of the family; and for very poor women, it is undoubtedly a means of livelihood.... If the well-to do women of India were to spin a certain quantity daily, they would make yarn cheap.[23] Indeed, Gandhi felt that the restoration of spinning to its central place in India's peaceful campaign for deliverance from the imperial yoke gave her women a special status, especially because in spinning they had a natural advantage over men. 'Spinning is essentially a slow and comparatively silent process', he said,' and woman is the embodiment of sacrifice and, therefore, non-violence. Her occupations must therefore be, as they are, more conducive to peace than war'.[24] Gandhi's relentless propaganda in favour of *Charka,* spinning and wearing of *Khadi,* was designed to bring the spirit of nationalism and freedom into every home, even in the remotest village. In this way, abstract political ideas such as struggle against colonial rule assumed concrete form for ordinary people. This was, indeed, a remarkable way of reaching out to women and bridging the gap between their private life and the country's economic and political struggle. It was with remarkable insight that Gandhi, without challenging their traditional role in society, could make women an important social base for the movement.

It was not enough that the women of India should just achieve political freedom like their male counterparts but that they should also be socially liberated from the web of superstition and rigid ancient customs and economically self-sufficient. To those who argued that the political struggle ought to have primacy over everything else, Gandhi answered:' To postpone social reform till after the attainment of *Swaraj*, is not to know the meaning of *Swaraj*'.[25] Gandhi had suspicion that though not openly hostile to women's issues, Congressmen often tended to shelve or sidetrack these. Gandhi wanted the Congressmen to give the women of India 'a lifting hand' and enable them to realise their full status and play their part as the equals of men.[26] Gandhi told them that regeneration would come only through faith in *Ahimsa* and if only they carried out the non-violent programme faithfully and completely, then women would be automatically converted. In the process may arise one among them who 'will be able to go much further than I can hope to do'.[27]

During the Civil Disobedience movement, Gandhi's views on women underwent a positive change. This time Gandhi envisaged a more direct role for the women of India which would bring them into the arena of public activity. The period of apprenticeship was over and now women could be expected to contribute to the freedom struggle in equal measure to their male counterparts. Gandhi's memories of the Non-cooperation days convinced him that 'women could work wonders on behalf of the motherland. There was no guile about their word or work. Their purest sacrifice untainted by anger and hate and spontaneous loving response convinced him that God was with him'.[28] Over the years, Gandhi developed great faith in women's capacity for non-violence 'not because they are weak as men in their arrogance believe them to be, but because they have greater courage of the right type and immeasurably greater spirit of self-sacrifice'. Gandhi's message percolated to women and had the desired effect. Gandhi aimed to enthuse them and inject into them the hope that had so long eluded them. Indian women, on the other hand, found a reason for faith in their very existence, as Gandhi had reserved for them a special role in his schema.

Initially, Gandhi had certain reservations about women taking up frontline positions in the struggle for *Swaraj*. We gather from his writings that Gandhi faced some difficulty in selecting the first batch of *Satyagraha* for his Dandi march. Male Congress workers were anxious to enlist and women did not lag behind. Pondering on the issue for sometime Gandhi told the women that 'their time was not just yet'. Gandhi explained that since a sufficient number of men were likely to respond, the presence of women was not essential. They were likely to be outnumbered by men and so their services would neither be specifically noted not commended. Not only would they be lost in the crowd but also, there would be 'no suffering for which they are thirsting'. Other practical reasons for excluding women was Gandhi's sense of chivalry and his unwillingness to take advantage of his rivals. Justifying his action Gandhi said: ' I must be considerate to the opponent. We want to go in for suffering and there may even be torture. If we put the women in front, the Government may hesitate to inflict on us all that they might otherwise inflict. A delicate sense of chivalry towards the opponent is what decides me against women in the first batch'. Gandhi felt that if the British hesitated to attack the *Satyagrahis* because of women, then not only would the purpose of the *Satyagraha* be defeated, but the entire Congress would have to face the accusation of being cowards. Gandhi's logic was that just as Hindus do not harm a cow, the British do not attack women as far as possible; just as it would be cowardice to take a cow to the battlefield, in the same way it would be cowardice for us to have women accompany us.[29] It is not to suggest that Gandhi wanted to keep women as a reserve force – rather he had specially assigned tasks for women in this *Satyagraha* which, if carried out effectively, would bring to them no less recognition than if they went out to face police batons. In fact, Gandhi thought it required much greater courage to maintain self-control in the face of suffering than to assert oneself through a violent act.[30] His philosophy of non-violent resistance made him extraordinarily sensitive to the latent capacities of subordinate groups, whether they be colonial subjects, untouchables or women. He saw in the downtrodden the potential to develop an inner strength and ethical sense superior to those of dominant groups and this potential he wanted to put to use in his non-violent struggle for India's independence. Gandhi hoped that the *Satyagraha* movement would yield not only independence but reform and regeneration of all participating groups, or, in other words, of Indian life. It was with this remarkable insight that he made women an important constituent, a social base for the movement. As with other groups, such as students and the peasantry, he told women to take the responsibility for not just changing their own situation but that of society also. The innate qualities of women made them better leaders in 'a non-violent struggle for a just society'. It only remained for them to reject the role of being men's playthings and insist on their basic human rights, dignity and responsibility as equals and extend their love and compassion beyond their families to embrace the whole of humanity.

Gandhi did not see women only as objects of reform and humanitarianism but rather as conscious subjects who had a definite social role to fulfil as active self-conscious agents of social change. His desire was not limited to bringing about change in selected areas of life such as education and marriage as a way of regenerating Indian society as had been the case with most of the 19th century social reformers. These men saw women as passive recipients of more humane treatment through the initiative of enlightened male effort[31] Greatly concerned at the impact of modernisation which increased the gap between men and women and threatened the stability of the family, these reformers sought to strength women's position with education and limited rights to properly. The question of women's political power or equality between the sexes was not on their agenda. An urban middle class origin and bias is evident in their perception of women's problems. Traditional attitudes and obscurantist customs such as *purdah*, child marriage, denial of divorce or remarriage, the oppressed condition of widows, ignorance and lack of property rights were seen as the main enemies. Education and removal of these oppressive customs, the reformers claimed, would allow women to develop to be better wives and mothers. There was no questioning of women's traditional familial roles or dependence on others.[32]

Gandhi's main concern was to bring about a radical reconstruction of society by creating an atmosphere in which women would be able to regain the self-confidence she had lost through years of subjection. In the process she would cease to be passive recipients of more humane treatment through the initiative of enlightened male effort. While Bankimchandra and Vivekananda strove to accord recognition to the 'power of women' in Indian society by linking the traditional image of sacred motherhood, Gandhi tried to give a new dignity to women by striking a new equation between womanliness and political potency. In the process, he denied the Western association between maleness and control over public affairs and statecraft; rejected the martial tradition in India which debased womanhood; and abrogated the colonial identity which equated femininity with passivity, weakness, dependence, subjugation and absence of masculinity.[33] Gandhi thus made the political movement for national liberation a means, a weapon to achieve the social reconstruction he was aiming at and in this movement he saw women playing a major role. He was confident that in the process of restructuring the society, women of India would free themselves from the specific forms of bondage that affected them as women.

Any discourse on Gandhi's views on women is incomplete without its recent feminist criticism. Feminist writers [34] hold that the Gandhi-led nationalist movement is an example of his policy of first mobilising and then subordinating women. It is alleged that Gandhi knew that his fight for *Swaraj* would be incomplete without the support of women who constituted one half of the population. Moreover, who more than women, used to manoeuvring patiently through patriarchal authority, could offer better models of passive resistance in his scheme to dislodge the Raj. Gandhi drew out women from their homes to participate in his *Satyagraha*. Yet this remained only a part of his political strategy for national liberation. Gandhi did not challenge oppressive patriarchal traditions within the home. While Gandhi believed in the equality of sexes and said that 'woman is gifted with the same mental qualities' and that 'she has the same right of freedom and liberty as he', he also admitted that there are important physical and emotional differences. 'She is passive, he active', he said. It is an irony that Gandhi saw men and women in those terms that were used to reinforce the disability of women to acquire power in the family or society. By making woman a compliment to man Gandhi ended up by extending the domination from which he had tried to free women. Gandhi made a clear distinction between the home and the world, between woman's private domain or the household where 'she is the queen', and the 'outside', of which 'he is the master'. But it must be said, in fairness to Gandhi, that though he insisted on the sexual division of labour, with the home as woman's main sphere of activity, at the same time he actively created conditions which helped women break the shackles of domesticity. What Gandhi objected to was the excessive subordination of the wife to the husband, not the fact of women generally playing a subordinate role. He could envisage women being 'free' even while playing a socially subordinate role. As a good patriarch, the maximum he could bring himself to do was to rationalise authority, make it just and humane.[35] He found it difficult to accept that most forms of power engender discrimination and inequity, be it state power or that of the patriarch, and so the best that he could do was to advocate and expect harmony and not tyranny in the social division of labour.

What Gandhi sought to change was not so much the material condition of woman as their moral condition. He succeeded in creating a general atmosphere which was sympathetic to woman's problems but failed to see that if women were really to emerge the equals of men, then they would have to have control over economic resources within the family and even outside. Oppression is not always an 'abstract moral condition' but often relates to questions of economic power.Gandhi advocated *Khadi* as an area of employment and means of livelihood for women. But spinning could never become a viable means of livelihood just as *Khadi* could not be a real alternative to cloth produced in mills for mass consumption.

Critics of Gandhi consider the case of the Salt Satyagraha as an instance of reinforcement of gender inequality. Why would women, whom he considered fit for picketing, be excluded from the *Satyagraha* programme? It is difficult to match Gandhi's stance as the upholder and defender of equal rights with his decision to keep women away from taking a position by the side of men. Gandhi certainly had his justification for having acted thus, and we have discussed it earlier. On close scrutiny, it appears that this decision stemmed from an error of judgement. Gandhi was wrong to expect that the civilization and culture of the British race would hold them back from striking a *Satyagrahi* simply because she is a woman. In reality, thousands of women were arrested, beaten, faced repression and went to prison. The Bengal Congress Committee reported, 'being female was no protection from police brutality'.[36] In fact, the British were certainly not pleased at women's participation in the struggle. The 1932 Annual Report of Police Administration characterised the presence of women as 'calculated to prove an embarrassment to the police'. Perhaps this is what Gandhi felt morally bound to avoid. However when the confrontation did take place, it helped to lay bare British hypocrisy over Indian men's maltreatment of women since the British police and army officers were quite prepared to intimidate, beat, and shoot women demonstrators. In a way, their presence in the campaigns upset British stereotypes of Indian women and exposed police brutality. These actions also 'undermined the legitimacy of Britain's rejection of independence, since the very women the British had claimed they were there to liberate from the abuses of Indian men, were taking up the fight against their foreign protectors'.[37] As astute as he was, Gandhi should, have understood this and allowed women to participate in the first instance.

Gandhi knew that no movement could succeed if one half of the population remained indifferent and passive and so he attempted to feminise the movement by inducting into it certain symbols which were essentially feminine. It is said that such symbols as the *'charka'* and *'khadi'* were strategically gendered through his evocation of mythological figures like Sita, Draupadi and Savitri which embodied roles for women in the nationalist movement. The identification of Sita with *Swadeshi* (Sita only wore *swadeshi*) demonstrates how the female body and what it is clothed in can become a symbol of national liberation.[38] Gandhi knew that the choice of clothes was generally a woman's decision. He thus raised this mundane sphere of life to a new poetical and, moral plane. While the choice to spin and wear *khadi* called for no heroism, at the same time it symbolised each individual's choice of a philosophy of life. Thus by initiating women into spinning and wearing *khadi* he was helping men to 'be in a position to take, the vow of *swadeshi*'[39]. And *khadi*, in Gandhi's own words seems extremely gendered--- 'In spinning they (women) have a natural advantage over men... spinning is essentially a slow and comparatively silent process. Women is the embodiment of sacrifice and non-violence'.[40] Often, Gandhi projected the 'female' in him by performing 'feminine' roles like spinning, nursing and even cooking in the Ashram. The image of the Mahatma sitting before the *Charka* patiently spinning *Khadi* was calculated to inspire women and men and mentally prepare them for the otherwise tedious passive resistance.

It appears that, outside the perimeter of *Satyagraha*, that is, in public life, Gandhi saw women only as selfless and committed social workers. He saw all around him men who were power loving and selfish and felt that women alone could selflessly undertake the task of reconstruction. He was convinced that woman's entry to public life would purify it and restrain unbridled ambition and accumulation of property. Participation in political life, Gandhi thought had brought with it a new prestige and status for women *vis-a-vis* their male counterpart. Moreover, the Karachi Congress of 1931 had committed itself to equality of women irrespective of their status and qualifications. Perhaps Gandhi considered these to be an advance great enough to satisfy women's desire to have a taste of public life and so, now, they were to leave politics and professions exclusively for the males. With independence round the corner, Gandhi grew apprehensive of an imminent clash of interests between man and women. He feared that women, enthused with her newly acquired voting rights and legal status, may decide to have a say in the political deliberations of the nation. As if to coax and cajole women out of such a course of action, Gandhi said: 'And you sisters, what would you do by going to Parliament? Do you aspire after the collectorships, commissionerships or even the Viceroyalty?'[41] Gandhi went further; he virtually sealed the fate of those millions whose uplift was the goal of his mission. Gandhi's words betray a latent patriarchal zeal to decide what is good for women whether or not the decision actually resulted in the good of those for whom it was intended. He said: 'I know that you would not care to, for the Viceroy has got to order executions–and hangings, a thing that you would heartily detest.'[42]

Standing on the threshold of the 21st Century we criticise Gandhi's views on women's role in the domestic and public sphere as essentially narrow and constricted. We pass verdict on the man for what he wrote and spoke about women almost half a century ago on the basis of current feminist ideas. It is strange no doubt that in the years of the freedom struggle, though there was much divergence from the Gandhian mode of operation by women participants, there was no raucous criticism of the man or his ideas. No one, not even women revolutionaries or communists could either ignore Gandhi's ideas or presence or deny the support he gave them to break out of domesticity and participate in the national struggle. While Kamala Das Gupta, a revolutionary, considers Gandhi to be the 'harbinger of modern age for women',[43] Lakshmi Bahgal, the leader of the Rani of Jhansi regiment in Subhas Bose's I.N.A. acknowledges that without the support of Gandhi, women's participation could not have blossomed as it did during the independence movement.[44] It is thus unfair on our part today to decry Gandhi for having selfishly appropriated women's body and mind for political purposes. It is for us to realise and understand that like any other person Gandhi too was the product of the age in which he lived and struggled. Moreover he came from a traditional, patriarchal Bania family, which was certainly not free from the structural bias conducive to the subordination of women. Perhaps Gandhi could rise over some limitations and could not over others which he unconsciously imbibed from his family. Thus Gandhi did not see his advocacy of women's participation in non-violent campaigns as contradictory to his basic concept of woman as the nurturer and care-taker of the home and the family. In fact he considered women's participation in *Satyagraha* as an extension of her special mission as the care-taker of humanity. But though Gandhi did not advocate radical reform of the family structure, he was certainly aware that the problem of female subordination lay deeply ingrained in the very fabric of society. He thus advocated fundamental changes in Hindu inheritance laws to give men and women equal property rights. What Gandhi failed to perceive was that the capacity for silent self-suffering which he so idealised in woman, whether within the domestic structure or in the public sphere, happened to be one of 'the key symptoms of her subordination.' Gandhi visualised women surmounting the obstacles that impeded their full expression as human beings, yet his programme of reform cannot be seen as a revolutionary doctrine aiming at radical change of those institutions of Indian society which uphold and perpetuate inequality. Himself being the product of a culture and institution so steeped in conservatism, perhaps Gandhi could never rise above this contradiction. Perhaps too, he never realised the contradiction implicit in the situation and remained satisfied at having been able to draw women out of the confines of domesticity by involving them in the freedom struggle.

Gandhi's real achievement with regard to the women's issue lies not in the extent to which he materially altered their situation but on the process of self-realisation which he worked up in their minds. This was not limited to the educated elite and urban middle class woman only, but extended also to ordinary women from traditional domestic backgrounds in rural areas. It is difficult to gauge exactly what Gandhi's impact meant in each case; whether it meant the assertion of equal rights to some or simply a response to the call of a nation in need to others, it certainly brought about some personal transformation in them. Nehru succinctly sums up the impact of Gandhi's call to women when he says: '. . . it always had a double meaning for women, and the enthusiasm and energy with which they threw themselves into the struggle had no doubt their springs in the vague and hardly conscious, yet nevertheless intense desire to rid themselves of domestic slavery also.'[45] That domestic slavery for women did not end in the post-independence period and that women's uplift remained merely a political slogan to be paid lip-service to by leaders does not necessarily mark the defeat of Gandhi's perception nor does it indicate a narrowness of vision as critics would have us believe. Where Gandhi failed was in understanding that once freedom was achieved there would be others to reckon with in deciding such issues, leaders who perhaps would not see eye to eye with him. There were in fact, within the Congress, men like Rajendra Prasad, who were against the reform of women's legal position. Factors such as this are seldom taken into account and Gandhi's sincerity towards issues concerning women is often questioned. In fact, it is an irony of Gandhian criticism that he is either deified or torn to shreads much like the women who were either revered as goddesses or doomed to subjection and for whose uplift Gandhi had worked.

Notes and References

1. S. Bhattacharya, Fighting the Purdah and the British in *The Statesman*, Calcutta Tercentenary Issue, 1990.

2. Meredith Borthwick, *The Changing Role of Women in Bengal, 1849-1905*, Princeton, 1984, p. 354.

3. Interview with Kamala Mukherjee, Calcutta, 26.4.90.

4. Kamaladevi Chattopadhyay, The Struggle for Freedom in Tara Ali Baig ed. *Women of India*, New Delhi, 1958.

5. Rajkumari Amrit Kaur, Gandhi and Women in Kshitis Roy ed. *Gandhi Memorial Peace Number*, Vishwa Bharati Quaterly, October 1949, pp. 167-68.

6. Interview with Phulrenu Guha, Calcutta, 9.3.90.

7. Interview with Shantisudha Ghosh, Calcutta, 22.4.90.

8. D.G. Tendulkar, *Mahatma, Life of M.K. Gandhi*, New Delhi, pp. 132-37.

9. *Harijan*, February 24, 1940.

10. *Collected Works of Gandhi*, Volume 40, pp. 416-17.

11. A.L. Basham, Traditional influences on the thought of M.K. Gandhi, in R. Kumar ed. *Essays on Gandhian Politics, The Rowlatt Satyagraha of 1919*, Oxford, 1971, p. 41.

12. B.R. Nanda, *Mahatma Gandhi. A Biography*, New Delhi, 1981, pp. 19-20.

13. Krishna Kripalani, *Gandhi A Life*. New Delhi, 1968, p. 2.

14. B.R. Nanda, op. cit, p. 21.

15. C.W.G. Volume 13, p. 442.

16. M.K. Gandhi, *Women and Social Injustice*, Ahmedabad, 1942, pp. 4-5.

17. Barbara Southard, The feminism of Mahatma Gandhi, *Gandhi Marg*, Vol. 3, No.7, October 1981, pp. 402-21.

18. Speeches and Writings of Mahatma Gandhi, p. 423 quoted in To the Women, *Gandhi Series* Vol. 2, ed. A. Hingorani, Karachi, 1943.

19. *Harijan*, February 24, 1940.

20. *Speeches and Writings*, op. cit.

21. Treatment of Women, *Young India*, July 21, 1921.

22. *Harijan*, November 5, 1938.

23. *Young India*, August 11, 1921.

24. *Harijan*, December 2, 1939.

25. *Young India*, India 28, 1928.

26. Tendulkar, op cit. Vol. 4, p.24.

27. *Harijan*, November 5, 1938.

28. *Young India*, August 5, 1921.

29. C.W.G. Vol. 43, pp. 154-55. Extract from Navjivan, April 6, 1930.

30. Lloyd and Susanne Rudolph, *Gandhi The Traditional Roots of Charisma*, Chicago, 1967, pp. 1991-92.

31. Madhu Kishwar, Gandhi on Women in *Economic and Political Weekly*, October 5, 1985.

32. Vina Majumdar ed: *Symbols of Power: Studies on the Political Status of Women in India*, New Delhi, 1979, Editor's Note, pp. X-XI.

33. Ashis Nandy, Woman Versus Womanliness in India: An Essay in Cultural and Political Psychology in A. Nandy ed. *At the Edge of Psychology, Essays in Politics and Cultural*, New Delhi, 1980, p. 41.

34. Barbara Southard, Madhu Kishwar, Ketu H. Katrak and others in recent times have tried to analyse the feminism of Gandhi.

35. Madhu Kishwar, op cit.

36. M. Kaur, Role of Women in Freedom Movement, New Delhi, 1968, p. 168.

37. Joanna Liddle and Rama Joshi, Gender and Imperialism in British India, in *Review of Women Studies Economic and Political Weekly*, October, 1995.

38. Ketu, H. Katrak, Indian Nationalism, Gandhian Satyagraha and Representations of Female Sexuality, in Nupur Chaudhuri and Margaret Strobel ed. *Western Women and Imperialism: Complicity and Resistance*, Indianapolis, 1992, p. 397.

39. C.W.G. Vol. 15, p. 291.

40. *Harijan*, December 2, 1931.

41. Cited in Tendulkar, Vol 3, p. 61.

42. Ibid.

43. Interview with Kamala Dasgupta, Calcutta, 4.6.90.

44. Interview with Rajani Alexander quoted in her 'A Rich and Colourful Tapestry: Women's Participation in the Independence Movement' in Ravi Dayal ed. *We Fought Together For Freedom, Chapters from the Indian National Movement*, Oxford, New Delhi, 1995, p. 263.

45. Jawaharlal Nehru, Thoughts on Women, Nehru Memorial Museum and Library, New Delhi, 1975.

Norman Scotney

Gandhi's Lifeline-Belief: Towards Religious Pluralism

In the coming century the example set by Gandhi will be more deeply appreciated than in this century. The world has need and will have more need to study and learn from both his thought and his unrelenting commitment to his beliefs. Currently we do not lack ideas; what we lack is the faith that could give us the courage to grapple with the world torn endlessly by wars and violence. The next generation is threatened by animosity and greed. Almost the only solutions proposed seriously are those of Mohandas Karamchand Gandhi.

The West has chosen to consider Gandhi primarily as a politician; a politician with a unique style but one whose dramatic achievement was to secure for his country independence from British colonial rule. Further, in this century he was the first to succeed where many others have followed. Some, depreciating his achievement, have suggested independence for India was 'in the pipeline' anyway. This, though, arises from such a superficial view that it cannot much longer persist. The elements of a more profound view are already in place and waiting at the door.

Central to a mature Western view of Gandhi, of his personal and family life, of his relations with co-workers, of his ashrams and relations with the Indian people is his religious commitment, his faith and prayer. He maintained days of silence, committed himself and Kasturbai, his childbride, eventually to a form of abstinence – *brahmacharya*, he rejected violence, trained co-workers for non-violent programmes, insisted always that methods must fit ends not be conditioned by means, and worked to overcome the sin of untouchability. In a thousand ways he was undeniably a deeply religious man. The West, except for a small minority, has still to learn who Gandhi was.

Gandhi does not fit the Western concept of a religious man. Committed to a life of prayer, a monk or a nun is also expected to live in detachment from much of society and above all not to intervene in politics. Charitable assistance to the needy is acceptable. Intervention in political campaigns and publicly acknowledging membership of a political party, these are not. Gandhi did not wear any distinctive religious clothes and he did not frequent temples or mosques.

In the western press Gandhi attracted attention when he participated in public demonstrations–burning imported cloth, and especially the Salt March – but not in his prayer meetings. That he drew huge crowds to public meetings seemed to confirm his role as a political leader. When in 1921 he decided to wear only the loin cloth, with sometimes a shawl – he called it his 'mourning costume' – he identified himself with the poorest not with the educated and wealthy classes, so powerfully represented in the leadership of Congress. But this commitment to the needs of the poorest was not understood by western journalists. In the West, that the religious basis of Gandhi's life was integrated with his political commitment made it incomprehensible. He wrote: 'Religion which takes no account of practical affairs and does not help them is no religion. Not until and unless we have fed and clothed the skeletons of India will religion have any meaning for them. Religion is the service of the helpless. God manifests himself to us in the form of the helpless and the stricken'. (Young India, 5.5.25).

In most Western countries there appears to be a retreat from all religious preoccupation. There is evidence, though, that this affects mostly the beliefs and life of traditional churches. In 1909, returning by ship from London to South Africa, Gandhi wrote a short book *Hind Swaraj* later translated into English with a title extended to include *Indian Home Rule*. Of western civilization he wrote (p. 33): 'This civilization takes note neither of morality nor of religion. Its votaries calmly state that their business is not to teach religion. Some even consider it to be a superstitious growth. Others put on the cloak of religion and prate about morality'. Recently a Birmingham theologian, Rex Ambler, (p. 67) wrote: 'The elevation of a natural and proper concern to the status of an absolute - suggests Paul Tillich - is one way of defining idolatry.... Modern Western society seems to be unique in the history of the world in elevating material values to the point where they virtually exclude all others'. Though the churches have a unique position in education, effectively they are being silenced or ignored. This uneasy relation began with urban factory workers. Churches came to be regarded by many urban workers as part of the power base of the property-owning classes.

The deeply disturbing component of this Western insensitivity is that the sequence of greed, violence, war and demagoguery preparing the way for pseudo-religious dictatorship, must follow, unless a religious awareness supervenes. Gandhi was conscious, even in 1909, that Britain had gone far along that path. 'This civilization is irreligious, and it has taken such a hold on the people of Europe that those who are in it appear to be half mad. This civilization is such that one has only to be patient and it will be self destroyed. According to the teaching of Mahommed this would be considered a Satanic Civilization. Hinduism calls it the Black Age. It is eating in to the vitals of the English nation.... Civilization is not an incurable disease but it should never be forgotten that the English people are at present afflicted by it'. (*Hind Swaraj*. p.33 & 34).

Gandhi particularly stressed the need for simplicity: 'To see a universal and all pervading spirit of Truth face to face one must be able to love the meanest of creation as oneself'. (Bakle p. 140). He believed that *ahimsa* and training for commitment to *Satyagraha* – the soul-force oriented life – was the only path that could lead to the progressive elimination of the greed-violence complex destroying the life of the West. Whilst in the West the need for religion and purpose in people's lives has, from one point of view, been forgotten or buried there has developed an important but less obvious rebirth of belief. One manifestation of this is the surge of interest in Eastern religions.

The foundation of Gandhi's challenge to Western societies was his belief in the power of love expressed in non-violence to overcome self-centred behaviour.

In London in 1889 Gandhi had discovered almost simultaneously Tolstoy's *The Kingdom of Heaven is Within You* and *The Sermon on the Mount*. Tolstoy insists that the essential message of Jesus is 'Resist not evil' and, if assaulted, turn the other cheek. From arriving in Durban and being forced off a train at Pietermaritzburg, Gandhi, until his death, developed both his commitment to and understanding of non-violence in action. From the problems and failures of mass protests he learned that such protests may be demanding, even to costing people's lives, and therefore training must include attention to faith and beliefs. After the Salt March he sent from Yeravada Prison in 1930 a message to *satyagrahis* at his Sabarmati Ashram a list of eleven vows to which they should commit themselves. The four principal vows were Truth, Non-violence, Chastity and Non-possession (or Renunciation). He wrote: 'God is the very image of the vow. God would cease to be God if he swerved from his own laws even by a hairsbreadth... We should therefore never doubt the necessity of vows for the purpose of self-realization' (*Non-violent Resistance* p. 37-38).

To participate effectively in non-violent action participants must believe so deeply in what they are undertaking that they are prepared, if there is no other way, to 'put their lives on the line'. This requirement of faith often leads to a limitation in non-violent action in the West.

In Britain the long campaign for nuclear disarmament pioneered large scale passive resistance. A long sequence of non-violent protests drawing attention to objectionable legislation and Government programme has followed. Sometimes non-violent protests have led to violence, as was the experience of Gandhi. He wrote, 'Intoxicated by my success in South Africa I came to India. Here too the struggle has borne fruit but I have now realised it was not based on the non-violence of the brave. If I had known so then I would not have launched the struggle.' (*Harijan* 27.7.1947, p253).

A deeper understanding of Gandhi's faith, with its challenge to Western religious opportunism and divisiveness is needed to form the basis of a new religious consciousness. Gandhi valued all religions and refused to make judgment of their comparative worth. 'Religions are different roads converging at the same point. What does it matter that we take different roads so long as we reach the same goal? I believe in the fundamental truth of all great religions of the world. I believe they are all God given and I believe they were necessary for the people to whom they were revealed' (Saiyidain p. 34 & p. 25).

Gandhi was, though, intimately aware of the destructive, satanic nature of religious struggles and saw that each religion had its limitations: 'I came to the conclusion that all religions were right and every one of them imperfect because they were interpreted with our poor intellects, sometimes with our poor hearts, and more often misinterpreted' (*To Missionaries*. Calcutta -1925). He was deeply opposed to those whose aim was conversion. 'All religions are as dear to me as my own Hinduism. My veneration for other faiths is the same as for my own faith, consequently the thought of conversion is impossible. The object of the Fellowship ought to be to help a Hindu to be a better Hindu, a Christian a better Christian, etc. An attitude of protective tolerance is opposed to the Spirit of the International Fellowships... Our attitude ought to be, God has given to them all the light and truth they need for their highest development'. (Satyagraha Ashram, Sabarmati January 13-15, 1928).

He was equally opposed to those who would grade religions. Asked in Bengal if Christianity and Islam were not progressive religions and Hinduism static or retrogressive he replied, 'No! I have noticed no definite progress in any religion. The world would not be the shambles it has become if the religions of the world were progressive.' (Fischer, p. 56).

Gandhi was not, however, vague about the nature of religion. It is well known that he hoped his last word would be said smiling in praise of God. (And so it was, '*Hey Rama*'). Of his personal concept of God he said: 'There is an indefinable mysterious power that pervades everything. I feel it though I do not see it. It is this unseen power which makes itself felt and yet defies all proof because it is so unlike to all that I perceive through my senses... But it is possible to reason out God to a certain extent... There is an unalterable law governing everything or every being that exists or lives. That law, then, which governs all life is God. Law and the law-giver are one. I may not deny the law or the lawyer because I know so little about it or him. Just as my denial or ignorance of any earthly power will avail me nothing, even so my denial of God will not liberate me from its operation; whereas humble and mute acceptance of divine authority makes life's journey easier even as the acceptance of earthly rule makes life under it easier.... God is not a person... He is the essence of life. He is pure and undefiled consciousness. To seek God one need not go on pilgrimage or light lamps and burn incense before or around the image of the deity or paint it with red vermilion. For He resides in our hearts. If we would completely obliterate in us the consciousness of our physical body we would see Him face to face' (Fischer p. 113 -114). 'The only way to find God is to see him in his creation and to be one with it.' (*Harijan*, 28 Aug. 1936).

Gandhi saw in all religions belief-concepts that have the same objective. This is to help all to come nearer to a holy, God-centered life. Gandhi believed with Jesus 'By their fruit ye shall know them (Matthew 7v 20). Gandhi wrote: 'To me the Gita became an infallible guide of conduct... I turned to this dictionary of conduct for a ready solution of all my troubles and trials'. (*Autobiography*, p.244). He also said that the last nineteen verses of the second chapter of the Bhagavadgita set the goal for his life. There Krishna tells Arjuna that the key to divine wisdom is to renounce all selfish desires, to live in peace of mind. Then, undisturbed, Arjuna will find his wisdom is firmly established because although desires enter, like rivers flowing into the ocean, they cannot disturb him. He attains peace. In the divine state he reaches to the bliss of God and is one with him. One is reminded of St Augustine's: 'Thou hast made us for thyself and our hearts are restless until they find their rest in thee.'

Gandhi would certainly approve the changing attitude to 'Comparative Religion'. The Encyclopaedia Britannica has six pages devoted to the 'The Classification of Religions' but after considering a range of possibilities the writer concludes: 'Normative classifications have no scientific value because they are arbitrary and subjective in as much as there is no agreed method for selecting the criteria by which such judgments should be made '(15th Edition. *The Classification of Religions* p628). There has also been in universities a move away from 'Comparative' to 'Religious Studies'. Increasingly the major faiths are each studied as having their own validity. But in the schools the dilemma of what to teach in a multi-faith society persists. A widely used textbook *Philosophy of Religion* by John Hick has a word of warning: 'It is not appropriate to speak of a religion as being true or false, anymore than it is to speak of a civilization as being true or false. For the religions in the sense of distinguishable religion-cultural streams within man's history are expressions of the diversity of human types, temperaments and thought forms' (p. 124).

One of the major questions for anyone seeking to understand Gandhi must be his response to Christian beliefs and Christian Churches. Extravagant and unjustified claims have been made even to claiming Gandhi was, in fact, a Christian. That Gandhi attracted and was in turn attracted by Christians is apparent. Many of his Christian friends published accounts of their friendship. The very close association of twenty-six years of Gandhi with Charlie Andrews reveals how Gandhi could relate to and understand the thinking of a convinced Christian. As a schoolboy Gandhi was offended by the evangelical preachers who tried 'in a corner near the high school' proclaiming Christ to make converts (*Autobiography* p. 46). In London as a student, and especially in South Africa, well-meaning Christians felt that his interest in their faith meant they might convert him, and they tried to effect this. In London he was given a Bible. The result of his serious attempts to read this through from the beginning was foreseeable. 'I could not possibly read through the Old Testament.... The chapters that followed Genesis invariably sent me to sleep. I disliked reading the book of Numbers'. Then came the surprise! 'But the New Testament produced a different impression, especially the Sermon on the Mount which went straight to my heart. I compared it with the Gita. The verses "But I say unto thee, that ye resist not evil: but whoever shall smite thee on thy right-cheek turn to him the other also" delighted me beyond measure' (*Autobiography* p. 78).

In South Africa the contradictions between the profession of Christianity made by Christians and the customary and, eventually, legalized discrimination daily practiced against Indians and Africans changed the direction of his life.

Gandhi's 'Christianity' became the Christianity–banned in its own country–of Tolstoy's *The Kingdom of God is Within You*'. Written in 1891 this was circulated in typed copies from 1893. On page three Tolstoy announces his theme. He calls the Christianity current in Russia 'an ecclesiastical faith... a delusion' and instances as the chief deviation from the teachings of Christ 'the failure to acknowledge the commandment of non-resistance of evil'. This theme he pursues, often with vehemence, through 350 pages. The Christianity of the Sermon on the Mount, of the life of Jesus and of the crucifixion Tolstoy contrasts with the professions of the church leaders and the degrading social conditions they permitted. This view remained with Gandhi colouring his view of Christianity to his death. He was careful though, as always, not to offend friends.

Gandhi explained when asked why whilst respecting Christianity he was not a Christian: 'Jesus was a Jew. He was the finest flower of Judaism. You can see that from the stories of the four apostles. They had untutored minds. They told the truth about Jesus. Paul was not (in his thinking) a Jew; he was a Greek. He has an oratorical mind, a dialectical mind, and he distorted Jesus. Jesus possessed a great force, the love force, but Christianity became disfigured when it went to the West. It became the religion of Kings.' (At Dr. Divishah Mehta's Nature Cure Clinic, Poona 2 July 1946). 'It was impossible for me to believe that Jesus was the only incarnate son of God and that only he who believed in him would have everlasting life. If God could have sons all of us were his sons. If Jesus was like God, or God himself then all men were like God and could be God himself. That Jesus by his death and by his blood redeemed the sins of the world; metaphorically there might be some truth in it... but that only human beings had souls and not other living beings... I had a contrary belief I would accept Jesus as a martyr, an embodiment of sacrifice and a divine teacher but not as the most perfect man ever born... The pious lives of Christians did not give me anything that men of other faiths had failed to give..."(*Autobiography* p. 13 5).

Gandhi saw Jesus as an example to follow but did not agree with worshiping him. Dogmas like the virgin birth and the physical resurrection he could not accept. They are, as he realized, an integral part of the claim to Christian uniqueness, to Christianity as the only true religion and to the exclusiveness that has been a problem to so many people. When, for example, the former Bishop of Durham tried to explain these tenets as not physical facts but of deep theological significance, he was widely criticised. (*Freedom to Believe*, David Jenkins, especially pp. 4 & 5). He states: 'It should not be forgotten that religion saves no one. It is God who saves. Religion and what religious people say has often been against God' (Idem p 56). Another Christian theologian pointed out: 'The plain fact is that no picture of the historical Jesus has yet emerged–or even seems likely to–which comes anywhere near commanding universal or even general agreement... In what they say about Jesus' resurrection the New Testament writers are more divergent than on almost any other subject'. (Nineham, pp. 165 & 167). Gandhi saw missions as divisive and firmly set himself, as has been mentioned, against conversion. Yet he frequently showed his awareness of Christian sensitivities. Of Jesus, 'He was a servant of the people or a spiritual aspirant. The first lesson he took through baptism at the hands of John was that of humility and self-purification. He thought of aligning himself with the millions by taking baptism and a bath in the Jordan' (Desai's *Diary*, vol VIII p. 242). The example of Christ's suffering was throughout 'a factor in the composition of my undying faith in nonviolence' (Chatterjee p56). That 'When I survey the wondrous cross' was a favourite hymn of Gandhi is well known.

One suggestion is that Gandhi may have found the overriding importance he came to attribute to love and compassion in life in Christianity. The Gita, though, is a devotional book revealing the requirements of a fully rounded love. Krishna tells Arjuna what he must do. 'Fix your heart on me, love me, sacrifice all for me, give yourself to me and thus you will surely come to me. I promise you my dearest friend' (Gita 18.65). It could not be more explicit. The Gita and Jesus are agreed: love of God and love of human beings are the same. Gandhi was sure that we must also love the whole creation.

Another suggestion is that it is from Christianity that Gandhi acquired a spring of energy lacking in lethargic Hinduism. Aware of its great diversity some have concluded that Hinduism is not a distinguishable entity, but the cultural bases are so dissimilar, comparison is not realistic, with either the Christian or the Moslem faith. Each has to be accepted for its own intrinsic worth. Certainly the mind of Gandhi was influenced by his training as a lawyer but the spring of energy that characterized his life must surely have derived more from the inhumanity he experienced and encountered in South Africa than from any personal association there. That inhumane society, however, purported to be Christian. His energy and determination sprang from his confrontation with a 'Christian' society of which Christians have now become ashamed.

The phenomenon of Gandhi is that of a man who thought seriously, who wrote intensively, but above all believed, and then made the actions of his life conform to his belief.. He played a key role in one country and a vital role in another at a turning point in the history of each country.

Those who came to know Gandhi could not resist the power of his friendliness and of his sincerity. Inevitably they wrote about him. With his own collected works in ninety-three volumes, and those of his friends, his is an exceptionally documented life. But it is the reality of his life that is overwhelming. To build a livable, humane world we have to meet violence and greed with love, courage and forbearance. 'God is light not darkness. God is love not hate. God is truth not untruth' (Saiyidain p. 44). 'Every experiment of mine has deepened my faith in non-violence as the greatest force at the disposal of mankind... The more I work at this law the more I feel delight in life, delight in the scheme of this universe. It gives meaning to the mysteries of nature; it gives me peace that I have no power to describe.' (*Young India*, 1. 10. 1931).

'If I may say so without arrogance my message and my methods are indeed, in their essentials, for the whole world. I believe myself to be a revolutionary, a non-violent revolutionary. I am aspiring after a new order of things that will astonish the world' (Patel/Sykes, p. 195). 'As long as my faith burns bright, as I hope it will even if I stand alone, I shall be alive in the grave and, what is more, speaking from it' (Patel/Sykes, p. 120 from *Harijan* 17.8.47). This last was written five months before his death.

In Johannesburg in 1908 Gandhi was struck to the ground by an Indian opposed to Gandhi's compromises with the repressive governmental regime. A Baptist Minister ran to the scene and took the seriously injured Gandhi into his home. The Reverend Joseph J Doke subsequently wrote, largely based on his conversations with Gandhi, '*An Indian Patriot in South Africa*', which was published the next year. Doke wrote: 'I question whether any system of religion can absolutely hold him. His views are too closely allied to Christianity to be entirely Hindu and too deeply saturated with Hinduism to be called Christian, while his sympathies are so wide and catholic that one would imagine he has reached a point where the formulae of sects are meaningless' (Doke, p. 106). But a much admired Christian missionary forty years later wrote an epitaph. An American Methodist missionary to India, he declined a bishopric, established in India two Christian ashrams and a psychiatric centre and also supported Indian independence. His name was E Stanley Jones. He wrote: 'and so one of the most Christ-like men in history is not called a Christian at all.' (Fischer, p. 418).

Two of Gandhi's collaborators, Jehangir Patel and Marjorie Sykes, wrote in 1987: 'Gandhi believed there was an unbreakable bond between all truly religious men and that therefore religion should bridge differences and make possible a genuine 'secular' polity', (Patel/Sykes p. 35). They knew his unrelenting efforts to make a single united India had been frustrated and that in the months before his death looting, violence and murder on an unprecedented scale had accompanied the partition of the sub-continent.

Religious strife has been a component of wars without number. Gandhi believed, nevertheless, that non-violence, which was for him an expression of love in action, would erode and eventually subdue wars and minimize violence. That was the purpose of religion.

Chatterjee in her remarkable study *Gandhi's Religious Thought* says 'Gandhi's own solution was learned from the ancient Jain tradition of his native Gujarat'. This held that all religious awareness is inevitably partial and incomplete so that different traditions can complement and enrich one another. (Chatterjee px). Gandhi himself wrote, 'I came to the conclusion long ago, after prayerful search and study.... that all religions were true and also all had some error in them and, whilst I hold my own dear, I should hold others as dear as Hinduism. Our innermost prayer should be that a Hindu should be a better Hindu, a Muslim a better Muslim, a Christian a better Christian. I broaden my Hinduism by loving other religions as my own'. (Saiyidain p.34).

In a world where all of us are neighbours Christianity has to choose between claiming exclusiveness (e.g. Jesus our Lord and Saviour, unique and final. All must come to him to be saved.) and claiming to be inclusive (e.g. Jesus is Lord but the divine logos John 1 v. I to 5 , which is love, is the true light which gives light to everyone) and pluralism (e.g. all faiths are one, and all are revelations of Truth, of the real).

Gandhi adhered, in his own way, to both the inclusive and the pluralist positions. He said of Christianity to his faithful secretary, Mahadev Desai: 'I do not experience spiritual consciousness in my life through that Jesus (the historical Jesus). But if by Jesus you mean the eternal Jesus, if by Jesus you understand the religion of universal love that dwells in the heart, then that Jesus lives in my heart to the same extent that Krishna lives, that Rama lives. If I did not feel the presence of that living God; at the painful sights I see in the world I would be a raving maniac and my destiny would be the Hooghli (River). As that Indweller shines in the heart I have not been a pessimist now, or ever before'. (Desai's *Diary* vol. VIII, pl35). John Hick in his textbook *Problems of Religious Pluralism* sees currently a transformation taking place 'in response to the great world faiths' which are to be regarded as alternative ways along which men and women can find salvation / liberation / fulfilment (Hick, p47). He also says, 'It may be that different conceptualizations of the Real – Christian, Muslim, Buddhist and so on – may enable people to begin the personal transformation from self-centredness to Reality centredness' (Hick, p108). But he sees a sticking point in the transformation process: 'To a great extent the actual attitudes of Christians in inter-faith dialogue have (since the 1950's) been implicitly pluralistic, treating the other world religions in practice as valid alternative contexts of salvation. But this attitude... has not yet worked back either into the structures of Christian theology or into an accepted philosophy of religious pluralism' (Hick p 109). It seems that the tree that Gandhi planted has yet to bear its true fruit.

A positive change has occurred, though, in the orientation of Christian concern for third world countries. Effort is now mostly directed to trying to bring life' s essentials to the poorest people. Christian Aid, its Catholic counterpart CAFOD, Oxfam, Save the Children Fund and many other agencies derive their funding from Christian – often church–sources. Conventional missionary activity has been reduced.

Will learning from other faiths undermine one's own faith? Gandhi believed the contrary and in his life seemed to prove it. Loving regard for other faiths would, he believed deepen your fundamental belief and increase commitment to your own faith. Sensitivity to the commands of God in the world would increase.

The chief Rabbi of the United Kingdom, Jonathan Sacks, says: 'Pluralism should not simply be neutral between values. Rather, it must recognize the very specific values of Christians, Muslims, Buddhists, Sikhs, Hindus and Jews growing up in their respective heritages. Traditions are part of our moral ecology, and they should be conserved (Gandhi would say 'enriched') not dissolved by education,' (Sacks, pp65-66). Sacks' conclusions concerning 'moral ecology' echo the thought of the Mahatma who was convinced that toleration was not enough, there must be sympathetic awareness.

Gandhi's whole life was an expression in action, including political action, of the values he absorbed as a youth and reinforced continually by prayer, study and his *Experiments with Truth*. A devout Hindu yet he worked and prayed with men and women of many faiths. He found commitment to common ethical values was never incompatible with diversity of religious belief.

The German theologian Hans Kung thinks that humanists, scientists and anyone who is responsible and cares can develop a personal code of values, but he also says; 'They cannot give a reason for the absoluteness and universality of ethical obligation'. (Kung p. 51). He is thinking of crises 'where action is required of human beings which is in no way to their advantage; a 'sacrifice' which in an extreme case can even call for the sacrifice of their life' (Kung p43). Jesus is the example. But so is the lifelong commitment of Gandhi. The essential human struggle is for the realization of values.

When returning from the Round Table conference, at a public meeting in Switzerland, Gandhi said: 'I observed throughout the West a sickness of heart. You seem to be tired of the military burden under which Europe is groaning and also tired of the prospect of shedding the blood of your fellowmen. The last war, falsely called "great", has taught you and humanity many a rich lesson. ... You found that no fraud, no lies, no deceit was considered too bad to use to win the war, no cruelty was considered too great; there were no unfair ways and means of encompassing the destructions of your so-called enemy... The civilization of the west was weighed in the balance and found wanting' (Lester *Entertaining Gandhi* p165-66).

Though his mind was on India's need for freedom he was clear that the West provided no moral pattern for the sub-continent. Gandhi's further insight was that if values, not creeds or dogmas, are the true backbone of religion then all faiths are seeking the same goals. Honesty, truthfulness, love and compassion are not the monopoly of any one religion but the pure water of all. Then religious dialogue between faiths should be concerned not with the origins and significance of various belief statements and customs but with working together for values. Out of the fire comes the iron white hot. Edward Said, the Palestinian philosopher, says: 'We must stop thinking in collective passions and try to concentrate instead on transcendental values, universally applicable to all peoples.' (Cristina Odone, Ed. 'Catholic Herald' in 'Amnesty' Nov. 1994). Hans Kung has a slogan: 'No world peace without religious peace'. He points to the existence of trans-national, trans-cultural and trans-religious legal structures, and continues 'but what is a world order without a binding and obligatory ethic for the whole of human kind . . . i.e. without a world ethic'. (Kung, p. 34). He instances the United Nations' special agencies and similar bodies as the precursors of such an ethic, and also the 'World Conference of the Religions for Peace' of Kyoto, Japan, 1970, but he does not underestimate the lengthy road to be travelled.

Gandhi appeals to us to develop individual value systems. 'I feel morality consists in following the path which we know to be true, which our "inner voice" tell us to be so. Conscience, inner voice, God and Truth are synonymous terms.' (*Harijan* 8 March 1933). He devoted the last months of his life to trying to heal the wounds and stop the bloodshed that had followed the partition of India, the partition that for twenty years he had tried to avoid. Though there were many points of conflict, Hindus and Moslems were seeking the same goals, he thought, and demonstrably could live side by side. That he died from the bullets of an aggrieved Hindu shows the world needs his witness. His death reinforced the message of his life.

Bibliography

Ambler, Rex *Global Theology* London -1990

Bakle, S.W. *Hinduism* New Delhi - 1991

Chatterjee, Margaret *Gandhi's Religious Thought* Basingstoke - 1983

Doke, Joseph J *An Indian Patriot in S. Africa* New Delhi - 1967

Fischer. Louis *The Life of Mahatma Gandhi* London - 1982

Gracie, David Mcl *Gandhi and Charlie* Cambridge, Mass - 1989

Gandhi, M.K *Hind Swaraj etc* Ahmedabad - 1938

Gandhi,M.K *Hindu Dharma* Delhi - 1978

Gandhi, M.K. *The Bhagvadgita* Delhi - 1980

Gandhi, M.K. *An Autobiography or My Experiments with Truth* London – 1982

Hick, John *Problems of Religious Pluralism* London - 1985

Hick, John *Religious Philosophy* London - 1981

Jenkins, David & Rebecca *Free to Believe* London - 1991

Kung, Hans *Global Responsibility* London - 1990

Nineham Dennis *The Use and Abuse of the Bible* London - 1976

Patel, Jehangir & Sykes Marjorie *Gandhi-His Gift of the Fight* Rasulia - 1987

Payne, Robert *The Life and Death of Mahatma Gandhi* London - 1969

Sacks, Jonathan *The Persistence of Faith* London - 1991

Sayidain, K.G *The Significance of Gandhi* New Delhi -1970

Sheean, Vincent *Lead Kindly Light* New York - 1949

Tendulkar DG *Mahatma - Life of MK Gandhi* New Delhi - 1960

Tolstoy, Leo N. *The Kingdom of God is Within You* Trans. Weiner, L. London - 1905

Thomas Daffern

Gandhi's Influence on Religious and Philosophical Thought in the Modern World

Gandhi casts a long shadow, this much is certain......

In each of the various religious and philosophical traditions of the world, there has been some significant kind of impression left behind by the life and teaching of Gandhi. The purpose of this paper is to examine something of this legacy by considering each of the major religious communities in turn and asking what form the influence has taken.

A few general points are in order to begin with: Gandhi was not in fact really a religious leader. He had no formal training in the Hindu priesthood, for example, and not being of the Brahmin caste, that position was denied him. His mother, Putali Bai Gandhi, was in fact apparently strongly influenced by the Jains, although she no doubt conformed to the Vaishnava Hindu tenets of the household as a whole. Erik Erikson tells us: 'Putali Ba belonged to small sect which prided itself on having unified the Koran with the Hindu scriptures and which abhorred any regression to the idolatry of either, to the point of not allowing any images at all in its temple'. No doubt some significant influence on Gandhi's ideas of *ahimsa* can be traced to her early influence, although the full details remain to be researched. Romain Rolland also tells us that it was his mother's Jain faith which made her make him swear the three vows of the Jain, to abstain from alcohol, meat and sexual intercourse, during his visit to London when aged 19 in 1888. His father was from the Vaishnava sect of Hinduism.

Nor, it must be said, had Gandhi any significant formal training in philosophy, since he chose rather to study law. He did nevertheless undertake a great deal of philosophical and religious study on his own, of both Western and Eastern thought, and eventually pieced together a living ethical and spiritual faith based on the reconciliation of theory and practice.

As we might expect, given his background the details of Gandhi's relationship to Hinduism were complex. In *Ethical Religion* he stated: 'I do not believe in the exclusive divinity of the Vedas. I believe the Bible, the Koran and the Zend-Avesta to be as divinely inspired as the Vedas. . . . Hinduism is not a missionary religion. In it there is room for the worship of all the prophets in the world... Hinduism allows everyone to worship God according to his own faith or *Dharma* and so it lives in peace with all religions.' In this regard then, Gandhi is situating himself on what we could call the 'progressive wing' of the Hindu community, a far cry from the radical nationalistic and narrow definition of Hinduism revived by militant Hindu nationalist movements today. It is also worth remembering that it was a Hindu nationalist who killed Gandhi.

It is, therefore, as we might expect, on the reformist wing of modern Hindu thought that the influence of Gandhi has been greatest. Rabindranath Tagore (1861-1941), who first gave the title Mahatma to Gandhi, was a good friend and admirer of Gandhi, and like him he emphasised the preeminence of love in human and cosmic affairs: 'Tagore was a prophet of divine love on earth. . . Love is not the antithesis or external to cognition. It is the summit of consciousness. Thus the realisation of the immanence of divine love in the rhythmic manifestations of the world supplements the view which interprets the universe as governed by an abstract, inexorable law......... Like Gandhi, Tagore believed in an immanental cosmic law of moral governance in the world and felt that injury to the least of worldly objects or living beings was an offence against the beneficent providence of God.... For Tagore, the essential purpose of human existence and moral striving is to be able to attain freedom, through the attainment of a universality of consciousness which is above all sects, dogmas and narrow definitions:' (*Modern Indian Political Thought*, V.P.Vamma, 1993 11th edition). For Tagore, as for Gandhi, 'Freedom is only attained through the recognition of pervasive interdependence of all beings, enlargement of perspective, expansion of consciousness, and acceptance of responsibility... The essence of freedom is the illumination of the soul by a process of self realisation. It lies in the attainment of universality. Hence love is the pathway to freedom.' (ibid p89)

It is then in the company of the Hindu philosophical sages that Gandhi finds his best company, and certainly a number of modern Hindu thinkers and spiritual leaders have developed their work with considerable influence from Gandhi's life and teachings.

One such spiritual teacher was Dr Bhagwan Das (1869 - 1959). Theosophist, author of *The Essential Unity of all Religions* and other similar writings, he preached the idea of *Swaraj*, self-government, along with Gandhi, and advocated a spiritually based socialism as the preferred form of social and economic organisation: 'The heart must be filled with the religious emotion of benevolence, sympathy.... only this quality of heart can establish the longed for millenium of true socialism, as distinguished from artificial and forced communism on the one hand and on the other from oppressive individualism manifesting as heartless capitalism and ruthless militarism... True socialism can be founded only upon the sense of the Oneness of all life, which means realisation of the Supreme Self... Self government (eg. Raj of the Higher Swa, government by the higher self of the people) in the collective and individual intelligence of mankind....'

One could think of a number of living Hindu religious and spiritual leaders who share similar ideals with Gandhi, and whose message has influenced many people worldwide, and who, like Gandhi, are essentially universal in the appeal of their teachings; rather that 'Hindu' within a narrow definition of adherence to the divinity of the Vedas, etc. The Spiritual teacher Sri Mataji Nirmala Devi, the founder of Sahaj Yoga, for example, is someone who Gandhi knew when she was a young girl, and of whom he spoke highly. (Her husband worked as head of the United Nations Maritime Office and as personal secretary to former India Prime Minister Lal Bahadur Shastri)

The spiritual teacher,Sri Chinmoy, who studied with Aurobindo, and who travels tirelessly throughout the world teaching meditation and preaching world peace, is another contemporary Hindu thinker whose writings evoke Gandhian ideals.

A further contemporary such teacher is Sai Baba, whose ashram in Southern India has become a Mecca for many spiritual seekers from throughout the world, and who counts among his disciples and friends the former Indian Prime Minister, N.Rao. In his religious eclecticism, and his stress on non-violence and peace, Sai Baba has certainly felt some Gandhian influences.

Ramana Maharshi (1879-1950) and Sri Aurobindo (1872-1950) were two other great Hindu mystics and teachers whose ideas overlapped in many ways with those of Gandhi. Maharshi adopted more the path of the recluse and saint, living the spiritual path in Arunachala away from the difficult social and political context in which Gandhi was operative. Yet the same fundamental moral and spiritual energy, and rigorous introspection and self inquiry, can be detected behind the two thinkers.

Aurobindo likewise, after an initial period of revolutionary activity in Bengal, chose to devote himself to philosophical introspection, and to the cultivation of spiritual knowledge. He shared with Gandhi a negative appraisal of over–centralised state government, and both could be classified as spiritual anarchists in terms of their political philosophy. 'Sri Aurobindo is a critic of the very idea of the State. He is highly critical of the socialist cult of the state. The State is to him a machine lacking in tact, taste and delicacy... By its very nature it is unable to go deep into human nature and get in touch with that reach of human consciousness where alone man knows himself and his fellow human beings as an expression of a common spiritual unity. Underlying the political unity is a social unity. And underlying that social unity is an invisible spiritual unity' (*Sri Aurobindo and Karl Marx: Integral sociology and dialectical sociology* by D.P. Chattopadhyaya, 1976 p111).

Sri Swami Sivananda (1887-1963) is a further religious leader who should be mentioned as someone interested the Gandhian legacy. Founder of the Divine Life Society. 'Religion is the pathway to universal peace and brotherhood ... the essentials of all religions are the same..... there is only one caste, the caste of humanity, there is only one religion, the religion of love, there is only one righteousness, that is truthfulness... all the great religions of the world preach the gospel of peace. Peace can only be found within... anger, greed, jealousy and hatred are enemies of peace. Develop goodwill, cooperation, mercy, compassion, non-resistance or non-retaliation to injuries done to you, forgiveness, contentment, nobility and cosmic love. Pray for him who has done you harm, send thought currents of peace and goodwill to him and to the whole world' (Swami Sivananda, *Religious Education*, 1963, 4th edition) Such words could have come direct from Gandhi himself.

Another great modern Hindu religious teacher was Swami Chinmayananda. Born in 1916 in Kerala, as Balakrishna Menon, he graduated in science and political thought, later studying as a post graduate in literature and law. At the age of 27, influenced by Nehru's' *National Herald* he joined India's freedom struggle, and played a significant role in Gandhi's campaigns. Influenced by Swami Sivananda, in 1943 he took *sanyas* under him. Committed to advanced Hindu scholarship he later worked under Swami Tapovanam of Uttarkashi, studying Sanskrit philosophy. Chinmayananda's path was that of the traditional Vedic rishi, and he spent 7 years in the Himalayan mountains studying spirituality, until he returned to the normal social world and gave his first religious lecture in 1951 in Poona.

The other main group of 'Hindu' Political leaders who managed to combine a religious and spiritual element, 'Gandhian' in ideal if not always in style and content, includes a large number of eminent names, whose influence has been central to the shaping of modern Indian society and politics. It would be fair to say that Gandhi has influenced the whole field of Indian politics as much as, if not more than, its religious life, yet in the political sphere, the influence has been more in the ideal than in the reality. Yet there have been exceptions in that several major figures have tried in their ways to enact the essence of Gandhi's vision for society including figures such as:

- Pandit Nehru, (1889-1964) Prime Minister of India from 1947-1964;
- Desai, Moraji Ranchodji (1896-), Prime Minister of India from 1977-79;
- L.B. Shastri (1904-1966), Prime Minister of India;
- Dr. Rajendra Prasad, President of India, (1950-1962);
- Narayan, Jaya Prakash (1902-1979);
- Achariya Vinoba Bhave, (1895-1982) a key figure in any study of Gandhi's legacy, and the *Sarvodaya* movement;
- Mahadev Desai - secretary to Gandhi, a teacher who joined Gandhi in India in about 1916, and stayed till his death in 1943;
- Sardar Vallabhbhai Patel, (1875-1950) Deputy Prime Minister of India.

All these figures, in their diverse ways took the ideas of Gandhi and applied them in the political, social and economic spheres of Indian life. All of them were essentially

Hindu in orientation, but their religious activities were generally subordinated to their other work.

In the Christian world, Gandhi's influence has also been strong. Many writers have commented upon the close relationship between Gandhi and Christian thought, and indeed, when asked which book had influenced him most, replied *The New Testament*. But the relationship between Gandhi's thought and Christianity needs qualifying, since it is with heterodox, or 'esoteric' Christianity that Gandhi found himself most at home. Those thinkers who had particularly influenced him, such as Thoreau, Ruskin, and Tolstoy, were what could be called 'radical Christians' inspired by the ideals of Jesus rather than the forms of the church, or the traditions of conventional theology. In this sense it has been with individual Christians rather than with the body politic of 'The Church' that Gandhi has had most influence.

Any comprehensive survey of modern Christians influenced by Gandhi would be too vast for the purposes of this paper, so I will rather be selective and highlight a few particular individuals who stand out. Even so the list is formidable:

> Schumacher, E.F. whose work in revisioning economics is well known, and although a Roman Catholic, was deeply influenced by Gandhian thought.
>
> Rev. Jesse Jackson whose leadership of the American civil rights movement is significant both politically and religiously.
>
> Homer Jack, an American Unitarian who served as a long running founder of WCRP and who edited *The Gandhi Reader* in 1958.
>
> Bede Griffiths, the Benedictine monk who left Prinknash Abbey and went to live in an ashram in India, and has spent years working out a theological and mystical reconciliation of Eastern and Western thought.
>
> Rev Dick Sheppard, born in 1880, he volunteered for Boer War but was unable to go as hurt in accident, he worked in east End, being ordained in 1909, he became the vicar of St Martins in the Fields and was a moving force behind the Peace Pledge Union; he died in 1937 aged 57.
>
> Thomas Merton, the great Christian contemplative monk whose work attempted to reconcile Eastern mysticism and Western social and political action, and whose commitment to peace and non-violence was profound.
>
> Bishop Trevor Huddleston whose tireless work in campaigning for peace and justice in South Africa, and for an end to the system of apartheid, has at last born fruit.

Albert Schweitzer, the great Christian scholar, missionary, musicologist, medical doctor and philosopher, whose links to Gandhian thought were profound, and whose ethic of reverence for life acts as a Western complement to Gandhi's principle of *ahimsa.*

Louis Massignon, the great Christian Franciscan scholar of Sufism, who authored a study of Al Hallaj, and who agonized over a way of reconciling the great Abrahamic faiths of the middle east, hoping that Gandhi's ideas could be a beacon of light to help heal a bitterly divided landscape.

Nelson Mandela, the great South Africa political leader who has emerged to lead the African National Congress into the forging of a new South Africa.

Bruce Kent, the British Canadian Catholic peace campaigner.

Rev. Dr. Martin Luther King, perhaps the greatest of all those inspired by Gandhi's example in modern times, and who led the Black Americans struggle for full civil equality, and who ultimately paid for it with his life.

Prof Hans Kung, the German Catholic scholar whose work in the pursuit of inter-religious tolerance and understanding is seminal.

Lester, Muriel (1883-1967), born in Leytonstone, a British leader of Christian opinion she was present at the FOR (Fellowship of Reconciliation) launch in 1915, established Kingsley Hall in the 1920's in Bow, where Gandhi lived during his visit to London in 1931.

Thomas Berry, the great scholar of the divinity of the natural world; he founded the Riverdale Centre for Religious Research in 1970, and in 1975 was elected President of American Teilhard Foundation; he also studied American Indian world and Sanskrit and Hinduism.

Berdyaev, Nicholas, the Russian existentialist Christian thinker.

Toynbee Arnold Joseph (1886--1975) Director of RIIA from 1925-1955; History of the World 1934-1954, whose eclectic style of historical philosophy ended in a Gandhian affirmation of love as the primal energy underlying society and spirituality and indeed all of history.

Inge, Dean William 1860-1950, the great Christian mystic thinker and pacifist.

Paul Tillich, (1886-1965) who emigrated to USA in 1933 and who thought through the profound roots of peace and justice in the complexities of the modern world.

Kenneth Boulding, the Quaker economist and founding father of peace research.

Rev. Marcus Braybrooke, the scholar and practitioner of interfaith dialogue and action, who lived many years in India and was inspired to his work partly by Gandhi's example.

Elise Boulding, wife of the late Kenneth Boulding, a tireless Quaker peace educator and feminist historian.

Bishop Desmond Tutu, renowned for his spiritual leadership in the South African struggle against apartheid.

Mubarak Awad, a Palestinian non-violence leader, born 1943 in Jerusalem, raised as a Quaker, held in solitary confinement in Israeli prison in 1988, he was about to be expelled but messages from around the world led to his release; he has established a centre for nonviolence research in Jerusalam.

Danilo Dolci, born 1924, whose work in Sicily to advance the conditions of the poor, in spite of the opposition of the Mafia and the established church has become world famous.

Matthew Fox, inspirer of creation theology and the notion of 'original blessing' as opposed to original sin.

Rev Dorothy Soelle, among the leading contemporary theorists on non-violence.

Lanza del Vasto, the colourful Christian pilgrim, who met Gandhi in India and founded the Community of the Ark as a series of communal religious houses where Gandhian ideals can be put into practice.

Teilhard de Chardin (1881-1955), the great Jesuit scholar and thinker who agreed with Gandhi in identifying love as the hidden energy underlying the universe.

Rev Donald Soper, the unstoppable Methodist pacifist preacher.

Richard Henry Tawney, 1880-1962; who tried to work out the details of his Christian beliefs in social, political and economic terms, and whose thinking underlies many of the ideals of Christian socialist thought in the UK.

The relationship between Gandhi and Buddhist thought is complex: indirectly, through Theosophy, Buddhist ideas had a large part in the shaping of his own views on non-violence and the meaning of the spiritual life. A large number of Buddhists from different parts of the Buddhist world have found in Gandhi an exemplar in the political sphere of many of the ideas of Buddhist thought. The Dalai Lama, spiritual head in exile of the Tibetan people, is perhaps the best known of the Buddhist Gandhians who espouse *ahimsa* and refuse resolutely to countenance the normal political way of resolving disputes through force.

In Japan also, Gandhi's ideas have had an indirect appeal and resonance. Tsunesaburo Makiguchi, (1871-1944) was the distant founder behind Soka Gakkai and whose ideas share certain common themes with Gandhi's. Born in North West Japan, at the age of 14 he went to Hokkaido and educated at Hokkaido University of Education. He served as a teacher to several schools in Sapporo and Tokyo and formed a small organisation of educators and converted to Nichiren Shoshu Buddhism in 1928. In 1930 he established Soka Kyoiku Gakkai (Value Creating Education Society) working to spread knowledge of Nichiren's teachings. In 1943 he was arrested with other leaders for opposing Shintoism and for criticising the Japanese war effort. At this point he can be regarded as having been involved at a different end point of the same struggle as Gandhi in India. He died in prison in 1944 aged 73. His publications include -*The System of Value Creating Pedagogy*.

Following Makiguchi's death, Josei Toda, (1900-1958) became the 2nd President of Soka Gakkai. In the 1920's he had joined school where Makiguchi worked; in 1928 he converted along with him to Nichiren Buddhism, and went also to prison during the war, after he emerged in 1945 he swore to rebuild lay society and founded new launched Soka Gakkai, which grew to number some 750,000 members by his death.

Daisaku Ikeda became the 3rd President of Sokka Gakai after him. Born in 1928, son of a seaweed farmer, he left school aged 12; introduced to Soka Gakkai and influenced by Toda, by 1964 he had raised the membership to 3 million; in 1975 he formed an international offshoot. In 1983 he won the UN peace award from UN Secretary General Perez de Cuellar. He engaged in various dialogues with world leaders including Arnold Toynbee which was published as the book *Choose Life*.

Another Japanese Buddhist religious leader, Most Venerable Nichidatsu Fujii, 1884-1985, in 1903 became a monk and in 1918 began to preach Buddhism publicly, travelling widely to Manchuria, China, Korea, etc. Warning of the growing militarism in Japan, he and his disciples took to the beating of hand drums and chanting the prayer for peace '*Namu myoho renge kyo*' (meaning 'Veneration to the Sutra of the Lotus of the Good Law'). He founded the first Nipponzan Myohoji near Mt Fuji in 1931-1933. He travelled to India to regenerate Buddhism there and met Gandhi in person. Throughout World War Two he fasted and prayed for peace. After the end of the war he began building peace pagodas, such as those at Milton Keynes and Battersea Park in the United Kingdom. His books include *Buddhism for World Peace*.

Another crucial neo-Buddhist thinker who has made a great contribution to the development of peace research as a field is the Norwegian thinker and academic, Professor Johan Galtung, currently teaching at the University of Hawaii, and who is married to a Japanese wife.

Joanna Macy is a contemporary Californian neo-Buddhist thinker who has been influenced by Gandhian thought in her work against militarism and the despair induced by the prevalence of weapons of mass destruction. Drawing also on the ideas of psychosynthesis and other contemporary transpersonal psychologies, she has developed a subtle and powerful form of 'despair work' in which one is encouraged to move through and beyond feelings of despair, disempowerment, suffering etc. so as to be able to reattain a basic sense of human solidarity and universal compassion.

Chris Titmus the founder of Gaia House and contemporary British teacher of Buddhist meditation would be another Buddhist in this same tradition, of commitment to inner and outer peace in equal balance.

Ken Wilber is another transpersonal psychologist and philosopher of religion who warrants a mention in this context. Born in 1949 he has been influenced by Krishnamurti, Ramana Maharshi, Gandhi, Aurobindo, Da Free John, as well as Western philosophical thinkers such as Heidegger. He also studied with Kalu Rinpoche, the great ecumenical Tibetan Buddhist scholar.

Petra Kelly, influential in the modern Green movement, was another neo-Buddhist inspired greatly by Gandhi's example, as have been many of the Green movement campaigners in recent years.

Some Buddhist figures have been less kind to Gandhi. Dr Bhim Rao Ambedkar, 1891-1956, wrote a book very critical of what he saw as Gandhi's reactionary acceptance of the caste system. He essentially complains that Gandhi was too orthodox a Hindu in his orientation, and left the caste system essentially as it was. His argument was that although Gandhi had sentimentalised the lower castes, by designating them as *Harijans* etc., he had in fact left their relative status untouched, and by idealising poverty and humility had merely reinforced the traditional class-ridden consciousness of Hindu Indian society. Ambedkar publicly embraced Buddhism partly as a conscious rejection of Gandhi's own special brand of Hinduism. It seems a double irony and tragedy that Gandhi should on the one hand receive criticism for being 'too Hindu' and on the other be assassinated for not being 'Hindu enough'!

Thich Nhat Hanh, the Vietnamese Buddhist peace activist, is another figure whose work has been to continue the development of the ideals of peace and non-violence in the modern world, whether through writings (eg. *Being Peace*) or through meditation instruction, holding retreats, or organising political actions for peace.

Rev. Nikkyo Niwwano is perhaps the one Japanese Buddhist figure above all others most deeply influenced by Gandhi's ideals. Born in 1906, of farming stock, he served in Japanese navy, without higher education. In 1923 he went to Tokyo and studied religion and Chinese thought. He joined the Buddhist group, Reiyukai, after his daughter's illness in 1920's/30's. In 1934 he set up a dairy shop in order to 'meet people'. In 1938 he seceded to form his own organisation and with Mrs Naganuma he established Dai Nippon Rissho

Kosei-Kai and became its Ist President. Currently its membership has enlarged to some 5 million people. Rev. Niwwano was one of the original founders and proposers for the formation of the World Conference on Religion and Peace (WCRP) which has played a highly significant role in international campaigns for peace through collaboration between religions since it was founded in 1969, on the centenary of Gandhi's birth.

In the Islamic community the influence of Gandhian thought has not been perhaps as significant as with some other religions. This is partly due to historical circumstances with the close proximity of large Muslim populations in Northern India and the role of Hindu-Muslim relations during the struggle for independence from the British Empire. Mohammad Iqbal, the intellectual architect of Pakistan, and a noted modern Islamic philosopher, felt that Gandhi's ideas on non-violence were too passive. Islam lays great stress on active resistance to evil and injustice; it is indeed a religious duty in Islam to defend oneself if attacked and to defend the weak and poor from oppression.

President Zakir Husain actually became the first Muslim leader of India, and took an active part in the inaugural meeting of the World Conference on Religion and Peace in 1968 in New Delhi. Sir Zafrullah Khan is another Muslim intellectual leader who has been active in the cause of world peace and understanding.

Yet in spite of this, a significant number of Muslims did realise that Gandhi's's philosophy in fact coincides with statements in the Koran and the Hadith that the greatest *jihad* (struggle) is actually against one's own lowest nature, not against outer enemies.

Particularly in the Sufi tradition have Gandhi's ideas found a special resonance, and those many schools of Muslims interested in the spiritual path have found resonance with Gandhi's teachings. M.R.Bawa Muhaiyaddeen has written: 'Peace can only be found within the heart. Good qualities, wisdom and clarity must provide that explanation within each heart. Man will only know peace when he brings God's justice and his qualities into himself. Therefore, before we speak of peace, let us try and acquire God's words within ourselves. Let us find tranquillity within ourselves. If we can do that, our speech will be fruitful. Then the whole world will be at peace. Man must find peace, tranquillity, happiness, unity, love and every good quality within his own life, within his innermost heart. Only a person who does that can understand the difficulties, the pain, and the misery of others. A man of wisdom will know this, understand this, and rectify his own mistakes. Then he can help others.' (*Islam and World Peace*, 1987.)

The famous Pathan leader from Afghanistan, Abdul Ghaffar Khan, was born in 1890 in the North West Frontier Province of India. Educated in Peshawar, he later founded the Pathan independence movement, the Red Shirts or the Servants of God. Frequently imprisoned by the British, the founder of the movement was honoured by the Afghan nation for his tireless struggle for independence for the Pathan peoples of the frontier. Yet in the end it has been a hopeless task. When he died finally in the 1980's, and was buried in Jalalabad, the Afghanistan he loved was racked with violent conflict due to the Russian invasion, and the path of non-violence was not perceived as an option in the struggle against the invaders. Perhaps it is only now, in the chaos of the aftermath of the invasion, with the exhaustion of witnessing pointless struggles between rival mujahadin gangs, that the people of Afghanistan may be willing to heed the voice of non-violence at last.

In the Jain religion, a number of eminent religious leaders have paid particular stress on Gandhian ideals; yet they would argue that these are in fact at the heart of the Jain faith anyway.

Acharya Tulsi and Acharya Sushil Kumar Ji are two of the most eminent of such religious peace leaders in recent decades.

In Judaism, a number of thinkers have been significantly influenced by Gandhi's philosophy of *ahimsa*, including: Martin Buber who lived from 1878-1965. Austrian born, he studied Philosophy and History of Art in Vienna and Berlin. His great work *I and Thou* was published in 1923. Politically, he approved of the ideal of peace between Arabs and Jews and he campaigned tirelessly for reconciliation between the two peoples as a practical application of his metaphysics of reconciled otherness held in the tension of divinely sanctioned love. His ideas have also inspired a number of contemporary Jewish peace activists. Yet Buber exchanged correspondence with Gandhi and disagreed with him over Gandhi's reluctance to see the validity behind a Zionist position. With the difficult and tragic history of the recent Arab-Israeli conflicts still being played out, it is difficult to pronounce straightforward judgement on the rights and wrongs of this historic exchange of opinions. But one thing at least is certain: if there is to be a genuinely workable future for people to be able to live at ease with one another in the Middle East, then Gandhi's legacy of non-violence cannot fail to make its essential contribution.

Albert Einstein is another great Jewish thinker who was inspired by the example of Gandhi; although a scientist rather than a religious thinker, Einstein in fact regarded his scientific work as a form of mystical worship and in a number of writings revealed that his mind had a deeply mystical cast. Above all, he advocated an ethical world view, based on compassion and reverence for life, and in social and political affairs likewise, advocated an ethical socialism similar to Gandhi.

Sir Victor Gollancz 1893-1967, a socialist and a pacifist, founded the Left Book Club to expose Nazism and to strengthen the intellectual forces against militarism and fascism in 1936; he was active in many humanitarian causes throughout his long life, including helping refugees after World War 2, and Arab refugees after Israel's War of Independence in 1948.

Rabbi Kook, the first chief Rabbi of Palestine under the British Mandate, was a profound Jewish philosopher and mystic, who wrote among other things a treatise on the meaning of redemption, and who advocated the urgent ethical imperative of finding a just peace between Jew and Arab in their common holy land.

Rabbi Abraham Heschel 1901-1972, who taught at the Jewish Theological Seminary in New York, was another influential Jewish thinker who advocated Gandhian approaches in both politics and metaphysics, and who campaigned tirelessly in the American civil rights and anti-war movements for peace at home and abroad.

The experience of the holocaust was obviously a unique feature of modern history which has shaped Jewish thought and from which different thinkers have deduced different conclusions. Some have hardened their Judaism as a result, arguing that never again will Judaism allow itself to become soft and yielding in the face of injustice and oppression, but will rather fight to preserve its identity even in the face of overwhelming odds. Others have taken the view that the holocaust teaches the final folly and stupidity of racism, of violence and militarism carried to their ultimate degree, and that its final lesson is the imperative to do all one can to avoid a repetition of such barbarism ever again, to any peoples. Rabbi Hugo Gryn, for example, an Auschwitz survivor, and Rabbi Albert Friedlander, a President of WCRP, in the United Kingdom, argue for the latter conclusion.

Other religious traditions have also had their Gandhian peace wings, inspired by the life and work of the Mahatma, but space shortage does not permit a full exploration here. These include the Sikh tradition, with the Namdhari branch of the Sikhs also claiming that several of the key Gandhian tactics eg. non-cooperation, actually originated with them in the first place. Zoroastrians, who in the Indian situation play an active role in welfare and social development work alongside their Gandhian colleagues. The Bahai's also see their own faith as having many features in common with the ideals of Gandhi. Shinto, Taoism, Confucianism, all likewise have their peace devotees.

These numerous religious traditions find a common platform of concerted endeavour for peace in the major international interfaith peace organisation, the World Conference on Religion and Peace. Founded in 1969, in the centenary of Gandhi's birth, partly as a result of a commemorative seminar in New Delhi hosted by the Gandhi Peace Foundation under the direction of G. Ramachandran. Since the first World Assembly held in Kyoto in 1970, there have been six such assemblies which have met to deliberate the details of inter-religious collaboration for peace and justice in this fractured and troubled world. At the most recent such World Assembly, which took place in November 1994, over 900 religious leaders from all the major religious traditions of the world, and from many nations, met to discuss the state of the global community.

Among the proposals decided upon was the creation of a Standing Commission on interreligious cooperation for conflict resolution and peace building, which will involve the major faith communities in undertaking a self appraisal as to their resources both human and spiritual towards conflict resolution, and then working together in this regard in troubled regions around the globe.

The author was also involved in a proposal which was approved at the conference to establish a Commonwealth Interfaith Council of religious leaders and activists working for peace and interfaith harmony. Religious leaders from Commonwealth countries such as India, Bangladesh, Pakistan, Sri Lanka, Malaysia, Australia, Canada, New Zealand, Kenya, Nigeria, South Africa all agreed to participate. Many of them, from all different religious backgrounds, were in fact Gandhian inspired. Gandhi's granddaughter, who is herself active in the South African chapter of WCRP, spoke movingly at the conference in the College of Cardinals in Vatican City, at the first such large interfaith gathering ever held there.

Certainly, Gandhi casts a long shadow .....

The Individual, Society and the State

Sadiq Ali

Political and Economic Decentralisation in India

Gandhiji came upon the world scene in the first decade of the twentieth century as the discoverer of a new civilised method of fighting and redressing social and political wrongs. He called it *Satyagraha* – Truth force or Soul force. He sought to apply it later in almost every field of life – social, political or economic, domestic, national or international. The success he achieved in his non-violent struggles against wrong drew world-wide attention. His weapon of civil resistance has its votaries to-day in several parts of the world. There are quite a few concrete examples of its successful application which the world has furnished in recent times. By this discovery alone the world would have perpetuated Gandhi's memory and message. Violence is becoming highly dangerous and destructive in whatever field it is sought to be used. The emergence of a more humane equivalent especially in the field of redressing social and political wrongs is greeted with relief in not a few quarters. But Gandhi did not stop here. He went much further and deeper into the current state of the world and came upon some startling ideas about life in general, human living and a good, decent free and democratic society which he compendiously described as a non-violent society.

One principal source of his ideas was his religion or religion and spirituality in general. This gave him his basic conception of human nature. It was this conception which drove him to declare that his aim in life was self-realisation, in other words, to see God face to face. Normally it would seem that a person who kept self-realisation as their aim would be lost to the social or political concerns of human kind. But Gandhi's self-realisation involved him deeply and continuously in every concern of humanity. In fact it took him beyond the human world. He yearned to realise his identity with all that lives. This explains why he lived such an active life. He was, as it were, the supreme activist of his time. Gandhi's conception of human nature led him to lay stress on the continuous growth of one's soul. This did not require the support of large material possessions. Nor was intellectual growth by itself a thing of great appeal to him. It was welcome as an aid to the soul's growth. The basic material wants of people in this view were easy of fulfilment if there existed a well-ordered society.

This was one aspect of the kind of society he wished to build. With his spiritual background the kind of society which he would wish to advocate could only be democracy where alone men and women had opportunities for full intellectual, moral or spiritual growth. He explained often enough what he meant by democracy. It was the western type of democracy which was mostly in people's minds when they had occasion to discuss it with him. Gandhi had practical experience of British democracy when he was in South Africa carrying on his struggle against racial discrimination. The view that he expressed on British democracy in his *Hind Swaraj* which he brought out in 1909 was far from favourable. It could have borne the marks of hasty thinking. It was contrary to what Indian leadership thought and felt in those days. They found in it a great source of inspiration in their endeavour to attain Home Rule. Gandhi's perspective in commenting on British democracy, the way he did, was however different. His mature view of democracy, the various parts of its content, became clear as India advanced towards its goal of freedom. Much that constitutes the distinguishing marks of democracy, such as freedom of speech, assembly, regular elections. Fundamental Rights had his warm endorsement. He also accepted the need for political parties with their own distinctive programmes and policies. He had strong views about how ministers should function and what example in honesty and integrity they had to set. He believed in adult suffrage. With all his zeal for religion he advocated its separation from politics. These and much else were common points of agreement between him and the normal advocates of democracy.

It was, however, the special stress Gandhi laid on certain aspects of democratic thought that marked him out from the rest. Basically he would have gone for enlightened anarchy. He was impatient of every kind of yoke. He cherished self-rule. Freedom, accompanied by self-restraint, and which took account of his neighbour's equal right to freedom, was what he would have wished to achieve. The acquisition of minimum material wants by everybody ruled out any form of exploitation and made for peace and concord. Since this enlightened anarchy was not, for one reason or another, a practical proposition, he opted for minimum government. Even this minimum government could be a lot of government, the society being as complex as it had become. 'I look upon an increase in the power of the state with the greatest fear, because although while apparently doing good by minimising exploitation it does the greatest harm to mankind by destroying individuality which lies at the root of all progress'. In the very first year of freedom Gandhi spoke out against controls by government when there was scarcity of food in the country.

Gandhi was also no great advocate of planning at the Central level. He did not take any special interest in the planning activities of Pandit Jawaharlal Nehru. This was planning from above which did not go well with his whole trend of thinking on the subject of India's social and economic reconstruction. The Central Government had, of course, a crucial role to play in demarcating the spheres of activity as between the private and public sector and leaving a wide field for cottage and village industries which were capable of being revived. But, basically, the centre of planning and development in Gandhi's mind was in the five lakh villages of India. Once the great inertia in villages was broken and the abundance of energy that lay hidden and suppressed there was released, a vast vista of possibilities would open out, and his dream of self-sufficient and self-governing villages would be realised. There was nothing utopian about it. It could go along with large scale industrialisation in the country in spheres in which the use of modern, sophisticated technology was in order. Villages could well be left to take care of certain basic necessities of life.

What kind of impact did Gandhi's fervent advocacy of decentralisation or *Panchayati Raj* have on the course of events in India? Had it formed the basis of India's Constitution when it was being drawn up by the Constituent Assembly soon after India became free, India's political and even economic structure would have been different from what it is to-day. The partition of India had further created a certain new atmosphere in the country. A strong centre was felt necessary to meet internal and external challenges. The Constitution-making body could, for a variety of reasons, think only in terms of the Union Government and the Constituent States, some of which were still in the process of formation as units of government. Gandhi, as intensely occupied as he was with meeting the menace of communal violence in the country which accompanied partition, was hardly in a position to play any active role in framing the Constitution of the country. There were also several trends of thinking in the Constituent Assembly which were not in harmony with his basic approach. Gandhi was, however, taken by surprise and deeply distressed when he was told that there wasn't even any mention of *Panchayati Raj* in the Constitution that was being drawn up for the governance of the country. Our Constitution makers saw Gandhi's point and found a place for self-government at the village level in the directive principles of the Constitution. This was no effective substitute for the comprehensive self-government which Gandhi aimed at, but it was some acknowledgement of its importance.

Panchayats were in action in some form in parts of the country even during British rule, but they were all effete, powerless bodies. When the country became free, the Government of India realised the need and importance of taking some initiative to rouse and awaken the vast countryside so to tackle in some effective way a whole host of problems which it was faced with. A movement called community development was set in motion. It did create a temporary stir and yielded some results but it was felt that a more systematic and country-wide effort was necessary for promoting local development. A Committee chaired by Balwantrai Mehta, who later became the Chief Minister of Gujarat, was appointed to go more deeply into the whole question of economic and social development at the village level. Its recommendations formed the basis of a well thought out scheme of self-government in rural India. It contemplated the existence and functioning of three layers of government at the local level. The district in a state formed one level. There was one intermediate body between the district and the lowest village unit. A certain division of powers and responsibilities between these units of self-government was broadly indicated. It was by no means any highly vigorous or extensive self-government but it did hold out possibilities of moving forward in the direction of local self rule .

These possibilities unfortunately were not realised except in some limited areas. The early phase of enthusiasm gave way to stagnation and later to decay. I may, without going into the cause of this decline, mention that in the late seventies a new Committee, chaired by Ashok Mehta, was appointed to have a fresh look at the whole experiment of village self-government. This Committee did submit its report but political developments in the country came in the way of any serious consideration of its recommendations. Time for fresh serious thinking on the subject came when the results of planning in the country and the work of the Planning Commission and the way the government worked came under review. There were several schemes for rural development and regeneration and enough monies were set apart for them and yet the results were meagre. The villages, with all the development that had taken place, did not present any attractive picture of growth or welfare of the people. Poverty, unemployment, diseases, illiteracy, insanitation and other ills still persisted in the countryside. There was a continual exodus from rural India to urban India making the latter less and less livable. Large scale industry, however necessary for the development of the country, held out no hope of absorbing any considerable chunk of the unemployed population, especially its educated fragment which was continually growing in numbers. The value of what Gandhi had said on this subject from time to time was brought home to our people in a new forceful manner.

Further the country had seen democracy in action at the Central and State levels. It realised that democracy in theory is one thing and democracy in action is another. The latter's level of achievement depends on the quality of the human material which is called upon to practise it. It is also judged by the fruits it yields. Those who govern at the political and administrative level are answerable to the vast mass of the governed. How far this answerability has been achieved is partly reflected in elections which are held from time to time and which are an essential part of democracy. But elections alone are not the total meaning of democracy. Their quality also matters a great deal. In India now, there is a search for more effective people's participation in the democratic process. The absence of this participation produces apathy which is good neither for democracy nor for progress and development in economic and social fields in almost three quarters of India.

Gandhi aimed at the reconstruction of the village in every field of life. It is good to know what his picture of what he called the village republic was. One or two quotations from his writings will give us some idea of this picture.

'Independence must begin at the bottom. Thus every village will be a republic or *panchayat* having full powers. It follows, therefore, that every village has to be self-sustained and capable of managing its affairs... This does not exclude dependence on, and willing help from neighbours or from the world. It will be free and voluntary play of mutual forces.. In this structure, composed of innumerable villages, there will be ever-widening, never-ascending circles. Life will not be a pyramid with the apex sustained by the bottom. But it will be an oceanic circle whose centre will be the individual always ready to perish for the village, the latter ready to perish for the circle of villages, till at last the whole becomes one life composed of individuals, never aggressive in their arrogance but ever humble, sharing the majesty of the oceanic circle of which they are integral units. Therefore the outermost circumference will not wield power to crush the inner circle but will give strength to all within and derive its own strength from it.' (*Harijan*, 28-7-1946)

'My idea of Village Swaraj is that it is a complete republic independent of its neighbours for its own vital wants, and yet interdependent for many others in which dependence is a necessity. Thus every village's first concern will be to grow its own food crops and cotton for its cloth. It should have a reserve for its cattle, recreation and playground for adults and children. Then if there is more land available, it will grow *useful* money crops, thus excluding *ganja*, tobacco, opium and the like. The village will maintain a village theatre, school and public hall. It will have its own water-works ensuring water supply. This can be done through controlled wells and tanks. Education will be compulsory up to the final basic course. As far as possible every activity will be conducted on the co-operative basis. There will be no castes such as we have today with their graded untouchability.' (*Harijan*, 26-7-1942)

There was fresh thinking on the subject among all political parties. In the late eighties both Congress and Non-Congress Governments at the centre brought forward legislation which sought to ensure maximum participation of the people by a maximum number of people in the administration of their own affairs at local levels. Central intervention was thought necessary for devolution of power and authority. But even this intervention was not enough unless the Constitution itself was amended. This constitutional amendment bill was introduced in September 1991. It was, referred to a Joint Committee of Parliament. On the basis of their report the bill was passed in December 1992. It had to be ratified by more than half the states. This was done. This now forms a part of the Constitution itself. This amendment has corrected many of the weaknesses of the old system and given new strength to local village self-government in several directions. It provides for regular and timely elections. It provides for reservation of seats in *panchayats* for Scheduled Castes and Scheduled Tribes proportionate to their numerical strength in the general population. There is a similar reservation in the distribution of top-posts of the various *panchayat* institutions. There is also reservation for women to the extent of one third of the total number of seats and top posts. The amendment calls for the appointment of a Finance Commission to recommend principles which should govern distribution of resources between the State Government and *Panchayats* at different levels. This should ensure that these self-governing bodies at the lower levels are endowed with enough financial resources and also with adequate powers and authority. There will be a State Election Commission to ensure free and fair elections.

The Amendment, if carried out in the right spirit by the State Legislatures and the State Administrations can go a long way to taking rural India towards the goal Gandhi had in mind. Gandhi thought in more radical terms, especially in the economic field, but this will have to wait on future developments at the national and international level and the pressure that the village units themselves might feel inclined to exert to achieve economic self-sufficiency. The way is now clear for the building up of this pressure.

There were critics throughout these more than four decades who maintained that *Panchayati Raj*, with all its strong points, would increase the power of the elite at the expense of weaker elements in society. The social order in villages did suffer from serious inequalities in social and economic fields. These inequalities could be reflected in the actual working of the *panchayats* and they did so in no small measure. In the constitutional amendment a serious effort has been made to neutralise to a fair extent the effects of this inequality with the device of special representation for women and the weaker elements of society. The latter can make themselves more effectively felt in the more equalitarian atmosphere which has been sought to be created by the amendment.

With all the forces of modernisation and industrialisation at work in the country ever since India attained its political freedom some village industries with all the handicaps to which they were subjected showed their staying power. The new forces could have overwhelmed and annihilated them but, thanks largely to Gandhi, they still have a place in the industrial map of India. But this place has to be enlarged and fortified in many ways. I give here a few figures which will illustrate the present position. Let me first take *Khadi* which means hand-spun and hand-woven cloth. It was something novel that Gandhi talked of *Khadi* in the new industrial age of machines and steam and electric power and modern inventiveness. Gandhi, however, argued with passion, as well as with logic based on facts and figures, and had some success in popularising *Khadi*. The *Khadi* movement he initiated acquired a certain momentum. This momentum had to acquire much greater strength in independent India. It did gather strength but it has fallen short of the legitimate expectations of its zealous champions. Still, it has some success to its credit. *Khadi* production which in 1955-56 was at the level of Rs.5.54 crores has now increased to Rs. 365 crores. Other village industries have produced goods valued at around 2,490 crores in 1992-93 when in 1955 did not exceed eleven crores. The employment level has gone up to 51.58 lakhs persons (*Khadi* 14.28 lakhs and village industries 37.30 lakhs) from the level of 9.64 lakh persons (*Khadi* 6.57 lakhs and village industries 3.07 lakhs) in 1955.

How far village and tiny industries should be encouraged and developed is an area of controversy but it is becoming more and more plain to an increasing number of people that large scale industry is unable to absorb the large number of people seeking employment. Modern industry, in order to be competitive, needs a smaller work force and more mechanisation and automation. India can hardly afford doles, much less doles on the western scale, to unemployed people in the country. They all can be a heavy liability for democracy if work is not provided for them. The law and order situation in the country can be under heavy strain especially when the unemployed are educated. Modernisation in India cannot go the western way. There is no escape from advanced and sophisticated technologies in several fields of life like defence, telecommunications, transport and some other areas. There are certain basic necessities of life which can be met in villages through traditional techniques with such changes in them as will improve their productivity and minimise drudgery. This will make it possible for every part of India to be industrialised through varying technologies. This kind of economic decentralisation is a highly practical proposition.

Gandhi's concept of decentralisation is part of his larger vision which embraces in its scope the creation of a non-violent society. In the present context of growing and widespread violence and all it connotes, Gandhi thought it inevitable, if humanity is to survive, that the world should think and act in terms of non-violence. This should be the way of life of the future, else there could be only war or several bloody revolutions.

This way of life has much to do with respect for Nature and its Laws. Wanton violations of these laws have brought humankind much misery. Deeper thought will reveal the close relevance of what Gandhi has said on a good life and a good society to the serious environmental issues the world is facing to-day. Gandhi's message has relevance to a whole variety of issues which concern humankind today.

Bunker Roy

Gandhi and The Last Man : In Indian Villages Today

Violence is bred by inequality
Non-violence by equality

- *Gandhi.*

I was born in 1945. I never got the opportunity to be part of the Freedom Movement. I was too young to absorb the historic developments that took place as a result of which we got our Independence. For all those men and women who gave their living fighting for the cause, for all the men and women who sacrificed their future by leaving secure well planned lives, I can only express my admiration and respect.

But the very people who took it upon themselves to keep Gandhian values and messages alive when we got our Independence must seriously question themselves and ask their inner voice, 'To what extent have they succeeded in their mission in keeping Gandhi's essential message alive today?'

Without having known Gandhi or seen Gandhi and felt the aura of his presence but being a sensible follower of Gandhi I can only speak for myself. My inner voice tells me we have failed miserably. We can only blame ourselves for this failure.

I had heard of Gandhi's writings on rural development, on *Gram Swaraj*, on self-reliance and on the emancipation of women but I did not want to be influenced before starting my work in villages. Now when I read Gandhi it makes eminent sense. What vision and inner strength the man had; what common sense he showed; and what grace and dignity he displayed under pressure.

But for Attenborough's Gandhi and at one stage the pointless Kudal Commission in the early 80s we hear and read very little of the Gandhians in India today. At the national level it appears they have ceased to matter: at the village level–again but for a few packets of splendid work–they are no longer a force to reckon with. The credibility of Mahatma Gandhi's thoughts and ideas has never been higher and more relevant in the world today. But the two giants JP and Vinoba Bhave are dead and the moral leadership that they provided evidently died with them. The rest are squabbling dispirited and disorganised. What sort of example are they setting for the youth of today? Can it be that these people are the only ones left to copy, to look up to?

Gandhian thought will never die so long as it can be used for selfish reasons: Gandhian action regrettably is dead. Cleaning public latrines is out of the question and the Gandhians are the last, by the looks of it, to set an example. *Shramdan* (voluntary labour) identified with the dignity and value of physical labour which is as important and necessary as intellect according to Gandhi is rarely practiced and sadly in many places even this is subsidised by the Government. The opportunities they let slip away, the favourable environment that once existed to allow these people in the villages to do constructive work, the stature that they once had among the people who were prepared to follow the Gandhians and give the spirit of volunteerism a respectable and dignified name has disappeared. Genuine Gandhian action survives in a few pockets all over the country and that too depends on a handful of charismatic individuals with the common fatal flaw of not being able to decentralise. So there is every likelihood of the organisation collapsing once they die. The movement of getting the rural poor together, the effort at getting voluntary agencies to sit on a common platform and the realisation that it can only be done without getting involved in party politics, has come a decade and a half too late.

On 10th September, 1931, in *Young India* Gandhi wrote: 'I shall work for an India in which the poorest shall feel it is their country in whose making they have an effective voice, an India in which all communities shall live in perfect harmony. There can be no room in such an India for the curse of untouchability or the curse of intoxicating drinks and drugs. Women will enjoy the same rights as men.... This is the India of my dreams'.

Choose any city, village, town suburb, mohalla or hamlet and can we claim that any part of Gandhi's dream has come true? It is not that half a century later there are none of his followers left. In fact they are to be found everywhere in politics, in business, in industry, in administration, in voluntary agencies. Indeed only in action have we been found wanting. It is almost as if we do not want untouchability to be eradicated and it is enough to pass a law against practising untouchability. We do not want the poor to feel this is their country–all our actions so far have shown this to be true. We must only appear to be doing something about it.

Gandhian values are universal. It is not necessary that one has to be a Gandhian to practice it. It is not required to wear *khadi* or only appear to be simple or read the Mahatma's Collective Works to follow Gandhian values. The Supreme Consideration was Man and how to get to the last man.

In October 1935 in *Modern Review* he wrote, 'I look upon an increase in the power of the state with the greatest fear because, while apparently doing good by minimizing exploitation, it does the greatest harm to mankind by destroying individuality which lies at the root of progress.'

Have not the Gandhians slowly but surely given way to let the state encroach on the independence and identity of the individual?

Gandhian Institutions like the Khadi and Village Industries Commission (KVIC) are under total government control: lack of professionalism and mismanagement has weakened their position to demand any autonomy or identity of their own–and they are happy to be dictated to by the state. It is even more bureaucratic than government and so long as they can extend their patronage to select Gandhian institutions and keep them operational that is as far as their vision goes. To think ahead, to multiply Gandhian action and give it greater relevance and to make the KVIC more accessible in human terms are issues that must worry them now.

Gandhi and The Village Councils (Panchayats)

Gandhi had talked of the village *panchayat* as being a responsible unit for the development of people in the villages. Later the idea was developed further by the *Sarvodaya* to *Lok Shakti* (power of the people) and *Lok-Niti* (partyless government). Perhaps at Gandhiji's instance and influence the Directive Principles of State Policy contains Article 40 in Part IV which reads:

'The State shall take steps to organise village *panchayats* and endow them with such powers and authority as may be necessary to enable them to function as units of self-government'.

But the operative word is self-government *not* at the pleasure of the State Legislature.

The *Gram Sabha* of a *village panchayat* does not need the legislature of a State to decide what powers they should have and functions they can perform. This is what has been approved in the 73rd Amendment. It is a travesty of Gandhiji's concept and dream of self-government. How could the Gandhians let this slip by without raising it as a fundamental issue? If the power of the people in the village is supreme and they have made a mistake with some candidates, they should, through the *Gram Sabha*, have the power to recall their candidate, especially if the *sarpanch* or member has done something criminally wrong or anti-social. The hiring is by the people but the firing is not within the powers of the people in the *Panchayat*! What sort of self-government is that?

Given the composition of the Legislature of the States–moneylenders, *banias*, people with criminal records accused of rape, cutting trees, grabbing land, believing in child marriage, untouchability and violence as a means of solving problems–it is hardly likely that village *panchayats* are going to be given the freedom and flexibility to decide for themselves. *Panchayati Raj* institutions do not start and end at the village *panchayats*. One of the MPs behind the Seventy-third Amendment is on record as having said, it is a move to empower the people to control the bureaucracy and make the government servant answerable. In other words, should there be any problem with teachers, engineers, doctors, *patwaris* and *gram sevaks*, the Panchayat Act will empower the people to transfer the problem to another *panchayat* as a solution. It is not for want of trying that government servants have refused to be answerable and accountable to the rural community they are suppossed to serve. The importance and constitutional protection being given to women on *panchayats* would have received Gandhi's support.

My Personal Experience In Following Gandhi's Ideas - The Barefoot College.

Almost everything that you do will be
insignificant but it is important that you do it.

- *Gandhi*

Almost 25 years ago soon after College I started living and working in a village in Ajmer District called Tilonia. At that time I had not read Marx. I had not read Gandhi. I had not read anyone who could have told me what the rural areas was going to be like. It wasn't a part of our college curriculum. The village was a total area of darkness for me. I went with an open mind. I just wanted to do something and I knew after my traumatic experience in helping out in a small way during the terrible famine in Bihar in 1966-67 I would be able to contribute. I did not know what I could do but I had a vague idea in my head. There was no clear blueprint only the will and the determination. It had to be simple, that one person could accomplish. It had to start simple. By living in a village for instance. It had to start from there. The motivation to do, to act, was very strong, I remember.

Now I look back these two and a half decades and it's possible to see the whole experience from a distance. Look at it a bit objectively and sum up what I feel. It's a personal journey back through time, all based on an interaction with a vast cross-section of very ordinary people who are never heard–always seen as a target or as beneficiary- but never consulted and given a serious hearing as a human being: someone who can think and also come up with a idea worth trying: someone who has been through very trying and tense times. The person Mahatma Gandhi called the last man, who is exploited, suppressed and never treated fairly or justly by the better off in the village. It is still true today. They are by far the most easy to identify but the most difficult to reach.

So the first impression which is strongest in my mind is that there are two Indias. There is the India of the cities – the filthily rich, the destroyers of the environment, the exploiters of the natural resources who have a criminal surplus of everything and who have the arrogance to think they can plan and decide for others. This India knows how to waste but does not know how to live; they know their rights but have no idea of their duties; they are literate but not educated. They have emotions but no compassion: they know how to take and grab out of sheer greed but don't know how to give gracefully and share; they know how to abuse and exploit the law so that their lifestyles are not affected and they would use all the power and money and even adopt criminal illegal means to ensure the poor remain poor.

Then there is *Bharat*, the vast majority of the poor who live, only survive, in the villages of this country. This is another universe which India has made no attempt to understand. India likes reading about it, seeing it in films from a respectable distance but not feeling and living through an actual experience in a village. It's too much to ask these unfortunate people to see how the other half lives–and dies. This was the first shock.

For many living in a village it is the entire universe. They have never gone out of their village. How do we treat the poor in one village, in their own vast universe, and do something tangible to improve the quality of their lives, address basic needs, tackle the social problems of caste and class and yet do it non-violently, without tension, and without repercussions on the poor after the process begins? Is there time? Do we have the skill? Indeed, do we have the right to interfere with the lives of the poor and upset the delicate balance in the village?

It was a challenge that couldn't be rushed. It had to be thought out very slowly. It wasn't projects and programmes that was going to make any lasting difference: the key element was sparking processes through changing attitudes in the mind and then letting them sort it out on their own, in their own pace and time. The important thing was to be accessible and available all the time to discuss: to meet, to clarify, to ensure you are with them, to remove doubts and fears and to lead them through to thinking in the right direction. It was a 26 hour job that one school building, road, dispensary or the construction of a dam could never accomplish.

In the process I went through a great unlearning process. I had to put away all I thought I had learnt in the Doon School and St Stephen's College and start from scratch again. I had learnt arrogance and had a misplaced notion that I knew the answer to all problems. I had learnt to do everything in a hurry. I had no respect for other people's time and opinions. I thought organisation management systems, orderly organised plans, was everything and I was God's chosen instrument to instil this message into the natives. I was told speed, precision, planning was the answer. A 100 mph lifestyle where there was no time to waste..

The first lesson I learnt painfully, slowly and surely was that only if I had the ability to listen gently and quietly would I have the ability to learn and absorb and be taken seriously.

The second lesson I learnt was the great difference between Literacy and Education. What is taught in schools is literacy but the real education you receive is from the family, from the environment and from the community. The educated person I found was more courageous, more positive and a more constructive contributor to society than a literate person. It is the literate who do not want to act. It is the educated who has no choice but to act.

It is the literate who do not want change. It is the literate in the village who do not have faith in their age old institutions; who look down on the people in the village and see them as illiterate, backward and primitive. It is the doctor and nurse who are never to be found in the dispensary while patients wait: the teacher who is missing while children patiently wait: the engineer who makes roads and bridges that never survive the monsoon. It is the literate policeman who breaks the law in the village: the cooperative inspector who embezzles funds and the forest guard who cuts trees for contractors and forests disappear.

These crimes are committed, please note, by the literate not the educated poor in the village. They have tremendous faith in their own institutions, in their panchayats, in their indigenous knowledge, in their wisdom and they are totally mystified by the behaviour of the literate man. If this is what reading and writing leads to, then much better to stay away from schools and adult literacy classes.

The fact is the educated have survived for so many centuries without literacy – hundreds of years villages survived without the engineer, the doctor, the teacher, the cooperative inspector and the policeman. As a result indigenous institutions made laws, observed them and enforced discipline without interference from outside. Their judgement was respected. Today, in the destruction and devaluing of multi-caste community institutions, single caste-based institutions have become very important and social ostracisation is still feared.

It appears India has given up trying to understand *Bharat*. This is evident by the absence of any sincere move towards dialogue, to trying to understand what to do and respect their decisions, even if it doesn't agree with preconceived policies and projects decided in urban areas of what they need. In the absence of any serious effort to listen to them directly (without intermediaries and self-interested politicians) we see the tragedy of the same short-sighted projects, leading to duplication and colossal wastage of funds benefitting a few.

It was a double tragedy. The poor knew the answers to improving the situation. But no one was prepared to listen to what they had to say. The difference is, I listened to what they had to say and put it in practice in Tilonia. Not immediately but over a period of time.

It's important to make mistakes – go through the process of learning and unlearning yourself. But what is even more crucial is the ability to confess you made a mistake–and start again. Make corrections, make changes half way–not alone, but carry the whole organisation with you. This requires humility: it requires transparency and openness, to share information and knowledge with other colleagues and discuss endlessly what needs to be done slowly. Most of all, it requires flexibility, to be able to change priorities, innovate, recruit new types of people, share responsibility of success and failure. Underlining all these processes initiated simultaneously is the basic and inherent need to trust and treat with respect the opinion, ideas, and suggestions of others however high or low the person may be in the organisation. In this case Tilonia.

What we asked ourselves was the question–how is it possible to do without the literate man? The engineer, doctor and teacher has an equivalent in the village. Can they be replaced and made redundant? Can we show it is possible?

Take the problem of drinking water, a basic need. We have hand pumps everywhere. Do we need an engineer, trained driller to install and repair and maintain it? Do we need a man with a paper degree who has never touched a hand pump, doesn't take water from a hand pump, because he prefers to live in a city, to understand how important it is in a village to keep it running all the time? For months hundreds of hand pumps are out of order because it is dependent on the engineer to come and repair it. Government has said the hand pump is government property and the community cannot repair it themselves.

So what did Tilonia do? Took an illiterate cycle repairer and electric pump motor re-winding repairer, living in the village, and trained them to take the hand pump apart, identify the parts that needed replacement and put it back again. One month's training. Demystified the whole process. When the engineer was saying it was 21st century technology and it needed years of training in an engineering college to be competent to instal and repair it here was Tilonia simplifying it to the illiterate, rural youth, village level. They were scandalised and the engineering fraternity in Rajasthan in the Public Health Engineering Department were up in arms against it. Now several years later the 'barefoot mechanic' the hand pump *mistri*, is a familiar sight and accepted. Women are now being trained to repair their own hand pumps: the urban trained literate engineer has finally received a good education.

Take the problem of children never going to school. On an average 60 to 70% of the poorer children in a village cannot afford to go to school in the morning because they are needed to graze cattle, look after sheep and goats and be a part of the economic activity of the family. The teacher has no time to run schools in the evening. It cuts into the private tuition fees he charges to coach weak students in government schools to pass exams. It is a known fact that schools run in the morning are run for the convenience of the teacher not for the students. They would commute from nearby towns.

What was Tilonia's answer to this problem? Starting schools at night for the drop out kids, shepherd boys and girls, who would never have had an opportunity to go to school. It is run by an unemployed rural youth from the same village, after being trained in Tilonia on how to run a rural night primary school. It is very different. The teacher comes from the village. The person is not formally trained in a college, but a person rejected or failed by the formal system to qualify for any government job. What the children are exposed to is how government systems function; the curriculum concentrates on the village insitutions and how the post office, the bank, the police station and cooperative works. 150 schools are running today. Most of them in villages where there are no schools. They run at night and the attendance of girls has increased. It has angered the teachers' union that now their monopoly has been broken and they have to prove their worth in the eyes of the community. This scheme of using failed rural youth to run night schools has been accepted by the State Government and it has been replicated all over the State in another form.

The development of the human being is all. How do we provide an environment for a non-person to develop himself and become a thinking responsible human being? That should be the goal. Even if it takes years we should not be in a hurry. It's a costly but risky and invisible investment that we must believe in as primary and crucial. It is non-negotiable.

The use and application of technology should be seen keeping this faith in mind all the time. Should we allow technology to control our lives? Should we be scared of it or should we treat it with respect without being intimidated by it? How do we demystify the most sophisticated of technologies and use it to our benefit?

The conventional view of solar energy is much too complicated and expensive to be introduced in the rural areas. It needs government. It needs highly trained solar and electronic engineers. It needs a back-up support to repair and maintain that is just not available in the rural areas. In short, it is madness to try generating electricity from the sun. There are other much more important needs to be met. Right now it is not possible.

It's time to try and explode this myth. With humble beginnings in 1986 till today in 1994 Tilonia, I am pleased to say, has baffled the technologists in the urban areas and left them fumbling. A fully solar electrified campus is in fact operational today in Tilonia running 500 lights, 8 computers, a water testing laboratory and a solar pump installed and maintained by rural youth from the village who have never studied beyond primary school. The head of the section is a village priest who still looks after the temple in a nearby village. It's possibly the only centre of its kind in the country.

Here rural youth, illiterate and semi-literate have been trained to instal solar units for electricity in non-electrified villages from Ladakh in Kashmir to Trichy in Tamil Nadu. 500 houses have been electrified in 25 villages in Ladakh in villages located 10,000 to 15,000 ft in the Himalayas. Abdul Karim, the first Ladakhi to install solar units in 1989 was the master trainer who has installed over 300 units himself: he can barely sign his name. But the units he has installed still produce 3 hours of light a day.

The point being made is, India is responsible for perpetuating myths that *Bharat* is still suffering from till today. The mystification of paper degrees required to develop the poor in *Bharat* is a myth. The need to bring alien expertise from the urban areas to the rural areas is a myth. The need to over-plan and formulate projects and policies sitting in Delhi is a myth. The fact that illiterate people do not know how to think and plan for themselves is a myth. The fact that we need such urban trained professional people in the village *at all* who have no respect for the poor is the most expensive myth.

Give the poor the space to develop themselves. Leave them alone so that they can develop their self confidence in their own pace and time. These are not issues that can be tackled in one financial year. There is no doubt the biggest threat to developing the poor is the Literate Man.

I like to think the way the Barefoot College has evolved in thought and action and in the process developed some self-respect in the last man, Gandhiji would have approved.

Traveller, there is no Path
Paths are made by Walking

Lakshmi Krishnamurti

Gandhi's Ideal of Gram Swaraj

Mohandas Karamchand Gandhi, barrister, had to give up his lucrative legal practice. His battles with the white South African Government left him with no time to attend to it. Leading the highly oppressed Indian Community to fight for its right to survive with its self-respect intact was time-consuming. His selfless and relentless opposition to governmental repression attracted hundreds of volunteers totally committed to the cause. Having established the Phoenix Farm and helped in organising local leadership to carry on the movement, his thoughts returned to his mother-land. There, the stirrings of a sullen anger had started smouldering against the British ruler.

Arousing reception waited for Gandhi when he landed at the Bombay port, for his fame had preceded his arrival. Gokhale advised Gandhi to tour India, see the villages and get to know the people before involving himself in the struggle for freedom. When touring the then Madras presidency, the sight of hungry looking peasants ploughing their tiny patches of land, clad just in a loin cloth, shocked Gandhi as nothing else did. The utter poverty of these peasants and their miserable hovels touched his heart. Like Prince Siddhartha who gave up a Royal life to become the Buddha, Mohandas Karamchand Gandhi shed all his fine clothes and the turban he sported and wore only minimum attire. This complete renunciation of a life of comfort gave him total identity with the poor and downtrodden masses of India. Thus Mr. M. K. Gandhi became the Mahatma.

Adopting a life of privation was only the beginning of his struggle not only against the alien ruler, but also against a society ridden with superstition, sub-human and inhuman traditions and cruel conventions, which in the name of religious sanction held a vast majority of the sons and daughters of India oppressed and treated as untouchables. This tore his heart and goaded him to carry on the long haul for decades to come, to set right the centuries old wrong done. But he wanted no short cuts, for Gandhi the moralist the means should always justify the end. Gandhian thought and ideas rest on the foundations of certain eternal truths which are practical, realistic, bound by love for every living being.

Gandhi's goal was to establish friendship with the world. He said: 'we shall live for world brotherhood and die for world brotherhood'. He urged us to widen the circle of our love till it embraces the whole village. The village in its turn must take into its fold the district, the district the state, and so on till the scope of love envelops the whole universe.

Gandhi had strongly advocated the decentralisation of political and economic power in favour of more or less self-sufficient and self-governing village councils known in India as *panchayats*. He regarded these local institutions as models of non-violent organisation. His concept of "*Gram Swaraj*" was based on Humanism, Truth and Non-violence pervading the whole of human society where moral values count most.

Gandhi wrote at length what he visualised as a model village republic. Extracts are given here.

His idea of village *swaraj* is that it is a complete republic, independent of its neighbours for its own vital wants and yet interdependent for many others where dependence is necessary. Thus every village's first concern will be to grow its own food crops, and cotton for its cloth. It should have a grazing reserve for its cattle, recreation and playground for adults and children. Then if there is more land available, it will grow useful money crops, but excluding ganja, tobacco, opium and such narcotics.

The village will maintain a theatre, school, reading-room and public hall. It will have its own water works ensuring clean water supply. Education will be compulsory up to the final Basic Course. As far as possible every activity will be conducted on a cooperative basis. There will be no castes such as we have today with their graded untouchability.

Non-violence with its technique of *Satyagraha* and non-cooperation will be at the sanction of the village community. There will be a compulsory service of village guards who will be selected by rotation from the register maintained by the village. The government of the village will be conducted by a *Panchayat* of five persons annually elected by the adult villagers, male and female, possessing minimum prescribed qualifications. These will have all the authority and jurisdiction required. Since there will be no system of punishments in the accepted sense, this *Panchayat* will be the legislature, judiciary and executive combined to operate for its year of office.

Craft, art, health and education should all be integrated into one scheme. *Nai Talim* is a beautiful blend of all the four and covers the whole education of the individual from the time of conception to the moment of death. Therefore, I would not divide village uplift work into water-tight compartments from the very beginning but undertake an activity which will combine all four. Instead of regarding craft and industry as different from education, I will regard the former as the medium for the latter. *Nai Talim* therefore ought to be integrated into the scheme.

A village unit as conceived by me is as strong as the strongest. My imaginary village consists of 1,000 souls. Such a unit can give a good account of itself, if it is well organized on a basis of self-sufficiency.

An ideal Indian village will be so constructed as to lend itself to perfect sanitation. It will have cottages with sufficient light and ventilation, built of a material obtainable within a radius of five miles. The cottages will have courtyards enabling the householders to plant vegetables for domestic use and to house their cattle. The village lanes and streets will be free of all avoidable dust. It will have wells according to its needs and accessible to all. It will have houses of worship for all, also a common meeting place, a village common for grazing its cattle, a cooperative dairy, primary and secondary schools in which industrial education will be the central factor, and it will have *Nyaya Panchayats* or Village Panchayats for settling disputes. It will produce its own grains, vegetables and fruits and its own *Khadi.* (hand spun and hand woven cloth).

This society must naturally be based on Truth and Non-violence which, in my opinion, are not possible without a living belief in God, meaning a self-existent, all-knowing living force which inherits every other force known to the world but which depends on none and which will live when all other forces may conceivably perish or cease to act. I am unable to account for my life without belief in this all embracing living light.

In this structure composed of innumerable villages there will be ever widening, never ascending circles. Life will not be a pyramid with the apex sustained by the bottom. But it will be an oceanic circle whose centre will be the individual always ready to perish for the village, the latter ready to perish for the circle of villages, till at last the whole becomes one life composed of individuals, never aggressive in their arrogance but ever humble sharing the majesty of the oceanic circle of which they are integral units.

Therefore, the outermost circumference will not wield power to crush the inner circle but give strength to all within and derive its own from the Centre. I may be taunted with the retort that this is all Utopian and therefore not worth a single thought. If Euclid's point, though incapable of being drawn by human agency has an imperishable value, my picture has its own for mankind to live. Let India live for this true Picture, though never realizable in its completeness. We must have a proper picture of what we want before we can have something approaching it. If there ever is to be a republic of every village in India, then I claim verily for my picture in which the last is equal to the first, or in other words, none is to be the first and none the last. In this picture every religion has its full and equal place.

When *Panchayat Raj* is established, public opinion will do what violence can never do. In *Panchayat Raj* only the *Panchayat* will be obeyed and the *Panchayat* can only work through the law of its own making."

Therefore, politically, Gandhi advocated a democratic form of government and wanted to take this system nearest to the people, giving them more responsibilities to govern themselves in small communities. So his vision of future India is based on village republics, or village *swaraj*, and extending it to world government, which require that the political and economic order, consisting of village republics, federate themselves into higher and higher unions, until, there is a federation embracing the whole country and, in course of time, the whole world–each higher union enjoying only such powers as its units agree to confer on it. In that case, the highest union would have minimum of functions. The least governed is the best governed.

The Constituent Assembly set up soon after His Majesty's government decided to hand over power to Indians for self-government, consisting of many legal and economic experts in addition to the political leaders of the highest order, made no mention of local self-governing bodies. The omission was more glaring as it was drawn up mostly by the close associates of Mahatma Gandhi himself, whose vision of *"Gram Swaraj"* was widely known and he had clearly written about it in the *Harijan*, the weekly, in which he wrote his views on all matters. Some of the Constituent assembly members strongly objected to giving any powers to local self-government on the grounds that illiterate and innocent villagers were not competent to take up this responsibility.

Eventually, they gave in to saner counsel and conceded that the establishment of *Panchayat Raj* Institutions (Local self-government bodies) be included in the Directive Principles. The advocates of *Panchayat Raj* Institutions had to content themselves with this in spite of their disappointment. This step-motherly treatment of *Panchayat Raj* Institutions continues to the present day.

Article 40 in Part IV (Directive Principles of State Policy) of the Constitution States: "The States shall take steps to organise village *Panchayats* and endow them with such powers and authority as may be necessary to enable them to function as units of self-government". But the institutions at district, block and state levels have not been able to acquire the status and dignity of viable and responsive bodies.

Many discrepancies have crept into these grass-root institutions. One is forced to think of them as but a mockery of what was conceived originally by the Constitution framers. These institutions were not truly representative of the whole village but were dominated in most instances by socially and economically privileged sections.

Several committeees, starting from the Balwant Rai Mehta Study Team of 1957, the Ashok Mehta Committee of 1977, followed by other committees headed by Dr. G.V.K. Rao, the economist, Dr. L. M.Singhvi, the legal expert, and the Sarkaria Commission reviewed the functioning of these *Panchayats* and suggested strengthening them by devolving necessary powers and authority to function as self-governments. In 1989, the late Rajiv Gandhi the then Prime Minister introduced the 64th amendment to the Constitution, which was later enacted as The 73rd Constitutional Amendment, enabling these institutions to survive, thrive and to ensure "Power where it belongs", to quote his own words.

Even during British rule there was some semblance of local government in India in general and particularly in Tamilnadu with nominated members to what were called District Boards. Maintenance of roads, school level education and primary health were all entrusted to them. District Board members were considered quite powerful. With the dawn of independence the elections to local bodies was revived. Village *Panchayats* and *Panchayat* Unions, co-terminous with the community block came into existence. There was only a two tier system and District Development Councils as purely advisory bodies were formed with the District Collector presiding, including local members of the State assembly, Members of Parliament and prominent social workers. One big advantage noted was that since heads of all the District Departments like Health, Education, Public works etc., were all present at these review meetings held once in two months, correction of acts of commission and omission by the Departmental machinery was possible. All this was good while it lasted.

With the introduction of the Community Development programmes in 1957 during the Prime Ministership of Jawaharlal Nehru, the late S.K.Dey the Minister in charge, with great dynamism, introduced multifarious schemes throughout the country. For the first time, villages were brought into developmental projects. This.was supplemented by the emergence of a Central Social Welfare Board under Dr.Durgabhai Deshmukh, Minister in charge. The Board formed similar bodies in all the States, roping in thousands of voluntary women social workers. A new vista was opened for all the bottled up energy, capacity and capability of a hitherto untapped source. With the opening of mid-wifery centres, creche, pre-primary classes (Balwadies 0-4 age) craft classes and formation of rural women's associations (Mahila Mandals), the process of bringing these women into the mainstream of progress and activity had commenced.

The initial enthusiasm seen in the first two decades started waning, vested interests started creeping into the local self-government area. Politicisation, greed, and power mongering started corroding all the good that was introduced.

What was seen as the introduction to making Gandhiji's dream of *Gram Swaraj* a reality, slowly begun to crumble . Now with the enactment of the 73rd Constitutional Amendment to these *Panchayat Raj* Institutions, new hope dawns that grass root democracy,so clearly spelt out by Gandhiji the visionary, will get a fresh lease of life. About 2,25,000 *Gram Panchayats* (Village Councils) 5,100 intermediate level *Panchayats* and 475 District *Panchayats* will be constituted all over the country. Due to one-third reservation for women, about 80,000 women chairpersons in *Panchayats* at different levels and over 50,000 chairpersons from the weaker sections of society will be taking up leadership positions and be involved in the development process at the grassroot level.

As the late Rajiv Gandhi, the then Prime Minister of India, was very keen in reviving the village *panchayats,* he promoted the 64th Amendment to the Constitution Bill 1989. The Bill provided for Constitution of *Panchayats* in every State at the village, intermediate and district levels. The Bill proposed that these *panchayats* are statutorily given adequate powers and authority enabling them to function as institutions of self-government. The Bill made additional provision for the appointment of a Finance Commission to review the financial provision and entrusted the Election Commission of the State with the superintendance, direction and control of elections to the *panchayats*. Unfortunately this Bill never became an act, as it was not approved by the Rajya Sabha (Council of States).

Again in September 1990 a Bill providing for a "*Gram Sabha*" in each village was introduced but it also lapsed due to the dissolution of Parliament.

The present government soon after assuming office introduced the 72nd amendment Bill on 16th September 1991, which was referred to the Joint Parliamentary Committee in December. This Committee's report was presented to Parliament in July 1992, and this Bill was passed with near unanimity in the 3rd week of December. A little over a year since its introduction, ratified by 17 State Assemblies it has emerged as the 73rd Amendment, 1993, coming into force from April 24, 1993. As of this writing all the states have discussed, approved and enacted the Bill in their respective states.

The salient provisions of the Act are:-

1. There shall be a *Gram Sabha* in each village.
2. *Panchayats* shall be constituted in every State at the Village, intermediate and District levels. Thus bringing uniformity in the structure.
3. Members of all the 3 tiers of the *Panchayats* will be directly elected. The chairpersons at the intermediate and district levels will be chosen by indirect election.
4. Reservation of one-third seats for Scheduled Castes/ Scheduled Tribes has been provided in proportion to their population at each level.
5. The term of office will be 5 years and in the event of dissolution, elections should be completed before the expiry of six months from the date of dissolution.
6. There shall be a State election commission and a State Finance Commission exclusively for *Panchayat Raj* Institutions. This body will review the financial positions, recommend on the distribution of funds, and suggest measures to supplement their resources . Thus a large amount of assured funds will flow to the *Panchayat Raj* Institutions which will strengthen peoples involvement in the planning process.
7. Rural development programmes will get a boost as a result of this Act. *Gram Panchayats*, who get an assured allotment will decide upon the schemes to be taken-up under the Jawahar Rozgar Yojana. This will provide employment to

rural youth, involving them in all the village improvement schemes. The enhancement of the outlay for rural development to Rs.30,000 crores in the Eighth plan assumes much wider significance. The *Panchayats* will now have adequate powers and finances to implement the economic development programmes meant for the people.

8. The addition of the 11th schedule in the 72nd amendment lists out clearly 29 subjects which are to be entrusted to the elected *panchayat* officials. Starting from agriculture, rural industries, electrification, health it is a long comprehensive list. In fact Kerala State has included 73 subjects in this schedule.

Nothing seems to have been left to chance. If only this is backed up by sufficient financial and manpower resources, with technicians and other experts from the line departments, an impetus to improve the quality of life in rural India would have been given.

More than all these new responsibilities, what is so great about the 73rd amendment, is the one-third reservation of seats to women, Scheduled Castes and Scheduled Tribes in all the 3 tiers of the *Panchayat Raj* Institutions. This empowerment of women will ensure a great change and make grass-root level democracy meaningful.

There, of course, have been women with exceptional leadership qualities who were members of Parliament, Ministers in the Central and State cabinets, women who have held honourabily various public posts. Considering that 50 percent of Indian population is women, their representation has been very microscopic. Even at the *Panchayat* level, where there were specific provisions as in Tamilnadu for at least one woman either to be elected or, failing which, nominated, their participation was minimal. Some of those nominated were the relatives of the *Panchayat* Presidents, and they merely affixed their signature in the attendance register for meetings even without stirring out of their houses. The women's representation was a mere token. Conservative traditions, patriarchal system, illiteracy and little exposure to the outside world are great handicaps which economically and socially backward rural women more than their urban sisters face. For the present at least reservation is the only way to ensure their adequate representation in the *Panchayat Raj* Institutions.

In the last 5 or 6 years there is a new awakening. The spread of adult literacy, in comparatively progressive states like Kerala, Karnataka, Andhra Pradesh and Tamil Nadu has given these women a certain amount of exposure to activities outside their homes. Given the opportunity and backing, women have the inherent qualities in them to face the challenges when they are placed in responsible positions. Following in the footsteps of the Mahatma, by adhering to non-violent *Satyagraha* women have met with a great measure of success in leading resistance like the *Chipko, Apiko* movements to save trees from destruction by rapacious contractors. and the anti-liquor lobby of Andhra Pradesh has succeeded in forcing the ruling party to declare in their election manifesto that total prohibition will be introduced.

The Satyamurti Centre for Democratic Studies, highly concerned about the important role of *Panchayat* members, conducted in 1989-90, before the term of office of the elected representatives in *Panchayats* ended, 12 women *panchayat* and *panchayat* union member's training camps. They were attended by 900 members. The field experience of Satyamurti Centre strengthens the belief in women becoming instruments of change in improving the quality of life in the countryside of India.

The effective strategies pursued by some of the women participants' narrated in the training camps, to solve the local problems is worthy of citation. Just 3 incidents detailed here show, that if empowered adequately and exposed to the outer-world, even simple rustic women will rise to the occasion and the leadership qualities dormant in them can be successfully harnessed.

(a) A middle aged woman member of a *Panchayat* near Erode with little formal education but highly motivated, shared her experience in an awareness generation camp at Tiruchirappally.

There was a small Ganesha Temple in her village and only a male heir could officiate as priest. This was a hereditary responsibility unchallenged till then. With the sudden demise of the priest, with just 3 daughters of his own, a problem arose. But this woman *Panchayat* member stood up in favour of the eldest daughter inheriting the priest's post, which was stoutly opposed. She persisted and created such a stir that the police had to lock her up as a disturber of peace.

Her comments at this juncture are very revealing and eloquent. She said: "After all, many times Gandhi was put behind bars, ate only gruel, cannot I a humble village woman suffer this for a worthy cause just for a short while?" Eventually she succeeded in convincing the public and had the girl appointed as priest, breaking the tradition. What an example of courage and determination! A great lady.

(b) The second memorable incident was narrated by a woman who was a *Panchayat* President belonging to South Arcot District. She was a Christian but classified as Scheduled Caste (an untouchable) and was very shrewd and courageous.

Seeing the same man being elected President term after term unopposed in her village and his complete lack of interest in the welfare of the *panchayat*, she decided to contest. She filed her nomination to the surprise of everybody, and the over-confident male candidate defaulted by filing his nomination paper late.

This, of course, was contested by him, but she persisted, fought a legal battle with him and she was declared elected unopposed by the court. She did not stop with that. She was able to evict the influential persons of the village from occupying the communal land. Despite stout opposition she persuaded the Revenue Divisional Officer and the Collector and succeeded in her attempt to get the land back to the *Panchayat* and planted trees on these lands.

(c) These are two success stories. The third was about a traditional woman from a very orthodox conservative family, who lacked family support, and who belonged to the so called forward community and was not being backed by other communities even when the public welfare of the village was threatened. She knew her rights and powers, but was helpless due to lack of support.

This is where a *Gram Sabha* consisting of local senior citizens can play a very positive role, as they are normally a group of senior people, non partisan who will be heard with great respect.

These three experiences have been cited just to show how things would be if successful power devolution takes place, and more women are entrusted with village administration. The whole system would have a good chance of being humanised as women are pragmatic, and compassionate.

In raising local resources and in drawing up village plans, the *gram sabhas* play a very important role. Under the new Act the *gram sabhas* have to function and are obliged to meet twice a year. All persons who are enlisted in the electoral roles of the village are its members. *Gram Sabhas* have always been existing and meeting on every new moon day. They are an integral part of rural India. The significant role they play in the village can never be under - estimated. One glaring omission in the present Act is that the Nyaya Panchayat, conferring judicial powers on the village *panchayat*, has not been included. Justice S.Krishnaswami Reddy, Chairman of the Police Commission appointed by the Central Government, says that 141 crimes which come under the Indian Penal code are petty crimes and can be handled by the *Panchayats*. If this had been done a lot of time, energy and money would be saved by the villagers while also speeding up justice.

At a Colloquium organised by the Satyamurti Centre in 1993 on the 73rd Constitution Amendment Bill, attended by regional representatives from five major national political parties, Mr.Ramakrishna Hegde, former Chief Minister of Karnataka State, cited the positive role of the *Gram Sabhas* in his home State. During his term, elections were held for all *Panchayat* Raj Institutions. *Gram Sabhas* were given freedom to draw the village development plans and prioritise them as they deem fit and to implement the schemes. During this period, due to total involvement of the community there was marked improvement in attendance at school, not only of students but teachers also, and of nurses and doctors discharging their duties in the rural, public health centres. Adequate financial support was given to the *Gram sabhas* for successful implementation of the projects.

One outstanding example narrated by Mr.Ramakrishna Hegde was of a particular village. All village *panchayats* to augment their coffers try to raise resources locally by the sale of the produce from trees in public lands, auctioning of trees and fish in the local tank or lake. In this village previously the annual income derived from fishing rights was uniformly only Rs.35,000, because interested contractors saw to it that nobody bid for a higher amount. With the intervention of the *gram sabha*, they realised thrice the amount and prioritised the requirements of the village on which the money would be spent. First came the repair of the school building, second repairs to the road to the school and third provision of good drinking water. "Leave it to them" he said, this is exactly what Gandhiji had chalked out. The age old wisdom of the villagers backed by an effective support system will usher in devolution of power and decentralise democracy.

All this may sound utopian and even naive. Statutorily in 1995, elections to *Panchayat Raj* Institutions have to be held in all States and there will be tremendous opposition to a fair and free election from all vested interests. Everyone declares that elections to the village councils would be fought on non-party basis. But there is a big gap between profession and practice. Attempts will be made to divide the electorate in the name of religion, caste, community and political affinity and gender. But the inertia of the earlier years is getting shaken up. Several voluntary organisations, groups and individuals, helpless witnesses to the attrocities perpetrated and the breakdown of law and order and increase in violence in the land of the Mahatma, are gearing themselves to prepare the rural voters to stand up for their rights, Determined and motivated local activists have begun to network to ensure the change so eagerly looked forward to by all concerned. Sustained, planned pre-and post–election training of both electors and candidates is imperative. Quite a few organisations have drawn up plans. Even training modules and posters and charts are ready.

The National Institute of Rural Development, Hyderabad, and its counterparts in the states, have begun in right earnest, focusing their training programmes on the working of the *Panchayat Raj* Institutions. Various seminars, workshops, panel discussion are held all over the country on the subject by voluntary organisations. There is an air of expectancy coupled with a determination to involve more and more people in this far reaching experiment. At the risk of being dubbed *Panchayat Raj* Institutions fundamentalists, a large number of dedicated persons, cutting across all other affiliations, are coming together, determined to see that persons of known integrity, character and ability get elected to the *Panchayat Raj* Institutions. This must become a mass movement like the "Quit India Movement" of Mahatma Gandhi in 1942, like the anti-emergency movement led by Lok Nayak Jaya Prakash Narayan in 1976-77. This is one chance for extricating the country from its present stalemate rescuing it from criminals who have wormed their way to seats of power.

Once 'Sree Shakti' (Woman power) is aroused and harnessed to the progress of the village community there will be no stopping it. A change for the better, when India will take rightful place in the polity of nations by her achievements is bound to follow. Resurrection of *Gram Swaraj* is the most fitting homage to Mahatma Gandhi on his 125th Birth anniversary.

Anthony J. Parel

A Gandhian Liberalism?

The object of this paper is to raise the question of whether there is a Gandhian type of liberalism. Even raising such a question may scandalise the Gandhians and amuse the liberals. It may scandalise the Gandhians because they tend to identify Gandhi's ideology with anti-modernism. Some of them even believe that what Gandhi offers is an alternative to liberalism. It may amuse the liberals because they tend to identify liberalism with one or more of the following: capitalism, scepticism, agnosticism, atheism, negative liberty and unfettered individualism. Each of these goes counter to what Gandhi stood for. Yet the question is worth raising if only because there are elements in his thought and practice that seem to have a *prima facie* affinity with liberalism broadly considered, than with any other political ideology. Besides, liberalism itself is not a monolithic ideology.

To take the point that liberalism is not a single, monolithic ideology. During its long history of over three hundred years liberalism has evolved a surprising array of different doctrines, often inconsistent with each other. To a sceptical liberal such as John Stuart Mill one can oppose a believing liberal such as Lord Acton. By the turn of the twentieth century liberalism in England had shed part of its radical individualist aura and acquired instead a quasi-collectivist one. Liberalism began to develop distinctive cultural features as well, depending on the particular national culture in which it wished to establish itself. Thus British liberalism is not the same as French or Italian or American or Japanese liberalism. Even within British liberalism we find significant differences between eighteenth century and contemporary liberalism. Given these tendencies within liberalism itself, it should not come as a surprise if historians of ideas should come across an Indian brand of liberalism, and even such a thing as Gandhian liberalism. What the historians of ideas would look for here is not so much uniformity of ideas as points of difference. How liberalism adapts itself to various cultural settings is a question worth careful investigation.

As far as the question of a Gandhian liberalism is concerned, perhaps a feasible way to proceed would be to take a close look first, at his practical politics and, secondly, at his political thought.

As for Gandhi's political practice, South Africa and colonial India offer ample raw materials. What kind of political ideology was he trying to implement in these two theatres of action? There is little doubt that in South Africa he was implementing a basically liberal programme. To begin with, the British Constitution (the object of one of his two 'passions', as he called them, in his *Autobiography*) remained for him the general framework of his various campaigns against the regimes in Pietermaritzburg and in Pretoria. And in the late nineteenth-century that Constitution enshrined the basic principles of British liberalism. One is not surprised to find that the single most important objective of his South African campaigns was the securing of the rights, the liberal rights, it may be emphasised, of the Indian settlers considered as British citizens--the right to trade, to settle as immigrants, to acquire and enjoy private property, to vote, and to participate in the politics of the colonies. While the British Constitution provided the general framework for his political campaigns, the narrower framework was provided by Queen Victoria's celebrated Proclamation of 1858. The latter too is an eminently liberal document, setting out the equal rights and privileges of the Crown's Indian subjects everywhere in the British Empire. At least that was how Gandhi interpreted it. These rights, again were liberal in nature. And Gandhi considered the Proclamation the *magna carta* of Indians in South Africa. Whatever the degree of success of Gandhi's South African politics in securing these rights, the South African experience gave Gandhi two very valuable opportunities. First, it give him the opportunity to digest liberal ideas and to develop a political strategy based on those ideas; and second, even more important, it gave him the opportunity to educate South African Indians in the art of implementing liberal principles to their best advantage.

Examine the numerous petitions to the local and imperial governments that he drafted, or the constitutions of the Natal Indian Congress and the Transvaal British Indian Association which he helped to draw up, or the significant pamphlets that he wrote during this period (for example, the *Green Pamphlet, Appeal to Every Briton*), and the many articles and letters to newspapers. We find that the argument and the ideology underlying them are uniformly liberal in character--vindication of individual liberty, equal protection under the law, freedom from discrimination based on religion or race. *Satyagraha* itself emerged, as everyone knows, in the course of his practice of liberal politics. Taking a strictly historical perspective, one cannot imagine how *satyagraha* could have emerged in any other ideological context.

When we turn our attention to the Indian scene, the picture becomes somewhat clouded because of the central position *satyagraha* and non-cooperation occupy in it. If in South Africa Gandhi was a litigant, one trying to rectify things within the system, in India he was a rebel, one trying to wreck the system. But would that make him any less a liberal? For rebellion itself has an honourable place within the liberal tradition. Even apart from this, if one were to ask what the ultimate aim of Gandhi's Indian politics taken as a whole was, one cannot but admit that it was the securing of self-government for India. He wanted the principle of self-determination applied to India. But self-government achieved through self-determination is preeminently a liberal idea.

Or take the Indian National Congress during the pre-independence days, the period relevant to our question. It was and it remained a non-sectarian, liberal institution. Its fundamentally liberal character distinguished it from the Muslim League. Both in his analysis of the ideology of the Congress in *Hind Swaraj*, an analysis which covers its history from 1885 to 1909, and in his practical leadership of it from 1920 to 1947, Gandhi did nothing to change its liberal orientation. And he did this within full view of the socialist and Marxist experiments taking place elsewhere in the world. Even more remarkable is his firm stand against the challenges from both the socialists within the Congress, and from open, orthodox Marxists outside it such as M. N. Roy.

Or consider Gandhi's attitude towards the various constitutional reforms and discussions--the Morley–Minto Reforms of 1909, the Montagu-Chelmsford Reforms of 1919, the Round Table Conference of 1931, and the Government of India Act of 1935. To begin with these reforms were inspired as much by liberal ideals as by political necessities. Though often critical as to their details, Gandhi was never wholly negative about them on ideological grounds. He criticised them where he felt criticism was necessary, not because they did not reflect a socialistic programme but because they were not sufficiently liberal. Likewise, his attitude towards the Muslim League and to the question of Minorities in general was guided by the liberal principles of non-sectarianism and one 'man' one vote. His lack of enthusiasm for the idea of separate electorates ultimately sprung from his faith in the liberal notion of adult franchise.

All the above issues notwithstanding, we have, as mentioned already, the problem of reconciling the policy of non-cooperation with the principles of liberalism. Indian liberals parted company with Gandhi on the question of non-cooperation as being inconsistent with liberalism, believing, as they did, that always and everywhere, constitutionalism was the *only* policy consistent with liberalism. Gandhi disagreed. As far as he was concerned disciplined, non-violent, and principled non-cooperation was but an Indian form of extra-parliamentary rebellion, rebellion consistent with the best norms of liberal ideology. Gandhian non-cooperation was one way, and a significant way, that liberalism took shape in India during the anti-colonial period. The pursuit of *swaraj,* under the conditions in which India found itself in the period 1920-1947, was better conducted, he believed, through a prudential mixture of non-cooperation and constitutional cooperation. The difference between Gandhi and Indian liberals affected only the means of attaining *swaraj,* not the end itself. Gokhale the preeminent Indian liberal remained his acknowledge political *guru.* Srinivasa Sastri, the second most important Indian liberal, remained a trusted friend and consultant.

There are a host of Gandhian documents that would support the claim that Gandhi's political practice was more in harmony with liberalism than with any other political ideology. If one were to select one specific document to illustrate our claim, perhaps none would be better suited than the 1931 Karachi Congress resolution respecting fundamental rights. The draft of this resolution was prepared by Jawaharlal Nehru (see *Selected Works of Jawaharlal Nehru*, vol. IV, ed. S. Gopal, Delhi: Orient Longmans, 1973, pp. 511-3), and amended by Gandhi (for the amended version see *The Collected Works of Mahatma Gandhi*, vol. 45: 370-2). It was the Nehru/ Gandhi version that was presented to, and passed by, the Karachi Congress. The presenter was Gandhi himself. In moving the resolution he said that it 'meant to indicate to the poor, inarticulate Indian the broad features of *swaraj* or *Ramarajya*. . . . . By passing this resolution we make clear to the world and to our own people what we propose to do as soon as we come to power.' (Ibid., p. 372).

'*What we propose to do as soon as we come to power*': here we have Gandhi giving us, as it were, a preview of his programme for India, a programme that would be consistent with his theory of *swaraj*. And the programme reflects a liberal outlook. If one takes Gandhi seriously at his word, and we should do so here as elsewhere, one is struck by the basically liberal character of what he was proposing to do when he would come to power. The Constructive Programme and the document enshrining the ideal of the 'oceanic circle' are ideologically an extension of the principles of the 1931 Karachi resolution.

For reasons of space a detailed analysis of this resolution is not possible here. It dealt with a wide range of issues, ranging from fundamental rights, the religious neutrality of the state, adult franchise, gender equality, to the right of labour to be free from conditions of serfdom, etc. In all it contained twenty clauses, of which only one, clause 19, is perhaps not of orthodox liberal parentage. It read: 'Control by the State of key industries and ownership of mineral resources.' For the rest, the resolution is soundly liberal in its temper:

Parts of the resolution read as follows:

> Preamble.
> This Congress is of opinion that to enable the masses to appreciate what *swaraj*, as conceived by the Congress, will mean to them, it is desirable to state the position of the Congress in a manner easily understood by them. In order to end the exploitation of the masses, political freedom must include real economic freedom of the starving millions. The Congress, therefore, declare that any constitution which may be agreed to on its behalf should prove, or enable the *Swaraj* Government to provide the following:

1. *Fundamental rights of people, including*:
   a) freedom of association and combination;
   b) freedom of speech and of the Press;
   c) freedom of conscience and the free professions and practice of religion, subject to public order and morality;
   d) protection of the culture, language and scripts of minorities;
   e) equal rights and obligations of all citizens, without any bar on account of sex;
   f) no disability to attach to any citizen by reason of his or her religion, caste, creed or sex in regard to public employment;
   g) equal rights to all citizens in regard to public roads, wells, schools and other places of public resort;
   h) *right to keep and bear arms in accordance with regulations and reservations made in that behalf*;
   i) no person shall be deprived of his liberty nor shall his dwelling or property be entered, sequestered or confiscated, save in accordance with law. (Gandhi, *The Collected Works of Mahatma Gandhi*, vol. 45, pp3, 72-4. Italics mine).

Gandhi was not a doctrinaire liberal in the way for example, Gokhale or Srinivas Sastri or Tej Bahadur Sapru were liberals. Nor was he a member of the Indian Liberal Party. All this notwithstanding, there is little doubt that his basic vision of politics was inspired by a liberal view of the state, law, and citizenship. That Gandhi's political outlook was liberal was a point not lost on his Marxist and Socialist critics, such as M. N. Roy, Palme Dutt and E.M.S. Namboodiripad. In short, Gandhi's practical politics, despite *satyagraha* and non-cooperation, followed a liberal direction.

For the purposes of our enquiry, Gandhi's political thought is even more interesting than is his political practice. An enquiry into his philosophical ideas is too large an undertaking to be attempted here. For reasons of space, let me limit myself to a brief consideration of just three of them--individualism, *swaraj* and *satyagraha*.

Individualism is generally taken to be an essential element of the liberal ideology. But there is a bewildering array of doctrines respecting this element in the literature, ranging from the Hobbesian 'nasty, short and brutish' variety to the Millian individualism of self-realisation. Besides, there is economic individualism and the broader individualism of natural rights. Sometimes liberal individualism is taken to be the source of all ethical values, which, pushed to the extreme, brings with it certain nihilistic or atheistic implications. Sometimes liberal individualism stands for the autonomy of the individual, which, however, leaves the question of the source of values open-ended, open even to transcendence. Given the complex nature of this notion, how, one may ask, could Gandhian individualism fit into a liberal mould, if it could fit into it at all?

Perhaps a manageable way of addressing the issue is by way of a close look at Louis Dumont's influential analysis of individualism in India and in the West. Dumont distinguishes between what he calls 'outworldly individualism' and 'inworldly individualism'. The first, according to him, is characteristic of India, and the second, of the modern West. In the Indian tradition, according to Dumont, 'the man in the world" is not an individual in the modern Western sense of individual, interdependent as he is on society and subject to the order of *dharma*. In India individuality is achieved only by those who renounce the world, by 'the individual-outside-the-world'. For such individuals, the socio-political world is something 'devoid of reality'. For them the discovery of individuality brings with it the notion of the need for 'liberation from the fetters of life as commonly experienced in this world'. They are concerned only with themselves, and in this they resemble the individuals in modern West. But the Indian individual, unlike his Western counter-part, is the world renouncer, who does not desire to change the socio-political reality, much less to act on and/or in it. If he is interested in any change at all, it is only to bring changes in the sphere of popular religion. Thus the Indian individual is essentially a world-renouncer, who may recommend to those who listen to him a religion of individual choice superimposed on the popular religion. But otherwise he is in this world, but not of it. Liberalism is not possible for him. This explains, argues Dumont, why liberalism is not part of the Indian tradition, and why it is essentially a modern Western ideology. (Dumont, *Essays on Individualism*, Chicago, University of Chicago Press, 1972, pp. 25-6).

Assuming for argument's sake that Dumont diagnosis is valid, how would the diagnosis affect our search for a Gandhian type of liberalism? Is there an individualism compatible with liberalism in his philosophy? Does Gandhi's individualism affirm or renounce the socio-political world?

In one sense Gandhi does renounce the socio-political world, for the *final* human destiny, *moksha*, is not to be found in the historical process. Yet in another, and deeper, sense, he affirms the world, in that his very renunciation brings him back into the world. And he is back in the world not to reform religion, but to reform society and to engage in politics. It is through action in the socio-political world that *moksha* is to be attained. What he regulates are only negative forces in the human psyche--greed, lust, desire for domination–forces, if not regulated, could threaten himself as well as others. *Artha* and *kama* are still pursued, but they are pursued only within the framework of *dharma*. That is why his world affirmation does not pose a threat to others, as happens in the case of modern Western type of world affirmation. Instead of making him a 'possessive individualist', his moral renunciation frees him, to a sufficient degree, from the hostile tendencies within him. The attainment of this inner freedom contributes to his becoming a truly liberal individualist, such that his actions remain non-violent and non-threatening. His liberalism consists in being able to choose freely what *dharma* requires. The possibility of error still remains, and it is recognised as such. That is why he relies on spiritual exercises--vows, daily prayers, good reading and meditation. Without them the danger of lapsing into possessive or aggressive or destructive individualism would remain.

The recognition and voluntary acceptance of *dharma*, (in the form of *swadharma*) is consistent with the principle of internal autonomy. As Gandhi stated, commenting on his spiritual adviser, Rajchandbhai, *dharma* is neither a creed nor a dogma, nor learnt by rote from reading the *Shastras*; it is rather an internal quality of the soul, by which one recognises the basic principles of right and wrong. It is not gained solely from sensory or inferential knowledge, it is, to repeat, gained ultimately through the inner 'quality of the soul'. As such, the power to know its basic principles is internal to the individual. *Dharma* is not something imposed externally by an alien agent. It is something which a free individual is capable of recognising and accepting freely. *Dharma* then does not infringe on individual autonomy. It is in this spiritual freedom that Gandhi grounds his liberal, political, freedom--the freedom to act as one rightly desires to act in one's socio-political relations with other citizens and the state.

One can see how closely Gandhi's political philosophy is connected to his philosophy of religion. And this connectedness has a good deal to do with his liberalism. The classic statement of this connectedness of religion and politics is found in the last chapter of his *Autobiography*, where he speaks of how the desire to see the Universal Spirit of Truth face to face has made him love his neighbour, even the humblest of them. It is because of this desire that there is a deep connection between one's religion (*dharma*) and politics. Those who say that there is no such connection, he asserts, do not know what religion really means. For ultimately religion, as he understands it, (religion as *dharma* and not as sect), is the most reliable repository of ethical values. And it is *dharma* which inculcates and promotes the desire to see the Universal Spirit of Truth face to face, which is assessed to be the deepest of desires active in humans, and which therefore requires them to renounce the world morally, if only to rediscover it in a most positive and political way.

Gandhi has accomplished two things here. The first is to modify the traditional Indian notion of individualism so as to bring the morally transformed individual back into the socio-political world. Secondly, he has also modified the modern Western notion of individualism so as to free it from its anti-social possessive, aggressive and dominative attributes. In so far as this is the case, in Gandhi's political philosophy we see a peculiar type of individualism, the Gandhian type, one no longer fully traditional in the Indian sense nor one any longer fully liberal in the modern Western sense. And here we come to the heart of Gandhian individualism as it characterises his liberalism:

an individualism which is detached from this world in one sense and yet engaged with it in another sense.

Turning now to the theory of *satyagraha*, we notice a curious fact, so curious indeed that commentators and interpreters often seem to overlook it. It is Gandhi's own simple definition of it given in his most authoritative text, *Hind Swaraj*. There in chapter XVII he defines it as follows: 'Passive resistance (*satyagraha* in the Gujarati original) is a method of securing rights by personal suffering.' The key word here, from our perspective, is 'rights'--liberal rights. What distinguishes *satyagraha* from other modes of securing rights is 'personal suffering'. Rights are the end, *satyagraha* and non-violence, the means. Critics have sometimes tended to overemphasise non-violence and to build such theories as 'conquest of violence' (Joan Bondurant) and 'conflict resolution' (Arne Naess) around *satyagraha*. These theories are no doubt derived from *satyagraha* and throw much light on our understanding of how it can actually work. The fact remains, however, that in Gandhi's mind *satyagraha* was only a means, and that it had a liberal aim, namely the securing of rights. And historically, it has worked effectively only in liberal regimes or where an institution of a liberal regime (such as the British Parliament) had the ultimate say in political matters. I would go so far as to say that *satyagraha* presupposes a liberal state, one that recognises the sovereignty of rights.

If we now move to a consideration of Gandhi's conception of liberty as enshrined in the notion of *swaraj*, here too we can find a certain affinity between his notion of *swaraj* and a liberal notion of liberty. Gandhi uses *swaraj* in two distinct, though related, senses: as self-rule and as self-government. Self-rule is the rule of the individual by the individual; self-government is the rule of the nation by the nation. The two notions of freedom are morally linked. In other words, both inner freedom of the soul and the outer freedom of the nation are basic to Gandhi's concept of liberty. That is to say, he has a distinct theory of liberty, which may not be the same as Mill's or Berlin's or Rawls'. But that does not make it any less a theory of liberty.

To conclude this discussion. We raised at the beginning of this paper whether there could be such thing as Gandhian liberalism. We noticed that there were different types of liberalism, and that despite the differences between them, they engaged as it were in a common enterprise of making individualism, rights, the limited state and, above all, liberty, the basic issues of politics.

Gandhi too made these issues the foci of his thought and action. He has a theory of individualism, whose end is self-realisation. He has a theory of economic welfare and economic freedom which would carry the liberal notions on these matters to their ultimate limit--the welfare of all. He has a theory of rights. Only that in his case rights are best secured in a specific way and within a framework of duties. He has a theory of the state, the limited state, as his famous analogy of the 'oceanic circle' attests. Finally, he has a theory of liberty, which combines negative liberty and positive liberty. This may not entitle him to belong to the Berlin school of liberalism. But that in itself should not disqualify him from starting a school of his own.

Our main aim in this paper has been to raise the question of whether there could be a liberalism with a Gandhian face. The answer is beyond reasonable doubt. Our aim was not to assess Gandhian liberalism critically. No doubt, it needs a critical assessment, but meeting that need has not been our object here.

If our discussion leads to one general conclusion it is that there is a Gandhian type of liberalism. Indeed, the cherished ideals of Gandhi's thought can be best realised in a liberal regime, i.e. a parliamentary regime. This had been his own view of the matter. For as he stated in 1921, his 'corporate activity' in India was dedicated 'to the attainment of parliamentary *swaraj* in accordance with the wishes of the people of India.' (*Young India*, 26-1-1921).

Vasudha Dhagamwar

Gandhi and the Last Woman: Is Gandhi relevant for Independent India?

Of all Gandhiji's teachings two seem to be seminal to his thinking. One was in the manner of touchstone. 'Wherever you are in doubt over some course of action', said Gandhiji, 'remember the poorest, weakest man you know and ask yourself if this action will benefit him'. That advice is poignantly valid today, except that with feminist perceptions one would speak of the poorest, weakest woman. His second lesson was to fight the might of the British empire non-violently with the united strength of the people. In their different ways both lessons have come to grief.

The lesson about keeping the poorest person in one's mental view was perhaps never learnt by most of us. So minute is the stratification of our society and so great is our pride in it that the person who gets only half a *roti* (loaf) a day considers himself superior to one who gets less than him - superior and therefore untouched by the latter's woes. In two very different areas of public policy is our neglect of Gandhiji's touchstone made evident. Railways and criminal justice.

Gandhiji insisted on travelling third class and not without reason. It is said that his companions would capture a carriage and would not allow ordinary travellers to board it. Never the less he did travel by the most uncomfortable class with hard wooden seats and few other comforts. In those days the railways provided four classes for passengers. Third class for the poor, intermediate class for not so poor, second class for the not so rich, and first class for the wealthy.

After independence the intermediate class was the first to go, followed by the second class. The old third class was instead renamed second. Then came a succession of long distance trains, taking travellers faster and faster still from Delhi to various state capitals. Air–conditioned first class was introduced in late 1950's followed by

Air–conditioned chair cars and Air-conditioned second class sleepers. Now Air-conditioned three tier second class sleepers are being introduced. The railways serve the affluent to such an extent that Rajdhani Air–conditioned first class fare between Calcutta and Delhi or Bombay and Delhi is higher than aeroplane fare for the same distance.

All that remains for the poor is the three tier, non Air-conditioned, second class. Not so poor, for that matter. For almost all the long distance trains, reservations are a must, something the illiterate or ignorant traveller cannot handle. The quotas for stations in between the terminus are in any case minuscule. It is not on those trains that one meets the average Indian, not even in the second class three tier sleeper. He and his wife travel by passenger trains, whose condition is deplorable. Lights, fans, water in toilets, emergency chains, bars on the window, or bolts on the door – any or all of them can be missing from a single carriage. The platforms of mofussil stations are barely raised above mother earth so that children, as well as old, ailing or pregnant travellers, have a hard time boarding or disembarking. Nor is food easily available at these wayside stations. But as the long distance Rajdhani or Shatabdi trains never stop at those stations, no one bothers about them or their users.

The second and even more serious example is of our criminal justice system. This author had occasion to study it in Bihar, admittedly one of the worst administered states at present. But Santhal Parganas on which one focused was a peaceful district compared to many others, with little crime taking place. After examining the records of six sub-divisional courts one realised that the tribal population in jail was much less than their ratio to the non-tribal population. In other words, fewer tribals were wanted by the law for breaking it. Yet those who were arrested tended to stay in for much longer. Their trials were not pursued vigorously. They had hardly any property to put up as surety so they were not able to get bail.

There was already more than one Supreme Court judgement directing subordinate courts to give bail on personal bond after verifying the antecedents of the prisoner; but the district courts - both bench and bar - were so uncomfortable about bail for a man without property which could detached if he absconded that they refused to give it or even to apply for it. The net result was that the poor stayed in jail, most of them being tribal or of the scheduled castes. There were, for example, a couple of 80 year old men in some of prisons. They had been there for 10 years on charges of decoity and rape and they were waiting to be tried. There were boys who were growing up in jail for equally long periods. Non-tribals, especially those who could afford lawyers' fees and could arrange for their bail, came and went. Their trials were expedited. The poorest and weakest men stayed in jail. Many of the prisoners were also wanted in Marxist West Bengal in connection with other offenses. Once they were sent to Bengal to stand trial - even as their trial in Bihar was in progress - they disappeared for years on end. In both states the story was the same. The poor prisoner was incarcerated for much longer periods as an under trial.

During the Emergency (1974-76) many political leaders were imprisoned. After the Emergency was lifted, much was written by them about horrendous jail conditions. The Congress was defeated and a non-Congress Government came in at the Centre. No attempt was made to streamline criminal justice administration or to improve conditions in jail. One dare say that even under so called populist Governments of Uttar Pradesh, Bihar, Tamil Nadu and Andhra Pradesh the situation is no different today.

For a long time the number of Indians under trial has exceeded that of convicts. In 1960 there were 2,93,398 undertrial in India as against 4,12,198 convicts. By 1970 the proportion had been reversed: there were 9,38,598 undertrials in the country as against only 4,40,059 convicts. In 1978 of the 1,85,000 prisoners throughout India, 1,20,000 were undertrials and only 65,000 were convicts. Although the total population in jails had come down remarkably the inverse proportion of undertrials to convicts remained the same.[1] In September 1980 the Bihar Minister of State for Jails told a press conference that out of 25,000 prisoners in Bihar 4,000 were convicts and that the rest were undertrials.[2] At the end of 1993 there were approximately 2,00,000 prisoners in the whole of India of them about 90% were undertrials.[3] Only 500 of this jail population was female. At the end of 1994 in the single jail of Delhi state alone, namely the Tihar jail, out of total population of 9000 prisoners only 1000 were convicts. 300 of the inmates were women both as undertrials and prisoners.[4]

All these figures are a sad commentary on our criminal justice system. They tell us, loud and clear, that a large number of people are being deprived of their liberty without being tried and convicted. This is so despite the fact that the law holds everyone innocent unless proved guilty. Almost all of them are prototypes of Gandhiji's poorest and weakest man.

Gandhiji's second lesson was of nonviolence

From Gandhiji we learnt how to fight a colonial Government nonviolently, with popular might, and wrest our independence from foreign conquerors. All the world over and, indeed, even on the subcontinent wars of independence have been bloody and bitter, and often they have actually become wars of attribution and annihilation. But in India we managed to hate British rule without hating the Englishman, keeping on friendly terms with Great Britain both during the freedom struggle and after attaining independence.

If nonviolence was one part of the lesson, the other part, inevitably, was that the Government was not of us. This indeed was nothing new. It has been the lesson of Indian history for hundreds of years well before the British arrived. A good or benign Government was a blessing but it was still an outsider. It and the people looked upon each other from a distance, across a chasm. The Government of British India was projected as being other than a friend, in fact an enemy, even when it behaved well, because it was a colonial Government. All its doings were suspect. Naturally to work with it was to sell out one's people and to be a traitor. It was 'us' against 'them'.

Over forty-seven years have passed since independence and almost forty-seven since Gandhiji was assassinated on 30th January 1948. In these forty-seven years non-violence has received more lipservice than practical application. It is said that more people have died in police firings since independence than they did in the entire British rule of 250 years. The peace of the subcontinent has been shattered by terrorism garbed with patriotism but of a variety quite different from the philosophy of Bhagat Singh, Chandra Shekhar Azad or V.D. Savarkar - men who refused to shoot at even the wives of British officers, let alone lob bombs into market places or kill travellers on long distance buses simply because they belonged to a particular religon. We remember the Mahatma, we remember the revolutionaries like Bhagat Singh, and all the while use violence, indiscriminate violence, as a tool for conveying our demands or expressing our opinions. But perhaps, even the terrorists pale into insignificance in comparison with the endemic deterioration of law and order in large parts of the country.

While we have abandoned Gandhiji's teachings on this front, we have clung to the other one, viz. the Government is our enemy, and we have to fight it. People from all walks of life have a strong sense of being denied their (not always legitimate) demands. In a marked contradiction people accuse the Government of doing all that is wrong *knowingly* and at the same time believe that the Government cannot really ever deliver the goods. If the Government is omniscient and omnipotent – which it must be to be always doing the wrong thing deliberately – then surely if it so wishes it can do the right thing! But most people are not willing to admit this.

An outcome of this complex and confused set of perceptions is that any Government policy is seen as misguided, or indeed deliberately intended to be harmful. Be it identity cards for voters, be it setting up of trading corporations to buy forest produce from tribals – so that traders may not cheat them – or a proposal to make registration of marriages compulsory, the knee jerk response is that the Government has harmed us and that too deliberately, wickedly, almost evilly.

To be fair, the Government too believes that people have to be kept at a distance. Information is routinely withheld, almost anything is stamped confidential or secret. Obstruction, at worst and patronising charity at best characterise the bureaucracy – especially at the lower levels with which alone most people interact. Most Government servants are conscious of the shear, naked power they possess, and do not hesitate to show it. The process does not stop here. During a workshop to sensitise trainee Sub-inspectors, both men and women, to human rights, this author had suggested that one should have 'respect' for other people. The immediate reaction of the class, without exception, was: 'But unless we torture them a little, how can we get the truth out of them?'

If the State is our enemy, it follows that the law is also our foe, for does it not express the will of the State? Aren't laws made by that arch enemy of the people, the Government? Finding acceptance for law and obtaining its self-monitored implementation has become next to impossible. Common sense tells us that in order to be effective law must be willingly followed by the majority. Obedience can only be exacted from a small number. If the large number violate or even disregard the law, it fails. Instead there is anarchy, not civil disobedience.

This is the position that we are fast approaching in India. We now have a situation where one half of Gandhiji's message has stayed with us, viz, the Government is alien and hostile to our interests and that we should fight against it. The message has long become out of place in a sovereign democratic republic. But we have retained it in our collective memory. The second half of Gandhiji's message was to fight the public fight nonviolently. That part of the message is totally forgotten.

If the state is our enemy, its agent, the government cannot be expected to look after the people's interests. Someone has to do this job, however. Thus it is that Non Governmental Organisations emerge as the saviours and champions of the ordinary people. They too believe that the government is our enemy. In order to acquire and then retain their image as fighters of injustice, takers on of government, they are required and indeed require of it themselves – not to cooperate with the Government. To work with the Government is to be 'coopted'. One must criticise the Government but if one is asked to implement one's suggestions or in any way be of help then one must not do so, because that is the slippery path to cooption and corruption. So goes the logic of Non Governmental Organisations most of which are led by middle class intellectuals.

Such logic is totally blind to the fact that this is not a colonial Government; we have elected it and are as such responsible for its being in power and therefore have a duty to make it behave itself or else refuse to vote it back into power a second time round. What the middle class intellectuals say is passed on to others more accustomed to using their hands, stones, sticks and other sundry weapons. What then comes to pass is often a tragedy we ourselves wish to disown, and for which we blame the Government. Destruction of public property by protesters is now almost passé. Kidnappings of civil servants are not unknown. Murder of bureaucrats, though not commonplace, do occur from time to time. Krishnaiah, the young District Magistrate who was killed in Bihar in December 1994, by a mob, in retaliation for the killing of some gangsters in another district, was one such example. To that mob, out for revenge, the District Magistrate represented the state, their arch enemy. Small matter that he was not the administrative head of Muzzafarpur but of Gopla Ganj. He stood for the state and as such deserved to be killed. It is not without significance amongst the people arrested for the murder of Krishnaiah, there was a couple, the wife being a member of Parliament and her husband being a member of the State Legislative Assembly of Bihar.

We therefore get a situation which Gandhiji wished so desperately to avoid. One refers to his suspending the civil disobedience movement in 1922 because the public had set a fire a police station at Chauri Chaura in Uttar Pradesh, albeit in retaliation to police firing. Now there is no Gandhiji, no Gandhian courage in the face of a very real danger of being misunderstood by even his own followers, when he cried halt to the civil disobedience movement. The movement was for *civil* disobedience, not *criminal* disobedience, not a challenge to the prime duty of the State to maintain law and order within its boundaries. Nor was it disobedience for personal gain, but for public good. In a curious way the call to disobey the law and therefore bring the colonial Government to its knees still respected the legal frame work.

The individual Indian who disobeys the law so easily, and so frequently in his or her daily life does it for personal gain, however small. Both the silent majority and the violent protester are destroying the legal framework on which public peace rests.

Chesterton had once remarked that forerunners of many movements would be quite horrified to see what they foreran. There is no doubt whatsovever that Gandhiji would not have been at all happy with the anarchical and basically *selfish* disregard for the law that prevails today in India. And yet the current situation is something that is heir to Gandhiji's teachings. Strategies that succeed when one is trying to wrest power, do not work when one is exercising that power.

The Mahatma's teachings saw us up to independence. He gave us our collective role as subjects of a colonial state that we wished to get rid of from our midst. Now our needs have changed radically. We are citizens of a free India. Perhaps what we now need is a fresh reading of Gandhiji's works, to discover our new roles as citizens and voters in a democracy.

But that has to be done with minds cleared of all cobwebs. In other words minds that are analytical, perceptive, able to think holistically and, above all, free of adulation for Gandhiji. Perhaps minds that have never come across Gandhian philosophy with any seriousness.

If at the end of the exercise we find that Gandhi has nothing to say in this matter, we have to be prepared to leave him behind, albeit with gratitude and love for all that he has done for us. We will then have to forge our own way ahead. That will be the truest homage by far to Mohandas Karamchand Gandhi the father of our nation.

Notes and References

1. Baxi V. The Supreme Court undertrial: The undertrials and the Supreme Court 1980 (1) SCC (Jour) 35. All figures above are taken from this article.

2. *The Search Light*, Patna, 28.09.1998.

3. Figures given at an International Workshop on, Police, Prisons and Human Rights organised by Commonwealth Human Rights Initiative, 9-10 December, 1994, Delhi.

4. Ibid. Figures given by Inspector General Prisons, Tihar Jail.

Conflict Resolution

Sunderlal Bahuguna

Treading the Gandhian Path

Born in a remote Himalayan village and that too in a princely state, I could know about Gandhi when I was a High School student at the age of 13. My inquisitiveness to know about a strangely dressed young man, who was dressed neither like the officers of the state nor like the poor subjects with loin cloth, but was putting on white Khadi cap, Kurta, Jacket, dhoti and chappal, inspired me to chase him. He had a small box in one hand and a bag in another hand. I guessed he must be somebody like an archer, who had demonstrated his feats in archery and we were so much impressed that we left going to the school for some days and followed him. The idea came to my mind that his small box must contain something of our interest. I along with a few friends asked, 'what are you carrying in your small box?'. He very gently replied, 'come I will show you'. He sat under a banyan tree, opened the box and demonstrated his feat. He was spinning yarn. Looking at this new wonder, we said, 'It may take you a year to produce yearn sufficient for a shirt'. He promptly replied, whether I get enough yarn for my shirt or not, Gandhi with confidence says that we can end the British rule and become independent, if every Indian starts spinning. This is Gandhi's Yarvada Charka (the spinning wheel he invented inside Yarvada prison).

'What else does Gandhi say? How can a spinning wheel bring freedom'. The young man said, "if you want to know more, you can buy these small booklets". I spent the whole amount of six annas (about five pennies), which my mother had given me for a week's breakfast on three small booklets. One was by Gandhi - *How to achieve Swaraj*? Other was of national songs and the *A word to young men* by Prince Kroptkin.

The young man was Sri Dev Suman - a smart hillman of 25, who had become Gandhi's follower at the age of 15. He asked me, 'what are you going to do after finishing studies?' I said, 'service of the ruler'. And he again asked, 'But who will serve these poor with loin cloth?' I immediately replied 'we will also serve them too'. 'How can a person serve two masters?' He silenced me by asking this. 'Then what should I do?' He said, 'That you have to decide, but I ask you, will you sell yourself for a few silver coins?' And I firmly said, 'No, never. I also join the army of Gandhi'.

It occurred to me that the soldier of Gandhi's army should wear *Khadi* (hand-spun, hand woven cloth), know spinning and above all know more about Gandhi's life. Our small group could manage to get a spinning wheel, Gandhi's autobiography and some other books. We were cautious not to be detected, so we practised spinning and study of Gandhi's autobiography in the cemetery.

Sri Dev Suman after three years was arrested and charged with treason. He was tried inside the prison, where he undertook fast unto death for the protection of civil liberties. I myself was arrested for getting his statement published in the press and kept in the police lockup for five months. Gandhi's writings and Suman's penance strengthened me and as a boy of 17, I felt glorified in being imprisoned for being a humble soldier of Gandhi's army.

Another opportunity to study Gandhi and practice his teachings came, when I went underground from Lahore, where I was studying in the University. I was in a remote village in Lyallpur district teaching children of a Sikh family. I felt I should take up Gandhi's constructive work programme. I started spinning for self-sufficiency and scavenging the village streets. Though I was laughed at, I felt very much satisfied.

The British had left India, but slavery in the native states continued and thus the freedom struggle in the states was intensified. I was prevented by the Army from entering into Tehri town. I went on a fast. They dragged me some distance and I remained sitting. My fast continued for a week and finally they had to yield. I had seen Gandhi during his last days in his prayer meetings in Birla House. We met him a day before his martyrdom. He expressed his happiness over the success of non-violent struggle of Tehri-Garhwal state's freedom.

Gandhi in his last will had called upon the freedom fighters to settle down in villages, liquidate the Congress and take up constructive work among the villagers. I could not do so. I was working as a general secretary of the Congress party in my district but this work did not give me satisfaction. Untouchability was still there. Scavengers were regarded as untouchable. They, in order to forget their miserable life, used to take liquor and fight among themselves. The police would not intervene. On Gandhi's birthday, Oct. 2nd, 1949, I started a night school in their colony. We used to sing the devotional songs and Ramayan. Now they were under a new type of intoxication - the intoxication of Ram-nam – so dear to Gandhi.

I met Thakkar Bapa in Delhi. He had devoted his life for the upliftment of tribals and untouchables. He asked me, 'Have you seen the cells in which those where you teach live?' I admitted, I never saw these. Shewing his stick he told me that he had measured thousands of dark and dirty cells where these servants of the society lived. This was a practical lesson to me. We launched a programme of making better houses for them. Untouchability was in practice in the school hostel. There was a scheduled caste boy, who was served food outside. Two young caste students raised voice against this, but their protest was not paid heed. So we started a hostel where students of all castes could live together. It was later named as Thakkar Bapa Hostel. We started the construction of its building when the number of students increased. I used to work as a construction labourer, helper to the masons. The students also worked after their school hours. Within five years, we could construct a building. This become the centre of anti-untouchability movement. We had a group of young students, who led the temple entry in the holy shrines of Gangotri and Yamunotri. Spinning and other manual labour along with their studies became a part of their routine and these students could be recognised separate from others.

But it was Mira Behn, the English disciple of Gandhi, daughter of Admiral Slade, who persuaded me to work in the villages. She established her Pashulok (Animal's World) Ashram in the Himalayan foothills at Rishikesh. In 1949 Ganga was in spate and damaged the Ashram. Mira Behn rode on horse back towards the source of Ganga in the hills to find out the causes of the flood. She could see it was deforestation and, more than that, conversion of natural broad leaved oak forests into commercial Chir-pine forests. She wound up her foothill Ashram and set up a new Ashram–Gopal Ashram (Ashram for the service of cow) in the remote hill village of Geonli. To reach there one had to walk 40 Kms. Mira Behn looked after the cows, worked in the kitchen garden and simultaneously could find time to listen to scriptures, read books and write articles. In her life I could see a balance between head, heart and the hands.

Tehri-Garhwal was the poorest district of India. There were forests, but of no use to the people. The contractors made fortune out of these forests. Mira Behn had a plan to change the land use in which tree species giving fodder, fuel and fertilizers were to be encouraged, but bureaucracy came in the way, in spite of Pandit Nehru's full support. Finally she left the area and settled in Kashmir. But she created in me a village worker, passionate for Ashram life.

Finally my dreams were fulfilled, when I and Vimala–an assistant of Gandhi's other British disciple, Sarala Behn, who had established an Ashram to train women workers in Kumaon hills–were married. I left party and power politics forever on June 19th, 1956. We constructed huts, with the help of Thakkar Bapa Hostel students, on a degraded piece of land covered with thorny bushes. Two huts were made–one for living and other for kitchen. Vimala found work for herself. She gathered cow herd children and taught them during the night. I tended cow, worked with the villagers in the fields, sat with the villagers for evening prayers. Gandhi's prayer of the Sevak (peoples' servant) sustained me. One of the sentences of the prayer was, 'Oh God give me strength and eagerness to be one with the common masses of India'. Common people earned their livelihood by doing manual labour. We formed a labour co-operative and worked through it in constructing the canal and the roads. The villagers were addicted to liquor and used to distill liquor. The ladies were the worst sufferers. They could not speak anything against their drunk husbands, but in our evening prayer meetings the issue was raised. Women become vocal and the men took pledge to give up this bad habit. When complaint of their breaking the pledge came, I went on fast in lonely place and they repented.

In 1960, in the wake of Chinese aggression, Acharya Vinoba Bhave–the spiritual heir of Gandhi–called me to Agra, where he was halting during his *padyatra* (foot march). He said in a challenging tone, 'look here, I am an old man walking all over the country but you being a youngman are sitting in your Ashram. The threat from China is psychological more than physical. China is not a tiger to be threatened by the guns. China has a philosophy of alleviating poverty. We have the superior philosophy of Gandhi's *Gram Swaraj* (village rule). You should go from village to village in Uttarakhand (Central Himalayan) region with this message.' Nehru and Vinoba came out with a similar statement that *Gram Swaraj* was a defence measure.

Exactly four years after we had started the Ashram, I left it to go from village to village. We would tell villagers to free themselves from three shops–liquor shop, courts, the shop of litigation, and cloth shop. They should give up liquor, settle their own disputes and spin their own cloth. But the government was encouraging liquor to earn revenue. A new liquor shop was proposed near our Ashram in Ghansali. I sought Vinoba's permission to suspend my wandering in the region and offer *satyagraha* at the liquor shop. He immediately responded, 'you have to organise people for picketing the liquor shop. The government should think how can they confront China freed from opium by making people drunkards'.

Men were not serious, but the ladies were determined to fight the liquor. They had to look after the family, the farm and the cattle. The main problem was of creating leadership from among them. We organised Ram Lila (the play of Ramayan) during the night. Ladies in hundreds thronged.

After day's hard work and feeding the family, they would walk 7 to 8 Kms. with torchwoods in their hands. We encouraged them to come on the platform. They would also come with a handful of rice to help the movement. A retired judge–an old man, the most respected in the area–came forward to lead the movement. Seeing the dedication, determination and devotion of the people, the government changed the decision. This was the peoples' first victory and their faith in non-violence was established.

We multiplied this experiment. For seven years, we fought against liquor. There were mass movements against the liquor, picketing by ladies everywhere. One after another the liquor shops were closed and finally the government declared five hill districts dry in 1970. But the High Court revoked the prohibition. Everywhere an atmosphere of terror was created. The women were told that if they picketed the liquor-shops after High Court orders, they will be sent to jail for many years. We were keeping vigil at the spot where the shop was to open, but the liquor-vendors eluded us by opening it at a new place. Immediately we rushed to the spot. Acharya Vinoba Bhave had made a rule to chant one thousand names of Lord Vishnu (Vishnu Shahastranam) at 10.30 a.m. all over the country. I sat in front of the liquor shop and started chanting Vishnu Shahastranam. As soon as I finished and opened my eyes I was shocked to see the ghastly scene. The head of the son of the liquor vendor was bleeding. He was beaten with an empty bottle by his own servant, who had taken the full bottle to rejoice the reopening of the shop.

Liquor is the cause of violence and bloodshed. Is it going to happen all around? What to do? Because everybody around us said that it was impossible to close down the liquor shops now. I was reminded of a devotional song of blind saint Surdass. He sang long-long ago.

I bow to the feet of Almighty.
With whose kindness, the lame crosses the mountain.
The blind sees everything.,
The deaf hears and the dumb speaks.
The poor wanders as a crowned king.

At least a blind man had experienced that the impossible can become possible. When all our worldly efforts had failed, why not go on a prayerful fast.

Thus, started my prayerful fast in front of the liquor shop on Nov. 5th, 1971. It was an open place on the road. People laughed at me. The drunkards created noise. They became more vocal and remarked what right I had to create hindrance in their way; but gradually some senior citizens came to persuade me to give up the fast. Later women started coming. I asked them were they still afraid of the prison. They said, 'no'. If so, go from village to village and bring thousands to protest against the liquor shop. Their number went on increasing. They sang devotional songs near the place of fast. On 16th day, 20th November, more than twenty thousand people, mostly ladies, assembled in Tehri town. They had come fully prepared to court arrest. A public meeting was held, which passed a resolution asking me to give up the fast as they will picket the liquor shop. Thus, I concluded my fast. The people, the most oppressed in the society, the women, had come forward to fight for the cause. This is what Gandhi wished. Scores of these women, including my six year old son Pradeep, along with his mother, were arrested and sent to far off prison. My wife's old mother was also arrested. In this way the three generations had come together for a common cause.

While working for *Gram Swaraj* in the border villages, we had seen a bigger threat to the country in the shape of ever-increasing floods due to deforestation in higher Himalayas. We took up forest problem in 1972. We thought the unscrupulous contractors were responsible for overfelling the trees. So the demand was to replace the contractor system with forest labourers' co-operative, supplying raw material to local forest based industries. The idea to pressurize the government by hugging the trees marked for selling came from the villagers. This was the result of 12 year long efforts of peoples' education in non-violence. *Chipko* means hug–feel the heartbeats of the trees. Women, who were trained in non-violent method of protest came forward to save the trees, but their vision was different than that of men's economic demand. They said, forest is our 'mothers' home–a place, which a lady remembers when in trouble. After five years our illusion was cleared, when we saw that there were land slides even if the trees were felled by the forest co-operatives. Women's participation and our long foot marches to educate the people, a fifteen days' fast in 1974, gave birth to a new concept - a new slogan:

> What do the forest bear? soil, water and pure air.
> Soil, water and pure air, are the basis of Life.

On 9th January 1979 was my 53rd birthday. We were camping in villages of Alaknanda valley. Thousands of green trees had been marked for felling. The axemen were at work. The villages were scattered. I sat under a tree marked for felling. The axeman was to come there to start his work. I felt I had become so insensitive that I was doing nothing when my sons are being slaughtered before my eyes. The holy Upanished says, 'A tree is equal to ten sons.' I hugged the tree and the axeman went to the next. I chased him. For some time this continued. Finally I followed them to their huts, but nobody would give me shelter. They were told I was their enemy–an obstacle in their way to earn money. I sent my two colleagues to go to the village and declare my fast unto death till tree felling was stopped. I squeezed under a heap of hay. Next day people from the villages came. The news spread far and wide. On the fourth day to my surprise the hay was burning. I saved my life by running away with the sleeping bag, my only belonging. Thereafter we could find shelter under a hut. Vimala, along with some ladies from my Ashram, had come. On the 13th day of my fast, they took me to jail. I continued my fast and gave a statement that force feeding and medicines would cause my death as I was naturalist. This baffled the authorities, who were pressing the doctors to do force-feeding. When I did not yield, they sent me to Dehra Dun jail. Groups of doctors came every day to examine me. They would feel my pulse, the heart, measure the blood pressure; but found everything alright. I observed silence and listened to devotional songs. This strengthened me. Doctors asked me the secret of this. I said there is a hidden power–the power of self–to measure which you have no instruments. On the 24th day, the government decided to stop tree feeling and talk with me on the issue on management of hill forests. Thus ended my prayerful fast. I came out stronger from this ordeal.

It was finally in April 1981, when felling of green trees for commercial purposes was banned. But it was only in the state of Uttar Pradesh. Himalaya extends from Kashmir to Kohima. How to spread this message? I finally decided to undertake *padyatra* (foot march). During this foot-march, the first to join me was 72 year old Gandhian activist, Sri Ratanchand Dehloo. Later many more people joined and we could complete this 4,870 km march in 300 days. Besides Indian Himalaya, we walked through Nepal and Bhutan, about 2000 kms. We carried our luggage on our backs and lived upon whatever the villagers offered. We could take the message to the hearts of the people, impress upon them the vital importance of forests for their survival.

The slogan given by *Chipko* attracted international attention. Richard St. Barbe Baker, celebrated Man of the Trees, the veteran forester came to India to greet the movement. He was a saint scientist. He declared that this was a scientific movement. Later, Indian Science Congress also passed a unanimous resolution supporting the movement. Thus the way for *Sarvodaya*–well being of all–was paved. Science had come in support of self knowledge (Atma-Gyan).

A 260.5 meter high dam, Tehri dam, the highest in Asia was planned over River Bhagirathi in 1960s. When it was sanctioned by the Planning Commission in 1972, people who were going to be displaced by this monstrous dam launched a movement against it. Work on it was started in 1978. The movement slowed down. People went to the court, but in spite of all scientific opinions against it and the apprehension of a big earthquake, work continued. Sri V.D. Saklani, the spirit behind the movement, asked me to devote full time to this issue as he had become old and weak. On November 24th, 1989, I left Silyara Ashram, the base of my 33 years work, with a decision not to return till Tehri dam was stopped. Now I was a homeless wanderer. I went from village to village listening to the people and to the nature around. Is this all going to vanish if the dam is built? Nobody was listening to the people.

On Christmas day, 25th December, 1989, I went on a week's fast. This was a call to attention motion on my part. I was fasting outside the dam site. Nobody was allowed to go to the site. On the fourth day of my fast, I walked to the work site. Gigantic machines were at work. First I made gesture to stop these, but they continued. Finally, I jumped upon a bull-dozer which was in action. They had do stop it. It was evening and the frosty winter night was to fall. My sitting there made people brave. They came in hundreds. We made fire around. Next morning a temporary shelter was made, but I made the wheel of the bulldozer my permanent seat. I would offer my prayers, speak for an hour and observe silence for the whole day. When nothing happened for seven days, I declared an indefinite fast. On the 11th day, message came from Delhi for talks. The talks were not decisive. Our protest continued.

I repaired to my ancestral deserted house, which is in the submergence area of the dam. Later, through foot marches from the source of Ganga to Hardwar, where it descends down from the hills to the plains, we walked spreading the message from village to village. River Ganga is worshipped by millions as the holy mother. It is the symbol of India's Aryan Culture, which sees life in all creation and advocates a worshipful attitude towards all forms of life. Moreover, behind the story of the origin of Ganga is the story of penance of a king, who left everything for the welfare of humankind. The river is suffering from the dual onslaughts of exploitation and pollution. To make people conscious about it, we set out on a cycle rally on September 11, 1991, from Ganga Sagar, Bay of Bengal, where Ganga joins the sea, to Gaumukh in Himalayas. Again, teaching and preaching through our action. We covered 2300 kilometers in 46 days, when a big earthquake rocked the hill region on October 21st, 1991. This put a big question mark on the construction of Tehri dam on a highly seismic zone.

On October 29th, we decided to sit in protest near the dam site and finally, on Dec. 14th, 1991, along with more than two thousand people, we stalled the work at dam site.

The monstrous machines were again stopped. We pitched our tents at the work site, keeping 24 hours vigil. They tried to dislodge us, brought a bull-dozer to demolish our camp. We again climbed upon the bull-dozer. The work remained stalled for 75 days, when in the dark of night the police came and invaded our camp, arrested forty of us and took us to the jail. Among those arrested were Vimala, my wife, two minor girls of our Ashram and three ladies. This was an attack on civil liberties. I started indefinite fast in the prison. Vimala and Diksha Bisht, a lady worker, joined me. We were shifted to Roorkee jail the fourth day and later to Megrut Medical College, finally released and brought back to Tehri. I continued my fast and insisted to be taken to the spot, where our camp was demolished. But everywhere armed police were posted to prevent our entry. We pitched our camp on the road side. All methods of torture were adopted. The fast generated countrywide interest in the problem of Tehri dam. It was discussed in the parliament and finally George Fernandes, a socialist leader and member of the Parliament, visited me with an appeal from the President of Lok Sabha to break the fast. We wanted an assurance from the Prime Minister that blasting of explosives at the dam site will be stopped and a review of the project undertaken. It took another two weeks. On the forty-fifth day when this came, I broke my fast and shifted to the bank of the river near the dam site.

Here I live in a shanty since April 1992. People from different parts of the country and world visit this spot. Near our shanty is a red flag– the flag is not the flag of socialists, but railwayman's danger signal, to caution people about the dangers from a high dam in Himalaya, in particular, and from destructive development. People often ask what is the alternative. Gandhi had foreseen the domesday as early as 1908, when he wrote *Hind Swaraj*. The objective of development is economic growth or prosperity but to achieve this temporary economic prosperity, we have lost peace and happiness. We have created a world, which is confronted with the problems of threat of war and internal in security, pollution and depletion of resources, and poverty and hunger. The concept of development had made man the butcher of nature. Gandhi's vision of an ideal society was based upon the Indian culture. Development is a state in the life of individual and society in which they enjoy permanent peace, happiness and fulfillment. This can be achieved if science and technology is applied to sublimate nature. Thus the ultimate goal of humankind, to march from nature to culture, will be achieved. The seed was sown by Gandhi. He nurtured it and left tender plant to our generation to rear and help the tree to grow. I have been devoting myself to this during these 55 years.

Peter Cadogan

The Troubles of Northern Ireland seen as a manifestation of Fundamentalism

Homo sapiens is a religious animal. This, as a universal truth, does not refer to any particular faith but to religion as a phenomenon; just as art, science and philosophy/history are comparable phenomena.

It follows that those who successfully reach down to the religious depths of the human psyche tap the greatest creative or destructive powers known to humankind. Religion is the name we give to the ways in which the person individually, and people collectively, relate to the sacred i.e. to that which is set apart, infinite, eternal. Or to use A.N.Whitehead's plain English, to that which is most important. And clearly that which is most important determines the fate of all else.

The IRA/Sinn Fein have no received religious or political theory. Up to 1970, when the Provos took over the leadership from the Officials, they had their own version of marxism based on the class struggle i.e. *not* on nationalism. The supposed object was to get the Catholic and Protestant working classes to combine against their capitalist masters regardless of sectarian differences. The success of the Provos meant a return to nationalism as such, the identification of the Protestants with the British and an avowed acceptance of the communal divide.

There were then two simple inter-related beliefs, the first being that the British Government and its Army should be expelled from the Six Counties (as Republicans call Northern Ireland) and that in the process, those Six Counties be re-united with the Twenty-Six Counties (as Republicans call the Republic of Ireland).

The mode of attainment was to be 'blood and sacrifice' i.e. war. The twin objectives enjoy the status of the immaculate. They are sacralised by the blood of those who have died for them. We are therefore into the realm of the non-rational (not the irrational); and this makes it virtually unintelligible to the empirical British, who simply avert their eyes. British public opinion plays no part in anything to do with The Troubles and Her Majesty's Opposition gives full support to Her Majesty's Government over all essentials in Northern Ireland.

There is a small group (who don't make three figures) in London, round the *Gandhi Foundation, New Dialogue* and the *National Peace Council,* who have been very active since 1988, and who are quite disproportionately influential, but the response throughout the country is quite negligible.

Of the Nature of Fundamentalism

Fundamentalism requires a faith, a Leader, a vision and a mythology. To compound these four successfully is to create a base of immense potential power. People who then identify with it render themselves exclusive, different, cut off from ordinary mortals and prepared to make the ultimate sacrifice - that of their own lives. Their immortality will lie in that sacrifice. We are in the presence of the possessed; they have a mysterium, so it is believed, for which it is right to live and die.

We need to look back to the beginning and invoke the aid of the anthropology of religion. None of us are so far from tribalism as we are wont to believe. Historically it was as yesterday.

In the religious faith of tribal pre-civilised times i.e. before the arrival of towns, life was lived at two levels at one and the same time. There was this world – material, organic, social and personal – a physical reality. A close observance of it yielded an extensive knowledge of natural history. At the same time behind that world was another one of in–dwelling spirits that motivated everything in the material world. The material world was only apparent – the real world was that of the spirits.

Every stick, every stone, every plant, every animal, every natural force and everything human was moved from within by a spirit. If the spirits were displeased the results were apparent in sickness, accident, disasters, death and all things evil. If the spirits were pleased we enjoyed the bonuses of health, happiness, concord and all life's blessings. Life therefore turned upon thanking and gratifying the good spirits by worship and gifts i.e. sacrifice and casting out the bad spirits by exorcism. And all this happened in a static society.

Since it is some five million years since our proto-hominid ancestors broke with the primates (so the latest DNA research indicates) we are looking at psychological precedents of immense antiquity and presumably with some genetic base. By way of contrast civilisation, round the Tigris, Euphrates, Indus and Yang Tse Kiang, has a history of the order of a mere 6000 years. We tread on thin ice. We have presumed over a few millenia, to throw patterns of behaviour established over millions of years. And what if our throwing exercise comes apart? There is bound to be some reversion to type. But to what type? People cannot go back to traditions they have lost because imperial masters have destroyed them. The result can only be total disorientation. In that context fundamentalism is, *inter alia*, a search for roots when alien lids, those of empires and the Cold War, have suddenly been taken off. But there is then another deeper factor.

The Politics of Fundamentalism

Homo sapiens is also a political animal i.e. he needs, of his nature, to live under government of some kind. Instinct is not enough. Instinct serves the primates well enough; it is good enough to sustain the extended family. But that is all. Primates live within the parameters of nature. *Homo sapiens* does not.

It is the inventive power of the imagination that distinguishes us from the rest of the animal kingdom. How it happened no one yet knows. The original humans devised the artifice: music and dance, language, colour, design, mythology, ritual, heritage, tools and weapons. It was thus possible to make and unmake the world of nature, domesticate animals and plants, irrigate, build, store and trade. But this made for something new–surpluses over subsistence, the possibilities of greed, inequality, conquest and empire. Warriors became kings, medicine-men became priests. It has all happened since the departure of the last Ice Age, a mere 11,000 years ago. The first town, Jericho, dates back for some 10,000 years.

The suddenness of it all is alarming. It can so easily come apart. The State, the creation of warrior-kings, was devised to hold it all together. What the Army did for external authority the priesthood did for the mind–and the two corresponded. The result was Caesar and he is still with us. States bred empires and the rivalries of empires bred wars, until in our time the sheer cost and destructiveness of war–weapons of mass destruction has put an end to international war between the industrial powers. But elsewhere some twenty-six conventional wars are being waged at huge cost in terms of life, limb, dispossession and habitat. We have sown the whirlwind of post-imperial collapse. The result is that the world abounds in would–be emperors making fanatical nationalisms out of ethnic identities, exclusivity, tribal-type loyalties and access to AK47s. Todays fundamentalism is a greater killer than the Cold War ever was.

How then are the two natures, religious and political, to relate? The arbitrary power bred of civilisation, military and priestly, has escaped the imperial compound and turned populist. The old imperial powers, having lost their imperial vocation and focused their attention on the market values and goals of high-tech society, stand by indifferently while what was their imperial world tears itself apart in regional wars. And they are not going to change. The answers to regional crises will have to come from the regions themselves. It might take fifty years. The task is huge.

Ireland as a Case in Point

Ireland was England's first colony. The year was 1169 AD. Wales and Scotland followed. It was all a very complex mix of dynastic deals and military conquests. It is important to see that there was an English empire of these three realms, centuries before the British Empire was born.

That first empire was a failure. Over a period of some 200 years the Irish absorbed it. English men fell for Irish girls, married them and their children were soon more Irish than English. Also Ireland proved unconquerable. It was ruled by some sixty to ninety princes and lords, as often as not fighting each other. The society was tribal and so without any sense of unity against a common enemy. When the English took one part it made no difference to the others. It was rather like the recent Russian experience in Afghanistan. What does a single victory mean when there are dozens or other unbeaten armies in the field? So the English withdrew to the Pale of Dublin, a stretch of territory along the East Coast, north and south of Dublin; and there they stayed.

The four provinces of Ireland were Ulster, Munster, Leinster and Connaught and Ulster in the far north was the most Gaelic of all. It was from Ulster that the Northern Earls rose against the English in the 1590s, the last decade of Elizabeth's reign. They allied with Spain and a Spanish Army, 4000 strong, landed on the southern coast in the year 1601. The Earl of Tyrone's forces were supposed to join up with them but never made it. The English Army dealt with them separately and smashed them both. As the result of this defeat the Lords of Ireland went into exile of their own accord and left Gaelic Ireland leaderless. James I then decided on a massive plantation of Anglo-Scottish colonists, but this time there was to be no assimilation. A whole self-sufficient community moved in: farmers, craftsmen, families, traders, teachers, ministers of religion–and with them the Anglican and Presbyterian Protestant faiths. This was new and this was permanent.

The Irish rose against the new Planters in 1641 and massacred them. No one knows how many died, a conservative estimate is about 2000. When the Civil Wars (1642/48) in England were over, Cromwell reconquered Ireland in bloody style and the Second Plantation took place from 1649. Finally after James II was defeated at the Battle of the Boyne in 1690 the Third Plantation (bigger than the first two put together) confirmed Ireland's English political identity for over a hundred years–and the beautiful Georgian city of Dublin, as we know it today, was built.

The fateful seventeenth century established todays mythology for both communities. The memories are amazingly alive–it is as though it was yesterday. To the Catholics Cromwell is synonymous with Satan. To the Protestants King Billy (William III), the victor of the Boyne, is the saviour hugely celebrated every year in the spectacular marches of the Orange Order (named after him). A hard-line Unionist is today as fanatical and as fundamentalist as his republican opposite number. There is no way this can be properly conveyed on paper–it has to be seen and heard, in Northern Ireland itself, to be believed. So religion (not necessarily Christian) underwrites politics in a Gael-Planter confrontation, the product of 800 years of unhappy history. The situation is essentially colonial and post-colonial.

Blood and Sacrifice

Patrick Pearse was the presiding genius of Dublin's Easter Rising of 1916, the inspiration and the founding father of the IRA. On Christmas Day 1915 he said:

> Here be ghosts that I have raised this Christmastide, ghosts of dead men that have bequeathed a trust to us living men. Ghosts are troublesome things, in a house or, in a family, as we knew even before Ibsen taught us. There is only one way to appease a ghost. You must do the thing it asks. The ghosts of a nation sometimes ask very big things and they must be appeased, at whatever cost.[1]

Less than six months later he and fifteen of his fellow rebels were condemned to death and executed after the failure of their Rising. The choice of Easter was part of the mystique–the festival of Resurrection, the resurrection of Ireland. The firing squads turned failed revolutionaries into national martyrs. The cause was sealed in blood, and it still is. It is only enough to fight and die...

There used to be something called eschatology i.e. knowledge of the Four Last Things: Death, Judgement, Heaven and Hell. Today the very word is known only to specialists. It provided a civilised equivalent to a universe of in-dwelling spirits, providing divine sanctions for life on earth and the promise of life hereafter. Now it has gone. What has taken it place? Nothing. That is our problem vis-a-vis fundamentalism. They have their own answer and it works with their own people. The voice of sanity and social justice has to find its own response. We cannot take anything for granted.

The authentic republican, working with either the bullet or the ballot, has a mission in life and it gives his life meaning. It may be wholly mistaken, inhuman, reactionary and utterly wasteful–but no matter. It is how he *feels* that counts. A Catholic priest of my acquaintance went to see one of the H-Block prisoners during his fast to death in 1982. The young man, wasted away, had just lost his sight and had only a few days to live. The priest said to him: 'And how will you feel when you are up there in Heaven and looking down on us?' The reply: 'Father, when I see the British troops leaving the Six Counties I will say to myself: "I helped to get them out".' And with that he was more than content to die, his nine friends likewise. And it was not just his decision. It was not an act of conscience as with Gandhi. He had to apply to his Commanding Officer in the prison and to the Army Council outside the prison for permission to fast, for permission to die. He was a soldier under orders. He could only abandon the fast under instructions. Discipline is fundamental to fundamentalism. We need something of a different order which is, nevertheless, its equal and opposite.

Ways of Life

When there are two peoples living in the same territory, the common ethnic dilemma all over the world, there is culture clash. Traditions, customs, life-styles can be as different as religions and languages. The original Gaels, close to the land with their cattle and their tribal culture were happy to miss the Renaissance, the Reformation, the Discoveries, the Scientific and Industrial Revolutions. They had their music and dancing, their myths and stories, their perennial in-fighting, their religion (half-pagan, half-Catholic), the whiskey that was their own invention, later copied by the Scots (notice that the word is spelt differently in Ireland). They had warmth, hospitality and a powerful sense of belonging but not as people, that had to await the nineteenth century. They had no name for themselves, the words Ireland and Irish, like the name Dublin, were given them by their ninth century conquerors, the Danes.

Belfast was industrialised well over a hundred years ago. Dublin was not. It was not until the 1960s, after the departure of de Valera, that the industrialisation of the Republic got under way.

Then Protestant Ulster is not all of a piece. For centuries, as in England, the land was ruled by its aristocracy and gentry, but the industrial development of Belfast meant the rise of an industrial, commercial and professional complex of classes that bred a different politics. And thirdly there arose a new Protestant working class in the shipyards and factories of Belfast, Derry and elsewhere. In the mid-sixties the landed classes were ousted by the Ulster Unionist Party and then Paisley Democratic Unionist Party broke away from the UUP and underpinned by his own Free Presbyterian Church fanned the flames of a new virulent brand of Unionism, round the slogan: 'No Surrender' (to Dublin). His fundamentalism prepared the way for paramilitary rebirth. It was the Unionist UVF, not the IRA, that was first in the field in 1966. The IRA had wound up in 1962, dissolved its structure in the field and buried its arms and ammunition. And that condition obtained for seven years until the Provos surfaced in 1969 in face of acute Protestant provocation i.e. the burning and destruction of Catholic houses.

Stormont, the Parliament of Northern Ireland, was an English idea imposed on Ulster. Protestant Ulster didn't want it. Carson's successors would have been more than happy with government from Westminister, as was the case with Wales and Scotland. But Ireland has always baffled the English and Westminster was determined to pass the buck, which it did. It only made things worse. Ulster Catholics would have been perfectly content (most of them) to be governed by London, but to be governed by local anti-Catholic bigots – that was just asking for trouble. In 1972 the Heath Government at last read the writing on the wall and abolished Stormont; but by that time the worst of the damage had been done.

Internal Divisions

If the Protestants have a four-way split (the fourth element being that of their paramilitaries) with further religious denominational differences, the situation on the Catholic side is no better i.e comparably divided. Before the 'sixties (and Vatican II), there was much orthodox conformity. The young were successfully discouraged from undertaking higher education because that meant Queens University, Belfast, mixing with Protestants, getting ideas other than Catholic and possibly being lost to the Church.

Thus when I was first in Belfast, speaking to a students meeting in Queens (about the war in Biafra) it was 1969. I asked what proportion of the students were Catholic and the answer was 19%. Today that figure is 51% – an historic change. It signifies the arrival of a Catholic, middle class. Today there are parts of Belfast where violence is virtually unknown, along the Malone Road where Protestant and Catholics, middle class, live quite happily side by side. They speak the same language.

At the same time, affecting Ireland as a whole, the country has been rocked by sex scandals concerning the clergy, in association with an extensive public debate, about contraception, abortion and divorce. The once immaculate Church is seen to be most mortal. The young have decamped in droves.

So there is the great gulf between the two communities and any number of minor internal gulfs internal to each. To what extent is the difference fundamentalist?

From Catholicism to Fundamentalism

As from the eighteenth century there have been four distinct phases of Irish nationalism.

The first took off as from the American Declaration of Independence in 1776. In support of the new USA, France and the Netherlands declared war on England. The English/British Government was hard put to it to find troops for America, never mind to defend Ireland. Ireland at that time was semi-sovereign in the sense that it had its own Lords, Commons and Executive with limited powers. They raised their own Army for self-defence and that put them in a peculiarly strong position vis-a-vis London. The Irish, led by Planters, dreamt and prepared for independence and when the French Revolution broke out they made an alliance with the French. So it was the Protestant *United Irishmen*, with the Protestant Wolfe Tone as its best-known voice, who founded Irish nationalism. The revolt was crushed by force in 1798. Ireland's self-government was then abolished by an Act of Union, 1800. Ireland was granted 100 seats in the London *House of Commons* and 26 life peers in the *Lords*. Thus the parliamentary Irish Party was born, and when the *Act of Catholic Emancipation* was passed in 1829 the way was open to the Catholicisation of Irish nationalism; and so it happened under the leadership of O'Connell. Its subsequent militancy was occasioned by the appalling suffering endured as the result of the potato famine of 1845/6. A million died, another million emigrated. In the US the new exiles formed the *Irish Republican Brotherhood* (also known as the Fenians) and this caught on 'back home' as well. This second phase of nationalism, producing proto–republicanism, lasted till 1914 and covered the time, in the eighties, when the movement was led for the last time by a Protestant – Parnell.

It was in the third phase, in the build-up to 1916, that Republicanism became properly fundamentalist. Pearse restated its political philosophy and mythology in deeply religious terms. He did this in his own name, as the leader of a religiously and politically autonomous movement. There was no question of Church control or inspiration. Consider the very language he used in his Address at the grave of Wolfe Tone on 22nd June 1913:

> We have come to the holiest place in Ireland; holier even than the place where Patrick sleeps in Down. Patrick brought us life, but this man died for us. He was the greatest of Irish Nationalists. We have come to renew our adhesion to the faith of Tone; to express once more our full acceptance of the gospel of Irish Nationalism which he was the first to formulate in worldly terms. This man's soul was a burning flame so ardent, so generous, so pure, that to come into communion with it is to come into a new baptism, into a new generation and cleansing.[2]

No one had ever used language like that before. Pearse was translating nationalism into a new dimension. Conor Cruise O'Brien's latest book: *Ancestral Voices; Religion and Nationalism in Ireland* (1994) is a study of that dimension.

Two years later Pearse produced a tract *Ghosts* in which he asks for blood:

> An aspiration of King David haunts my memory when I think on Ireland and her wrongs: "That thy foot may be dipped in the blood of thine enemies and that the tongue of thy dogs may be red through the same."[3]

The spiritual-political soil of Ireland was ready for the new seed. The Fenians had been entrenched for sixty years. Catholic nationalism had been long underwritten by an organisation surely unique in world politics – the GAA, *The Gaelic Athletic Association* founded in 1884, intensely hostile to the British, committed to promoting forms of sport that were distinctively Irish like hurling and Irish football (quite different to soccer). It was firmly linked to the Catholic Church. The movement to restore the Irish language, the success of the Abbey Theatre and the reclamation of Irish mythology provided a new cultural base while, economically, the old Protestants suffered a shattering defeat. Under the *Land Acts* of 1881 and 1903 the planter landlords were obliged to sell up. The base built up since the twelth century was lost. But this did not happen in Ulster where the Protestants were working farmers on their own land. *Ulster was different*.

Even so, the great majority of Irish nationalists were still Home Rulers, not republicans, not wanting separation from Great Britain. They would have been happy with a Kingdom of Great Britain and Ireland and in 1914 their political leaders fully supported Britain in World War I and vast numbers of Irish volunteered for war service. The Irish recognised the service done to Ireland by Gladstone and those that followed him up and until the passing of the *Home Rule Bill* in 1914.

On the eve of the Easter Rising, in *The Sovereign People* of March 1916, Pearse set his seal on fundamentalism:

> Let no man be mistaken as to who will be Lord in Ireland when Ireland is free. The people will be lord and master. The people who wept at Gethsemane, who trod the sorrowful way, who died naked on a cross, who went down into hell, will rise again glorious and immortal, will sit on the right hand of God, who will come in the end to give judgement, a judge just and terrible.[4]

Then James Connolly, marxist and fellow-martyr of 1916, yielded before the fundamentalism of his chief and wrote:

> Without the slightest trace of irreverence but in all humility and awe, we recognise that of us, as of mankind before Calvary, it may be truly said: "Without the shedding of blood there is no redemption."[5]

It was not the blood of his enemies that he was referring to. It was his own.

We are back with pagan roots, medieval chivalry and the Holy Grail – a thousand miles and a thousand years from the twentieth century. No such compound is to be taken lightly. To understand it one has to make one's own journey through space and time. It is hardly to be wondered at that so few make it. It is so much easier to switch off.

Stage four - Today's Fundamentalism

There was a long and bitter struggle from 1918 to 1922 in the course of which both *Northern Ireland* and *The Irish Free State* were born. This is not the place to tell that story, save to say at the end of it there was civil war in *The Irish Free State* between the Nationalists who accepted the existence of Northern Ireland and a section of the Republicans who did not.

The out-and-out Republicans lost and, led by de Valera, they went into temporary political exile from which they emerged ten years later, still led by the same leader, but this time with a new Party of his creation: *Fianna Fail*. It is still with us. Republicanism ceased to be fundamentalist and eventually became marxist.

The return to fundamentalism was at the hands of the Provos in the years 1969/72. Its religio-political character was rendered beyond doubt by the H-block fast to death of 1982. This was blood and sacrifice in the fullest Tone-Pearse tradition.

I saw something of it for myself some four years ago. Every year there is a big meeting in Conway Hall, Red Lion Square, London, in honour of Wolfe Tone and 1916. On this occasion the main speaker was Gerry Adams. He spoke at length but never mentioned the political situation. He spoke only of the Easter story as told in the New Testament of the struggle against tyranny, of the suffering of the innocent, of sacrifice, of the indestructibility of the cause, of blood, of crucifixion, of death and resurrection and of ultimate triumph against all odds. He told the story well, he is an excellent raconteur in the famous Irish bardic tradition – *and he never mentioned Ireland once.* Yet 500 London-Irish and one Englishman knew exactly what he was talking about.

So how does a constitutionally governed society deal with a victory or death situation? For many years now Conor Cruise O'Brien has been famous (some would say infamous!) for his answer: Selective internment of the paramilitary godfathers. This could only be undertaken by British and Irish Government simultaneously. For the Irish Government it would indeed be the last resort and to date it has been vetoed. O'Brien expects the civil war to recur (exactly on the grounds of its fundamentalism) and sticks to his last. We have yet to know what the final outcome might be.

The Present Situation

On the 26th March, the Secretary of State for Northern Ireland, Peter Brooke, speaking in the House of Commons set out the ground rules for talks leading to a peace settlement. Nothing would be agreed until everything had been agreed; the final settlement would have to have the support of the people of Northern Ireland: there were to be three strands (a) within NI and with the British Government (b) between Belfast and Dublin (c) between London and Dublin. They would eventually all come together.

In 1993 came the Adams-Hume initiative. The IRA/Sinn Fein party saw that it had enough political capital in hand in Dublin and the US to make a peace bid. They were also under heavy pressure from their 500 members in jail and who wanted out. They got through to the Taoiseach Albert Reynolds and through him to John Major. The result was the Joint Declaration of December 1993. The IRA cease-fire came at the end of August 1994 to be followed some weeks later by the UDA/UVF cease-fire and long months of peace up to the time of writing this at the end of March 1995. The *Frameworks for the Future*, the latest statement by the British Government, is now under debate.

The critical issues are the surrender of IRA weapons, the release of prisoners and the future of the police force,the Royal Ulster Constabulary. The constitutional matters are Articles 2 and 3 of the Irish Constitution under which the Republic lays claim to the North, and Section 75 of the *Government of Ireland Act 1920* under which Ulster is incorporated in the UK.

At a deeper level is the half-hidden agenda of the IRA/SF – the unification of Ireland and the final expulsion of Britain from Ulster. There is also the Adams-Hume thesis that the responsibility of the British Government is to pressurise, 'persuade', the Protestant Unionist[3] to accept unification. This has the Unionists very alarmed indeed and makes for a very dangerous situation. The Republicans have also ruled out any internal settlement that will leave NI in the UK. Inter-communal communication is, if anything, worse than before. All these matters are, however, dressed up in political double-speak. The IRA/SF are extremely conscious that everything they say will be closely monitored by their friends in Dublin, Washington and New York.

The Voice of Non-Violence

Coming through all the double-speak and hidden agendas that plague the discourse of Northern Ireland there is a voice of non-violence. It has been there for centuries, but too often too still and too small. It comes through the Quakers, the Fellowship of Reconciliation, Corrymeela, Pax Christi, the Cornerstone Community, Peace and Reconciliation Derry, the Peace People, Enniskillen Together, Bryson House, The Columbanus Community, The Community Relations Council – hundreds of groups scattered throughout all the six counties of Ulster, Catholic and Protestant. It kills no one and so is not news.

Its clearest expression today comes through the voice and pen of one man–Ciaran McKeown - who was one of the three founders of *The Peace People* in 1976. The other two, Mairead Corrigan (now Maguire) and Betty Williams, were awarded the Nobel Peace Prize. By 1980 Ciaran had to withdraw temporarily from the scene to meet the demands of a large young family. As from last year, and a major shake–up in the ranks of *The Peace People*, he has been back, this time as the Editor of a new paper–*The Citizen*. He clearly embodies the spirit and intellect of Gandhi in contemporary Ulster.

> Whether or not we succeed, as the militarised world measures success, is utterly beside the point. What matters is that we try our utmost to live truthfully and therefore to act out the truth of our lives.
>
> Living truthfully means living in the light of a truth greater than ourselves.
>
> The overwhelming imperative for our time, for our culture, for humankind, is a radically new beginning that must be rigorously non-violent.
>
> And as well as cutting down the great cankers of oppression of the human being, we are called to build up communities of the nonviolent... communities on all levels that are tangible so that no-one feels alone, yet are not deluded into the false community of tribal imprisonment.

> Each generation must ask the questions anew, find the answers anew. Freedom is always fresh or it is not freedom. Only action, testing our abilities to deal with our own frustrations, helping each other through the minefield, may make us better at behaving nonviolently.
>
> We are in danger of being torn apart between the bonds of our ethnic belonging and the powerful bond of conscience of the immediacy of the sacred. Now the practical question arises: what difference does it make if we behave as if life is sacred?
>
> We should NOT surrender to any other human being. The surrender involved is a surrender to our own individual truth, when we have perceived that we are part of a reality which is greater than ourselves, whether from mystical or pragmatic perceptions.
>
> The prophet is almost always killed or banished. But of much greater interest is the fact that nonviolence, rooted in an awe-filled reverence, has always been part and parcel of great moments of renewal.
>
> Our ethnicity fills the great need we have for belonging, to be part of the crowd. Ethnicity, therefore is neither good not bad: it is a powerful force for murder or for building the community.
>
> The culture of a nonviolent world will be one which seeks enduring beauty as the very texture of its everyday ethos. The role of non-violent pioneers of a nonviolent millenium is to distill what is true from our inheritance and to fashion for that truth the most powerful and the most beautiful expression which we can possibly achieve.[6]

Applying these ideas to the actual situation in the light of the *Frameworks* document he comes to an important conclusion: "The people of Northern Ireland CANNOT enter freely, by consent, into a relationship with anybody else until they have established a cónsenual relationship among themselves."[7] This is the heart of the matter.

The Prospect

If Ciaran McKeown is right, and I am sure he is, then everything turns on the present and future state of the 'consensual relationship' between the two communities. *As of now (Spring 1995) it does not exist*. The gap, if anything, is wider than ever and this is because of mounting fear in the hearts of Protestants, fear that they are being deserted by the British Government. Whether they are right or not about that is almost beside the point. The fear is felt. The fear will be acted on. That is what counts.

There is a strange mixture of feelings among the Republicans and Nationalists. There is euphoria at success in Dublin and Washington – they feel they are winning. Gerry Adams has proved himself a master of public relations. But there is a deep contradiction in their policy. They are committed to the unification of Ireland now i.e.

not as an aspiration. At the same time they depend upon Dublin and Washington's support and that emphatically does *not* extend to instant unification. They simply cannot have it both ways. If they stick to unification they will lose Dublin and the US – and the battle. If they abandon unification they will betray their own dead and cause mayhem in their own ranks. And that means Republicans killing each other. Over arms, prisoners, and the future of the RUC, the future status of NI and the presence of British troops, there is a whole series of matters of major dispute that can now be as divisive as they have been unifying in the past.

A conclusion? Peace, a lasting settlement, depends upon inter-communal consensus. What happens in London, Dublin, Washington is important, but at the end of the day it all turns on Belfast and Derry. If consensus means that Ulster will once more have to journey through the valley of the shadow of death then there will be such a journey. Yet at the same time there is such overwhelming support for the cease-fire from all sides that there has to be hope. But that hope has to be articulated by political leaders and there is no present sign that that is happening. NI needs a new leadership that will match the new imperatives of peace. There are small signs that it is emerging. Twenty-five years of contained sub-civil war is long enough. It means that the paradigm shift, the emergence of a new generation of leaders, becomes a factor of politics.

A change of heart, a change of head, a change of Northern Ireland identity to one that is shared rather than divided, these will come in time – and with them peace. The tragedy is that peace, non-violence, comes dropping slow.

Notes and References

1. Quoted by Conor Cruise O'Brien in the book mentioned P.7. (Dublin 1994)
2. *ibid* p. 99.
3. *ibid* p. 103.
4. *ibid* p. 104.
5. *ibid* p. 113.
6. *The Citizen* March 1995.
7. *The Citizen* March 1995.

Ted Dunn

Unity and Diversity in South Asia: A paradigm for Social and Economic Harmony

There is a delicate balance of opposites in nature between order and chaos, unity and diversity, individuality and community. If we fail to recognise these diverse laws of nature or to work in harmony with them, we cannot create a peaceful world order.

If this diagnosis is true our task is to find the right structure within which our diverse human needs can be harmonized to create something greater than the parts alone can achieve. Or, as John Donne observed, "No man is an island, entire of itself, every man is part of the continent". Gandhi implicitly recognised these objectives in a philosophy he called *Satyagraha.*

Structures are vitally important to encourage cooperation at every level, between individuals, villages, regions, and continents. Looking to the future of the United Nations we want a global organization that encourages and respects local and community aspirations to create that is known as "natural law" without which humankind cannot survive. Cooperation by its very nature creates respect for the rights of others, the only true basis of law, if only for reasons of enlightened self-interest. The reality is that idealism must be married to self-interest and, good administration to good structures that encourages respect for social, economic and political justice, if the law we seek is to be upheld.

Unfortunately Gandhi's ideas about nonviolence and self-sufficiency were ignored after his death in favour of large scale market-led industrialization and the manufacture of nuclear bombs. A rearmament programme was started because of the hostility between India and Pakistan over Kashmir and other bordering states. Any peaceful solution must deal with this continuing problem by dealing with causes. Far too often politicians respond to symptoms and attempt to suppress them by force. This may have the effect of suppressing the problem temporarily. Far better to change the underlying causes of poverty and war.

Today, the people of the Indian continent have the opportunity to return to Gandhian principles by supporting self-sufficiency within new structures based on the idea of regional peace and development programmes. Regional peace and development programmes would encourage each village and state to be self-governing within a cooperating largely self-sufficient South-Asian regional community embracing India, Pakistan, Bangladesh, Nepal and Sri Lanka. Something similar to the Council of Europe is needed where problems common to all can be overcome. The importance of self-sufficiency and self-government is that it would free the Asian governments from the stranglehold of the international financiers. That enables billions of dollars to flow from one country to another at the touch of a few buttons on a computer. Today no one country, rich or poor, is immune from this state of affairs. No one state can remain an island unto itself and therefore structures must be created to enable, and encourage, common problems to be overcome cooperatively for the benefit of all.

This policy could become a reality once the divisions that have plagued the Indian continent for so long are resolved especially over Kashmir. It is essential to encourage all states to express their own identity, but equally it is essential for them to cooperate for their mutual good. Cooperation cannot, however, be imposed from above but nurtured gradually within well-conceived regional peace and development programmes.

Cooperation, however, must be based on consent, not coercion. Idealism is not enough; it must be founded on a combination of wisdom, knowledge, practical experience, and enlightened self-interest, or it will fail. How then can we translate these laudable aims into today's political situation and in particular to the problems of the Indian continent?

Today the United Nations stands at the cross-roads, holding the destiny of the world in its hands, undecided whether to follow the way of high technology and consumerism that is unsustainable, or adopt Gandhi's philosophy of sustainable local democracy within a structure that embraces local, regional, continental and international affairs.

Economic survival by many people with legitimate selfish interests also stands in the way. The population explosion is also creating a land problem which, if it is allowed to continue at the present rate, will destroy all our hopes. This problem is too big to be dealt with here but suffice to say that many people concerned with the population explosion believe the answer is basically economic. Raising the quality and the standard of life for the poor people through Regional Peace and Development Programmes of self-sufficiency could be the answer.

Economic debts owed by South Asian countries to the West also forces them into accepting policies dictated by foreign governments, the transnational corporations, the World Bank and the International Monetary Fund (IMF). When this happens poor countries are trapped in a situation from which it is difficult to escape. Difficult, but not impossible, once it is recognised that one of the main reasons for poverty is the arms race, costing billions of dollars every year. Far from adding to their peace and security this expenditure only succeeds in generating fear and suspicion when the same money could be used to encourage cooperation and mutual aid, true basis of security.

We need new forms of education where wisdom can be linked to knowledge to create a living democracy in which a true understanding about the nature of peace can be taught, as the example of Denmark has proved. Financial help, similar to that provided by UNESCO to help the Auroville Village Community, by the UN to buy land and basic equipment to enable Asian countries to follow the teachings of Gandhi and other great teachers would also be most helpful.

The first step should be for the United Nations to encourage all the countries of South Asia to cooperate by offering them generous economic aid similar to Marshall Aid to enable them to create a South Asia Council (similar to the Council of Europe) and the newly created European Community of Small States. Unfortunately there is a world of difference between aims and achievement. Past history has left us with a legacy of too many fears, hates and suspicions to allow cooperation to happen easily. This is why well-conceived UN help is so important.

Understanding and improving relationships between all the South Asian countries, especially between India and Pakistan, should be given priority, because as long as enmity remains between them, huge sums that should be spent on other more desirable projects will be squandered on defence. The problem is a vicious circle of fear and suspicion that could be broken by the United Nations offering the South Asian countries, as a region, financial help similar to the Marshall Plan, an idea that encouraged Western Europe to cooperate and create the European Community after the Second World War; but it was only given on the understanding that all the countries involved cooperated and agreed about an economic plan for the region.

The rich countries may complain that the cost of something similar for South Asia would be too high and therefore the idea is unrealistic. Closer study, however, shows that giving regional aid would be a far more cost effective way of helping these countries than the present unsatisfactory methods provided by the IMF and the World Bank or individual governments. The United Nations Conference on Trade and Development, (UNCTAD) in a recent report (*Guardian* 16.9.93), for instance, has called into question the work of the International Monetary Fund (IMF) and World Bank by saying its effect causes "*more shock than therapy.*" Oxfam has also said "*the activities of the IMF are increasingly damaging*".

The reasons for the failure of present policies are partly because aid is given to support short-term market-led principles, and partly because of the belief that wealth is best created by large scale industrialization, inappropriate for a population largely dependent on its largely rural population.

Uncontrolled market-led principles, almost inevitably, cause unemployment and create conditions where individuals are dehumanized and treated as cogs in a machine. South Asia however, has the opportunity to lead the world and demonstrate an alternative way of life based on Gandhian principles of local self-sufficiency and the examples of many Ashrams and local communities such as the Auroville community, as described earlier. In other words, Gandhian ideas for dealing with the economy of South Asia would reverse the "trickle down" theory, which has clearly failed. Although the rich have become richer the vast majority of the population remain poor.

This lesson is gradually being learnt because, according to information from the World Bank, aid in future will be given to help the rural poor as a first priority. This is a welcome step in the right direction. Doubt remains however, whether it will be implemented. Self-sufficiency programmes do not need expensive technology from the rich world. The spinning wheel, rural education, good water supplies, tree planting, education etc does not provide the rich exporting countries with a market for their capital goods, or a financial return on investments. Aid is also all too often linked to armaments and large scale capital imports ill-suited to dealing with the poor peoples real needs.

The lesson we must learn from the past is that development programmes cannot be considered in isolation from peace and many other issues such as human rights. Regional programmes offer the best, and possibly the only way of integrating them all to ensure that all the many aspects of peace are considered within one plan.

The international community should also be more alert and sympathetic to the needs of South Asia by modifying GATT (the General Agreement on Tarrifs and Trade) during the next three years available for modifications. To insist, for instance, on enforcing copyright on scientifically improved seeds, compelling small farmers to buy their seeds each year from seed companies controlled by multi-national firms, is threatening to cause havoc to the rural communities, so much so that "on Gandhi's birthday, October 2nd over 500,000 people assembled in Bangalore to hear protests from across the developing world". (*Guardian* March 11th) Provision should therefore be made for Asian countries to protect themselves by encouraging self-sufficiency; only then can they have control of their own destiny.

International aid should be channeled through the United Nations Development Programme, or alternatively, a United Nations Peace and Development Fund specially created to initiate and integrate regional peace with development programmes. To ensure the programmes are successfully conceived and administrated the region itself should appoint a Secretariat, in cooperation with the UN, with personnel drawn from the existing pool of experts, but not politicians. These experts should be able to command the respect and support of the people of South Asia and are available from many UN projects and from charities such as Oxfam.

But aid must be on a scale adequate to provide the incentive for them to cooperate and pool their resources for their mutual gain. Disarmament and peaceful relationships would then become natural process. The aim should be to jump-start the economy of South Asia and put it on an ecologically sound long-term basis. Aid should therefore be seen as a once-only way of helping the region to cooperate over a 5-10 year period. It should therefore be given in grant form, not as a loan, because loans invariably increase the region's debt beyond its ability to repay.

Aid, as at present being given, also discourages cooperation because when aid is given to individual countries there is usually an unstated agenda underlying the aid programme. This agenda has in the past used the developing countries as pawns in the Cold War, especially when it came to voting in the United Nations. Often they have been victims in more than a hundred Third World Wars as the so called "great" powers struggle for spheres of influence. Even when given with the best of intentions aid has often resulted in allowing countries to switch their own social expenditure to the purchasing of armaments from abroad.

A blatant illustration of the misuse of aid funds happened recently (1994) when it was discovered that aid given to Malaysia was misused to build a £417 million pound dam, (that experts in the Ministry of Overseas Aid and Development said was not appropriate) provided that country purchased military airplanes from Britain – a clear case of short-term selfish interests overriding the long-term good. The same short-term interests have also led rich and poor countries alike, to incur huge debts that have almost crippled them and left a legacy of debt it is impossible for the poor nations to repay. .

The only resolution to this huge debt problem facing the rich and the poor worlds alike must be to "write off" these debts within well conceived regional peace and development programmes. Cancelling debts by itself is no answer, but writing them off within a concept that puts the region on to a healthy long-term peace and development programme makes sense to both the lender and the recipient of aid.

Long-term economic programmes should be based on essentials, such as, human rights, an understanding about what development means, including a process of disarmament and an assurance of efficient administration but always in accordance with the aspirations of the mass of the people concerned. Wealth would then grow naturally and organically from the bottom upwards. Aid given in this way would be beneficial to everyone, rich and poor alike. With full employment and cooperation between all the countries in South Asia peace could become a reality, saving many millions of pounds to help finance the development programme.

It cannot be stressed too often the reason why regional economic programmes are practical and cost effective is primarily because aid is only given to a region on condition the countries involved cooperate and formulate an agreed economic programme. Also, that they agree to support social, economic and political human rights, and begin a process of disarmament with a well qualified Secretariat to formulate and help to administer the agreed programme. All these aims could be implemented along the lines advocated by Gandhi based on self-sufficiency, education, appropriate development, and population control. In exchange for this agreement the UN Development Programme would undertake to provide enough money to help jump-start the Programme on a scale similar to the Marshall Plan.

If this policy was adopted most of the money for the development programme could be found by the countries of South Asia themselves from savings made from disarmament. This would have the advantage of giving the people a feeling that the economic programme was their own, and not one imposed from outside; they would consequently be more enthusiastic for the idea and give it their support. By concentrating on direct "help to the people" (similar to aid given by Oxfam) instead of "help to governments" aid would also be more effective. What is wanted is for relevant, appropriate or intermediate technical help, for example, for trees, clean water education and environmental issues of all kinds.

The cost to the rich countries of supplying these basic needs would be less than present aid programmes that often include military equipment which in turn only serves to perpetuate fear and suspicions between Pakistan, India and Bangladesh and Sri Lanka. It is possible that if aid was given for direct aid to the rural population in preference to high technological programmes, such as nuclear power stations, huge dams, and all the shiny gloss of the Western world, the cost of aid programmes could be less than the 0.7% of GNP agreed by all countries in the United Nations. Each region would then be in a position to plan for its own economic needs on sound principles. This is difficult at present as the levers of economic power rest in the hands of the international gamblers on the stock-exchanges who are able to switch billions of pounds at the touch of a button, regardless of its effect on the lives of millions of people.

More self-sufficiency would also make the rich countries less vulnerable to the effects of war that may happen abroad, as in the Falklands and Gulf wars when arms supplied from Britain were used against Britain. If armaments must still be supplied to countries abroad the rich countries should agree to pay a high tax on them to the United Nations as proposed by the United Nations Secretary-General in his Report *An Agenda for Peace*. This tax could then help to finance regional peace and development programmes.

Nor does it make sense to sell high technology goods to South Asia, forcing millions to work under slave labour conditions, to produce crops that can only be sold at unrealistic prices in an overloaded market. Far better to reduce the supply by concentrating on self-sufficiency. With a reduced supply in the world market higher prices for their primary products would result. A 25% reduction in the exports of tea, for example could increase its price on the world market to a more realistic level. Reduced exports may therefore result in increased income!

The rich countries should therefore revise their philosophy about aid based on market-led economics, to one of cooperation and self-sufficiency. Market-led economics may be efficient in the short-term, but in South Asia where millions live at subsistence level it may do far more harm than good. For instance, combining a field of corn with a combine employing one man may throw hundreds out of work. This may be acceptable when there is alternative work but totally unacceptable if there is no alternative and no social security. Reliance on technology in developing countries is also a very expensive option. Tractors rust away for the want of a washer, or a new hospital lies empty because there is not the money to finance its running costs. Development, in other words, is a very complex matter demanding the reform of the economy and the infrastructure of the country from school to factory to communications, and the establishment of hundreds of service stations around the country. Far better for the economy of poor countries to grow organically (farmwise and economically) from a base, and at a pace, it can afford.

Unregulated free trade, however, is threatening even the established well-heeled Western world. Today all big firms are increasingly looking around the world for the cheapest way of making their goods. Cheap land, cheap labour, no regulations, and possible subsidies. All these are available in the poor world. The result is that whole industries are leaving Britain in searching of a "quick buck". All it needs is for a few dozen experts to direct and install new factories abroad and thousands will be made unemployed in Britain. This process is inevitable under unregulated free trade.

It is therefore in the interest of all the world's regions to become more self-sufficient and able to control and plan their economies. Leaving everything to the free market may reduce the price per unit of production in the short-term but it spells disaster to all countries in the long-term. The highly praised GATT agreement may increase world trade, moving goods and food around the world at an increasing speed and at great cost in pollution terms but it is fundamentally flawed and must be modified to encourage regional and continental cooperation.

In South Asia it must be better to offer economic aid to encourage village communities to be self-sufficient by giving aid in *Grant Form* in yearly installments over a period of, say, 5-10 years within an integrated plan, with most of the money being provided by the Asian countries themselves. If this procedure were to be adopted it would ensure the full cooperation of all involved so that the money would be spent wisely and well. To safeguard against the misuse of money there could be an understanding that if the spirit of the said agreement was not kept, aid could be stopped.

It is to be hoped that at the end of 5-10 years the Asian countries could attain a sustainable and successful economy and perhaps be in a similar position to Spain today. Only ten years ago Spain, for instance, was regarded as a developing country but by 1992 it threw off its legacy of isolation and became a full member of the UN Security Council increasing its aid programme from 203 million dollars in 1986 to 1261 dollars in

1993 (*Spur* March/April 1994). No doubt aid provided by the European Community aided this process.

In exchange for such an agreement the UN would provide enough money to provide the incentive to encourage the Asian countries to cooperate. The sums offered, however, must be generous and on a scale similar to the Marshall Plan if it is to succeed. The cost would be less, in the long-term, than present aid programmes that do little to remove the causes of conflict and poverty and have often proved a waste of money giving the rich people a feeling of "aid fatigue". Far better to give aid to a region on the understanding that the countries involved cooperate and where there is some real assurance that aid would have a direct effect on the poor. Of even greater importance is the assurance of successful regional peace and development. If this idea were to be 'sold' to world public opinion aid programmes would probably be given much more support.

Regional aid programmes would also have the advantage of decentralizing the work of the UN to the regions thus making its work more efficient. At present the work of the UN tends to be concentrated many miles away in New York and Geneva with all its bureaucracy. The work of its many agencies is often uncoordinated and lack any comprehensive overall plan resulting in overlapping and inefficiency. Far better for the UN to have a permanent resident UN Commission for South Asia to initiate, encourage and coordinate all its activities.

Mr. Boutros Boutros-Ghali, the UN Secretary-General, in his Report (requested by the Security Council on January 31st 1992), *An Agenda for Peace* supports this view by saying:

'regional arrangements, or agencies, in many cases possess a potential that should be utilized in serving the functions covered in this report: preventative diplomacy, peace-keeping, peacemaking and post-conflict peace building Regional action as a matter of decentralization, delegation and cooperation with the United Nations efforts could not only lighten the burden of the Council but also contribute to a deeper sense of participation, consensus and democratization in international affairs.'

The much maligned multinational firms would also welcome regional economic plans because (from their point of view) it is always easier and better to sell goods to a stable region than to one that is unstable. They may no longer have the same freedom to impose their will as now but a stable and prosperous region would enable them to play a more constructive and beneficial role for themselves and for the people of South Asia.

If this policy could be implemented each village would have a vested interest in cooperating with other villages over matters of mutual interest. Only when the people involved feel they have a direct involvement in the life of the local community and indirectly to the life of the national government will they give their support to the idea of law. Ideally law should not be necessary but, human nature being what it is, law is essential. But law cannot be enforced by violence, as any successful policeman can testify. Once the cooperation of the people is withdrawn law cannot be enforced. As an old Quaker poster declares "force may subdue but love gains".

Conclusion

The ideal law we seek cannot be accomplished quickly but must be nurtured over a period of time. The role of government should be to act as a provider and coordinator about matters that cannot be resolved locally. These issues should be kept to the minimum and limited to formulating regional and continental law. A regional Community, or Council similar to the European Community or the European Council of Europe, should not seek power, especially military power, because power corrupts and absolute power corrupts absolutely. What we want is world law based on cooperation, self-sufficiency, and a nurturing of social, economic and political justice. Excessive power in the hands of the few undermines and destroys these essential needs.

South Asian countries should therefore seek to become a Community or Commonwealth composed of small states to create something similar to the Council of Europe where countries cooperate and become members providing they agree to accept, as a basis of membership, social, economic and political human rights, the only sanction being that of being excluded from the benefits of cooperation. The Council of Europe is based on this principle and has already established a remarkable record of success in the European Court of Human Rights. The European Union (the old Community) has also enacted many law enforcement procedures all of which have been observed for self-interest reasons without the use of violence. This example should be followed by the countries of South Asia.

Regional cooperation must also be seen within the context of restructuring the United Nations, especially with regard to international law and its enforcement. But law must grow organically based on a sense of justice; only then will it be respected and obeyed. This means including the right of individuals to take their own government to a court of law. This idea is not as far fetched as it may at first appear because it is already in operation in the Council of Europe's European Court of Human Rights.

International law should also rest on the idea of individual responsibility under the law as provided for under the Nuremburg Principles. These principles have been in force for many years but because there has been no international court to which individuals who have committed crimes may be taken the law has fallen into disrepute. This deficiency in international law may soon be rectified because the UN has recently appointed judges to bring to justice those individuals who commit crimes. If this new development in international law is given the political support it so desperately needs by the regions of the world, war could be outlawed.

Despite all the major set-backs and all the gloom and doom around us, there are many signs of hope for the future. We cannot suppress conflict by violence but we can strive for a harmonious world by understanding and then obeying the economic and moral laws of non-violence and the structural idea of unity and diversity.

Alison Williams

Gandhi and Global Governance

'We must *be* the changes we wish to see in the world'.[1]

Fifty years from the end of World War II and the founding of the United Nations, forty-seven years after the assassination of Mahatma Gandhi, it is difficult to believe the world's peoples have made any progress towards peace. At the end of the 20th century as at the beginning the poet could say 'things fall apart'. But in this paper I shall argue that such a negative view is not the only one a reasonable person can hold; and, more importantly, that choosing a negative view produces only apathy, if not despair, where a positive one can help us build a better world together.

Creating effective Global Governance is a challenge worthy of the greatest human gifts: intelligence, imagination, generosity of spirit; vision, commitment, disciplined and determined will power. In the world as we know it those gifts are usually corrupted in practice by individual and collective self-interest, mutual suspicion and hostility, greed and sloth. Better Global Governance will be the achievement of better beings, and it is here that Gandhi's example may be at least as influential now and in the future as it was in his lifetime.

A few months before his death, Gandhi was among some threescore world thinkers invited by UNESCO to offer their opinions of the draft Universal Declaration of Human Rights. The substance of his reply was contained in one paragraph:

> I learned from my illiterate but wise mother that all rights to be deserved and preserved came from duty well done. Thus the very right to live accrues to us only when we do *the duty of citizenship to the world.* From this one fundamental statement, perhaps it is easy enough to define the duties of Man and Woman and correlate every right to some corresponding duty to be first performed. Every other right can be shown to be a usurpation hardly worth fighting for.[2]

Duty before rights: an unfashionable dictum in the late 20th century. And a duty of citizenship to the world: a concept which is fermenting here and there but has yet to reach the critical point necessary for general acceptance.

In addition to these broad principles, we should remember Gandhi's Constructive Programme, and his Philosophical Anarchism expressed in the familiar quotation 'that government is best which governs least. . . .'[3]; and the political ideal of a Federation of Villages. B R Nanda summed up Gandhi's ideal society as

> a federation of small village republics providing for the essential needs of the community. Based on a thorough-going decentralisation of the economic and political structures, it was to reduce the temptation for exploitation from within and aggression from without. . . It was to be designed for specifically Indian conditions, and to respect *'the sovereignty of the people based on pure moral authority*[4].

And that recalls what Gandhi is still best known for: insisting upon moral means to achieve the moral ends; that is to say, wherever possible, nonviolent means.

In all these respects, I believe Gandhi's example and teaching are relevant to the quest for better Global Governance. They offer us a vision and some practical guidance. But how would Gandhian Global Governance cope with the ego-maniacal tyrants of the world, with weapons of mass destruction and the readiness of criminals and terrorists to take innocent life at will; with economic structures backed by political and military force condemning hundreds of millions to poverty? In short, what have Gandhi's example and teaching to say about the abuse of naked power? There will be no easy answer to this question, but it cannot be avoided. In facing it we can again learn from Gandhi's principled pragmatism, his readiness to compromise in hopes of achieving the greater good, and to admit and learn from his mistakes.

What is Global Governance?

'Governance' is a new term for the glossary of political science, usefully defined by John E Fobes, a retired American diplomat and UNESCO official, in a paper to the Club of Rome in June, 1985. Fobes said it was a reconceptualisation of 'governing' to mean order in society created and maintained by a spectrum of institutions, of which *government* is just one. *Global* governance was the task not only of governments as such but also of intergovernmental organisations (eg, the United Nations and its Specialised Agencies), non-governmental organisations (NGOS, eg the Red Cross, the Worldwide Fund for Nature and Amnesty International), and transnational organisations (eg IBM, Shell and Unilever). The global capital market and the global mass media are part of it too, as are citizens' movements all over the world.

Fobes welcomed trends towards decentralisation and away from hierarchical structures, and asked whether international NGOs were handicapped by having parliamentary or industrial models of organisation and management. Was there, he wondered, some way that their capacities could be utilised more effectively in the interests of all humanity while retaining their valuable quantities of freedom and flexibility?[5]

The report of the independent international Commission on Global Governance, *Our Global Neighbourhood*, should help the concept reach a wider public. The Commission, co-chaired by Shridath Ramphal (former Commonwealth Secretary General) and Ingvar Carlsson (recently re-elected Swedish Prime Minister), began its work in 1992 at a time of 'profound, rapid and pervasive change in the international system'.[6] The report offers an Action Plan to follow the analyses of earlier independent Commissions chaired by Willi Brandt on North-South Development (1980), Olaf Palme on Common Security (1982), Gro Harlem Brundtland on Environmentally Sustainable Development (1987), Sadruddin Aga Khan and Hassan bin Talal on International Humanitarian Issues (1988), and Julius Nyerere on the Challenge to the South: how developing countries can help one another (1990).

In September 1993 the then Executive Director of the Commission, Peter Hansen, addressing an NGO conference, said with a wry smile that he and his colleagues cursed the term 'governance' as it existed only in the English language. However, he went on, 'we all know more or less what is meant by it', and the question before the Commission was clear: how do we strengthen the international institutional capacity to achieve objectives? Would it help, for example, to strengthen the World Court, or to set up an International Criminal Court? What about a Code of Practice for Multinational Organizations?

The principles on which Global Governance must be based were also clear: transparency, accountability, and respect for democratic values. The Commission was not about to propose a 'tinkering' with existing structures, or to seek 'technocratically correct solutions' that would make work for a few management consultants. Neither were they exclusively focused on the United Nations, like the drunk who looked for his lost keys under a lamp post just because that was where he could see best. Nor had they any notion of a World State in mind. Quite consistent with Gandhian principles, they were determined that all the proposals would be 'embedded in a value framework', and that the word 'universal' would be used with care, respecting the diversity of people and cultures.

The Commission on Global Governance set up working groups on Global Security, Global Development and the Environment, and Global Values; each of which reported to a fourth, on Global Governance, when it had completed its work. Submissions were invited from wide range of institutions, organizations and interested individuals; and it is hoped that the Commission's Report will now be as widely distributed and discussed.[7]

The United Nations Organization

The United Nations System clearly represents the highest level of Global Governance the world has known – and equally clearly, it does not work well enough. Let us recall, first of all, what the United Nations was designed to achieve and the historical context in which it was created.[8] The purposes are set forth in the noble preamble to the Charter:

> WE THE PEOPLES OF THE UNITED NATIONS determined to save succeeding generations from the scourge of war. . . . to reaffirm faith in fundamental human rights. . . . . in the equal rights of men and of nations large and small. . . . to establish conditions under which justice and respect for (international law) can be maintained. . . . to promote social progress and better standards of life in larger freedom. . . .

Chapter 1 concludes its list of Purposes saying the UN was to be 'a centre for harmonizing the actions of nations in the attainment of these common ends' (Article 1:4). It was *not* to be an authority directing the actions of its members. That was made quite clear in Article 2:1 (which affirms the sovereign equality of member states); and 2:7 (which forbids the Organization to interfere in matters of domestic jurisdiction).

The UN Charter was drafted as the Second World War was coming to an end. It was signed on 26 June, 1945 and came into force five months later, on October 24th. Inevitably, it reflected the historical and political conditions of its time. It was believed that among the chief reasons for the failure of the League of Nations was the refusal of the United States to join. The new organization, therefore, must be acceptable to the United States and all other great powers.

As is well known, the Security Council of the United Nations gave permanent seats to five World War Two allies, expected to champion and defend a New World Order, and insisted that the five must concur on all important ('substantive') issues. The Permanent Five were: the United States, the Soviet Union (now Russia), the United Kingdom, France and China. Their permanent membership of the Security Council and their veto power are among the chief targets of would-be UN Reformers, within and outside the Organization.

Another aspect of the UN organization which is worth considering in historical perspective is its financing. 'Lack of resources' is the perennial reason given for the UN system's failures to meet the world's needs; 'lack of political will' in governments with disposable means is the given reason for the lack of resources. Without entering into labyrinthine detail, we can see how the UN's budget mirrors the economic inequalities of member states.

Assessments for individual members are decided by the General Assembly every three years on the recommendation of a representative 18-member committee. The first criterion for deciding the scale of assessments is a member's ability to pay, and that is calculated on the basis of national income, population size and income per capita. Accordingly, the United States' assessment in 1946 was 49.89% - nearly half the total budget. A revision some years later reduced the United States' assessment to 39.89% and introduced a minimum contribution for members of 0.04%. As membership increased, the scale was again revised until the United States was assessed for 25% of the budget (1974) and the minimum contribution was reduced to 0.01% (1978). Without the maximum and minimum ceilings which were agreed, the United States would be assessed for more and the poorest developing countries for even less than they are.

The significance of those figures is apparent when we realize that member states contributing a total of less than 2% of the budget can command the two-thirds majority in the General Assembly necessary to approve that budget, as the great majority of member states are among the very poor. In one particular case (the programme budget for 1986-1987), member states assessed for 80% either cast a negative vote or abstained[9].

Given those circumstances, the reader will not be surprised to hear that assessments for the UN budget are one thing and payments something else again. It is widely known that the United States, assessed for the highest amount, is the organization's largest debtor. As of 30th November 1994, member states owed the UN a total of $2 billion; over $500 million for the regular budget and $1.5 billion for peace-keeping operations. Of that sum, the United States owed a total of $666 million to the regular and peacekeeping budgets.[10]

Before leaving the question of UN financing, it is worth getting the relative cost of running the organization into perspective. The governments which pay most (a small minority of the membership, as we have seen) are most concerned with efficiency and cost-cutting. Listening to them, or their sympathetic media, one would suppose the United Nations disposed of vast resources with reckless extravagence and routine corruption. It is therefore worth noting that in fact the regular UN budget compares with that of the world's major cities, not the member states: something over US$l billion per annum. The organization is routinely dependent on voluntary and ad hoc contributions to keep going. Peacekeeping operations in particular are dependent on such voluntary funding; and as Brian Urquhart, former Under Secretary General responsible for those operations, has said more than once, one and a half days of the Gulf War operation in 1991 would have paid all UN peacekeeping costs for a year.

The question of how to achieve a more just and effective distribution of the world's resources is one of the fundamental challenges awaiting Better Global Governance. And the question of how to improve financing of the UN and other international institutions is an essential part of that greater challenge.

Enough has been said to indicate the difficulties inherent in an international organization of sovereign states set up to achieve global objectives. In answer to the currently fashionable view that it is all a question of 'management', one experienced member of the UN Secretariat pointed out that the UN's 'Enterprise Board' consisted of 166 (now 185) Directors, each with a particular set of interests and priorities. The challenge to 'management' is thus unique in its complexity.[11]

In spite of the difficulties, it is possible to close this section on a positive note, briefly calling to mind some of the UN's achievements. In geopolitical terms, the chief of these is no doubt its role in the relatively peaceful process of decolonisation since the Second World War, a process reflected in the surging UN membership. There were 51 original Members in 1945. Twenty years later, there were 118. And by December 1994 there were 185. The United Nations aspired to universal membership and has virtually achieved that end.

On the peace-keeping side, the UN has undertaken a long list of operations: some have been successfully concluded, some have been underway for decades, and many have been undertaken since the end of the Cold War.[12] Under the same heading, we should recall the occasions when leaders of great powers have used the United Nations to get themselves out of dangerous corners. To offer just two examples: in 1956, Eisenhower used the UN to save face when having encouraged the Hungarians to revolt against the Soviet occupation, he decided not to support them. 'The UN had failed to live up to its Charter' he claimed. And many will recall the ignominious end to the Gulf War, when Bush encouraged the Iraqi people to rise against Saddam and then, in the name of Security Council resolutions, failed to support or protect them. Conor Cruise O'Brien, a UN-watcher from its beginnings, recently noted the organization's 'unacknowledged role as scapegoat for the vanities and follies of statesmen'.[13]

Assessing the United Nations' achievement in the field of development is more problematic. Much has been attempted (and spent), but the misuse of resources has at times been scandalous, and evidence of well-founded progress is patchy. My own view is that the greatest achievement here has been to begin learning from past mistakes and promoting a new attitude.

Until the beginning of this decade, the UN's financial agencies notably the World Bank and the International Monetary Fund dealt almost exclusively with governments concerning their national economic stability and growth while other parts of the UN system were concerned with development as it impacted directly on people. But since 1990 the World Bank, at least, has acknowledged the Abolition of Poverty as a goal and now sets aside funds to mitigate the social effects of its Structural Adjustment Programmes. To the same end, it is now open to consultation with some of the voluntary agencies in the field [14].

Equally encouraging, the Secretary-General's Agenda for Development, presented to the General Assembly in 1994, has moved well away from the largely macro-economic and governmental focus which has made so little impact on human need. It opens with two brief assertions: 'Development is a fundamental human right. Development is the most secure basis for peace.' The concluding chapter contains another significant generalization: '*Development has to be oriented towards each person in the world*' The report discusses the economy as 'the engine of progress' and the environment as 'a basis for sustainability'. It contains sections on 'Justice as the pillar of society' and 'Democracy as good governance'. The section on participants in the work of development assigns national governments the primary responsibility, sometimes assisting one another on a bilateral basis; or assisted by the UN and its Agencies, by regional organizations, NGOs, private international investment, the academic and scientific communities and grass-roots organizations.

> such as religious communities, neighbourhood associations and self-help groups. As they address the needs of small communities otherwise often overlooked, the learning process in development flows not only to but from their direction.[15]

Since the publication of the Brundtland Report in 1987 the phrase, 'sustainable development' has become familiar. Following the first-ever World Summit for Social Development, in March 1995, the phrase 'sustainable *human* development' should become equally familiar. The passage just quoted points up the dawning awareness that development is not primarily a matter of 'national wealth' an abstraction which in concrete terms benefits very few – but of meeting the basic human needs of the many.

The Secretary-General's new Agenda recognizes the current obstacles to the development process. He describes 'a confining cycle' of resistance to multilateralism, to spending which may not directly serve the contributor's interest, and to participating in difficult operations of uncertain duration. He concludes the section:

> *Without a new and compelling collective vision*, the international community will be unable to break out of this cycle...[16]

So we come to what is probably the least-regarded achievement of the UN, but one which should have the greatest long-term significance: inspiring that 'new and compelling collective vision'; in a word, consciousness-raising. In the quietest way, known only to specialists and activists in every field, there is the work of documentation. The information about human life on this planet recorded by the UN and its agencies gives us a uniquely Whole View to complement the now famous photograph of the earth taken from space.

Then there are the Declarations, affirmations of standards all humanity may aspire to. There are the well known ones, such as the Declaration of Human Rights (1948); and virtually unknown ones, such as the Declaration on the Right of Peoples to Peace (1984), and the Declaration on the Rights of Persons Belonging to National or Ethnic or Religious and Linguistic Minorities (1992). A lot of dry words, you may think: but then think of Rwanda or Bosnia, Kashmir, Northern Ireland or the area of conflict closest to you. And remember the words in the preamble to UNESCO's constitution:

> Since wars begin in the minds of men, it is in the minds of men that the defences of peace must be constructed.

An informed belief in the human *capacity* to live in peace inspired the following affirmation, endorsed by twenty international scientists who specialized in a range of disciplines from psychology and anthropology through sociology and biology to behaviour genetics. Their Statement on Violence, produced under the auspices of the Spanish section of UNESCO for the UN's International Year of Peace, challenged 'a number of alleged biological findings that have been used... to justify violence and war' and concluded:

> . . . that biology does not condemn humanity to war, and that humanity can be freed from the bondage of biological pessimism and empowered with confidence to undertake the transformative tasks needed... in the years to come ... The same species who invented war is capable of inventing peace. *The responsibility lies with each of us.*[17]

So we are back with Gandhi, and the personal duty of 'citizenship to the world.' And back to the need for international institutions which allow us to perform that duty effectively.

United Nations Reform: Intergovernmental Approaches

'I would not want to live in a world that was not one world.'[18]

For personal 'world citizenship' to be effective, the worldwide institutions, governmental and non-governmental, must be representative and accountable, honouring from globe to neighbourhood the principle of subsidiarity. Decisions must be taken at appropriate levels, as close as possible to the people they affect and with maximum participation from those people. If this can be achieved, we may see a global 'federation of villages', a Gandhian utopia for the 21st century. But given the complexity of the task it should surprise no one that in fifty years the United Nations system has not yet 'got it right'.

The most significant reforms which have been achieved to date have been in response to the growing membership. That led to the enlargement of the Economic and Social Council and the Security Council as well as the General Assembly, which of course seats all Member States. And it required the successive alterations in the budgetary assessments referred to above.

The most consistent pressure for reform has concerned the UN Secretariat: those 'international civil servants', the bureaucracy the world's media so love to hate, also have the misfortune of being the one target all member governments can agree upon when cost-cutting is top priority. Over the decades, reforms affecting the Secretariat have been attempted and are still underway. Inevitably, they have been resisted by those whose interests were threatened and challenged by those who see the great powers, above all the United States, exercising a dominant influence.

It is also criticized by those who point out that the United Nations and the 15 Specialized Agencies, with a worldwide total of 51,484 Professional and General Service staff combined, have nowhere near enough people to do the work required of them. Those staff numbers, related to work for some 5.5 billion people on earth, are comparable to the civil service of the American state of Wyoming with a population of 545,000.[19]

Proposals for UN Reform, more and less radical, have come from a wide variety of sources: from within the organization, from governments and non-governmental organizations, and from sections of the academic world. Governmental proposals naturally reflect the diversity of their interests. The main pay-masters, a small minority of the membership as already noted, consistently press for 'greater efficiency'. And when a group of Ambassadors were appointed to consider UN reform in the late 1980s they concentrated on their own field – politics and diplomacy – and paid little attention to economic and social priorities, finance and budgeting, or human rights.[20]

At the present time, the governmental proposal which has the strongest support, and which will almost certainly bear fruit in the near future, is the demand for a restructuring of the Security Council. It is argued in terms of UN Democratization, and readers must judge for themselves how far giving the world's existing governments more equal rights would contribute to that end.

Security Council reform has been an item on the General Assembly's agenda since 1979; and it was the subject of a debate in December 1992 which concluded with a consensus decision to invite all member governments to submit their views on the subject by June 1993. Of 16 speakers in the debate, 5 were from Asia, 5 from Africa, 3 from Latin America and 3 from Europe. The preponderance of speakers from developing countries indicates their impatience at how representation on the Security Council had failed to keep pace with the growing membership. The argument that a larger membership required a larger Security Council had been accepted in 1963, with an increase from 11 to 15. But there had been no change since then, with the result that the ratio of UN members to Security Council seats became ever-greater. This was pointed out by the Ambassador for India who introduced the debate with figures which may be tabulated thus:

1945 (with 51 members)	1 seat to 4.6 members
1963 (with 113 members)	1 seat to 7.5 members
1992 (with 179 members)	1 seat to 12 members

The Ambassador for Malaysia analysed the Security Council seats in geographical terms as follows:

Asia	22 members to 1 seat
Africa and Latin America	17 members to 1 seat
Western Europe and others	12 members to 1 seat
Eastern Europe	10 members to 1 seat

With the fusion of Eastern and Western Europe in particular, he concluded, 'the industrialized countries... are glaringly over-represented in the Council, holding 4 of the 5 permanent memberships.'

Most of the speeches were devoted to such analysis and criticism. In addition, they answered the familiar arguments against reform: a somewhat larger body need not be unmanageable and it would have the advantage of being more representative and attracting more support. Nor need reform open a 'Pandora's Box' of uncontrollable dangers – only Articles 23 and 27 of the Charter would require amendment, as had been done in 1963. Several speakers warned that if the Security Council wanted the support of the wider membership it would have to adopt reforms that gave it greater legitimacy.[21]

Other proposals from an intergovernmental perspective come from international civil servants, in post or recently retired. The critique and recommendations of Maurice Bertrand, a Secretariat member writing in a personal capacity, are noteworthy. He offered three proposals designed to overcome inadequacies in the administration of global economics and development: there should be an Economic Security Council; the Secretariats of the UN and the Agencies should be under a single authority staffed by 'independent persons of distinction'; and the Specialized Agencies, each with its own brief – Health, Food, Education and so on – should be replaced by Regional and Subregional Agencies responsible for all the needs of their areas. These proposals were strongly resisted by the Specialized Agencies but are part of the on-going debate on UN Reform.[22]

They are largely compatible with the conclusions of four papers coauthored by two high-ranking Secretariat officials after their retirement. Brian Urquhart, already cited, was a member of the Secretariat 1945-1986 with special expertise in peacekeeping, and Under Secretary-General for Special Political Affairs 1974-1986. Erskine Childers, a member of the Secretariat for 22 years, retired in 1989 as Senior Adviser to the UN Director-General for Development and International Economic Cooperation. His expertise is in UN problems of coordination, development operations, and public communication and constituency building. As well as drawing on their own experience at UN headquarters and in the field, the authors read and consulted widely so their work carries considerable authority.

Their first paper, published in 1990, deals with the subject of World Leadership in the UN context. For the UN system to work to its full potential, they say, inspired leadership and managerial skill must be applied to a rigorous agenda. The Secretary-General and his or her colleagues must work as a team, and persuade the public and private sectors as well as governments to support them. To find 'the best possible candidates' for top UN positions, 'parochial, national, geographical or political considerations should cease to dominate the process'. The authors urge 'far more imaginative and wider search procedures', and argue that a policy of single-term appointments for a maximum of seven years 'would do much to energize and facilitate the search and appointment process.'[23]

Their second and third studies, published together in 1992, offer recommendations for a reorganization of the Secretariat, and pointers to how the international response to humanitarian emergencies could be strengthened. Concerning the Secretariat, they concentrate on the need to introduce intermediate levels of management between the Secretary-General and Departmental Staff. At the time they were writing, over thirty units were supposed to report directly to the Secretary-General who had also assumed significant functions in political and security work. As they say, the office of the Secretary-General 'cannot also cope with the task of detailed substantive direction, coordination, and follow-up of the complex work of so many units which the present structure imposes upon it,' so they propose five additional senior posts to distribute that workload.[24]

Their paper on Humanitarian Relief opens with the daunting statement that 'Major humanitarian emergencies are likely to become more frequent.' They quote Red Cross data to the effect that a significant natural disaster occurs somewhere in the world on average once a week; and on average every three weeks, 'a disaster which exceeds the response capacities of the country afflicted'. In addition to natural disasters come the human-made ones, actual and potential, of technological breakdown (eg Bhopal and Chernobyl), economic imbalances and war.

All emergencies contribute to the waves of displaced people within and between countries. The paper has a solemn warning for the world's 'Haves' about the phenomenon of Economic Migration: '. . . until North-South economic disparities are adequately addressed, uncontrolled mass surges towards the comparatively prosperous and luxurious sectors of the planet must be added to the list of potential major humanitarian emergencies.'[25] The authors are mindful, too, of the estimated 24 million people (probably far more) who do not fall within the internationally recognized category of refugees, usually because they are displaced within their home countries. As for 'recognized' refugees, this paper gives figures for 1951 (1.5m), 1980 (8.2m) and 1991 (17m). By 1993 UN sources gave a figure of 20 million and readers will not need reminding that it has continued to rise .

The challenge to 'governance' is by definition extreme in emergency situations, and the authors list administrative obstacles to effective response: a lack of prompt and accurate information, too few competent personnel, and a situation which requires intergovernmental and voluntary agencies to compete with one another for funds from the same citizenry and governments. The constructive chapters of this paper discuss how emergencies may be prevented, mitigated and dealt with, each section concluding with suggested Improvements.

In a section on Media Liaison, they accept the vital role played by press and television in calling attention to humanitarian emergencies. Good journalists recognize their responsibility to identify new crises as early as possible; and the UN needs to improve its facilities for conveying to them an in-depth, overall picture.

In conclusion, the authors say their proposals are necessary because the initiatives taken in recent years have been too haphazard. It was now urgent to pull into coherent shape, and make the most of, the valuable capacities that existed and so ensure that in emergencies the UN is able to 'anticipate early, initiate immediately, and implement seriously'.[26]

How the UN system as a whole may be pulled into coherent shape is the subject of their fourth and longest paper. The introductory chapter opens with the Gandhian quotation at the head of this section and affirms, very much in his spirit, that 'the only hope of effectively dealing with the world's major problems in the interest of all humankind is through the progressive development of *a working world community*.'[27]

There is no space here for the details of their analysis and proposals but three things are worth noting: first, the disproportionate scale of the UN system's task and the resources committed to achieving it; second, the need to bring coherence to leadership within the system; and third, the need to improve the UN's relationship with 'We, the peoples'.

In a section responding to the familiar myth that the UN is 'a vast, sprawling bureaucracy', they give a table of staff figures and the comparison with the state of Wyoming cited above. The UN Secretariat, they continue, has a smaller staff than the civil service for the Canadian city of Winnipeg, or that of the international advertising firm, Saatchi and Saatchi. As for the supposedly huge budget, the total for regularly assessed and voluntarily contributed sums including the recent soaring increases for peace-keeping and humanitarian relief comes to some $10.5 billion a year. That is a great deal less than the United Kingdom spent in 1993-94 on General Public Services, £12.6 billion[28].

In response to the need for greater coherence in leadership, the authors recall that the original intention of the founders of the United Nations was for the heads of all the Specialized Agencies to be in the same place as the UN Headquarters itself. Early plans for the New York site include a second skyscraper for the purpose, but for a variety of practical, historical and political reasons that plan was not followed. As a result, one or more of the Agencies have headquarters in Washington DC, Geneva, Berne, Rome, Paris, London, Montreal and Vienna. Urqhuart and Childers argue the case for returning to the original plan. If Pakistan, Nigeria, Brazil and - before long - Germany can move their capital cities, the practical difficulties would not be insuperable; and the contribution to coordination and coherence would make it all worthwhile. In reply to the argument that the trend of the age is towards decentralization, they say

> The decentralization that is needed in the UN system is not between its various headquarters but from them to regional and country levels. The headquarters structure has been decentralized for nearly fifty years without significant advantage, and with considerable disadvantage. A common location would in fact facilitate the needed decentralization to regional, subregional and country levels . . .[29]

Accepting their argument, I would add 'subcountry and neighbourhood' levels to complete the picture.

Turning finally to the section on 'We, the peoples' we find that, apart from the preamble to the UN Charter, the peoples are almost entirely overlooked by the UN system. Article 71 does provide for non-governmental organizations to have consultative relations with the Economic and Social Council, and about a thousand of them do, in one category or another. Many are also associated with the Secretariat's Department of Public Information. But there is no provision for NGOs to work with the General Assembly or the Security Council. In the post-Cold War world, the authors take note of 'a new dynamic' between the UN system and the NGOs which must be 'actively nourished and built upon' in order to give the UN the support base it needs for political will and funding.

As a means of involving citizens more closely with the UN structure, they support a Canadian proposal for a UN Parliamentary Assembly. That is one of many proposals to 'democratize' the UN which have been discussed within the non-governmental framework of CAMDUN (originally Conferences, now Campaign, for a More Democratic United Nations).

United Nations Reform: Non-governmental Approaches

The CAMDUN process has drawn together NGOs, academics and other individuals from around the world to consider ways and means of achieving greater accountability of the UN to its peoples. It began in 1989 as a project to hold a series conferences and transformed itself into a campaign in 1993. The first CAMDUN conference was held in New York in 1990, the second in Vienna the following year, regional CAMDUNs took place in 1992, and in 1993 CAMDUN-4 was again in New York.[30]

Among the 50 or more organizations sponsoring the conferences were national and international ones, large and small, well-known and little known. They included The Gandhi Peace Foundation (India), The Campaign for Nuclear Disarmament (UK), The United Nations Association of the USSR, and the Robert Jungk Foundation (Austria). This diversity of the CAMDUN network makes it a representative guide to non-governmental interest in the questions of UN reform and global governance.

Most contributors to workshop sessions represented some organization or movement: the Universal Esperanto Association, the Asian Committee for Peace-Solidarity and Human Rights, the Conflict Resolution Network of Australia's UNA, and The Teilhard (de Chardin) Centre, to name a few. Some participants were academics with expertise in electoral reform, voting systems and international law. Each conference was an assemblage of 'We, the peoples...' with a common interest in democratic global governance and a variety of proposals for achieving that goal.

World Federalism had the largest body of supporters at CAMDUN conferences, particularly the two held in New York. It seems to many Americans to be the natural completion of a historical process: if a group of statesmen could get together and draft the United States Constitution in 1787, why should not the Whole World now receive a constitution in the same way? The world should be ruled by law, and the law should be applicable to individuals, not nations or states. This approach has considerable appeal for highly rational individuals, often with legal training. For some, the merits of their case are so transparently obvious they cannot understand why it is ignored or rejected by others.

Among World Federalists there is another stream of opinion which doubts the feasibility of 'one step to democratic world order' through a Constitutional Convention. They favour instead a gradualist approach, through reform of the existing United Nations and its Charter. Supporters of the UN Parliamentary Assembly (UNPA), which is enjoying some influential support as noted above, are of this persuasion, with a proposal modelled on the European Parliament.[31]

A quite different institutional approach is proposed by supporters of the International Network for a UN Second Assembly (INFUSA). Designed and developed by the English medical doctor and peace campaigner Jeffrey Segall, it calls for a non-governmental assembly representing the world's people as global inhabitants to complement the General Assembly which represents us as citizens of a state. Where the General Assembly is roughly analagous to the upper house of most federal systems, with equal representation for each Member State, the proposed Second Assembly would be comparable to a lower house, with seats allocated according to national population. If, for example, they were calculated according to the square root of the number of millions, populations of up to 1 million would have 1 seat; of 100 million, 10 seats; and of 1,000 million, 32 seats. That formula could produce a body of about 550 seats to establish dialogue among the world's people, able in that context to focus on *common* concerns and objectives without the accompanying duty to defend any *national* interest. Supporters of the Second, or Peoples' Assembly want a body free from the political constraints inescapable in any parliamentary, and so governmental, structure.[32]

Article 22 of the UN Charter allows the General Assembly to establish 'such subsidiary organs as it deems necessary for the performance of its functions'. A Parliamentary Assembly or a People's Assembly could be set up through that provision. So could an NGO Assembly, or an Assembly to represent Transnational Corporations, ideas which also have their supporters.

Not everyone in the CAMDUN network is primarily interested in such structural reform, however. The Association of World Citizens (AWC), another of the main participating organizations, has a wider brief; one which would certainly have had Gandhi's approval. It is '*dedicated to building a global village* of lasting peace and justice required for the 21st century.'[33] The fundamental concept is that human beings share a common responsibility for the future of the planet. By declaring ourselves to be World Citizens, we do not disown our allegiances to family, town or nation, we include them in a complex loyalty to the earth and all peoples.

Modern communications technology gives us the means to express that loyalty and responsibility in active cooperation. Three of the current commissions of the AWC reflect the working groups of the Commission on Global Governance with a fourth on Alternative Economics 'to produce more accountable, effective, just and democratic economics for the 21st century.' The AWC support the idea of a Peoples' Parliament '*to provide a moral voice at the UN*', and the establishment of global governance 'through the creation of world law'.

World Citizenship and Global Governance: A Personal View

Throughout this text I have italicized phrases which taken together, introduce a summary of my own perspective on global governance and the relevance of Gandhi to that daunting task.

the duty of citizenship to the world . . . . . (2)

the sovereignty of the people based on pure moral authority . . . . . (4)

development has to be oriented towards each person in the world . . (15)

a new and compelling collective vision . . . . (16)

the responsibility lies with each of us . . . . . (17)

a working world community . . . . . (27)

dedicated to building a global village . . . . . (33)

to provide a moral voice at the UN . . . . . (33)

Each phrase has its own implications and I could understand readers finding the list full of contradictions; or thinking the selection was prompted by naive idealism, utopianism even; that it showed ignorance of political and economic realities and absurd optimism about human capabilities. Hoping for the patience of such readers, I ask them to consider the sources of the items on the list: Gandhi and a historian of Gandhi, a report of the UN Secretary General, a statement by distinguished international scientists, a study by two long-term international civil servants, and the objectives of one non-governmental organization. Granted, what they say reflects a degree of idealism, and optimism about human capabilities. Faced with the world including all its horrors, they persist in believing things could be different – transformed for the better.

I said in my opening paragraph that a reasonable person could hold a positive view of the world's progress toward peace and I believe that is so. If the world is full of horrors, is it not reasonable to strive for something better? If one's own Good Life is threatened by the misery of others, is it not reasonable to relieve that misery? Surely persistent labours to those ends are reasonable enough. And not merely reasonable, but consistent with the best of human potentiality: our gifts of intellect, heart and spirit.

Returning to my list of phrases, I acknowledge its implied contradictions between the individual and the collective; duty and rights; authority and freedom. Most debate on these subjects has been conducted as a dialectic of opposites, but over the last twenty years or so I have noticed an increasing tendency to reject the 'either/or' approach in favour of a 'both/and' one. Some opposites are seen to be complementary and not mutually exclusive. I associate this change with the simultaneous rise of the Women's Movement throughout the world, and with the Western world's new openness to Eastern ways of seeing things. I do not mean to suggest a clear causal relationship among these changes. I see them rather as reciprocal influences occurring as the Human Family reaches the threshold of a new maturity.

As evidence of that maturing, look again at the list of phrases from their diverse sources. Where at the beginning of human history we cooperated for mutual well-being with members of our immediate family and tribe, we are now trying to cooperate globally for the same end. At all stages of that history, as today, there will have been conflict, more and less brutal. And from all times we have the record of saints and visionaries showing the way to a destiny beyond brutality. Take for example the prophet Isaiah, in the 8th century BC:

> They do no hurt, nor harm, on all my holy mountain, for the country is filled with the knowledge of Yahweh as the waters swell the sea.[34]

And the Sermon on the Mount, which presents the moral ideal of Jesus: it is said to have carried morality to the sublimest point attained, or even attainable, by humanity; and Gandhi's admiration for it is well-known. I cite examples from my own Judaeo-Christian tradition, sure that readers of other backgrounds can find similar ideals in their own.

Better global governance, as I said at the outset, will be the achievement of better human beings. In Gandhi we find the example of a man struggling to improve himself and to make what contribution he could to improving the world as well.

Psychologists continue to affirm that human beings are greatly influenced by example, from earliest infancy, so it is worth reflecting on that of Gandhi: do we acknowledge a 'duty of citizenship to the world' and if so, what does it mean to us? Have we the courage to insist upon moral means when others do not? Can moral means involve the use of lethal weapons? Have we anything like the conviction Gandhi had about what was Right and Wrong? And are we as open to self-criticism and experimentation? Do we believe the world can be peaceful and just, a beautiful home for us all and a safe place to raise children? If so, do we accept some personal responsibility for attaining those ends? Do we agree with Gandhi that 'We must *be* the changes we wish to see in the world'.

The United Nations Charter, like the list of phrases at the head of this section, expresses the human aspirations to achieve 'a better life for all' through orderly cooperation. Getting those aspirations into words is still an early stage of the process of achieving them. Getting them into the consciousness of ever greater numbers of people follows. And while the words are written and spoken the efforts go on to effect the necessary changes in social, economic and political realities. The history of social change shows us that as public consciousness rises, the efforts made become increasingly effective, and that in turn further raises consciousness. Once again we see the operation of reciprocal influences.

But not all reciprocal influences are progressive. We need to consider here three problems which present the greatest challenges to global governance: the problem of power, noted in the introduction; the problem of selfhood; and the problem of complexity. The humane ideal would have us exercise power with love in the common interest, 'doing no hurt nor harm' to any living creature; and expressing selfhood in mutually beneficial and freely chosen ways. Human history shows power in all its forms monopolized by a few in their own interests, and selfhood too often expressed in domineering and destructive ways. Even in families and villages relationships fall short of the ideal, and in larger social units the abuses and conflicts tend to occur on a correspondingly greater scale. The problem of complexity allows us to deny that we are, as John Donne put it, 'involved in Mankind'. 'What can *I* do about it?' people often ask, and stop listening before they are persuaded by any answer. Equally unhelpful are those who deny the complexity and insist the solution is obvious, if only others had the wit to see it.

It is clear that vested interests, individual and collective, are among the chief obstacles to better global governance. Jobs, money, high living standards and status are enjoyed by the 'haves' determined to use the power they command so as not to become 'have nots' in a competitive world seen as the setting for a 'zero-sum' game: if they win, we lose. A saying attributed to the American President Lyndon Johnson is relevant here: 'they want what we've got and we're not going to give it to them.'

In a different context, we have political leaders who murder their opponents and terrorize their citizens to maintain power: according to Amnesty International's report for 1994, 112 governments torture and otherwise ill-treat prisoners. And they all represent signatories of the United Nations Charter. One military leader, aspiring to political office but defeated in an election, has continued a campaign of slaughter ever since. He is reported to be 'psychologically unable to accept defeat'.

With economic, political and military power grasped by hands determined to hold onto it, with many people 'psychologically unable' to serve any interests but their own, and with multiple crises of unprecedented scale and complexity, what sense is made by those phrases at the head of this section? In the midst of such Chaos is there any point in aspiring towards humane Order?

Here again, developments in the past two decades or so give grounds for hope – this time, developments in technology and the sciences. I am thinking in particular of the new science of Chaos and the even newer one of Complexity, both dependent on state-of-the-art computer technology to produce and manipulate the information. Holding to the fundamental assumption that the universe is ultimately coherent and comprehensible, scientists use the language of mathematics in pursuit of greater understanding of its physical laws. What studies in Chaos and Complexity are revealing is a world of self-organizing patterns, sensitive and responsive to the slightest influences: the familiar example is the fluttering of a butterfly's wing. And the area where creative change occurs is the fine line between no change (stagnation) and constant, random change (anarchy), known as the Edge of Chaos.[35]

The human species lives on that line; and as we grow in collective self-awareness we improve upon the organization of our lives. My chosen phrases express age-old values and aspirations, with origins in intuition and the deep unconscious but in our time becoming deliberate goals. They are no longer largely confined to the religious and philosophical domain but are finding their way into discussions of political, economic and military affairs. All our institutions are subject to re-ordering, re-structuring and re-definition of their aims and objectives.

Gandhi's continuing influence is apparent in the range of people who quote him still: in this paper alone they include a then Senator of the United States (subsequently Vice President), an Executive Director of the UN Environment Programme, and two senior international civil servants, recently retired. Gandhi's supreme contribution was his, 'moral voice' backed by example. It is for people alive today to build 'a working world community' and I have indicated something of the extent of the on-going labours to that end, at international and grassroots levels.

Looking to the future, the Commission on Global Governance has now published its programme of action. In September 1994, a 20-year programme of action was adopted by the UN Conference on Population and Development, meeting in Cairo. In March 1995, the UN World Summit for Social Development will take place in Copenhagen to produce another programme of action.

Accepting a duty of world citizenship each of us can, according to our abilities and circumstances, help to achieve those programmes. We can acknowledge that promoting human solidarity responds to the deepest law of our own being. And we can choose to play a constructive part in better governance wherever we are until, in time, what "We, the peoples" were determined upon has been accomplished at last.

Notes and References

1. Al Gore, *Earth in the Balance* 1993, pl4; also cited by Elizabeth Dowdeswell (Executive Director, UNEP) in London, 4/11/93; reported *New World* Jan/March 1994, p.8

2. *New York Herald Tribune,* 31/1/48 p.6 (Gandhi to Julian Huxley, first Director of UNESCO)

3. *Young India*; Madras, April 1915

4. B R Nanda, *Gokhale, Gandhi and the Nehrus*, 1974

5. Reported, CAMDUN briefing paper for Conference, 26 June 1994

6. Commission on Global Governance, Terms of Reference; *Our Global Neighbourhood*, Oxford University Press, 1995

7. Conference notes, CAMDUN-3, New York, September 1993

8. see diagram of UN System, Annexe 1

9. Joachim W. Muller *The Reform of the United Nations*, A Volume in the Series Annual Review of UN Affairs, Vol. 1; Oceana Publications Inc. New York, London & Rome; 1992

10. UNIC News Summary, 5 August 1994 - 15 December 1994. It is fair to add that during September 1994 the US made payments to both the regular and peacekeeping accounts totalling $577 million; reducing a debt which in July stood at $531 million (regular) and nearly $956 million (peacekeeping)

11. Margaret Anstee in foreword to Muller, op cit.

12. see list of operations, Annexe 2

13. Conor Cruise O'Brien, Faithful Scapegoat to the World, *The Independent*, 1 October, 1993

14. *World Development Report 1990: Poverty*, World Bank, 1990; Notes of Christian Aid Conference, September 1994

15. "Development and International Economic Cooperation: An Agenda for Development", Report of the Secretary-General, General Assembly document A/48/935 (6 May, 1994), paras. 233 (italics added), 145

16. ibid. paras. 240-242, italics added

17. Statement on Violence, Medicine and War, Vol.3 191-193, 1987 (published elsewhere as the Seville Statement)

18. Gandhi, Introduction to Childers with Urquhart, note 23 below 1994, p.11

19. Childers with Urquhart, note 23 below; 1994, p.2; and Annexe 3

20. Muller, op cit, p.50 Childers with Urquhart, note 23 below, 1994, pp26-28 UN Observer, June 1993 (Critical report of Boutros Boutros Ghali's first 500 days)

21. Question of Equitable Representation on and Increase in the Membership of the Security Council; 47th Session of the General Assembly (1992), Document Number A/47/PV.69

22. Muller, op cit, pp. 35-36

23. Brian Urquhart & Erskine Childers, *A World in Need of Leadership: Tomorrow's United Nations*, 1990 *Towards a More Effective United Nations*, 1992 Erskine Childers with Brian Urquhart *Renewing the United Nations System*, 1994 all published by the Dag Hammarskjold Foundation, Uppsala

24. Urquhart & Childers, 1992, pp.16 & 37

25. ibid, p. 50

26. ibid, p.85; quoting Jan Eliasson, then UN Ambassador for Sweden

27. Childers with Urquhart 1994, p.21 (italics added)

28. ibid, p.29. John Logue, in his testimony to the US Commission on Improving the Effectiveness of the UN, said the total budget for the UN system approximated that of the state of Connecticut (Philadelphia Federalist, February 1993). UK Treasury figures, 1993-94: General Public Services cover Legislative Organs, Financial and Fiscal Affairs, External Affairs, Economic Aid, Fundamental Research and General Services. The costs of policing the UK, 1993-94, were £7.7 billion.

29. Childers with Urquhart 1994, p.52

30. ed. Frank Barnaby, *Building a More Democratic United Nations* Proceedings of the First International Conference on a More Democratic UN, Frank Cass, 1991; ed. Jeffrey J Segall & Harry H Lerner, *CAMDUN-2: The United Nations and a New World order for Peace and Justice*, CAMDUN, 1992

31. UNPA Information Update No.1, March 1993

32. INFUSA summary, 1989.

33. *World Citizen*, Fall 1993, p.12 (italics added)

34. Isaiah 11:9

35. useful introductions for the lay reader: James Gleich *Chaos: Making a New Science* (Cardinal, 1987) M Mitchell Waldrop *Complexity: the Emerging Science at the Edge of Order and Chaos* (Viking/Penguin 1992)

Annexure 1
Diagram of the United Nations System

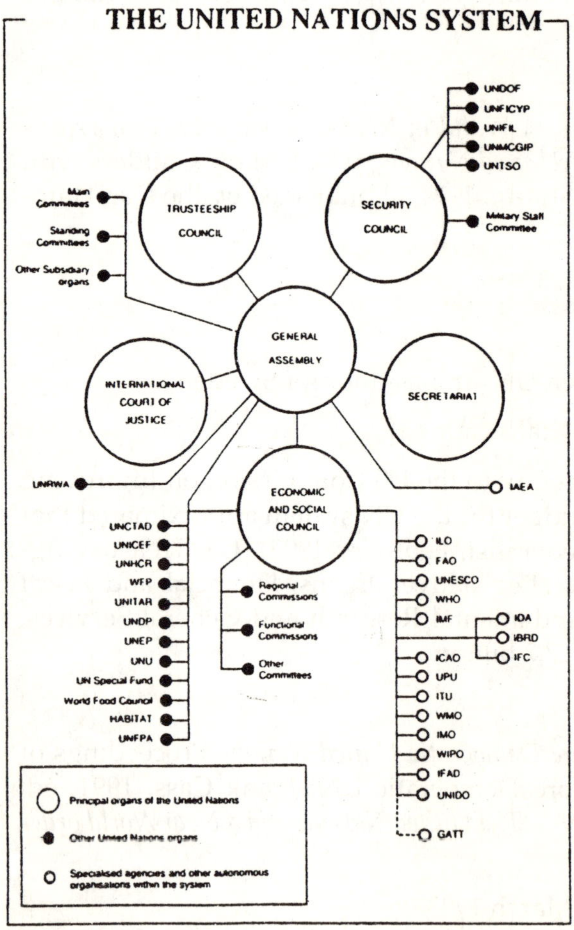

Glossary

ACC	Administrative Coordinating Committee
ECOSOC	United Nations Economic and Social Council
FAO	Food and Agriculture Organisation of the United Nations
G-7	Group of Seven most industrialised nations (Canada, France, Germany, Italy, Japan, United Kingdom and United States)
GATT	General Agreement on Tariffs and Trade
IAEA	International Atomic Energy Agency
IBRD	International Bank for Reconstruction and Development
ICAO	International Civil Aviation Organisation
IDA	International Development Association
IFAD	International Fund for Agricultural Development
IFC	International Finance Corporation
ILO	International Labour Office
IMF	International Monetary Fund
IMO	International Maritime Organisation
ITO	International Trade Organisation
ITU	International Telecommunication Union
OECD	Organisation for Economic Cooperation and Development
UN	United Nations
UNCHS (Habitat)	United Nations Centre for Human Settlements
UNCTAD	United Nations Conference on Trade and Development
UNDOF	United Nations Disengagement Observer Force
UNDP	United Nations Development Programme
UNEP	United Nations Environment Programme
UNESCO	United Nations Educational, Scientific and Cultural Organisation
UNFICYP	United Nations Peace-Keeping Force in Cyprus
UNFPA	United Nations Population Fund
UNHCR	Office of the United Nations High Commissioner for Refugees
UNICEF	United Nations Children's Fund
UNIDO	United Nations Industrial Development Organisation
UNIFIL	United Nations Interim Force in Lebanon
UNITAR	United Nations Institute for Training and Research
UNMOGIP	United Nations Military Observer Group in India and Pakistan
UNRWA	United Nations Relief and Works Agency for Palestine Refugees in the Near East
UNTSO	United Nations Truce Supervision Organisation
UNU	United Nations University
UPU	Universal Postal Union
WFP	World Food Programme
WHO	World Health Organisation
WIPO	World Intellectual Property Organisation
WMO	World Meteorological Organisation

Annexure 2
United Nations peace-keeping operations as of 24 February 1994

Title	Abbreviation	Area	Date Established	Date Terminated
UN Truce Supervision Organisation	UNTSO	Middle East	1948	Present
UN Military Observer Group in India and Pakistan	UNMOGIP	Jammu and Kashmir	1949	Present
UN Emergency Force	UNEF	Sinai	1956	1967
UN Observer Group in Lebanon	UNOGIL	Lebanon	1958	1958
UN Operation in the Congo	ONUC	Congo	1960	1964
UN Observers and Security Force in West Irian	UNSF	West Irian	1962	1963
UN Yemen Observation Mission	UNYOM	Yemen	1963	1964
UN Peace-keeping Force in Cyprus	UNFICYP	Cyprus	1964	Present
UN India-Pakistan Observer Mission	UNIPOM	India and Pakistan	1965	1966
Representative of the Secretary-General in the Dominican Republic	DOMREP	Dominican Republic	1965	1966
Second UN Emergency Force in the Middle East	UNEF II	Sinai	1973	1979
UN Disengagement Force	UNDOF	Golan Heights	1974	Present
UN Interim Force in Lebanon	UNIFIL	Southern Lebanon	1978	Present
UN Good Offices Mission in Afghanistan and Pakistan	UNGOMAP	Afghanistan and Pakistan	1988	1990
UN Iran-Iraq Military Observer Group	UNIIMOG	Iran-Iraq	1988	1992
UN Transition Assistance Group	UNTAG	Nambia and Angola	1989	1990
UN Observer Group in Central America	ONUCA	Central America	1989	1992
UN Observer Group for the Verification of the Elections in Haiti	ONUVEH	Haiti	1990	1991

Annexure 2
United Nations peace-keeping operations as of 24 February 1994 (*Contd.*)

Title	Abbreviation	Area	Date Established	Date Terminated
UN Angola Verification Mission	UNAVEM	Angola	1989	1991
UN Angola Verfication Mission	UNAVEM II	Angola	1991	Present
UN Mission for the Referendum in Western Sahara	MINURSO	Western Sahara	1991	Present
UN Observer Mission in EI Salvador	ONUSAL	EI Salvador	1991	Present
UN Iraq-Kuwait Observer Mission	UNIKOM	Iraq-Kuwait border	1991	Present
UN Advance Mission in Cambodia	UNAMIC	Cambodia	1991	1992
UN Transitional Authority in Cambodia	UNTAC	Cambodia	1992	1993
UN Observer Mission in South Africa	UNOMSA	South Africa	1992	Present
UN Operation in Mozambique	ONUMOZ	Mozambique	1992	Present
UN Operation in Somalia	UNOSOM	Somalia	1992	1993
UN Protection Force	UNPROFOR	Croatia, Bosnia and the Former Yugoslav Republic of Macedonia	1992	Present
UN Operation in Somalia	UNOSOM II	Somalia	1993	Present
UN Observer Mission in Georgia	UNOMIG	Georgia	1993	Present
UN Observer Mission in Liberia	UNOMIL	Liberia	1993	Present
UN Observer Mission in Uganda-Rwanda	UNOMUR	Border between Uganda and Rwanda	1993	1993
UN Mission in Haiti	UNMIH	Haiti	1993	Present
UN Assistance Mission for Rwanda	UNAMIR	Rwanda	1993	Present

Annexure 3

From Renewing the United Nations Systems,
Erskine Childers with Brian Urquhart,
Dag Hammarskjold Foundation, Uppsala, 1994, p.27

The staff numbers are divided into Professional ('Prof.') and General Service ('G.S.'). The table also distinguishes between those employed from Regular Budgets, who constitute the long-term worldwide civil service, and those employed from Extra-Budgetary funds contributed voluntarily for development and humanitarian operations.

Table 1
Staff of the United Nations System*

Organisation	Financed from Regular Budgets			Extra-budgetary (Voluntary Funds)			Total	
	Prof.	G.S.	Total	Prof.	G.S.	Total	Prof.	G.S.
United Nations	3,265	5,829	9,094	1,604	3,198	4,802	4,869	9,027
UNHCR	106	179	285	643	1,198	1,841	749	1,877
UNITAR		1		10	8	18	10	9
UNRWA	51	2	53	67	7	74	118	9
ITC	1		1	181	192	373	182	192
ICSC	18	22	40				18	22
ICJ	19	28	47				19	28
UNU				36,	65	101	36	65
UNDP				1,571	5,033	6,604	1,571	5,033
UNICEF				1,179	2,623	3,802	1,179	2,623
ILO	678	1,012	1,690	695	692	1,387	1,373	1,704
FAO	1,051	2,062	3,113	1,608	1,649	3,257	2,659	3,711
UNESCO	808	1,406	2,214	248	341	589	1,056	1,747
WHO	1,269	2,350	3,619	564	1,208	1,772	1,833	3,558
ICAO	248	350	598	231	223	454	479	573
UPU	62	84	146	25	1	26	87	85
ITU	240	395	635	135	99	234	375	494
WMO	104	124	228	78	72	150	182	196
IMO	88	146	234	34	47	81	122	193
WIPO	114	237	351	4	18	22	118	225
UNIDO	355	665	1020	305	458	763	660	1123
IAEA	684	958	1642	15	108	123	699	1066
TOTALS	9,161	15,850	25,011	9,233	17,240	26,473	18,394	33,090
GRAND TOTAL UN SYSTEM								51,484

Several important points emerge from these figures. The first is the very small size of the central professional-level civil service of the United Nations itself. Governments have authorized only 3,265 professional posts for the central UN Secretariat at New York, Geneva, Vienna, the five Regional Commissions, and its many other units around the world...

* As of the end of 1990. There have been no major changes since then. Data derived from ACC document on 'the Budgetary and Financial of organizations of the UN system', UN doc. A/47/593, 3 November 1992, and ACC/1991/Per/R.28.5 July 1991. Staff of the IMF and World Bank Group not included because not part of the UN common system.

Howard Horsburgh
Non-violence and Collective Security

When humans threaten one another, and feel that they need help to meet these threats, they can only receive that help from other humans, usually on the basis of mutual aid. This help is made possible by the fact that humans fear and distrust each other unequally, thereby making it possible for them to join with those whom they trust most against those whom they trust to a much lesser degree. If humans distrusted others equally, security organisations could not be formed.

Initially, before anything has been done to reduce distrust, people form alliances, giving and receiving assistance to and from other particular persons or powers in the event of any member of the resulting alliance coming under attack. Such an organisation is outward-looking in the sense that it is only designed (officially at least) to meet threats that come from outside itself. For example, in countries where street security is low, people tend to go about in pairs or even in groups, their expectation being that their joint strength will either deter would-be attackers or overpower them if they refuse to be deterred. Again, if countries go in fear of other countries, they tend to ally themselves with those powers which share their enemies. Thus, in the 1930s when many countries were increasingly afraid of Nazi Germany, some of them formed alliances with other countries, their hope being that the collective strength of these alliances might be sufficient to keep Germany at bay. Alliances, like the ones I have just mentioned, or NATO during the cold war, are often targetted against specific enemies. But this is not necessarily the case as is shown by street security alliances where the enemy may be any nameless stranger or group of strangers.

But alliances have many disadvantages. To begin with, they are not always possible. One cannot always walk with one's friends, and countries which fear other countries have not always been able to find suitable allies. Moreover, they often lack overwhelming strength. The three musketeers, with d'Artagnan's assistance, formed a powerful alliance. But Richelieu's guards sometimes formed a still more powerful alliance. Again, at the international level, alliances have sometimes been seen as threats to the security of the powers against which it is suspected that they are directed. They can then raise instead of lowering existing dangers. Furthermore, as distrust declines and some degree of pacification occurs, a simple division of powers or people into friends and foes ceases to be possible and it is more widely recognized that threats can come from anywhere -- from inside a security organization as well as from outside. And finally, as threats decline still further and pacification increases, it is widely felt that what is wanted is not so much a war-winning as a war-quelling combination of powers, and that this combination should include all possible members.

Street security, such as it is, offers us a possible model here: all those who journey through a city are at risk of attack, and ideally, they are protected by the great majority of other wayfarers, most of whom are to be thought of as possible sources of security rather than as threats to it. Between the world wars efforts were made to develop just such a system internationally through the League of Nations, the hope being that all the powers would belong to the system, and that in the event of any power being attacked by any other, all the other powers would ally themselves against the aggressor, quelling the conflict and also safeguarding the victim of the attack.

Such an organisation is a system of collective security. It seeks to be all-inclusive, having as members all those persons or powers who or which are qualified to join; and hence the threats it is designed to meet do not come from outside but from inside itself. Again, it does not aim at forming a victorious partnership but at building up such collective strength as to be able to protect all its members and to quell any conflict that may arise among them.

Unfortunately, the international experiment in collective security failed. This failure was due to many things including a lack of firm commitment to the League among its members, and to their having felt so threatened as to have formed alliances that cut across the system and reduced it to a farce.

Collective security has many advantages: its realism, its inclusiveness or non-divisiveness, its peace-promoting orientation. But, as so far described, it has a fatal disadvantage: it can only function effectively when the security stakes are low.

Suppose, for instance, that in the 1930s the principal powers in Europe had been, on the whole, of a peaceable bent, the Weimar Republic having thrown off Hitler and depression, and the Italians having thrown off Mussolini and his Fascist thugs. Some threats and counter threats may still have arisen. After all, the Treaty of Versailles would still have been unjustifiably resented, to mention only one possible source of strife. But if the great powers of Europe had not been easily divisible into groups, and had seemed on about equally good or bad terms with one another, they might have been willing to combine against aggressors. Similarly, if theft and violence were rare, the old hue and cry system might be an effective instrument of street security.

But humans have only attained to such levels of security in specially favoured times and places. Something more is needed, something which combines the advantages of the two basic varieties of security system, providing as much reliability as a good alliance and as much peace-promoting potential as a good system of collective security.

At the street level of security such a combination was achieved when police forces were instituted. Police forces are professional bodies of men and women whose task it is to come to the rescue of the injured and the attacked, to restore peace, and to enforce the law. They are not expected to serve these ends unaided: the citizen is still supposed to be there when needed -- to witness, to act in support of police efforts, to take the place of the police when, for any reason, no professionals are available. Clearly, what we have here is a two-tier system of street security, the old collective security system forming its lower (but indispensable) tier and a professional law-enforcing agency a new upper floor -- an addition which is supposed to give the law as many teeth as a powerful alliance.

In favourable circumstances, systems of this kind have produced unprecedented levels of security. But they are subject to many disorders. Whether things are going well or badly, at any given time, is most easily seen by assessing the relations between them. If these relations are good it is extremely probable that the system is working well; and equally, if these relations are bad -- as they often are these days -- the system is in danger of breaking down.

'But how are hostile relations to be avoided?' someone may ask. 'After all, the police are often bound to intervene in ways that make enemies'.

Yes, they are bound to make enemies in certain quarters: if they don't it's probably a symptom of widespread corruption. Crooks may very well see them as the enemy and hate them. But surely the relatively meek and honest majority should see them as their best hope of inheriting the earth?

The main virtues which a police force must have if it is to win or keep the affections of the general public are worth stating. First, the general public must have faith in its police force. This is mainly a matter of believing in the police force's good intentions towards the general public, believing that its personnel have been selected for brains and benevolence as well as brawn, and that it will not attempt to shield the rare officer who should not have been selected. This last condition is seldom enduringly fulfilled. For example, even in the democracies the police are often suspected of shielding their rogues and these suspicions have sometimes been justified. Second, it must be widely believed that the police are reasonably impartial and free from prejudice. For instance, if blacks have reason to believe that their tax dollar buys less security than whitey's, whitey's street security is bound to suffer. Third, -- and above all -- a law enforcement agency must not itself be perceived as a threat, as it would be if it were seen as an instrument of tyranny or revolution. In a democracy the good citizen glows with consciousness of safety in the shadow of a police officer, and even criminals may view him/her ambivalently. But in a police state, faced with a member of the Gestapo, knowing that you had honesty on your side would not be enough: you would also want to have party membership and an impeccable ancestry. Good police forces protect everybody, regardless of the extent to which any particular person may deserve to be protected. But they tend, in the middle and long run, to favour good citizens, ie. those who form the lower rung of the street security system. And so, ideally, a collective security system favours citizens who promise to add to the effectiveness of the system, considered as a two-tiered whole. Fourth, the system is not likely to function well unless risks are fairly low. For, if risks are high, witnesses refuse to witness and even Good Samaritans pass by on the other side, minding their own business when they should also be minding the community's.

Similar issues arise at other levels of security, and similar expedients for solving them have been either used or mooted. This is most easily seen by considering the process whereby alliances, as they become more and more inclusive, necessarily turn inwards and acquire the characteristics of a collective security system.

The American Civil War pitted two alliances against each other. The winning alliance, by overcoming bitterness and building up the singleness of the U.S., slowly turned into both a wider alliance and also a system of collective security. In relation to Britain or France it was a wider alliance. But in relation to its own affairs it became a system of collective security as soon as it came to be recognised that federal forces would intervene to crush any interstate violence regardless of the identity of the belligerents.

A similar process may be taking place internationally at the present time – in spite of all the wars which are also being fought. NATO, the West's present instrument of security, was founded in 1949 to meet the threat of the Soviet Union's military power. But now, with the collapse of the USSR and the emergence of several new states in Eastern Europe, it seems on the brink of acquiring new members. To avoid discrimination this enlargement of NATO is likely to precipitate a set of conditions that must be satisfied by those powers aspiring to membership. This in turn opens up the possibility of all the major powers of the world eventually becoming members of the same alliance. At that point, if it is ever reached, the alliance must become inward-looking, expecting such threats as still arise to come from disputes among its members and not from outside itself, thereby becoming primarily a system of collective security.

But what kind of system would it be? One tier or two? Like the system that proved futile in the '30s, or like an efficient police force, complete with a unified international army that is strong enough to deter or to quell all comers? At the present time couldn't the alliance go in either direction? But aren't there also good reasons (including the organisation of joint exercises and a unified system of command) for believing that something truly international is emerging, and that genuine planetary forces, buttressed by new loyalties, may eventually come into existence?

It should also be recognized that the role of armed forces has been significantly changed in recent years. Admittedly, they are still trained primarily for armed combat. But much of the work that they have been undertaking has been of a pacificatory and humanitarian nature -- and work of these kinds seems likely, ever increasingly, to become their principal business.

Except occasionally, at the street level of security, the alliance is clearly not an appropriate instrument of the non-violent. Its victory orientation, together with several other things that I have already noted, amply support this conclusion.

'But are systems of collective security any better? They, too, are violent, and potentially they are as violent as a military alliance. An international army -- for that's what we're really talking about -- would use the same weapons, and use them just as murderously'. All this is true. But it does not take account of the power to deter which would be exercised by a well-constituted international army. Armed resistance would be very rare, and if it occurred, one-sidedness would probably ensure that it would be of brief duration. Again, international armed forces would be in a position to impose disarmament on the whole planet, thereby ensuring its gradual pacification.

The non-violent are specially fitted to make certain vital contributions to such developments. They are naturally suited to the task of encouraging wider loyalties that transcend the nation-state -- loyalties similar to those which may be forming in response to customs unions, real and proposed. Again, the non-violent should be particularly concerned to promote enquiries into non-violent sanctions, how they can be made more effective, and what it is, here and now, which is preventing them from being as decisive as was once hoped. Finally, the non-violent movement has a special responsibility to end, or at least to reduce, the utterly vile armaments trade -- a trade that, even in the last few years, has been responsible for the deaths of millions in Somalia and Rwanda. It is true that without modern weapons tribal warfare may still have broken out in these countries. But the scale of death and human suffering would have been vastly less, and it would have been much easier for international forces to intervene since they could not have been seriously resisted.

These are the tasks which are open to the non-violent while they remain a small minority in all parts of the world. But if, at some future date, a particular country were to commit itself to non-violence, much more would be possible.

The gun is now the worst of social pollutants. If a non-violent country acted with uncompromising firmness on this issue, the effect on street security would be enormous. Murder would still occur occasionally: sharp instruments cannot be rounded up, let alone blunt ones. But it would be a noteworthy gain to cut back murder to isolated homicides. Also, when security stakes are low police forces can afford to act in a more conciliatory and considerate way -- especially if law enforcement personnel were selected as much for their non-violent is for their violent capabilities. Faced with officers who enforced the law with a light and humane hand the general public would really feel that its police force was wonderful, thereby giving the national community the stamp or hallmark of the good society: one in which the police force enjoys overwhelming popular support.

A sufficiently marked difference between the homicide rate of a non-violent country and homicide rates in other parts of the world, would be bound, under modern conditions, to attract a great deal of attention. Such a country would then be in a position to insist that its big lead in street security was due to the drastic measures it had taken against all instruments of multiple homicide. It is probable that this would precipitate legislation of the gun control variety -- perhaps only causing social ripples, but if carefully exploited, perhaps waves. If this legislation had little or no effect -- and mild legislation seems to do little -- it would only underline the case for really tight gun control -- and a world that is improving its methods of law enforcement is a world that is being pacified.

A non-violent country's defence system might also exercise a powerful influence on other countries. To begin with, the costs of non-violent defence would be minuscule compared with those of armed defence. Hence, if its defence system were successful, the country escaping attack and its methods gradually gaining the interest and attention of other powers, it is quite likely that it would find imitators. After all, one country, Costa Rica, has already disbanded its armed forces, and Switzerland, though it still depends for its security on force of arms, has actually held a national referendum on the subject.

If I seem to be willing to compromise on the issue of non-violence I am leaving a quite false impression. But it is vital to distinguish between what one advocates and is oneself willing to do, and what one recommends to people who reject non-violence and are in process of making choices involving violence. The non-violent must certainly witness to their belief in non-violence, and if they act at all they must act non-violently – these are the inescapable demands of consistency. But, in a world so overwhelmingly committed to violence, that is surely only the beginning of what the non-violent should do: for, above all, they must attempt to influence believers in violence, doing their best to incline them toward courses that seem likely to serve the unending pursuit of a more peaceable world.

A philosophy teacher of mine once said to a class I was in, 'There's no God, but there are still good and bad reasons for believing in Him.' This may sound paradoxical as well as witty. But it is useful in connexion with what I have been saying. For what he meant was: 'Although I don't believe in Him, if you start talking about God -- and you are all incorrigible believers -- I may still take part in your conversation. There are things still to be said and done when converts haven't been made, and you know that they are most unlikely to be made. In an age of faith the atheist must keep his mouth shut -- unless he thinks he's still qualified to say something useful and relevant, as my philosophy teacher thought he was. The world has chosen capitalism: it is pointless for socialists to quarrel with the way that most of the planet has chosen to run itself. If they have anything to say that may be heeded it must relate to the world in which they disbelieve. It must be aimed at making capitalism as tolerable as possible, recommending courses that are likely to abet the great ends underlying socialism. Similarly, the world has chosen the sword, and may well perish by it. But it is clearly the way that the world has chosen, and the non-violent can only make themselves relevant by recommending policies and alternatives which they themselves reject.

Consider the case of someone opposed to capital punishment living in a time when its abolition was still unthinkable. Certainly he must plead his cause and win converts, if only a few. But if he has the fate of prisoners at heart in opposing their execution, and society still insists on executing them, the least he can do is to try to influence his society towards more humane methods of execution--and similar things. The advocate who won't be listened to hasn't discovered a relevant way of intervening -- and can one really believe in a cause whose supporters cannot find occasion for valuable intervention even in a crazy society?

Reformers have to be interventionist if the world is ever to be reformed, and they cannot be interventionist if they only preach about causes to which the world of that time refuses to be converted. The world dictates the terms on which it really listens, dictates the policies it might be persuaded to adopt. To have any influence in the world, to reform it in any respect, you have to recommend changes that are against your own principles though not the principles of those to whom you are recommending them. If those who are making the decisions have narrowed the choice down to bad and worse, surely your own devotion to the good should not prevent you from recommending the bad to someone who would otherwise choose something worse?

Gandhi has been criticized for serious inconsistencies, above all for his recruiting efforts in the British cause during the First World War. I do not intend to examine these alleged inconsistencies, and I do not mean to imply that they are merely alleged. But I do wish to point out that they are exactly the kind of charges that one would expect to have brought against Gandhi -- who was, so clearly, an interventionist, and a man who had no intention of being side-lined by his idealist beliefs.

In Conclusion

Bhikhu Parekh

Is Gandhi still relevant?

Although Mahatma Gandhi has been dead for nearly four decades, opinions about him remain deeply divided. For some he was a man of action not thought, and was too hostile to modern civilisation to offer an adequate understanding of the nature of modernity let alone provide answers to its problems. For them his contribution as a man of action largely consisted in leading his country's struggle for independence. Some of his critics even wonder about this. They argue that his basically conservative, puritanical, pro-bourgeois and pacifist thought hindered the development of radical political movements, harmed the cause of the *Dalits*, burdened the Indian psyche with a paralysing sense of guilt about economic development, hampered the emergence of a strong and powerful state, created a national schizophrenia about the need to acquire and exercise political power, and perpetuated unrealistic and confused ideas about human sexuality.

Gandhi's admirers take a radically different view. For them he was a man of both thought and action, a rare combination. As a man of thought he saw through the malaise and madness of modernity, and offered an alternative vision that combined the best insights of both the pre-modern and modern world-views while avoiding the confusions and contradictions of the currently fashionable post-modernism. Indeed, argue his admirers, if Indians were to be asked to mention their greatest twentieth-century thinker, most would unhesitatingly refer to Gandhi and feel hard pressed to mention another. Gandhi was also a man of action, and his field of action was not only political but also personal. He led the greatest anti-colonial struggle in history, organised his deeply divided countrymen, gave them a sense of collective pride, forged tools of collective action that continue to stand India in good stead, and developed a unique method of struggle that combined the energy and effectiveness of violence with the peacefulness and humility of non-violence. At the personal or moral level, he restlessly strove to create a beautiful soul free of all that was petty, mean, coarse and vulgar, and successfully embarked upon a most heroic struggle to conquer all his senses including sexuality.

Some of Gandhi's admirers go even further and argue that we should not be surprised if one day he were to prove as influential, and be placed on the same footing, as Jesus of Nazareth and the Buddha. Einstein set the tone for such a view when he remarked in a tribute to Gandhi on his seventieth birthday: 'Generations to come, it may be, will scarce believe that such a one as this in flesh and blood walked upon this earth'.[1] Ralph Boultjens echoed Einstein's view in 1984:[2]

> Thirty-five years after the crucifixion of Jesus Christ there was no indication that Christianity would emerge as one of the great spiritual forces of history. Around 450 B.C., three decades after the death of Confucius, nobody could have predicted how influential his ideas eventually became. And around 1915, thirty years after Karl Marx, the Communist movement seemed doomed to be an inconsequential political aberration. Perhaps, then, we are too near Gandhi to evaluate his impact on history.

Although both assessments of Gandhi make valuable points, neither is fully satisfactory. Since I cannot here undertake their detailed critique, I shall concentrate on what I take to be some of his major theoretical and practical insights. They remain as relevant today as when they were first articulated, and any moral and political theory that ignores them is to that extent unsatisfactory.

I

Gandhi saw more clearly than most other writers both the interdependence of human beings and the ways in which systems of domination and exploitation were built up and sustained. He argued that all systems of domination rested on a profound misunderstanding of human nature, and wrongly assumed that it was possible for one man or group of men to harm another without also harming themselves. Human beings were necessarily interdependent and formed an organic whole.[3] An individual owed his existence to his parents without whose countless sacrifices he would neither survive nor grow into a sane human being. He grew and realised his potential in a stable and peaceful society, made possible by the efforts and sacrifices of thousands of anonymous men and women. He became a rational, reflective and moral human being only within a rich civilisation created by scores of sages, saints, savants and scientists. In short every human being owed his humanity to others, and benefitted from a world to the creation of which he contributed nothing, for Gandhi the most basic and incontrovertible fact about human existence. As Gandhi put it, every man was 'born a debtor', a beneficiary of others' gifts, and his inherited debts were too vast to be repaid. Even a whole lifetime was not enough to pay back what a man owed to his parents, let alone all others. Furthermore the creditors were by their very nature unspecifiable. Most of them were dead or remained anonymous, and those alive were so numerous and their contributions so varied and complex that it was impossible to decide what one owed to whom. To talk about repaying the debts did not therefore make sense except as a clumsy and metaphorical way of describing one's response to unsolicited but indispensable gifts.

Since the debts could never be 'repaid' and the favours 'returned', all a man could do was to 'recognise the conditions of his existence' and to continue the ongoing universal *yajna* or system of sacrifices by accepting his full share of collective responsibility. The only adequate response to the fact that he was born in and constantly sustained by *yajna* was to look upon his own life as *yajna* an offering at the universal altar, and to find profound joy in contributing to the maintenance and enrichment of both the human world and the cosmos. As Gandhi put it, '*Yajna* having come to us with our birth we are debtors all our lives, and thus for ever bound to serve the universe'.

Since humankind constituted an organic whole and since human beings were necessarily interdependent, every human action was both self - and other - regarding. Directly or indirectly, visibly or invisibly, it affected the collective ethos and shaped the quality of the prevailing pattern of human relationship. 'We cannot see this, near-sighted as we are', but it remained an inescapable feature of the necessarily interdepen dent world.,[4] 'Rot in one part must inevitably poison the whole system.' When human beings developed themselves they awakened others to their potentialities, and inspired, encouraged and raised them as well. And when they acted inhumanly, both they and others suffered. Even a trivial crime was enough to create a general sense of insecurity, to heighten mutual suspicions, and to lower the moral tone of the entire community. 'I believe that if one man gains spiritually the whole world gains with him, and if one man falls the world falls to that extent.'[5]

For Gandhi humanity was indivisible, in the sense that no man could degrade or brutalise another without also degrading or brutalising himself, or inflict psychic and moral damage on others without inflicting it on himself as well. This was so in at least three ways. First, to degrade others was to imply that a human being may be so treated, and thus to lower the expected level of the moral minimum due to every human being from which all alike suffered. 'To slight a single human being is ... to harm not only that human being but with him the whole world.' Second, to degrade and dehumanise others was to damage their pride, self-respect and potential for good, and thus both to deny oneself and the world the benefits of their possible contributions and to add to the collective moral, psychological and financial cost of repairing the damage they were likely to do to themselves and to others. Third, as beings capable of morality and critical self-reflection, human beings could not degrade or maltreat others without hardening themselves against the latter's suffering and cries for help, building up distorted systems of self-justification, coarsening their moral sensibilities, and lowering their own and the collective level of humanity. As Gandhi put it, no man 'takes another down a pit without descending into it himself and sinning in the bargain.' Since humanity was indivisible and since basic human interests were harmonious, every man was responsible to and for others and should be deeply concerned about how they lived.

Gandhi's concept of indivisible humanity formed the basis of his critique of systems of oppression and exploitation. Such dominant groups as the whites in South Africa, the colonial governments in India and elsewhere, and the rich and the powerful in every society, naively imagined that their exploitation and degradation of their respective victims did not in any way damage them as well. In fact they suffered as much as their victims and sometimes even more. The white South Africans could not deprive the blacks of their livelihood and dignity without suppressing their inner doubts and tender feelings, damaging their capacities for critical self-reflection and impartial self-assessment, and falling victim to moral conceit, morbid fears, and irrational obsessions. In brutalising the blacks they also brutalised themselves, and were only prevented by their arrogance from noticing how sad, empty and pitiable their lives had become. They did enjoy more material comforts, but they were neither happier nor better human beings. The colonial rulers met the same fate. They could not dismiss the natives as 'effeminate' and 'childlike' without thinking of themselves as tough, hypermasculine and unemotional adults, a self-image to which they could not conform without distorting and impoverishing their potential. In misrepresenting the natives, they misrepresented themselves and fell into their own traps. They also took home the attitudes, habits and styles of government acquired abroad, and corrupted their own society. Colonialism did promote their material interests, but only at the expense of their larger and infinitely more important moral and spiritual interests. For Gandhi material interests had only an instrumental significance, and were positively harmful when they hampered moral and spiritual development.

On the basis of his concept of human unity Gandhi arrived at a novel theory of social change.[6] He readily agreed that no dominant group ever gave up power without a struggle. However he was convinced that such a struggle could not be adequately conceptualised in terms of, and conducted by means advocated by, the fundamentally flawed traditional theory of revolution. In his view the fact that almost every revolution so far had led to terror, devoured its own children, and failed to create a better society was a proof of this. These failures were not accidental but sprang from the Manichean view of the world lying at the basis of the traditional theory of revolution. The theory neatly separated good and evil, and saw human existence as a mortal struggle between them. Since no cause could be nobler than the elimination of evil, everything done to achieve the latter including the use of massive violence was considered justified. The misguided belief that evil had no rights lay at the basis of revolutionary morality. Those identified as evil were deemed to have forfeited their humanity, and the concomitant claims on their fellow-men's understanding and charity.

Gandhi argued that far from being mutually exclusive, good and evil were conceptually and existentially inseparable. Pure good and pure evil were intellectual abstractions popularly represented by the figures of God and Satan. In the human world good and evil did not exist in isolation from each other and were contextual in nature. Nothing was good except in a specific context and within a specific pattern of human relationship; what was good in one context was not so in another; good turned into evil when pressed beyond a certain point; and what was good for one man might not be so for another. Given the scarcity of time, money, energy and emotional resources, a moral agent had to make choices, and sometimes had to sacrifice or forego good in order to achieve what in his view was better. Every moral deed had a price, and good was necessarily shadowed by evil. Furthermore, in a world full of evil, good could not exist let alone be effective without participating in evil, and no evil could last a day without some basis of goodness to give it strength and organisation. Since good and evil were inseparable and at times indistinguishable, they could not be socially separated and ascribed to different classes or groups. Groups were composed of men, each a bearer of good and evil properties. Even the apparently innocent victims of an unjust social order actively or passively, wittingly or unwittingly, collaborated in their oppression and bore some responsibility for their predicament. Mankind therefore could not be divided into two neat classes, one so fallen or corrupt that it forfeited its claim to humanity, the other so privileged that it had a right to punish the rest. This did not mean that some men or groups might not behave in an evil manner and deserve to be restrained, but rather that this reflected only one aspect of their personality and did not foreclose the possibility of their regeneration.

In Gandhi's view the traditional theory of revolution did not fully appreciate the subtle ways in which good suffered corruption in its struggle against evil. The theory located good in the ends of an action, judging the allegedly a moral means in exclusively instrumental forms. Since the so-called ends were in turn means to some other allegedly higher ends, everything ultimately got reduced to a mere means. Violence, mendacity, cunning, duplicity, manipulation of the opponent, and so on were all considered legitimate if used in the pursuit of good ends. By resorting to such means, good subtly became transformed into evil and its victory was really its defeat.

Gandhi argued that we needed a new theory of revolution that was free from the defects of the old and structurally protected against degeneration into terror. Such a theory had to be grounded in the three central principles of the unity of man, the indivisibility of means and ends, and a non-Manichean view of the world. It should stand up not just for the interests of the oppressed but for the shared interests of all including the oppressors, and aim at a society in which *all* alike led richer and more humane lives. For Gandhi imperialism damaged *both* the British and the Indians, and needed to be ended in the interests of *both*. Untouchability inflicted a grave moral and emotional damage not just on the untouchables but also on the caste Hindus, and its abolition promoted the interests of both. A revolution was justified only if the society it sought to establish did not replace one set of masters by another and put an end to all forms of class rule.

Like Marx Gandhi argued that revolutionary consciousness sprang from intense sensitivity to human suffering, and had a special affinity with the oppressed, its natural constituency and object of concern. Unlike Marx, however, he insisted that the oppressed were neither wholly innocent nor free from their share of human failings, and that the oppressors were not totally evil and devoid of their share of human virtues. Both alike were caught up in a self-reproducing system which debilitated and brutalised them all and from which they needed to be liberated. Being more deharmonised and brutalised than the rest, the oppressed were more acutely aware of the need for liberation and had to initiate the emancipatory process. However even as no oppressive system could last without the co-operation of its morally implicated victims, it could not be conclusively ended without the co-operation, however grudging, of its erstwhile masters. The latter had to be assured that the revolution did not intend to physically eliminate them, that it was concerned with their well-being as well, and that it recognised them as human beings entitled to decency and respect.

For Gandhi the means - end dichotomy lying at the heart of the traditional revolutionary theory was fundamentally false. In human life the so-called means consisted not of implements and inanimate tools but of human actions, and by definition these could not fall outside the jurisdiction of morality. Furthermore, the method of fighting for an objective was not external to but an integral part of it. Every step towards a desired goal shaped its character, and utmost care had to be taken to ensure that the steps taken to realise it did not distort or damage the goal. The goal did not exist *at the end* of a series of actions designed to achieve it; it shadowed them from the very beginning. The so-called means were really ends in an embryonic form, the seeds of which the so-called ends were a natural flowering. Since this was so, the fight for a just society could not be conducted by unjust means.

Gandhi's theory of *satyagraha*, the 'surgery of the soul' as he called it, was his alternative to the traditional theory of revolution.[7] It was not so much a non-violent method of achieving revolutionary ends as a novel way of *defining* the very idea of revolution. Like Trotsky's permanent revolution it was a form of gentle but sustained social pressure designed to break down emotional, ideological and moral barriers that different groups built around themselves, to unfreeze the flow of social sympathy, and to enrich and deepen their consciousness of interdependence.

Even as every community required a widespread sense of justice to hold it together, it presupposed a deeper sense of shared humanity to give meaning and energy to its sense of justice. The sense of humanity consisted in the recognition of the fundamental ontological fact that humanity was indivisible, that human beings grew and fell together, and that in degrading and brutalising others, they degraded and brutalised themselves. It constituted a community's vital moral capital without which it had no defence, and no resources to fight against the forces of injustice, exploitation and oppression. The slow and painful task of cultivating and consolidating the sense of humanity, and thereby laying the foundations of a truly moral community, was an essential collective responsibility, which the *satyagrahi* took it upon himself to discharge. He assumed the burden of the common evil, sought to liberate both himself and his opponent from its tyrannical automatism, and helped reduce the prevailing level of inhumanity. He overcame his opponent by refusing to see him as one, and by appealing instead to his sense of decency and their common humanity. As Gandhi put it, the old sages 'returned good for evil and killed it'. The *satyagrahi* took his stand on this 'fundamental moral truth'.

For Gandhi a *satyagrahi* relied on the power of suffering love. Confronted with untruth he sought a dialogue with his opponent. When this was denied or reduced to an insincere exercise in public relations, he took a stand and accepted whatever punishment was meted out to him. Since his sole concern was to evoke a moral response in his opponent, he did everything necessary to put him at ease and nothing to harass, embarrass, anger or frighten him. In the meantime he suffered the punishment without hatred or ill-will in the hope of triggering off in him a slow, intensely personal, and highly complex process of self-examination. The moment his opponent showed willingness to talk in a spirit of genuine good will, he suspended the struggle and gave reason a chance to work in a more hospitable climate.

With all its limitations which we cannot here explore, Gandhi's theory of *satyagraha* offered important insights into the nature of political *praxis*. Like the rationalists, he stressed the importance of rational discussion; unlike them, however, he realised that what passed as rational discussion was often little more than alternative monologues or a public relations exercise, and that sticking to it under such circumstances was an act of irrationality. Even as Gandhi was aware of the limits of rationality, he was acutely conscious of the dangers of violence. He knew that narrow rationalism and violence tended to feed off each other, and that the failure of rationality rendered violence morally respectable. Accordingly he sought to break through the narrow straitjacket of the reason-violence dichotomy lying at the basis of traditional rationalism. He imaginatively explored the uncharted terrain between reason and violence and arrived at novel forms of political *praxis*. His *satyagraha* was basically a new form of dialogue, a new conception of discussion, embedded in a richer and more realistic theory of rationality. Although not rational in the narrow sense of the term, it was not irrational either. It was a way of enabling human beings to realise their potential for rationality and goodness, and to reach and act on the basis of an inherently tentative and constantly deepening perception of consensual truth.

II

Gandhi's conceptualisation of political life and redefinitions of such central concepts as liberty (*swaraj*) equality (*samata*), citizenship (*nagarikata*), rights (*adhikar*), obligation (*dharma*) and tolerance (*sahishnuta*) also contain important insights and deserve close study. We shall take the first three by way of illustration.

Like many Hindu philosophers Gandhi took little interest in the concept of human nature, largely because he took a radically individualistic view of man. Each individual was unique, followed his own path of moral and spiritual evolution, and had a distinct *swabhava*, that is, a distinct and firm but relatively open and within limits malleable constitution or nature. It was true that all men shared certain *gunas* or qualities in common. However these were too general and indeterminate to account for the unique constitution of each. The qualities were also largely passive, capable of neither mechanical nor teleological causality, and unable to explain human conduct. Since the concept of human nature had no explanatory power, it had neither theoretical nor practical significance for Gandhi.

For Gandhi the individual's *swabhava* had two sources.[8] First, he was endowed at birth with a specific physical and mental constitution, temperament, tendencies and dispositions, which were all a legacy of his previous life. Second, he was a member of a specific community which deeply shared his habits, character, memories, ideals and values, and gave his personality a distinct tone and colour. His *swabhava* thus represented an unique blend of socially transcendental and socially acquired characteristics. It held him together, persisted over time, and formed the basis of his personal identity. Since it was the basis of his being and made him the person he was, it constituted his ontological foundation or truth (*satya*). The Sanskrit word *satya*, meaning truth, is derived from *sat* meaning reality or that which endures over time. The opposite of *sat* is *maya*, meaning illusory, ephemeral, transient or only relatively real.

The *satya* or truth of an individual limited and guided but did not predetermine his choices and decisions. As a rational being endowed with such capacities as introspection, critical self-reflection and choice, he was capable of becoming aware of some of his determinations, taking a critical and detached view of himself, and of changing himself. Many aspects of his constitution, however, were too deep to be excavated by even the most rigorous self-examination and remained beyond control. And some of those aspects of which he did become aware were often too deeply entrenched and tenacious to be changed without superhuman courage. Human beings were therefore neither absolutely free nor totally determined, but free within limits. The depth and extent of the limits depended on such factors as their capacity for self-analysis, will-power, and the kind of society in which they lived. A cooperative and relaxed society, whose members took an affectionate interest in each other, freely commented on each other's conduct and thus contributed to their self-knowledge, was more conducive to self-transformation and freedom than one in which they scrupulously kept their distance.

Not how to be absolutely free or fully autonomous but how to change in harmony with one's truth was the central moral problem for Gandhi, as for most Hindu thinkers. Faced with a ceaselessly changing world, the self must change or risk disintegration. And critical self-reflection discovered failings and limitations which a moral being should try to overcome. The central problem of human life was how to change and yet 'remain true to oneself', how to grow without losing one's ontological moorings, how to assimilate and integrate the new and constantly to reconstitute one's being. A wise man resisted attractive but impossible ideals, knew and lived within the limits of his constitution, and strove for goals that accorded with his 'truth'. The art of living consisted in knowing how to become a whole being, an integrated person, an individual in the strict sense of an undivided and unfragmented being.

Unlike the liberal concept of individuality which stresses differences from others and is necessarily comparative, integration or wholeness in Gandhi's sense stressed the individual's relation to himself and his manner of ontologically carrying himself in the world. An integrated individual had integrity and was always 'true' or 'honest' to himself. Individuality as the liberal understands it was a *necessary* by-product of becoming an integrated individual. It could not be consciously cultivated for to set out to be different from others was already to be determined by them, and only a self-reflective person was able to achieve it. An unreflective man, one not in the habit of reflecting on and reconstituting his being, was constantly in danger of becoming an eclectic collection of borrowed and discordant properties. Critical self-reflection was the source of self-knowledge, and hence a necessary condition of wholeness and individuality.

As an uniquely constituted and situated being, each individual necessarily saw and experienced the world differently and formed his own beliefs and opinions. To force him to act against his sincerely held beliefs was to violate his truth, to ask him to be untrue to himself, to plant a lie at the very heart of his being. He might be mistaken, but he must discover that for himself. Others might, indeed they had a duty to, argue with him and show him why he was mistaken. If he remained unpersuaded, they should leave him alone. For Gandhi respect for an individual's integrity or wholeness required that his views should grow out of his way of looking at the world and reflect his truth. That was why persuasion was qualitatively different from coercion. Unlike the latter, it respected and reinforced the other's wholeness, and ensured that the new way of looking at the world took roots in and grew out of his changed being. To seek to persuade someone was to cooperate in reconstituting his being. Gandhi thought that an individual could be legitimately compelled only when his conduct had grave social consequences and when he could not be deterred in any other way. And even then no euphemism or verbal sophistry should be allowed to obscure the fact that compulsion violated his truth or integrity and was a regrettable necessity.

For Gandhi freedom consisted in being true to oneself, in living by 'one's own light' and growing at one's own pace'. It was a form of wholeness or integrity. It involved knowing and accepting oneself as one was, recognising one's limits and possibilities, and making choices on the basis of that knowledge. If my way of life suited me and if I was content with it, I did not cease to be free simply because I had not chosen it. Or if I developed a desire for something but realised on reflection that it did not harmonise with my being and decided not to gratify it, I could not be said to be unfree simply because I had to restrain my desire. Freedom did not consist in choice *per se* as some liberals argue, nor in making choices considered to be higher as the idealists argue, but in making choices in harmony with and capable of being integrated into one's being. It had nothing to do with the number of alternatives available to the agent either. If they did not include the one he wanted, they had no significance for him. And if the one he wanted was the only one available to him, the absence of others in no way diminished his freedom.

Like many Hindu philosophers, Gandhi subsumed freedom under truth. To be free was to be truthful to oneself. To deny a man freedom was to deny his 'truth', to force him to be untrue to himself and to live by someone else's truth. For Gandhi the case for freedom was simple, and the same as that for truthfulness. Respect for truth implied respect for human beings as they were constituted at a given point in time, and for their desire to live by their truth. Love of truth involved love of one's fellow-men as they were constituted, and not as one would like them to be. It could never therefore justify 'forcing them to be free' or sacrificing them at the altar of an abstract and impersonal ideal.

Even as Gandhi radically redefined the concept of freedom, he redefined the concept of equality. In much of the liberal and socialist literature on the subject, equality is defined in comparative, contractual, competitive and individualist terms. As we saw earlier, for Gandhi men were necessarily interdependent, rose and fell together, and were born subject to nonrepayable debts. He located the idea of equality in this context. Relations between human beings were mediated by their membership of the social whole, and thus non-atomic and non-contractual in nature. Human beings grew and fell together, and hence their relations were necessarily non-competitive and non-conflictual. And since they were uniquely constituted and had different needs and capacities, they were inherently non-comparable and could not be treated according to a uniform standard.

Since society was necessarily a fellowship of unique and interdependent beings, the concept of equality had to be defined in non-comparative, non-competitive and non-atomic terms. For Gandhi it basically consisted in each individual enjoying full access to his community's economic, political, moral and cultural resources in order to realise his unique potential; that is, not an abstract human potential as determined by a philosophical conception of human nature or by an arbitrary moral standard, but his potential as an uniquely constituted being. As a progressive and reflecting being each individual 'grew from truth to truth' and strove to enrich, deepen and reconstitute his being. Equality of human beings consisted in all alike being able to do so. It did not mean that I should get what others get, but rather that I should get what I need for my development as I define it. It was not only in my interest but that of all others that they should treat me equally, for in degrading and demeaning me they degraded and demeaned themselves and deprived themselves of the contribution I would make as a rich human being. Equality thus was not a mechanical concept or a synonym for uniformity. It was at bottom a relationship of mutuality and fellowship.

Gandhi also redefined the concept of citizenship. As a political activist he knew that not consent, nor will, nor fear, but cooperation was the basis of the state.[9] Every state, democratic or otherwise, depended on the cooperation of its citizens, be it silent or vocal, passive or active, willing or unwilling. Since the state was an agency of action, their co-operation consisted in rendering it such specific services as carrying out its orders, paying taxes, and obeying the law. The state did not exist independently of its citizens, and was ultimately nothing more than a system of institutionalised cooperation between them. Since the state was a vast and complex organisation, they did not notice that it was their acts of daily cooperation that sustained it and that they were morally responsible for all it said and did.

Every government was tempted to misuse its power, and the democratic government was in that respect no better than the autocratic. What distinguished the two was the fact that one did and the other did not succumb to the temptation. And that was so because a democratic government knew that if it did, its citizens would refuse to cooperate with it. Notwithstanding all its institutional checks and balances, a democratic government could easily turn evil if its citizens became apathetic, vulnerable to corruption and manipulation, or lost their sense of moral responsibility. For Gandhi the virtues and vices of a government were not inherent in it but derived from those of its people. It was the coward who created the bully, the worm who encouraged others to trample on it, the morally irresponsible citizen who created a tyrant.

As a moral being the citizen had a duty to decide whom to give his loyalty and support and under what conditions. His self-respect and dignity required that his loyalty should not be unconditional or taken for granted. When a law was just, he had a 'sacred duty' to give it his 'willing and spontaneous obedience'. The duty had a dual basis. As a moral being he had a general duty to do or support good. And as a citizen he had a specific moral duty to the community into which he was born and rooted, by which he was profoundly shaped, whose benefits he had enjoyed, and to whose members he was bound by the ties of loyalty and mutual expectation. If a law was unjust or morally unacceptable, he had a duty to protest against and even to disobey it. To obey an unjust law was to 'participate in evil' and to incur moral responsibility for its immoral consequences.[10] In Gandhi's view it was a 'mere superstition' and an attitude worthy of a 'slave' to believe that a citizen should uncritically obey all laws. To be a citizen was to be co-responsible for the activities of the government.[11] And to obey a law was necessarily to support the government. Citizenship was not an autonomous and discrete role, but a mode of expressing and realising one's wholeness and humanity through the medium of the state. No human being could extend uncritical and absolute support to the state without forfeiting his humanity.

III

In the previous sections I discussed several important areas of Gandhi's moral and political thought and highlighted his central insights. Many of the insights are original to him and make an important contribution to our understanding of moral and political life. Like all such insights they were products of deep reflection on his experiences, and their persuasive power or 'validity' as he called it lay in their ability to illuminate and guide human experiences. He did not claim incorrigibility for his insights. Indeed he himself kept revising and reformulating them. He said that they represented the truth as he had discovered it, and were subject to correction in the light of new experiences. They were like a 'scientific hypothesis' which other individuals had to test against their own experiences and 'validate' for themselves. If they found them unhelpful, unilluminating or false, they should revise, even reject them and arrive at new ones of their own.

For Gandhi experience was the only true test of ideas and insights. And experiences varied from individual to individual. An idea stood alone, deriving its authority not from its creator, nor from the extent of its social support, nor from abstract arguments advanced in support of it, but solely from its ability to illuminate the relevant areas of human experiences. Even if he had been capable of it, which he was not, Gandhi was therefore deeply hostile to backing up his insights with a heavy philosophical ammunition bludgeoning his readers' intellect into submission. As a man who deeply cherished non-violence in life and in thought, he respected their intellectual and moral autonomy and advanced his views tentatively, gently, in great humility, and only to provide them with 'some useful material' in their solitary journey through life. As he put it, he was not a preacher, a teacher, a guru or even a guide, but an initiator of a conversation on moral and political matters and seeking not followers but fellow-seekers. In his view that was the only way in which free men should speak to one another, and the only morally acceptable manner in which moral and political philosophers should write about their subject.

Notes and References

1. See my Einstein's Assessment of Gandhi, *The Round Table*, 1991.

2. Gandhi: the other side of the balance sheet, in Krolik and Cannon, eds., *Gandhi in the Postmodern Age* (Golden, Colorado: Colorado School of Mines Press, 1984). p.15.

3. *From Yeravada Mandir*. (Ahmedabad: Navajivan, 1932) ch.s 1-5.

4. *Collected works*, Vol. 50, p.218; Raghavan lyer, *The Moral and Political Writings of Mahatma Gandhi* (Oxford; Clarendon Press, 1986) Vol.11, pp.552f.

5. *Young India*, 4 December 1924.

6. Raghavan lyer, *op.cit*. Vol.2, sec. VI

7. ibid., pp.298 ff.

8. *Harijan*, 2 June 1946 and 7 April 1946; see also preface to his *The Story of My Experiments with Truth* (Ahmedabad: Navajivan, 1956) and *Collected Works* Vol.50, P-216. I have discussed this more fully in my *Gandhi's Political Philosophy* op.cit., pp.92 f. As Shankara put it, the real nature or disposition of a thing constituted its truth (*Taṣya bhavah tattvam*)

9. Raghavan lyer, op.cit., Vol. 11, p.355.

10. *Young India* 22 July 1920.

11. *Young India* I December 1920, 1 June 1921 and 5 January 1922; see also *Hind Swaraj*, op.cit., pp.80 f.

Mahendra Kumar

Gandhi and Human Development in India

No theme has attracted so much attention in the post-colonial world as that of development. It has been an issue in ideological debates as well as a foreign-policy goal. It has provided a basis for international cooperation and has also led to the emergence of new areas of conflict and confrontation. It has been used as a convenient ploy establishing different forms of neo-colonial domination and has also facilitated a phenomenal flow of information and people from one place to another. It has been the major umbrella activity of the United Nations under which all other activities are covered. And it has produced numerous sophisticated theories of development.

This paper has a threefold purpose: (a) to discuss Gandhi's concept of human development; (b) to identify the distinctive characteristics of that concept; and (c) to examine the factors responsible for the failure of independent India to achieve a minimum level of human development of Gandhi's concept.

Whatever has been done in the name of development is considered deplorably inadequate. All through the several UN Development Decades, the concept of development itself has been changing, the emphasis has been shifting, and the strategy has been undergoing a constant revision. All this is reflected in the emergence of new areas of study such as "development dialogue", "development debate", and "development education". Opinion is growing that whatever development strategies have been followed so far, whether by national governments, regional groups or the United Nations, have hardly succeeded in ensuring even minimum socio-economic justice to the common man. It is, therefore, natural that right-minded people should now be addressing their attention to the question as to why is it so.

One attempt to answer this question whose relevance is now being increasingly appreciated is the one which is informed by the Gandhian perspective. This perspective makes a frontal attack on the contemporary development perspective. In all its fundamentals, this Gandhian attack on the contemporary development perspective is the same as the attack Gandhi levelled against modern civilization which he called "Satanic", in his *Hind Swaraj* more than eighty years ago. In fact, the contemporary development perspective represents a civilization whose Satanic dimensions are even serious and all-embracing. The contention of this paper is that the Gandhian angle provides not only a sound basis for identifying the ills of the contemporary development process but also a sound view of the true meaning of the concept of development itself as well as the strategy to be followed to achieve it. In order to distinguish the Gandhian concept of development from the usual run-of-the mill concept of development, one has to use the adjective "human" which marks out the Gandhian concept as a concept of "human development". Although Gandhi rarely, if at all, used the term "human development" or "humanism", a Gandhian theory of human development can easily be reconstructed on the basis of his views on the spiritual development of man and whatever he suggested as a strategy for achieving that spiritual development.

In the discussion that follows, it would be clear that the reconstructed Gandhian concept of human development would have four interrelated elements. One, development should directly be concerned with an overall development of the individual; two, individual development should be an agent and not a consequence of social development; three, individual development should cover the development of all men and women everywhere in the world; and, four, the process of achieving development should be "humane", that is to say that the development process should not involve in its trail the use of violence or coercion of any kind. In their essential, all these four elements are spiritual in nature. The first element discounts all those theories of development which over-emphasize the material aspect to the total exclusion of the moral-spiritual aspect, the second and the third elements emphasize the universal aspect of development, and the fourth element lends support to the concept of "sustainable development" which marks the latest entry into the lexicon of development debate. The reconstructed Gandhian concept of development would thus mean "human development humanely arrived at".

The Gandhian concept of human development has to be reconstructed along three major coordinates. The first coordinate is that it represents an enriched form of a particular ideological tradition in modern Indian political thought. The second is that whatever enrichment Gandhi provided to that ideological tradition was based on his own perception of the social crisis of his times. The third is that the Gandhian perception of the social crisis of his times, and the concept of human development resulting therefrom, are even more relevant in the global social crisis of the post-Gandhian period.

The Vivekananda-Aurobindo-Tagore Tradition

Irrespective of whatever influences Gandhi may have imbibed from the various ancient religious sources, the roots of the ideological tradition of modern India which was enriched by Gandhi go back to Swami Vivekananda who rejected the Western notion of power based on materialism and externality and who underlined the significance of the Indian concept of power. Vivekananda, thus, anticipated Gandhi's notion of soul force. "The power is all in the spirit," he said.[1] The spiritual power is far superior to what Gandhi later denounced as "brute force."[2] Vivekananda was of course not the first to emphasize the spiritual dimension of power. However, his genius lay in the fact that he signalled a significant and prophetic departure from the classical tradition by arguing that this spiritual power inhered in the masses. This clearly implies that the "only hope for the future of India is from the masses and that "the upper classes are physically and morally dead."[3] According to Vivekananda, the only path available to India to achieve greatness is the organization and coordination of the individual wills of people at large which, in turn, depends upon the cultivation of India's own inspired cultural and religious traditions which he called the "secret of power in India."[4]

Vivekananda's ideas influenced the ideology of the Indian National Movement in a significant way. This influence is clearly perceptible in so far as the Indian movement for independence under Gandhi treated. Western culture as inferior and emphasized the need for establishing a mass base of action with a simultaneous stress on social equality and reforms. Although Vivekananda's nationalism is sometimes characterized as aggressive nationalism, his emphasis on the spiritual basis of power and politics constitutes a distinctive contribution to political thought in modern India, particularly to the conceptualization of politics and power attempted by all the later political thinkers, including Gandhi. One of the foremost of these political thinkers accepting Vivekananda's conceptualization was Sri Aurobindo who asserted that the main idea governing all aspects of man's life has been the seeking of a true "spiritual self."[5]

As the "real intellectual heir of Vivekananda,"[6] Sri Aurobindo recognized the primacy of spirituality but attacked the monstrosity of the modern state which, according to him, promotes tyranny of "self-hypnotized mass over its constituent groups and units,"[7] usually manipulated by a small elite of demagogic politicians. This, he thought, was a realistic characterization of all States, whether one looks at Fascist Italy, Communist Russia, or even liberal Britain, France, and America. Sri Aurobindo viewed the history of the growth of the State as just a process of the development of a central authority and growing uniformity, regulation, and mechanization.[8] This is incorrect, for no centralized authority can ever represent, much less promote, the realization of the spiritual ends of man. Even a democratic system, Sri Aurobindo believed, tends to become a sort of march towards the annihilation of individual liberty which is an integral part of spiritual development.[9] He pressed that "the truest order is that which is founded on the greatest possible liberty,"[10] based on "the law of man's own divine nature."[11] In its essentials, Sri Aurobindo's philosophy reflects Vivekananda's vision of an ideal anarchist society, free from State authority and committed to promoting spiritual freedom.

Like Sri Aurobindo, Rabindranath Tagore also emulated Vivekananda's formulations by making a demarcation between society state and by associating the former with Indian civilization and the latter with the British civilization. Elaborating his view, he said: "England relies on the State for everything, from the relief of the destitute to the religious education of the public, whereas our country depends upon the people's sense of duty. Therefore, England has to exist by keeping the State alive, while we exist by preserving our social consciousness."[12]

Gandhi also accepted the basic distinctions between society and state and between Indian civilization and Western civilization articulated by Vivekananda and Tagore. As a matter of fact, he brought out these distinctions in a much sharper focus than his predecessors and even provided them with new, meaningful, and realistic justifications. Gandhi and Tagore both agreed that politics and law are "mechanical" and "artificial" and they usually corrupt and degrade men and that the price to be paid for it is self-sacrifice which alone could produce internal self-purification. But they differed on the issue of power. For Gandhi, power is of two kinds: one based on physical force and the other on truth force. But, for Tagore, "power in all its forms is irrational."[13] For the attainment of India's independence, Tagore favoured the use of moral power, not political power. In fact, he warned that even moral power becomes irrational and a temptation, once success has been achieved through it. Gandhi, on the contrary, believed that the practice of politics may be "wrestling with the snake," but it is only through politics that human society can improve itself. However, his notion of politics was different from the usual notion of power, in as much as he asserted that "my politics are not corrupt, they are inextricably bound up with truth."[14]

In broad agreement with Vivekananda, Sri Aurobindo, Tagore, and several philosophers of the anarchist tradition, Gandhi believed that the state represented the greatest hindrance to the realization of both individual freedom and social harmony. He said "The state represents violence in a concentrated form. The individual has a soul, but as the state is a soulless machine, it can never be weaned from violence to which it owes its very existence."[15] In an ideal society, therefore, there will be no political power, because there will be no state.[16] In the process of striving, to achieve such a stateless society, we may reduce the incidence and scope of violence and correspondingly widen the scope of individual freedom and voluntary action by decentralizing the authority of the State. Gandhi viewed the increasing centralization of power "with the greatest fear" because, he thought, it does the greatest harm "to mankind by destroying individuality which lies at the root of all progress."[17] He was convinced that "if India is to evolve along nonviolent lines, it will have to decentralize because centralization as a system is inconsistent with a nonviolent structure of society."[18] Therefore he pleaded for the "maximum possible decentralization of political and economic power" as the basis of restructuring the Indian society after it attains independence.

Refinement of the Concept of Human Development by Gandhi

The important point that emerges from the above discussion is that while Gandhi can be easily placed in the overall ideological tradition of Vivekananda, Sri Aurobindo, and Tagore as far as their general opposition to politics and power is concerned, he brought about a significant degree of enrichment to that tradition. This enrichment has several elements.

First, it moves away from the purely spiritual dimension of development and supplements it with the moral and social dimension. Thus, while the Vivekananda – Aurobindo – Tagore tradition would regard spiritual development as the essence of human development and would tend to advocate non-involvement in politics because of the evil character of the State, Gandhi would treat involvement in politics as an instrument for both spiritual advancement and social reform.

Secondly, as a corollary of the first, Gandhi would not accept the idea that the only source of danger to individual freedom is the state. Unlike his spiritual predecessors and also the classical liberal writers, he would insist that the assault to individual freedom comes not from state alone but also from gross economic inequalities, misdirected industrialization, an inflexible caste system, and colonial domination.[19] In other words, freedom from oppression and exploitation is also an essential ingredient of spiritual development. No one other than Gandhi understood better the stranglehold of oppression and exploitation and the human suffering resulting therefrom. A theory of suffering is, therefore, is as much a part of Gandhi's concept of human development as a theory of individual freedom and spiritual evolution.

Thirdly, Gandhi tried, more than anyone else in the present century, to actualize in practice what Vivekananda, Sri Aurobindo, Tagore, and many other sensitive thinkers had already rediscovered for the contemporary awareness. This awareness is about the existence of the fact that any oppressive system is characterized by a tri-faceted conflict among the oppressor, the victim of oppression, and the interpreter, the observer, or the 'onlooker' of the system. Apparently, each actor in this conflict tries to incorporate the other two. Herein lies Gandhi's genius, inasmuch as he asserted that the oppressor in a dehumanizing oppressive system is as much a victim of that system as the oppressed and that he, too, deserves to be liberated. Gandhi's emphasis on the victimhood of the oppressor himself and the need for his liberation, along with the liberation of the victim of oppression, constitutes a unique contribution to the theory of both human emancipation and human development. All through his life, Gandhi sought to free the British as much as the Indians from the clutches of the imperial system and the Brahmans as much as the untouchables from the degrading caste system. Behind this is reflected the belief that the perpetrators of evil and injustice deserve the same sympathy as do the oppressed and also the further belief that both the evil-doer and the evil-sufferer are amenable to change. The former needs human redemption and the latter human emancipation. Both human redemption and human emancipation become intertwined in Gandhi's theory of human development.

Fourthly, this kind of a human development would also constitute a stable basis of a new civilization because it would embrace non-exploitation as an integral part of a new world-view. It would make the task of reconstruction easier, both nationally and internationally. This aspect of the Gandhian concept of human development assumes particular significance in view of the fact that, as Ashis Nandy says, even after the formal end of an imperialist and an oppressive system, "the psychology of victimhood, and privilege continues and produces a second culture which is only manifestly non-violent or oppressive."[20] Within the framework of this observation, one can build a Gandhian theory of neo-colonialism which would suggest that neo-colonialism does not merely mean an informal domination of the former colonial powers on freed nations but also, and more importantly, the informal domination and exploitation of the new, local masters over the unprivileged local people. This form of neo-colonialism, which Ashis Nandy calls "the second culture", imparts the character of continuity to the whole task and process of human development. In that sense, the idea of human development has something in common with the idea of spiritual development that man's endeavour should be a constant search after perfection.

These charateristics of the Gandhian concept of human development are vividly reflected in Gandhi's critique of modern civilization. Gandhi made a frontal attack on the basic premise of modern civilization and made concrete proposals for re-ordering human society which would be free from the ills of modern civilization. He emphasized the uniqueness of "humanness" of all human beings and viewed modern civilization as a threat to this "humanness" which, in his view, could be promoted only through an ethico-religious pursuit of self-transformation.

The moral basis of Gandhi's concept of human development cannot be understood in isolation from his world-view. It is, therefore, necessary to appraise the moral foundations of his book *Hind Swaraj* in the context of his world-view.

For Gandhi, the propelling force of modern civilization is what he calls "the hunger for wealth and the greedy pursuit of worldly pleasures." In other words, the core of modern civilization is the craving for material aggrandisement and nothing else. The desire to amass unlimited wealth in a situation marked by resource limitations inevitably leads to violence at all levels. This means that every individual tries to prevent others from having access to the resources one wants for himself. Since modern civilization places self-interest at the centre of man's existence, the individual's entire effort focusses on acquiring as much riches as possible for his own use. This puts the pursuit of self-interest and the accumulation of wealth on the highest pedestal. Also, since the pursuit of self-interest is deemed as rational as well as desirable, any restraint on it is considered to be restrictive of the full flowering of individuality itself. If the pursuit of self-interest is recognised to be central in life, the pursuit of higher goals morality and spirituality gets crowded out of the individual's life. When the pursuit of self-interest becomes the central value, violence becomes the dominant characteristic of modern civilization and the only criterion for judging as to which desires to satisfy becomes a ceaseless struggle for acquiring more and more for one's own self. This, in turn, becomes a problem because resources are meagre and every desire cannot be satisfied without coming into conflict with others, with the result that there begins a process of what Gandhi calls "life-corroding competition" leading to exploitation, domination, inequality, and oppression. That is why Gandhi described modern civilization as something manifesting the maxims of "might is right" and "the survival of the fittest."[21] Modern civilization, according to Gandhi, "does not respect all life and, in its progress onwards, it has not hesitated to resort to wholesale destruction of even human life."[22]

The quest for material well-being leads to ceaseless activity as also to the annihilation of time and space. The growing hunger for material goods has wrought disaster for mankind because man's capacity to exploit Nature has not remained limited as it was before the onset of revolutions in science and technology which opened the way for technologically induced and sustained economic growth, based on mass production. This brought into operation the tendency towards physical and social mobility. The availability of quick modes of transportation has greatly removed the constraints on physical and social mobility. In the process of these constraints being overcome, the movement across space and time gets intensified. It has also made it possible for one country to expand outwards and colonise distant lands and people. That is why Gandhi detested "this mad desire to destroy distance and time, to increase animal appetites, and go to the ends of the earth in search of their satisfaction."[23]

More than everything else, Gandhi was greatly pained by the hypocrisy of modern civilization and argued that even though modern civilization promises to increase physical comforts, it fails miserably in doing so in any real sense. The projection of material acquisition as a desirable goal for everyone impels each individual to strive for an ever-rising level of bodily comforts and luxury and creates a situation where only a few can succeed, and that too, at the cost of millions of common people. Moreover, a large number of workers toil in miserable conditions for the sake of profits of the rich and, in the process, they suffer all kinds of oppression, suppression, exploitation, and indignity. That is why Gandhi points to the hypocrisy of modern civilization which, he thought, was "like a mouse gnawing while it is soothing us."[24]

In fact what Gandhi condemns in modern civilization is nothing more than the external manifestation of the Western world-view that became dominant in the seventeenth century with the onset of the Industrial Revolution. The source of Gandhi's critique of modern civilization is a world-view which is almost as old as human history itself and which has been eclipsed by the dominant Western world-view. Thus, at the back of *Hind Swaraj*, there is a confrontation between the two antithetical world-views. It is this confrontation that lends significance to *Hind Swaraj*.

Therefore, in order to comprehend the full significance of Gandhi's concept of human development, it is necessary to grasp the nature of this confrontation and see what the two antithetical world-views signify. The important point about these two world-views is that one makes a distinction between the world of here and now the real world and a conceptual world, while the other does not. The world-view on which modern civilization rests denies the existence of the larger world and the trans-individual authority as the source of norms and values. As a result, man emerged as a self-defining and a self-sufficient subject constituting society and using it for his own purpose. Also, with the denial of the existence of a larger order, the material world came to be viewed as devoid of any spiritual significance. Nature, then, obviously becomes a mere object for dissection and measurement by the observing mind. This marked a clear shift in the world-view which considered man as an integral part of a larger order and made man the centre of the universe. This shift, which Iris Murdoch calls a "broken totality,"[25] provides a significant clue to an understanding of Gandhi's concern for human development. Gandhi counterposed his own world-view in order to mend the "broken totality" and restore the fulness and wholesomeness of the human being. As stated earlier, Gandhi conceived the uniqueness of "being human" in terms of his ethical-religious pursuits. He recognized that man has the capacity to rise to a certain level to set on a journey to give free play to his moral and spiritual propensity for self-development or self-transformation.

Gandhi 's world-view projects an outlook which integrates everything into the fold of empathy, compassion, and fellow-feeling. However, to care for the world without turning to relate oneself to what is immediate and proximate is an anathema for Gandhi. Gandhi recognized the desirability of universalizing one's basic value commitment. But he also recognized the frailty of human nature and the strength of its attachments. The intimate relationship between the central pursuit of man means for Gandhi not the abnegation of the phenomenal world that surrounds us but the recognition of its compelling existence and its impingement on us and on our search for higher values.

To do good to others with the expectation of getting something in return is no morality since it is done not with the intention of doing good to others for its own sake but for advancing or promoting one's own interests. An action prompted by the motive of material gain, comfort, or personal happiness in another world is not moral. Morality requires rising above self-interest. Moreover, the desire for the pursuit of self-interest does usually conflict with and suppresses the desire for improving oneself and doing good to others. In order to be moral, therefore, it is necessary to discipline and regulate the desire for the pursuit of self-interest. This means transcending one's own powerful desires and aversions and making them subordinate to intelligence and thought purified by the process of self-transformation. It also means the taking of the decision to rise above self-interest against inclination, and against Nature. Such a decision must be conscious and must call for the application of will, intelligence, and thought. As such, such a decision cannot be mechanical and it must be free from fear or compulsion.

From the foregoing account it follows that Gandhi's objections to modern civilization are basically two: one, that it has stifled the process of the growth of human civilization by changing the moral-spiritual world-view; and two, as a consequence, it, by emphasizing the material aspect to the exclusion of the moral aspect, has created conditions of vulgar affluence for some at the cost of gross human degradation for many. At the highest level of generality, therefore, human development for Gandhi means nothing else but an all-round pursuit of man after such a state of affairs in which is established a proper balance between moral advancement and of the highest possible order and material survival at a reasonable level. In other words, the task of human development is the task of building or restoring what A.K. Saran calls "moral civilization."[26]

The Historical Context of Gandhi's Concept of Human Development

The historical context of Gandhi's thinking was India's struggle for human dignity and human rights; liberation of India from the bastion of alien and despotic rule, of women from the bane of male-dominated society, of the so-called "untouchables" from the tyranny of the upper castes, and of the Muslims from the induced apprehension of Hindu-domination under the cloak of democratic majority rule. The universal aspect of Gandhi's anti-imperialism has to be understood, first, as the assertion of the unity of mankind which British imperialism violated and, secondly, as the redemption of the human soul and as an effort to reveal the colonial man. Gandhi's anti- imperialism therefore was a magnificent protest against the soullessness of modern civilization.

Gandhi was not merely the philosophical heir of Vivekananda, Aurobindo, and Tagore. He was also the spiritual and political disciple of Justice Ranade and Gopal Krishna Gokhale. From the latter, he had learnt his lesson of the spiritualization and secularization of politics. While he was keen that the universally acceptable norms of ethics and morality must ever remain the basis of politics, politics must at the same time be delinked from religion and religious fundamentalism. He wished that the conduct of all those who are in authority should be guided by the common norms of morality and ethics so as to save the former from the canker of corruption. At the same time, he wished that every state allow the fullest opportunity to the followers of all religions. That is probably why he pronounced that "those who say that religion has nothing to do with politics do not know what religion means."[27]

In consonance with his own brand of religion, which emerged out of his extremely liberal Vaishnavite Hinduism and which he described as "ethical religion," Gandhi propounds the metaphysical and spiritual conception of human nature which by itself unfolds countless opportunities for all-round human development, for improving the quality of life.

In so far as Gandhi's concept of human nature is concerned, it is now widely known that he was deeply influenced by Greek political philosophy. He was so fascinated by its salient features that he went on to translate, for the benefit of his Gujarati countrymen, Plato's *Dialogues* into Gujarati. Like Plato and Aristotle, Gandhi too, described man essentially as a political and social animal. However, the unique characteristic of his political philosophy was that while he borrowed familiar concepts and phrases from wherever he could, he gave them a meaning which was so comprehensive and refreshing. For instance, when he called man "political," he meant that every human being has a potential for reasoning, by the continuous exercise of which he can immensely develop his personality and improve the quality not only of his own life but also of those who come in contact with him. This he can do by consciously discriminating between good and evil, just and unjust, right and wrong, non-violence and violence and choosing the former for ensuring an all-round human development on a durable basis. It is by virtue of his faculty of reason that man can choose, from a variety of available alternatives, the one which he feels is most conducive to human development.

It is, however, the metaphysical and spiritual input in his concept of human nature which not only makes it more comprehensive and positive than the Greek conception, but which also strikes a unique synthesis between the philosophies of the West and the East. To him, the basic nature of man is that he is essentially divine and good. Being probably the best and the most refined creation of the Omnipotent, Omnipresent, and Omniscient spiritual force of the God of Truth, man possesses, in the form of his soul, the little spark of this spiritual force, called the God of Truth. To Gandhi, what distinguishes man from other animals is not that the former possesses the soul force and the others do not, but that the former, like the latter, not only possesses the spark of this spiritual force, but, unlike the latter, he is also conscious of his unique divine possession. And, since man alone is aware or conscious of his divine potential, he can cultivate his divine attributes and mould his life and personality in accordance therewith. Man has the built-in potential of so developing his life and personality that he can make or unmake not only his own destiny but also that of his society, his polity, in fact the whole of the universe. He can so cultivate his virtues as to become someday a sort of mini-God himself and make his utmost contribution towards all-round human development.

The principal implication of man's divinity is that since the God of Truth is essentially "good," man who possesses the spark of this divine spiritual force is also implicitly "good". The greater the cultivation of this faculty on the part of man the greater would be the possibilities of all-round human development, through the unending chain of the steps taken to improve the quality of life.

In the direction of human development, not only can every individual make his own individual contribution, there is also immense scope for organized action at the level both of the state as well as voluntary organisations.

In so far as the question of the state effort in this direction is concerned, Gandhi did not find himself in agreement with the thesis of the Western utilitarian thinkers like Jeremy Bentham and John Stuart Mill. Gandhi had critically analyzed not only Bentham's thesis that the purpose of the state ought to be to provide "the greatest happiness of the greatest number"[28] (implying the material welfare of the majority of the people) as well as Mill's supplementary thesis of "the greatest good of the greatest number"[29] (meaning the welfare of the majority in all walks of life). Gandhi's first objection to Western liberal theory of the purpose of State was based on ethical grounds. He thought that the happiness or good of one person at the corresponding cost of another, whether of the majority at the cost of minority or vice-versa, would be immoral and undesirable. For, a "good" ceases to be "good," once it is sought to be realized at the corresponding cost of the "happiness" or "good" of another person. "Good" to be good must be the good of all. Secondly, the achievement of welfare in the economic or materialistic field at the cost of welfare in other fields of human activity would make the achievement of welfare an utterly imbalanced objective. Gandhi was unequivocal in rejecting the Benthamite as well as Marxian conceptions of human development as, in their own respective ways, they sought to define human development simply as human economic development. Gandhi goes beyond both of them and propounds his thesis of "total human development," i.e. improving the quality of man's life not only in the economic but in all walks of life.

Gandhi was also immensely influenced by John Ruskin's views concerning the theory of the purpose of state. In his celebrated treatise entitled *Unto This Last*,[30] Ruskin propounded his alternative view that the real purpose of the state ought to be the welfare of that section of society which is neglected, suppressed and oppressed, as no one needs it either to come into or remain in power. Hence, Ruskin thought that the state should strive to work for the welfare of the neglected minority. That would be indicative of the magnanimity of the majority towards the minority. However, Gandhi did not find himself in total agreement with Ruskin either. For, he thought that just as the welfare of the majority at the cost of minority would be sinful, the welfare of the minority at the cost of the welfare of the majority, too, would not only be immoral and undesirable but also unattainable. He asked the basic question that when the God of Truth does not himself discriminate between majority and minority, why should the state, which is the creation of God's creatures, human beings, discriminate between the majority and minority and strive to realise the welfare of one at the cost of another, especially in view of the fact that no group of people has ever been in perpetual majority or minority. In fact, the majority often gets reduced to minority and vice-versa. Moreover, the moment a government, which is elected by majority and remains in office so long as it enjoys the confidence of majority strives to realise the welfare of minority at the cost of majority, the majority would throw it out of office and its dream of serving the neglected minority at the cost of majority would always remain a distant dream, incapable of achieving the goal of human development. Gandhi interpreted Ruskin's views so as to make them look more humane. He said that what Ruskin really wanted was that while working for the welfare, good, or development of the people, the state should begin with the neglected minority, rather than remain confined to the development of the minority as that would make the entire state effort myopic. The significance of Gandhi's approach has been that he synthesized the views of both the majoritarians and the minoritarians, joining the 51% of the majoritarians with the 49% of the minoritarians or the 99% of the former with the 1% of the latter, and making it full cent-percent. In Gandhi's view, human development would be possible only if and when the state strives to attain the welfare of one and all, without distinction of majority and minority, and that too equally in all walks of life, rather than keeping it confined and restricted to the economic field, for, in the ultimate analysis, man is essentially a divine and rational being, and not simply an economic animal.

Thus we find the most striking synthesis of Western majoritarianism and minoritarianism resounding in Gandhi's concept of "*Sarvodaya*," the welfare of one and all in all walks of life. This, surely, is the most comprehensive theory on the basis of which the state apparatus can, in Gandhi's view, increasingly attain the goal of harmonious human development.

In his *Hind Swaraj*, Gandhi had also expressed his considered view that once human beings initiate the process of moulding their thoughts, words, and deeds in maximum possible harmony with their reason and conscience, i.e. once they start regulating their lives and activities themselves, their dependence on the State would slowly but surely indicate a declining curve. And, once that happens, probably in 9/10ths of our activities the state, as a machinery of coercion, would not be needed,[31] enabling the people to return to a stateless society, a self-regulated, soul-regulated, God-regulated, Truth-regulated polity, the *Ramrajya* or the Kingdom of God on Earth. Thus Gandhi, like Rousseau, romantically dreamt of realization of a stateless society through the agency of the ideal spirituo-secular decentralized democratic republic of his conception.

Though Gandhi thought of the distant possibility of a stateless society, he never discounted the necessity of corporate, organized, action on the part of voluntary organizations, working independently in various fields of life and activity. This would enable the largest number of people not only to participate at the level of executing social welfare plans and activities, but also at the level of decision-making and the raising of voluntary donations and contributions, rather than remain haplessly dependent on the meagre resources of the state which, in turn, provides the government with an opportunity to interfere with peoples' voluntary action.

Fearing at the same time, and perhaps rightly too, that in such developmental activities, the organized voluntary action may not be able to sustain itself for long, Gandhi was realistic enough to plead for the maximum decentralization of political power and economic resources. He, too, believed that power corrupts its possessor and absolute power corrupts absolutely. Being thus against the pyramidal structure of political power[32] under whose heavy weight the possibilities of human development get crushed, he asked for the ever-widening oceanic circular arrangement of political power[33] in which the goal of human development remains ever visible at all levels of government. He was against not only the concentration and centralization of political power and economic resources, but also against their division between the Centre and the States. In place of the traditional unitary and Federal systems of government, he asked for the establishment of *panchayati raj* (grassroot-level governing units) in which maximum political power and economic resources would rest with the *Gram Sabhas* and the *Gram Panchayats* (the village or grass-root level assembly of the people) in which all adults would not only freely and frequently participate but also determine their own priorities and pace of development. He believed that once political power and economic resources are under the direct and constant vigil of the people themselves, the possibilities of their misuse, disuse or abuse would tend to be minimized and the chances of the apparatus becoming corrupt would also be marginalised. In order to ensure human development in ever-increasing measure, Gandhi was, thus, in favour of the maximum possible decentralization of both political power and economic resources, reorganizing them on the basis of the maxim : *"nearer the level of government to the people, greater ought to be the political power and economic resources at its disposal."*

At the same time, like Plato, Gandhi also attached due emphasis to the significance of imparting proper education to the people. His whole scheme of education is reflected in his most celebrated Wardha Scheme of Education.[34] In terms of this scheme, not only was there provision of a seven-year free and compulsory vocational primary education which he thought was absolutely essential for ensuring a bare minimum level of human development, ensuring educational and employment opportunities equally for all. Having ensured this bare minimum level of human development equally to all, he asked for higher education not for all those who 'desire' but, in keeping with the typically Indian tradition, only for those who 'deserve' it on merit. Here, too, he would not make education dependent entirely on the resources of the state. In this case, he laid down a golden maxim: "he who needs the expertise would pay for it."[35] He thus laid the foundation of the partial privatization of higher education, not only to reduce dependence on and control and regulation by the state, but also to enlarge the scope of individual as well as voluntary organized action, so that each one may have a free and fair access to the kind of education he or she aspires and deserves. That, in turn, is a significant, peaceful and almost revolutionary step in the process of constructive, awakened, rational, and at least partially voluntary human development.

Human Development in Independent India

Gandhi approached the whole question of human development from a spiritual-moral point of view. The essence of this spiritual-moral point of view is that man should develop himself as a normal human being, devoting himself to social service, removal of injustice, creation of positive peace (both internal and external), and promotion of a quality of life commensurate with the requirements of both body and spirit. Such a concept of human development implies a certain discipline in life and a certain attitude to lifestyle. The code of conduct prescribed by Gandhi for a nonviolent resister and the constructive programme and trusteeship suggested by him both acquire significance in the context of this concept of human development. For the former inculcates in the mind of man, an understanding of the real meaning of human development, and the latter creates the necessary social conditions for the realization of the goal of human development. According to Gandhi, education plays a crucial role in shaping man's attitudes and also in promoting his commitment to the code of conduct, as well as his willing participation in the constructive programme and trusteeship.

All this is obviously different from the other variations of the modern concept of development that have sprung up in the last few decades. Gandhi's concept of development is different from the modern concept in so far as the former treats economic welfare as only one of its components, whereas economic welfare is the be-all and end-all of the modern concept of development. Thus, consumerism is the sole concern of the modern concept of development. Since Gandhi's concern was total "human" development and not just development, the whole debate about 'basic needs, minimum needs' and other such concepts becomes irrelevant. What is also important is that the unit of development in Gandhi is the individual, whereas under the modern concept it is a collectivity. That being so, the role of technology is also bound to be different in the Gandhian scheme of human development, in as much as technology is to serve as an instrument of human development without becoming a goal in itself.

Unfortunately, independent India has failed to achieve the goal of human development. This failure can be attributed to a variety of factors. First of all, India's education system has been modelled on the Western pattern which is grounded in a world view absolutely different from Gandhi's. This world view is informed by a search after the modern concept of development concerned only with materialism. A concern with the "human" dimension of development has been completely missing. Human development along Gandhian lines needs a certain value orientation which has not been provided by the system of education followed by India. Secondly, India has by and large surrendered itself to modern technology as the instrument of development. Although indigenous technology is encouraged to grow, it has not entered the area of large-scale planning for development. Thirdly, a total dependence on the physical aspect of development to the total neglect of the spiritual aspect, has made the entire development process "inhuman." The result is that India has been pursuing the path of "mass development" rather than "development by masses." The cumulative effect of all these factors is that India has not been able either to provide for a minimum satisfactory standard of living or to promote human virtues, both of which constitute the essence of human development.

Gandhi's perception of a normal polity has been delineated primarily in terms of human resources. The entire thrust of his *praxis* was on preserving and enriching humane and human components of Indian society and civilization on the one hand and on eliminating the sources of "inhumaneness" and dehumanization on the other. Even a random survey of his writings since 1909 when he wrote his *Hind Swaraj* clearly indicates the deep concern for "the human" which inspired his entire life work and his vision of the future.

His diagnosis of the ills of Indian polity is exclusively in terms of human ingredients of collective existence of man. He said: "We have to tackle the triple malady which holds our villages fast in its grips: (i) want of corporate sanitation; (ii) deficient diet; and (iii) inertia."[36] He further says: "An evil day dawned upon this unhappy country when labour began to be despised and therefore neglected... India suffered morally and materially... criminal neglect of the peasants and the artisans has reduced us to pauperism, dullness, and habitual idleness... The divorce of the intellect from body labour has made us perhaps the shortest-lived, most resourceless, and most exploited nation on earth."[37]

Discussing the priorities of work to be undertaken by municipal committees, Gandhi says: "No municipality can cope with insanitation and congestion by the simple process of taxation and paid services. This vital reform is possible only by wholesale and voluntary cooperation of the people, both rich and poor."[38]

Take another example, namely his concept of human settlements. An ideal village of Gandhi's conception was such as to promote perfect sanitation. Its cottages should have sufficient light and ventilation. They should be built of local material and its lanes and streets should be free of dust. It should have houses of worship for all, a cooperative dairy, primary and secondary schools, clear water supply, compulsory service of village guards, small manageable groups of people bound together in bonds of mutual cooperation and inter-dependence. Gandhi wanted to promote health and vigour of India's villages. He wanted human settlements in India as a whole to be in harmony with each other. What recommends itself most to Gandhi in an Indian village is the "human".

A cursory content analysis of all the eighteen items of Gandhi's Constructive Programme, which coupled with civil disobedience is based on Gandhi's faith that it will lead to Purna Swaraj aims at constructing a humane society by humane methods. The focus of the constructive programme is "the human" content of development and enrichment of the human content particularly through basic education, village sanitation, village industries, and through harnessing the human potentialities of the millions of people on the margins of Indian society Harijans, Adivasis, Women, Kisans etc.

After independence, Indian leaders and the articulate power elite failed to understand the essential characteristics of Gandhi's approach to construction of *Purna Swaraj*. Their perception of a normal society has been delineated primarily in terms other than the "human". A cursory look at the various Five-Year Plans confirms this impression. The national priorities have been described in terms of what may be called the "hardware" of economic, financial, and technological aspects of development. The "software" aspects of development, for example, education, village sanitation, improvement of quality of the vast labour force available in India, were relegated to the background. The education system in a country is the primary means of development of human resource and quality of life. But unfortunately it was only nineteen years after attaining independence that in 1966 India thought of drastically overhauling the colonial educational set-up from top to bottom in one sweep. The Kothari Commission emphasized the need in 1966. But prior to that a piecemeal approach was adopted in regard to educational reconstruction.

But even then the momentum of history prevails. Take, for example, the medical education system in India. The best talents are screened and admitted to medical courses. But after five years, the worst of human stuff comes out of these institutions good doctors and bad human beings. Professional education "dehumanizes" liberal education and promotes vulgarization and brutalization.

The budgetary allocation for education and such other software elements relating to development of human resources are very meagre. Even in the field of industrial development the "human factor" has never been the central issue. The question of labour participation in the management of industries was raised much later in the 1970s and that too has not been fully developed till today. All this reflects the basic approach of the power elite in India. It is assumed that "India's teeming millions" are the "objects" of history. The Nehruvian model assumed the primacy of the needs of the country over the needs of the people. This model was based on the assumption that if the country progresses, welfare will be promoted automatically. This is contrary to Gandhi's perception of human development in which the teeming millions were to be the agents of history and therefore India's reconstruction was to be undertaken by using vast reserves of human resources.

The entire concept of Indira Gandhi's twenty-point programme and the poverty alleviation programme of the present government assume that "the people in society are a passive factor and it is the state power and state resources which should play an active role in their upliftment". The balance between the state and society was disproportionately tilted in favour of the state. Consequently the society was emasculated and weakened and drained of its vitality.

The role of voluntary agencies in the reconstruction of rural society in India today does not present a rosy picture either. Gandhi left in 1947 a rich heritage of voluntary action in the form of a net of voluntary agencies committed to harnessing the energies of people in rural areas. About one lakh Gandhian workers were involved in voluntary work relating to constructive programmes in almost every major part of India. It could be the basis of further advancement of the "societal" sector as distinguished from state dominated "public sector." It had a vast potential for strengthening the "society" and hence for promoting human component of development. But unfortunately the Gandhian voluntary sector has got enfeebled and Gandhians are at best "estate" managers.

The situation of non-Gandhian voluntary agencies is worst still. It is totally at the mercy of the state and foreign funding agencies. The voluntary sector stands bureaucratized and professionalized and hence people's active participation in the development process is deplorably inhibited.

The events in the post-Gandhi era have, however, indicated a virtual failure of State as well as organized voluntary action to achieve even a basic minimum level of allround human development. This failure may be ascribed at least partially to the lack of enthusiasm on the part of the people to comprehend, understand, analyze and adapt the philosophy and strategy of Gandhi in keeping with the changing national and international scenario. In the post-Gandhi era, the number of people familiar with Gandhi's face, voice, views and constructive programme has indicated a sharp decline. Gandhi is becoming increasingly distanced.

Nevertheless, Gandhi, as he is understood and evaluated in academic circles, assures a more viable and humane alternative not only to Fascism and Communism, but even to the Western models of liberalism and democracy. Gandhi's alternative is more conducive to human development, vis-à-vis fascism and communism, as it minimizes the possibilities of organized and unorganized violence and correspondingly enhances the chances and possibilities of peaceful, constitutional, constructive change and transformation, irrespective of the process of its inevitable gradualism which is any day better than a sudden wholesome bloody revolution, resulting in countless destruction of life and property.

At the same time, Gandhi presents a better and a more viable alternative to Western conceptions of liberalism and democracy which are weighed rather heavily, on quantity at the cost of quality (on "how many" and not on "who" participate in the political process), on majority at the cost of suppressed and oppressed minority (often times, the reverse too has been a living reality) on men at the cost of women (even in states and geographical areas where their number is equal or even greater than that of their male counterparts), on the sustained legitimization of discrimination on grounds of race, colour, religion or language, and on the lack of will and effort to curb the rising trend of terrorism and religious fundamentalism. Gandhi's philosophy and strategy negates such glaring shortcomings of most of the dictatorial and democratic models widely prevalent even to this day.

Given the attention and trial it deserves, Gandhi, in most respects, would be found to be free from the glaring shortcomings of the prevalent political systems throughout the world. The philosophy and strategy of Gandhi is, in short, positive, constructive, peaceful, gradual, and consequently assimilative, allowing maximum opportunity of peaceful gradual change and transformation of the prevalent political, social, and economic systems into the ones which would, for sure, be more conducive to human development not only at the individual and collective levels, but also at the organized and unorganized voluntary levels. It assures constant development of human personality, institutions, traditions, practices and procedures, so as ultimately to enlarge the scope and increase the speed of constructive, comprehensive and peaceful human development which, in turn, would be a sure guarantee of peace and tranquillity on the one hand and preservation and prosperity on the other. The need of the hour is therefore to have a better understanding of, greater reliance on, and making an earnest worldwide effort to adopt and adapt the philosophy and strategy of Gandhi in keeping with the changing national and international scenario. "Understand, evaluate, adopt and adapt Gandhi" are thus the key words for ensuring and sustaining "human development" on a durable basis.

May I conclude by addressing a few questions for consideration:

(i) Have we not had enough of fascism, communism, Western liberalism, and welfarism?

(ii) Have not all these systems failed to ensure and enhance the cause of human development in any meaningful way?

(iii) Has not our experience of working with these systems brought us to the point of proclaiming: "enough is enough"?

(iv) Has not the time come for all of us to have the much needed conviction, will, and courage to give Gandhi's spiritual-secular, humane, democratic, constructive, peaceful, assimilative and ever-pleasant philosophy and strategy of human development the attention and the treatment it merits?

Notes and References

1. Swami Vivekananda, *Complete Works* (Calcutta: Advaita Ashram, 1960), Vol.II, P. 21.

2. *The Collected Works of Mahatma Gandhi* (Delhi: **of Information** and Broadcasting, Government of India, 1963) Vol. X, PP. 42-47.

3. Swami Vivekananda, *Complete Works*, Vol.V, P. 105.

4. Ibid. Vol.III, P. 299.

5. Sri Aurobindo, *The Spirit and Form of Indian Polity* (Pondicherry: Sri Aurobindo Ashram, 1966), P. 20.

6. Romain Rolland, *Prophets of the New India*, trans. by E.F.M. Malcolm-Smith London: Cassell & Co., 1930) P. 499.

7. Sri Aurobindo, *The Human Cycle and the Ideal of Human Unity* (Pondicherry: Sri Aurobindo Ashram, 1962), P.678.

8. *Ibid.*, P.673.

9. *Ibid.*, P.677.

10. *Ibid.*, P.685.

11. *Ibid.*, P.347.

12. Rabindranath Tagore, Society and State, in his *Towards Universal Man* (London: Asia Publishing House, 1961), PP. 51-52.

13. Rabindranath Tagore's letter to Gandhi dated 12 April 1919. See R.K. Prabhu and R. Kelkar, eds., *Truth Called Them Differently* (Ahmedabad: Navajivan Publishing House, 1961), P. 14.

14. Quoted in D.G. Tendulkar, *Mahatma: The Life of Mahatma Gandhi* (New Delhi: Publications Division, Government of India, 1961), Vol.III, P. 113.

15. *CWMG*, Vol.LIX, P. 318.

16. *Ibid.*, P. 319.

17. *Ibid.*, P. 319.

18. *Harijan*, 18 January, 1942.

19. For details, see, Ronald J. Terchek, The Psychoanalytic Basis of Gandhi's Politics, *Psychoanalytic Review*, Vol.LXII, P.226.

20. Ashis Nandy, "Oppression and Human Liberation: Towards a Post-Gandhian Utopia", in Thomas Pantham and Kenneth L. Deutsch , eds., *Political Thought In Modern India* (New Delhi: Sage Publications, 1986) P.356.

21. *CWMG*, Vol. VIII, P. 243.

22. *Ibid.*, Vol. XXII, PP. 243-44.

23. *Ibid.*, Vol. XLIII, PP. 113-15.

24. *Ibid.*, P. 129.

25. Quoted by Ramashray Roy, Moral Foundations of Hind Swaraj and Nonviolence, in Nageshwar Prasad, ed., *Hind Swaraj: A Fresh Look* (New Delhi: Gandhi Peace Foundation, 1985), P. 52.

26. See, A.K. Saran, Gandhi and the Concept of Politics: Towards a Normal Civilization, *Gandhi Marg*, (New Delhi), Special Issue, February 1980.

27. M.K. Gandhi, *An Autobiography or the Story of My Experiments with Truth*, trans by Mahadev Desai (Ahmedabad: Navajivan Publishing House, 1956), 2nd edn., P.504.

28. Jeremy Bentham, *An Introduction To The Principles of Morals and Legislation*, New York : Hafner Pub. Co., 1948, P.21.

29. John Stuart Mill,, *Utilitarianism*, ed, by Oskar Piest, (New York: The Bobbs Merril Co., 195) P.22.

30. M.K. Gandhi, *Ruskin: Unto This Last: A Paraphrase*, trans. by V.G. Desai (Ahmedabad: Navajivan Publishing House, 1962), P.V.

31. *Harijan*, 11 January 1936.

32. *Ibid.*, 28th July 1946.

33. *Ibid.*

34. *Ibid.*, 19 October 1937.

35. *Ibid.*, 31 July 1937; and *Ibid.* 9 July 1938.

36. *Young India*, 11 August 1927.

37. *Harijan*, 7 November 1929.

38. *Ibid.*

LM Singhvi

Gandhi in the 21st Century

I have captioned my theme as Mahatma Gandhi in the 21st Century not because I am an astrologer, nor because I am willing to venture forth in the role of a futurist. I shall emphasise what I consider to be the most significant Gandhian inputs into the 21st Century and focus on Gandhi in the later half of the 21st Century. I do, however, believe that to understand Gandhi we must try to understand him in the long perspective of time, in the context of his inheritance and with reference to the challenges he encountered as well as in terms of his relevance now and for succeeding generations of humankind. In the words of Shakespeare in *Macbeth.*

If you can look into the seeds of time,
And say which grain will grow and which will not,
Speak then to me, who neither beg nor fear,
Your favours nor your hate.

Taking you on a voyage into the 21st century in search of Gandhi, I should in all fairness enter the caveat that the high seas of future are uncharted, that the boat on which I am asking you to come aboard is only a twentieth century Indian contraption, and that my hesitating futurological sense of direction and destination is guided by a temperament and worldview which is essentially optimistic. I should also add that I do not see myself as a starry-eyed idealist dreaming of fairy castles with an uncritical faith in the human nature and human future. Nor do I wish to be a frowning, chilling cynic who glories intellectually in snarling and biting and in being generally indignant and bilious.

Mahatma Gandhi himself was ever an optimist and never a cynic. His faith in human nature was unbounded. In a thought for the Day on June 16, 1946, he said, "When we know that everything has two sides, let us look at the bright side only". Of course he was too much of a practical realist not to take into account the darker side. What he meant was to make his bright hope the loadstar. Remember that he was a *Karmayogi* and not a fatalist. He believed deeply in the power and efficiency of human endeavour to overcome weaknesses, adversities and injustices. He was neither a prisoner of the Past nor a hostage to an imaginary or utopian Future. His feet were firmly planted in the Present. He put his viewpoint with compelling and characteristic clarity, when he wrote on November 2, 1945: "The Past belongs to us but we do not belong to the Past. We belong to the Present. We are makers of the Future, but we do not belong to the Future". Thus Gandhiji had a sense of heritage and he had also an involvement in making the future unlike Marinetti's Italian-European Futurism which negated the past, and the Russian Velemir Khlebrikov's eccentric futurism which was anxious to give a slap in the face to public taste and advocated throwing Pushkin, Dostoyevsky and Tolstoy overboard. By contrast, Gandhi's futurism was constructive, humane and universal.

Gandhi had a vision and an ideology but he was not an ideologue. He was a man of abiding faith but he had not a trace of fanaticism. He knew deep down within himself that faith might transcend reason but was not opposed to it. He was an unflinching votary of Truth. Truth was his God. His life was dedicated to the quest of Truth. That is why he was not afraid of his experiments with Truth. He discovered the Truth of all truths in Non-violence. He discovered the many facets of Truth and the many facets of Non-violence and found them inextricably intertwined. He adjusted and evolved the science, technology, art and philosophy of Non-violence in all its ramifications in the life of the individuals, in the interactions of individual and society, in the pluralism of Society, Religion, State and Power, in the equations of Rights and Duties, and in the ultimate analysis, for the purpose of optimising Peace and Justice in the world. We might well say to Gandhiji in the poetic words of Longfellow in *Keramos*.

Thine was the prophet's vision,
Thine the exultation,
The divine insanity of noble minds,
That never falters nor abates,
But labours and endures and waits,
Till all that it foresees it finds,
Or what it cannot find creates!

Let me say that it is my conviction that Gandhi had the prophet's vision, he had the divine inspiration of a noble mind, which the ignorant might call insanity, and that his vision and inspiration will never falter, nor abate. It is my conviction that *the quintessential* Gandhi will endure, will be rediscovered, reinterpreted and restated and will help to catalyse and create a new world order and a new caring, sharing, compassionate, rational, reciprocating, free and fulfilling *persona* for the human individual, in the 21st century. I shall speak, briefly of that quintessential Gandhi in the 21st century, and in doing so I shall remember Emerson's wise thought that when God makes the prophet He does not unmake the man. Gandhi never accepted the status of a prophet but he was certainly a truly great human being. A poet has described him as the ripest contribution of Heaven to Earth. I would disagree. He was of the Earth, earthy. Truly was he a child of Mother Earth, in the Vedic words, "Mata Bhumih, Putroham Prithivya". Therefore I would say that Gandhi was a rare gift of Earth to Heaven.

Will this great and noble son of Mother Earth be remembered in the later half of the 21st century in India and the world? How and for what would he be remembered? And that takes us to the bundle of questions relating to the 21st century, more particularly to the later half of the 21st century? What would India and the rest of the world be like during that period? What would be the state of art in the institutions of governance from local to the global level, in the institutions of marriage and family, in the areas of creativity, culture, health, education, communication, environment, eating habits, law and order, religion, means of production and manner of consumption, and a whole range of other facets which coalesce to give us the contours and patterns of life in a given age? I shall not presume to answer these question here, except to say that they are intimately relevant issues to the theme of Gandhi in the 21st century. I would also add that Gandhian ideas will be reflected, merged, internalized and absorbed in the developments that will predictably take place during the coming decades. The Gandhian standpoint will, I am sure, be a part of the on-going dialectics of the developments leading up to the later half of the 21st century.

Mahatma Gandhi left no church, no Establishment, no Religion, no Political Movement, and no academic discipline or dogma. His legacy will nevertheless survive, in my humble opinion, for many centuries to come. It will survive not only in the archives, not merely in books of history, philosophy and other social sciences, but it will survive in every design and model of life which human being will make and unmake in the 21st century. The Gandhian legacy will survive not as a cut and dried package of ideas, not as a panacea or a universal solution to all problems, not as a manual of prescriptions, but as an approach to human and social engineering, as a philosophy of life for the purity of means as well as ends for the Individual, the State and the Society, and as a permanent revolution and a process of Catharsis and synthesis for a renewed moral and spiritual quest of Peace, Justice and Freedom in Fullness For All or *Sarvodaya*, as Gandhi called it. It is in the context of that luminous legacy that I say, Gandhi is dead, Long live Gandhiji.

Let me reflect on the theme I have chosen with reference to a bleak as well as a bright scenario in the imaginary year 2050 A.D.

The bleak scenario of the world at the mid-21st century would find the critical problems of today accentuated and magnified manifold. In that situation, let us imagine the people of the world living under the threat of something worse than a thermonuclear holocaust, poor nations of the world still severely handicapped and hamstrung by poverty, the affluent nations of the world more affluent than ever before but engulfed by a moral and spiritual crisis, environmental degradation hurtling towards its nadir, and fundamentalist fanaticism raging wild here and there. It would not make much of a difference to such a world if it were unipolar, bipolar or multipolar. In such a world, Gandhiji's concept and technique of Non-violence would have a vital role and relevance not only for nuclear and other kinds of disarmament but also for an equitable economic balance, environmental protection, multi-faith amity and moral rejuvenation. In such a bleak scenario, the Gandhian approach of Non-Violence could play a pivotal rescuing role.

If we now move to the alternative bright scenario, we would find a world without destructive arms, nations without sizable armies and without explosive confrontations, a healthier environment without anxieties of ozone depletion and greenhouse effect, and national economies without destitution and disabling deprivation. In that brighter world, which is well within our grasp, Gandhiji's Non-Violence would still have a very valuable role to play in progressively civilizing and humanizing social, economic and political institutions and in refining, redefining and readjusting individual human relationships. In other words, Gandhian precepts of non-violence and their application to the problem-solving tasks of humanity have the potential of making the utterly bleak somewhat bright, and the bright more lustrous and luminous.

In his epilogue in *Mahatma Gandhi, The Last Phase* by Pyarelal, a lifelong associate of Gandhiji, General Douglas MacArthur is referred to as describing Mahatma Gandhi as one of those prophets who lived far ahead of the time. General MacArthur is quoted for his significant view of Gandhian legacy that "In the evolution of civilization, if it is to survive, all men cannot fail eventually to adopt his belief that the process of mass application of force to resolve contentious issues is fundamentally not only wrong but contains within itself the germs of self-destruction". Gandhiji's greatest contribution is to envision a world without armaments, without wars and without violence. If and when war is outlawed and disarmament is achieved throughout the world, as I am sure it would be in the twentyfirst century, our posterity shall remember Gandhiji and his teachings.

Gandhiji was a true internationalist and believed in One World. Horace Alexander quotes Gandhiji writing in *Young India* in 1925: "It is not nationalism that is evil. It is the narrowness, selfishness, exclusiveness which is the bane of modern nations which is evil. Each wants to profit at the expense of, and rise on the ruin. Each wants to profit at the expense of, and rise on the ruin, of the other". He also quotes Gandhiji for the view he expressed in 1925 that the world should foster is universal interdependence rather than independence. The world is already working out the configurations of universal interdependence based on the precept of the world as one family. That precept will, I think, reach its fruition in the twenty-first century, and in that time and age, our posterity shall remember Gandhiji and his teachings.

Gandhiji rejected all religious chauvinism, exclusivism and fanaticism. He genuinely believed in the fundamental concepts of equal respect for all religions, protection of minorities and prevention of discrimination which have become the sheet anchor of Indian pluralism and secularism. He taught us that we must respect other religions as we respect our own and that mere tolerance of other religions is not enough. In his uniquely simple and elegant way, he summed up his multi-faith philosophy when he said: "Truly, there are as many religions as there are men. But when one goes to the root of one's religion, one finds that in reality religion is one".

Gandhiji wanted to unite the religions of the world with all their differences and divergences into a harmonious framework of togetherness. That is why every prayer meeting of Gandhiji became the hallowed ground of multi-faith sanctum and a temple of inter-faith understanding. "Ishwar Allah tere naam, subko sanmati de Bhagwan" sang of Mahatma and his disciples in a universal prayer. He drew upon all the holy scriptures of different faiths to preach his message of universal brotherhood, empathy and humanity. When all faiths meet and mingle in mutual amity, respect and understanding, and that dream, I think, will come true in all its splendour by the mid-21st century, our posterity shall acknowledge and remember Gandhiji and his teachings.

Gandhiji was a great apostle of equality for all humankind and of dignity and freedom for every human individual. In South Africa, he laid the foundation of a worldwide movement against racial arrogance, segregation and discrimination and for racial equality and inter-racial goodwill. When he came to India from South Africa, he made the cause of eradication of untouchability his life's mission. He worked not only for the temple entry of Harijans but also for their equal status and against all forms of discrimination, deprivation and disadvantage to which they were subjected. He wrote on November 28, 1944 that "removal of untouchability means not merely touching the Harijans (untouchables) but also looking upon them as our own kith and kin, in other words, treating them in the same way as we would our own brothers and sisters." In an article he wrote in 1921, he said that without the removal of the taint of untouchability, *Swaraj* was a meaningless dream. On another occasion he said "I would far rather that Hinduism died than that untouchability lived". The revolutionary significance of Gandhiji's mission for equality in all walks of life and at every step of life has to be understood in the context of every form of inequality and prejudice. At the Round Table Conference in London in 1931, he made it clear that he did not want freedom for his own country in order that India may exploit any other race upon earth or any single individual. He said that Indians would not be deserving freedom if they did not cherish and treasure the equal right of every other race, weak or strong, to the same freedom. He was also very firm and articulate on the equal rights of women. Long before the United Nations declared their allegiance to the concept of fundamental freedom and basic human rights, Gandhiji pioneered and espoused the cause of human rights, equality and human dignity. Long before Commissions for racial equality and for equal opportunities were established, he gave us a vision and a blueprint for rights and duties as the foundation for the edifice of human rights. When the human rights revolution, inaugurated in the 20th century its apotheosis in the mid-21st century, our posterity will acknowledge and remember the formative and far reaching role Gandhiji played in the process of decolonisation and in the endeavour to build a new world order based on the work and dignity of every human individual.

Gandhi's concept of Non-Violence paved the way for an harmonious relationship with nature and for the preservation of environment and wild life. He did not believe in subduing, conquering or destroying nature. Instead he taught the world to conquer one's passions and to practise self-restraint. His concept of Non-violence was based on the unique principle of reciprocity of all living creatures in the cosmos. He was guided by two basic precepts: 1. *Parasparopagraho Jivanam* (There is cosmic inter-dependence among all living beings and therefore they must live in reciprocity), and 2. *Atmavat Sarvabhuteshu* (Treat all living creatures as you treat yourself or would have yourself treated). Protection of environment, avoidance of violence and characterising waste and consumerist materialism as violence. Gandhiji illuminated the whole universe of situations and circumstances in which the principle of Non-Violence could be applied effectively and fruitfully.

I could multiply instances, areas and situations in which the Gandhian ideology of Non-Violence continues to be relevant and will be ever more relevant in the 21st century. His Non-Violence was a matter of principle and not merely transient expedience. Nor was it denominational. His Non-Violence was all embracing. It was Hindu, Jain, Buddhist, Jewish, Zoroastrian, Christian, Islamic, Sikh, Baha'i, and what have you. I hope the posterity of humankind will continue to discover and re-discover the universal and everlasting Gandhi rather than install his idol in a temple and become oblivious of his message. To remember and rediscover Gandhiji for every age is to remember and rediscover the best in ourselves and in our heritage, and to do that is indeed to pay a true tribute to Bapu.

Notes mainly autobiographical, on the Contributors

Ambler, Rex

Rex Ambler has been teaching theology at Birmingham University since 1968, having studied at Manchester, Oxford and Amsterdam. He visited India in 1976 to research the context and consequences of Gandhi's philosophy, and he has since written articles and booklets on Gandhi, mainly to indicate the centrality in his thought of the concept of truth, e.g. *The Relevance of Gandhi in the West* (Gandhi Foundation and Housmans, London, 1988). He has also written *Global Theology: the meaning of faith in the present world crisis* (SCM Press, London, 1990), and is presently working on a more philosophical book about faith and postmodernity.

Ali, Sadiq

Born at Udaipur on 4.4.1918 (Rajasthan); Graduate, Allahabad Univ; jailed several times during freedom movement, permanent Sec, AICC, 38-48, Gen Sec, 1958-62, and 1964-69; Member: Provisional Parliament, 1950-52, of Rajya Sabha, 1958-70; Chief Editor, AICC Econ Review 58-62, Editor, Political and Economic Review, 1960-62, 1964-69; President, Indian National Congress (O), 1971-73; Governor of Maharashtra, 77-60; Governor of Tamil Nadu, 1980-62; Chairman, Gandhi Smarak Sangrahalaya Samiti, since 1965; Chairman, Gandhi Smarak Nidhi, New Delhi since 1990; Chairman, Rajghat Samadhi Committee, New Delhi since 1992; Publs: *The Congress Ideology and Programme; Know Your Country; The Culture of India; The General Election, 1957; A Survey Towards Socialist Thinking in Congress ; Campaign Against Nuclear Arms.*

Bartolf, Christian

Born 1960. A scientific degree, university diplomas in educational science (adult education) and political science; compilation and five articles on "Pacifism in the USA" (John F. Kennedy Institute for North American Studies, Free University Berlin, 1986, ed. Prof. E. Krippendorff); essays on Gandhi's concept of emancipation, Gandhi's educational concept, about Bonhoeffer-Gandhi relationship (with D. Blondeau), about "Tolstoy and Gandhi" in our series of writings on non-violence; co-founder and president of Gandhi-Information-Centre, Berlin. This is a Research and Study Centre of Non-Violence. The

Centre's library and audio-visual archives are regarded as the most comprehensive of this kind outside India. Beside publishing an authorised series of essays, the activists support scientific research work, book and film projects.

Blum, Fred

Born in Germany in 1914, emigrated to the United States in 1939 where he became an American citizen, and came to Britain in 1959 on behalf of the Society of Friends (Quakers) to study new developments in mental health and religion with special reference to the organization of industry. He was a Member of the Society of Analytical Psychology in London and the Founder of the New Era Centre for the Development of a New Human Consciousness and Social Order. He was a leading figure in setting up the Gandhi Summer School. He died in 1990.

Bader, Godric

Godric is the son of Ernest Bader, founder of Scott Bader Ltd. Born in 1923, he has worked for Scott Bader since 1945, co-founding the Commonwealth, and is now Life President, having relinquished the roles of CEO and Chairman to promote the spirit of common-ownership within the business community. He is a Quaker, educated at the Friends School, Saffron Walden and Queen Mary College, London (evacuated to Kings College, Cambridge). He has written various articles for the World Business Academy, *The Guardian*, and *The Long Range Planning Journal*, and newsletters of the European Social Network, the London Business Network, and *Gandhi Way*.

Brotherton, Julian

Qualified in Agriculture at Aberdeen, in Education at Moray House, Edinburgh and the University of Newcastle upon Tyne, and in Philosophy at the University of London. He has taught in a wide variety of schools and was a College of Education lecturer. He also managed a Farm and School Project with a Gandhian emphasis. He has reviewed books for the *Times Educational Supplement* and written features for them on educational topics, the environment and natural history. His interests include rural life and ecology, community living and interfaith work. He has many connections in India and his wife is from Tamilnadu.

Bahuguna, Sunderlal

Born 9 January 1927. Graduated in Political Science, History, English from Lahore. Jailed 1944 for serving Independence Movement. 1945-46 in the underground Movement in Punjab. 1947-52 politically involved. 1956 set up Ashram in Silyara, in Himalayas. Thereafter to take up struggle for prohibition, and forest preservation – through the Chipko movement. 1981 declined Padma Shree Award: 'I do not deserve it till the flesh and blood, i.e. topsoil, is no longer flowing down to the sea due to tree felling in Himalaya'. Chipko movements spread in India. 1983 National Integration Award by Singhvi Memorial Trust. Takes the message of Chipko outside India. 1986 Jamnalal Bajaj Award for outstanding contribution to constructive work. Continues to work for his conviction that 'ecology is permanent economy' and that it can meet the triple demands of war, pollution and poverty facing humankind today. 1989 Sher-i-Kashmir Award. Honorary degree, Roorkee University of Engineering. 1991 launched direct action against the construction of Tehri Dam. 1992 Rathindra Award from Vishva Bharata University. 1995 Pride of Doon Award.

Copley, Antony

Born July 1937. Graduated from Oxford in History 1960. M. Phil. (Oxon) European History 1962. Has since taught in universities, at UCNW, Bangor, 1963-67, University of Kent 1967 till present. Became interested in Gandhi through writing about Rajagopalachari. His *Gandhi: Against The Tide* (Blackwells) published 1987. An Indian edition (OUP) published 1993. Is on the Executive Committee of the Gandhi Foundation. Has for a long time been involved with the Indo-British Review and is now its Associate Editor.

Chowdhry, Kamla

She is a graduate of the Universities of the Punjab, Calcutta and Michigan. She has played a key role in many Indian and international organisations dealing with development, ecology, women's issues, and people's participation. She is at present Chairperson of the Society for the Preservation of Wastelands Development, which sets policies and strategies for halting deforestation and promoting afforestation with people's involvement.

Cadogan, Peter

Peter Cadogan, a Tutor (retired) in the *History of Ideas* was introduced to Gandhi and his ideas by the works of Edward J. Thompson (1940) and then via the principled non-violent wing of Bertrand Russell's *Committee of 100* (1960/68). He then held leading office in the *Save Biafra Compaign* (1968/70); *The South Place Ethical Society* (1970/81); the Northern Ireland Project of the *Gandhi Foundation* (from 1988), *The William Blake Society* (from 1988) and *Values and Vision* (from 1991).

Dunn, Ted

Born 1919. Producer of a short film: Peace Through Law. One-time Coordinator of a Student Peace Project. During the Second World War worked in Ethiopia for the Friends' Ambulance Unit. Smallholder in a Cooperative when peace work allowed. Publications: Edited *Alternatives to War and Violence*, Edited *Foundations of Peace and Freedom*. Author of: *A Step by Step Approach to World Peace, A Step by Step Regional Peace and Development Programmes*. Contributor of articles and letters to journals and newspapers.

Daffern, Thomas

Thomas Daffern was born in Montreal, Canada, 1956. Educated in the UK, he studied philosophy at the University of Bristol and modern world history at the University of London. Actively engaged with the question of the role of intellectuals and educators in the search for peace and justice, he authored a detailed feasibility study into the development of an advanced research and teaching institute on Peace and World Order at the University of London. Involved for many years with study and teaching on the philosophical and academic dimensions of peace building and conflict resolution, he also serves as Secretary General of the World Conference on Religion and Peace (UK and Ireland) and International Coordinator of Philosophers for Peace and Global Responsibility, and is currently organising the development of the Gandhi Foundation School of Non-Violence and Conflict Resolution in London. He recently attended the World Summit for Social Development in his role as Director of the International Institute for Peace and Global Responsibility (University of London Institute of Education) and is concerned to develop new educational responses to the problems of global poverty, unemployment and social disintegration, in the spirit of Gandhi's holistic approach to truth, in which the spiritual and political dimensions have equal weight.

Dhagamwar, Vasudha

Is qualified in Sociology of Law, with special reference to Criminal Law, Family Law, Land, Women and Children, and published a book *Law Power and Justice* (1992) which looks at the theory and practice of Criminal Law. She currently runs an NGO, MARG (Multiple Action Research Group).

Eswaran, V. B.

Born 10 June 1928. Has a B.Sc. (Hons) degree in Chemistry, University of Madras. Civil servant, from 1950 to 1986, as a member of the Indian Administrative Service. Served the State Government of Gujarat, and the Government of India in executive and policy-making positions, including the permanent civil service. Head of the Finance Ministry of the Government of India.

After retirement, Executive Director of the well-known NGO, the Society for Promotion of Wastelands Development, New Delhi, from 1985 to 1991, was deeply involved in exploring and demonstrating appropriate methods of reclaiming and developing/managing degraded land and water resources of communities at local levels; and advising the government (formally and otherwise) on policies for land use and management.

Currently, among other things, is on the Governing Council of the Centre for Environment Education, Ahmedabad; the Board of Governors of the Indian Institute of Forest Management, Bhopal; the Governing Body of the Indo-German Social Service Society (IGSS), a large NGO; the Managing Committee of a couple of Voluntary Agencies engaged in need-based rural and community development work in the Central Himalayan region.

Horsburgh, Howard

Born in India. He was a conscientious objector in the Second World War. When it was over he studied philosophy at Glasgow and then at Oxford. Subsequently he taught philosophy at the University of Edinburgh, the Australian National University, Glasgow

University, the Universities of Guelph and Victoria in Canada, and at the International Christian University near Tokyo. He is an Emeritus Professor of the University of Victoria in British Columbia. He is the author of *Nonviolence and Aggression: A Study of Gandhi's Moral Equivalent of War* (OUP 1968), *Gandhi* (Lutterworth 1972), *Power Taming* (Gooday 1991), *Quenching Wrath* (Pax Books 1992).

Hart, Robert

A writer and pioneer of temperate agroforestry. He was born and educated in London and worked as sub-editor in Reuter's news agency. He is the author of *The Inviolable Hills* (Stuart and Watkins 1968), *Ecosociety* (Natraj 1984), *Forest Farming* (with James Shots Douglas, Robinson and Watkins 1980) and *Forest Gardening* (Green Books 1991). He now lives in Wenlock Edge, Shropshire, England.

Hoda, Surur

Born in Chapra - Bihar - India in May 1928. Graduated from Patna University, Bihar. Took active part in the student movement and India's struggle for independence. Inspired by J. P. Narayan, joined the All India Railwaymen's Federation (a leading Trade Union organisation of India) of which J.P. was the President. Was a Parliamentary candidate on behalf of the Praja Socialist Party of India. Worked for Rural Development with J. P. Narayan during his initial Gandhian Gramdan Movement. Came to Britain in 1965 as an official of the International Transport Workers Federation. Through J.P. came in contact with Dr. E. F. Schumacher and became a close friend. Helped in establishing the India Development Group (UK) and Appropriate Technology Development Association (India) with J. P. Narayan and Dr. E. F. Schumacher to promote Gandhian constructive programme of village industries. In 1983 helped in establishing the Gandhi Foundation with Richard Attenborough and David Ennals and became the founder General Secretary.

Jain, L. C.

Opted out of conventional politics on attainment of Independence; since then engaged in what may broadly be called Constructive Work, inspired by the Gandhian approach of strengthening the capacity of society for self-development. Has been involved actively with developing cooperatives (rural/urban) handicrafts, movements for decentralisation, environment and advancement of women. At the National Policy level, has tried to carry the influences of Gandhian views of socio-economic order. The advantages of Gandhian approach has also been attempted through books, papers, articles, teaching and lectures. He was Visiting Fellow at Harvard and Boston Universities (1984); Oxford University (1994). Member, National Planning Commission 1989-1990. (Age 69 years).

Krishnamurti, Lakshmi

Born July 1925. Educated: Annamalai University in the then Madras Presidency, left mid-way consequent on marriage, shifted residence to husband's state, Kerala, where she lived till 1975. Activities: Social Welfare Board work in Kerala from 1956 onwards. Chairperson of Kottayam District Project Implementing Committee of the state's Social

Welfare Board. Later member of the State Board. T. Nadu Activities: Member of the state legislature, Upper House (Legislative Council) from 1965 to 1970. Office bearer in the Congress Party (O) during the lifetime of the late Mr. K. Kamaraj and later until the party merged with the Janata Party formed under guidance of Jaya Prakash Narayan. Left active politics in the nineteen eighties, and since 1987 concentrating on the work of the Satyamurti Centre for Democratic Studies, a registered public charitable trust.

Kumar, Mahendra

Dr. Kumar is an Editor of *Gandhi Marg*.

Naidu, M. V.

Has taught for more than 20 years mostly at Brandon University. He has been a Visiting Professor at University of British Columbia; Carleton University; and Nehru University (New Delhi). He is currently head of the Department of Political Science at Brandon.

He has been President, Canadian Peace Research & Education Association; President, Canadian Asian Studies Association; Member, Board of Director, Social Science Federation of Canada; Member, Consultative Committee, Department of External Affairs Canada.

His publications include: *An Invitation to Think; Alliances and Balance of Power: A Search for Conceptual Clarity; Collective Security and the UN: A Definition of the UN Security System; Cruise Missile Testing in Canada; Gandhism on the Modern Industrial State; Dimensions of Peace & Militarism; Peace & Peace Studies: A Survey of Peace Studies in Canada; Rationalism, Religionism, & Peace Education.*

He is involved in non-academic and civic affairs in fields related to multiculturalism, medicare, municipal, provincial and federal elections, cultural festivals, mass media (TV, radio and newspapers).

Nanda, B. R.

Born in Rawalpindi (now in Pakistan) on 11 October 1917. He graduated from Government College, Lahore, with honours in History in 1937 and in 1979 a Master's Degree in History at the University of Punjab.

Shri Nanda joined the Indian Railways in 1942 and served as a senior executive in various positions.

In September 1965, Shri Nanda was selected to head the "Nehru Memorial Museum & Library". As its Founder-Director for fourteen years, he made it the premier institution for historical research in the country. His publications include: *Mahatma Gandhi: A Biography* (1958) (It has since been reprinted in the U.K., the U.S.A., India, and has been translated into French, Spanish, Italian, Hindi and several other Indian languages.); *The Nehrus: Motilal and Jawaharlal* (1962); *Gokhale, Gandhi and the Nehrus: Studies in Indian Nationalism* (London, 1974); *Gokhale, the Indian Moderates and the British Raj* (Oxford and Princeton, 1977); *Gandhi A Pictorial Biography* (1972); *Jawaharlal Nehru A*

Pictorial Biography (1980); *Gandhi and His Critics* (1985); *Gandhi, Pan-Islamism, Imperialism and Nationalism in India* (1989); *In Gandhi's Footsteps: The Life and Times of Jamnalal Bajaj* (1990); *Jawaharlal Nehru, Rebel and Statesman* (under print).

Shri Nanda was honoured with the National Fellowship of the Indian Council of Social Science Research, New Delhi in 1979; and the Dadabhai Naoroji Memorial Prize in 1961. He was awarded Padma Bhushan in 1988 for his contribution to English Literature.

Parel, Anthony Joseph

Born in Kerala, received his Ph.D. in Government from Harvard. He has been professor of Political Science at the University of Calgary since 1966. His publications include *The Machiavellian Cosmos* (Yale, 1992). He serves on the editorial board of *Gandhi Marg*. In the Lent term 1995 he delivered a series of lectures on Gandhi's political philosophy at Cambridge University, sponsored by Dharam Hindiya Institute of Indic Research. His critical edition of *Hind Swaraj*, with Introduction and Notes, will be published by Cambridge University Press.

Parekh, Bhikhu

Bhikhu Parekh is Professor of Political Theory at the University of Hull. He has been Vice-Chancellor of the University of Baroda (1981-84) and Visiting Professor at the University of British Columbia (1968-69), Concordia Univeristy, Montreal (1974-75), and McGill University (1976-77).

Professor Parekh has published several books and articles in the fields of political philosophy and Indian political thought. His publications include *Gandhi's Political Philosophy* (1989); *Colonialism, Tradition and Reform* (1989); *Contemporary Political Thinkers* (1982); *Karl Marx's Theory of Ideology* (1982); and *Hannah Arendt and the Search for a New Political Philosophy* (1981).

Paxton, George

Is a graduate of Glasgow University in physical sciences and the Open University in social sciences. His first, and conventional, career was in medical physics, his second, and unconventional, is in the voluntary sphere working for peace, human rights and fair trade organisations, and at one time bringing-up two children. He is the current editor of the Gandhi Foundation's quarterly newsletter, *The Gandhi Way*.

Power, Shahed

Born in the subcontinent of Anglo-Irish and Bengali parents. A first degree in Archaeology and over a decade's experience as a field archaeologist in Britain. A change of career was a result of contact with the late Professor Sugata Dasgupta in Calcutta during 1983-84. I gratefully acknowledge the encouragement and kindnesses received from Professors Dasgupta and Arne Naess of the University of Oslo. My teaching and research interests in the Environmental Resources Unit include environmental management – in particular, Environmental Impact Assessment, the origins of agriculture and the ecology of indigenous agriculture.

Roy, Ranjit Kumar

Dr. Ranjit Roy is a Reader in History at the Rabindra Bharati University, Calcutta. He was a Commonwealth Academic Visiting Fellow at St. Antony's College, Oxford. His doctorate, awarded in 1991, was on *Bengal's Response to Civil Disobedience: A Study on the Forms of Protest Amongst Women and Students, 1920-34*. His publications include his edition of *Bengal Yesterday and Today*, and *The Imperial Embrace: Society and Polity Under the Raj*. He is currently working on popular participation in the Quit India movement in Bengal.

Roy, Sanjit (Bunker)

Born 30th June 1945 in Burnpur, West Bengal. M.A. English Hons. St. Stephens College (1962-67). Indian National Squash Champion: 1965, 1968, 1970, 1971. Member of the Education Sub-Commission of the Indian National Commission for Cooperation with UNESCO. Member Rural Domestic Energy, Advisory Board of Energy, Ministry of Energy, Government of India. Between 1984 and the present he has served on a large number of committees at both State (Rajasthan) and national level concerned with development, both rural and urban, forests, wastelands, education and science.

In 1985 Jamnalal Bajaj Award for Promotion of Science & Technology in Rural Areas; 1986, Padma Shri; 1989, IDEA Laureate Award – Royal Swedish Academy of Engineering Sciences. He is Chairman Environmental Liaison Centre International (ELCI) 1992-93: 1993-94. ELCI is the largest southern based environmental network organisation in the world with 800 members in 90 countries.

Studdert-Kennedy, Gerald

Born Lucknow, 1933, and early education in Kashmir. Cambridge BA in English Literature. Assistant Producer for BBC Television Talks Department, 1958-62. Berkeley M.A. in Political Science. Doctor of Social Science, University of Birmingham. Reader in Politics at the University of Birmingham. Main research interest is in religion and politics. Main publications *Dog-Collar Democracy: the Industrial Christian Fellowship, 1919-1929* (Macmillan, 1982), and *British Christians, Indian Nationalists and the Raj*, (OUP, Delhi, 1991). Currently working on the 'Broad Church Tradition' in British politics.

Scotney, Norman

Early years – Huntingdon. Clerical work – London County Council. Conscientious objector – Agriculture. Teacher, Headmaster, Secondary School, North London. Principal Kivukoni College (adult education) Dar es Salaam. Consultant anthropologist rural health to W H O etc Africa and Asia. Head health behaviour research – African Medical Research Foundation, Nairobi. Lives in London with wife (Mozambiquan) and two children. Member of Society of Friends (Quakers).

Singhvi, L.M.

Dr. Singhvi is the Indian High Commissioner to Britain

Singh, Tarlok

Studied in Bombay University (1929-33), London School of Economics (1933-36) and School of Oriental and African Studies (1936-37). Entered Indian Civil Service 1937. Resigned 1962. Was Private Secretary to Vice-President, Interim Government and Prime Minister (1946-47) and Director-General, Rehabilitation in Punjab, India (1947-49). Served with the Indian Planning commission from its inception in 1950 until 1967, up to 1962 in official coordinating capacities and from 1962 as Member.

Was Visiting Senior Research Economist, Princeton University, Woodrow Wilson School for Public and International Affairs (1968-69); Fellow, Institute for International Economic Studies, University of Stockholm (1967 and 1969-70); Deputy Executive Director (Planning),. UNICEF New York (1970-74). First Chairman, Indian Association of Social Science Institutions (IASSI), 1979-61; since 1981, Chairman, Programme Committee; and edits the Association's interdisciplinary social science journal, *IASSI Quarterly*.

Author of *Poverty and Social Change* (1945, 1969), *Land Resettlement Manual for Displaced Persons* (1952), *The Planning Process* (1963), *Towards An Integrated Society* (1969), and *India's Development Experience* (1974), Edited *Social Science Research and Problem of Poverty* (1990).

First became committed to the study and understanding of problems of rural poverty as a college student in early 1931 to a large extent because of the emphasis on villages in Gandhiji's writings and in the national movement.

Williams, Alison

Born 1936. Lifelong interest in the UN since father joined Secretariat in 1945 with the first working party. MA and M.Phil (London) in modern Commonwealth and International History. Works as a teacher. Articles, reviews and reports in several journals, especially *The Teilhard Review* (1978-93).

Weber, Thomas

Was born in 1950 in Melbourne. He first became aware of Gandhi as a university student during the Australian anti-Vietnam War peace movement and had his first experiences of the Gandhian legacy during a visit to India in 1975. Since then he has spent a total of about two years in India, contacting Gandhians and learning about the Mahatma. In 1983 he retraced Gandhi's Salt March to Dandi (and has been working on the book ever since!). He is the author of *Hugging the Trees: The Story of the Chipko Movement, Conflict Resolution and Gandhian Ethics,* and the forthcoming *Unarmed Peacekeeping and Gandhi's Peace Army: The Shanti Sena,* as well as numerous articles on Gandhi and nonviolence. He currently teaches Legal Studies and Peace Studies at La Trobe University.

Index

Index of Concepts and Organisations

Index of People (A select list)